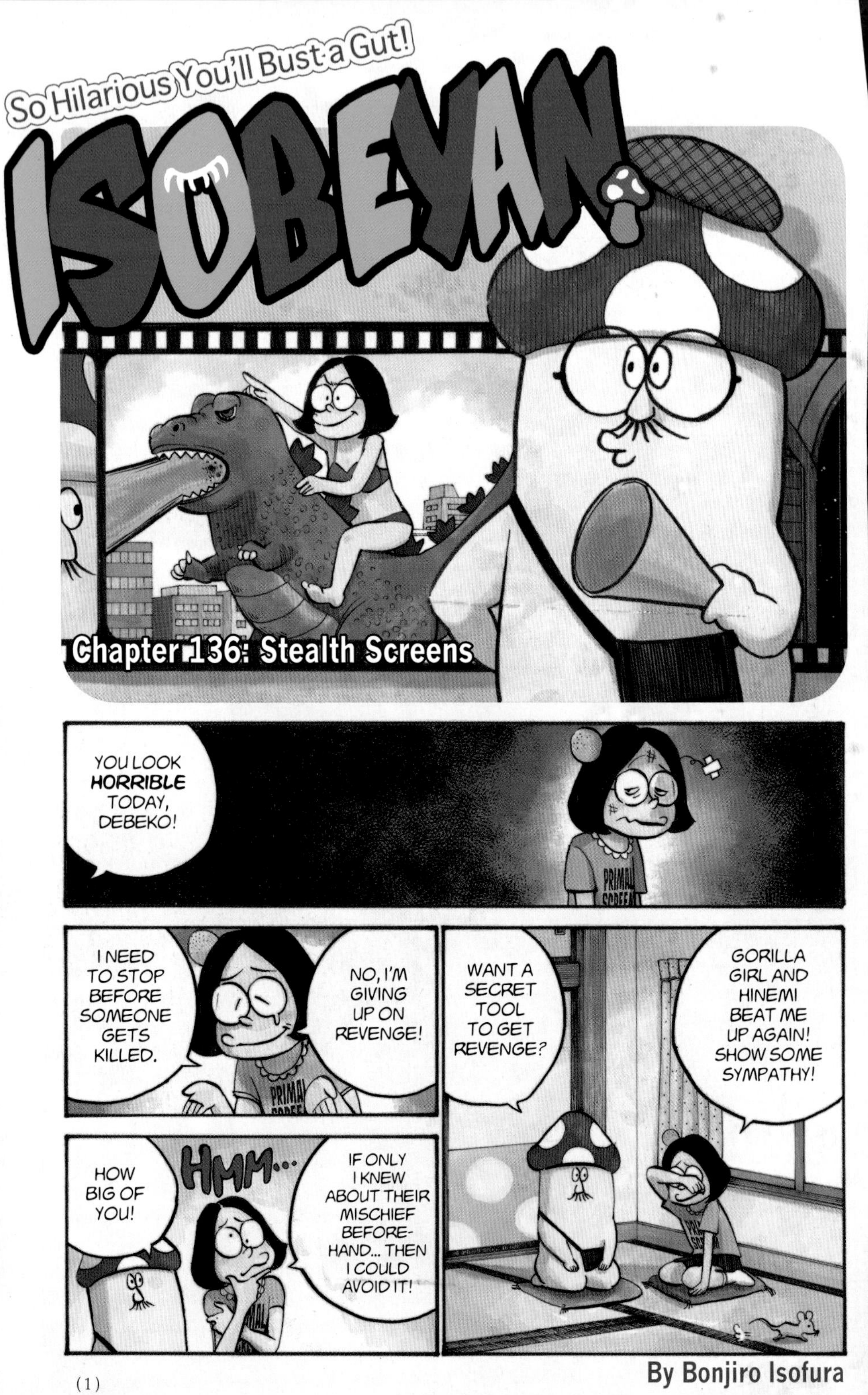
So Hilarious You'll Bust a Gut!
ISOBEYAN!
Chapter 136: Stealth Screens
YOU LOOK HORRIBLE TODAY, DEBEKO!
GORILLA GIRL AND HINEMI BEAT ME UP AGAIN! SHOW SOME SYMPATHY!
WANT A SECRET TOOL TO GET REVENGE?
NO, I'M GIVING UP ON REVENGE!
I NEED TO STOP BEFORE SOMEONE GETS KILLED.
IF ONLY I KNEW ABOUT THEIR MISCHIEF BEFORE-HAND... THEN I COULD AVOID IT!
HMM...
HOW BIG OF YOU!

By Bonjiro Isofura

☆Nietzsche says if you look into the abyss, it looks back at you! Scary, huh?

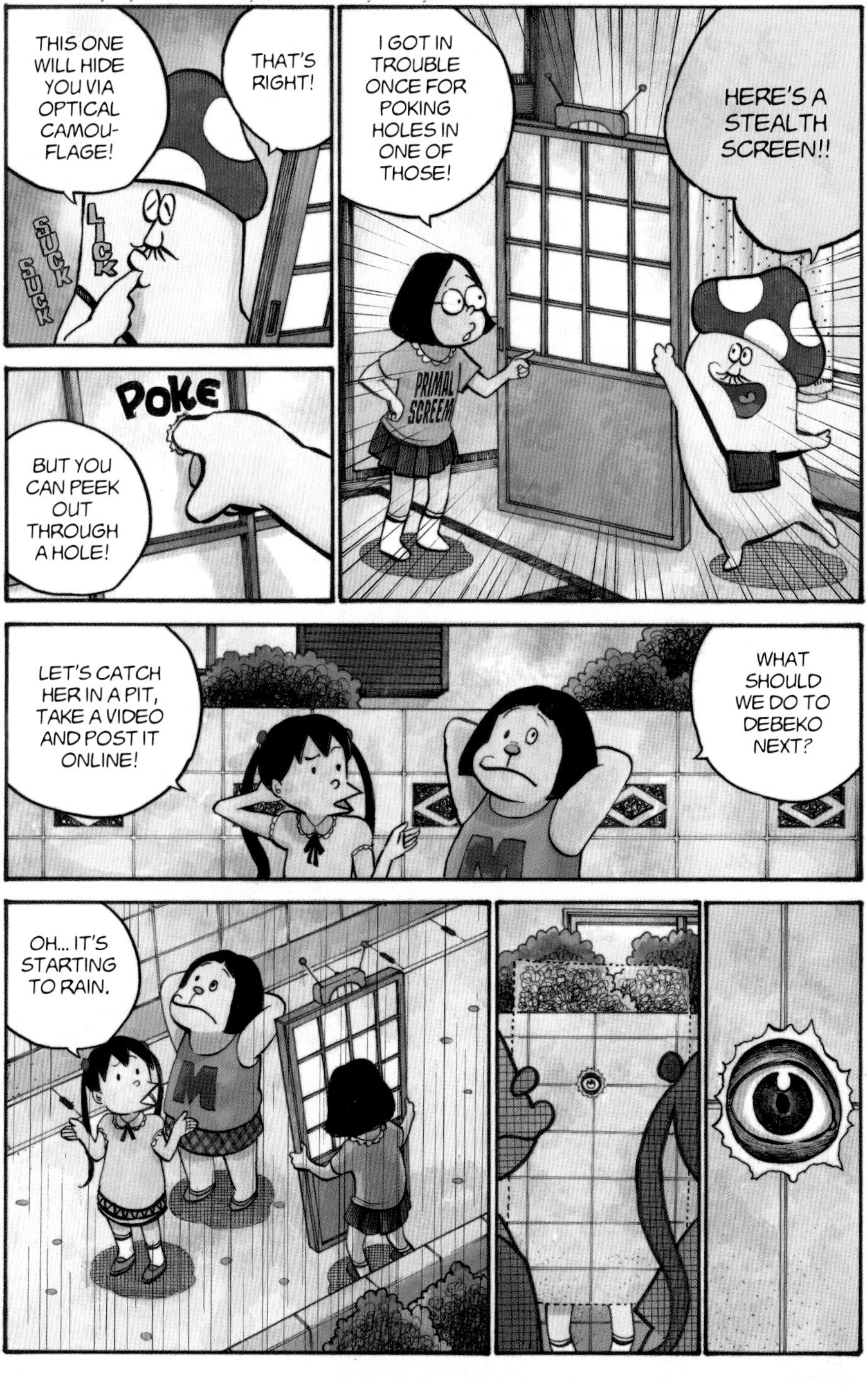
HERE'S A STEALTH SCREEN!!
I GOT IN TROUBLE ONCE FOR POKING HOLES IN ONE OF THOSE!
THAT'S RIGHT!
THIS ONE WILL HIDE YOU VIA OPTICAL CAMOU-FLAGE!
LICK
SUCK
SUCK
PRIMAL SCREEM
POKE
BUT YOU CAN PEEK OUT THROUGH A HOLE!
WHAT SHOULD WE DO TO DEBEKO NEXT?
LET'S CATCH HER IN A PIT, TAKE A VIDEO AND POST IT ONLINE!
OH... IT'S STARTING TO RAIN.

SUPER-POPULAR MASTERPIECE COMEDY **ISOBEYAN!**

☆Hey, everyone! Wear Isobeyan T-shirts! But when it's chilly, wear a jacket too.

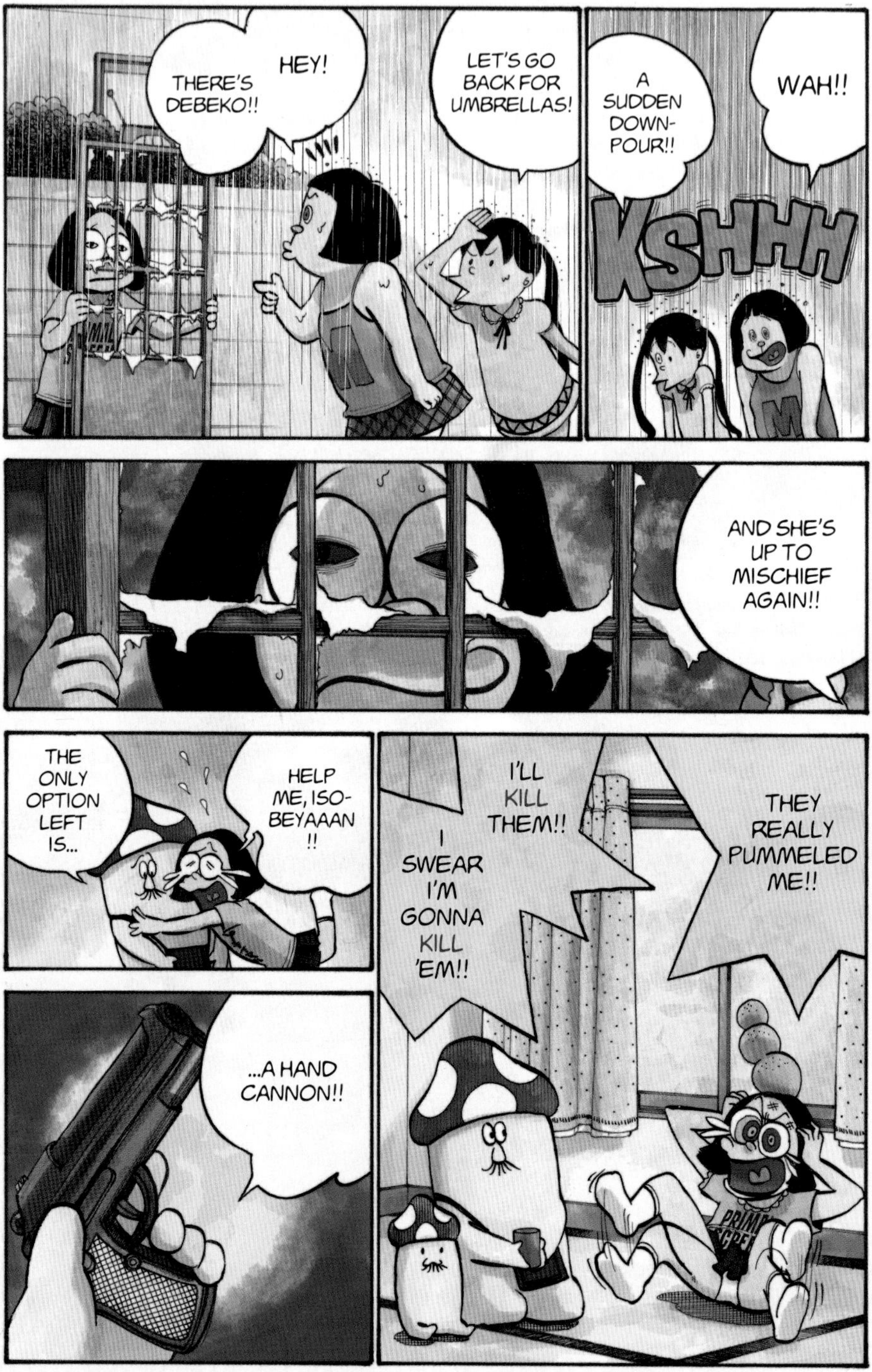
WAH!!
A SUDDEN DOWN-POUR!!
KSHHH
LET'S GO BACK FOR UMBRELLAS!
HEY!
THERE'S DEBEKO!!
AND SHE'S UP TO MISCHIEF AGAIN!!
THEY REALLY PUMMELED ME!!
I'LL KILL THEM!!
I SWEAR I'M GONNA KILL 'EM!!
HELP ME, ISO-BEYAAAN!!
THE ONLY OPTION LEFT IS...
...A HAND CANNON!!

☞ **Debeko brandishes her weapon! Continued on page 162...**

DEAD DEAD DEMON'S DEDEDEDE DESTRUCTION 6

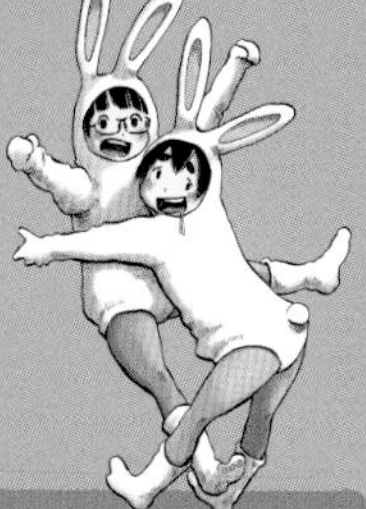

CHAPTER 41

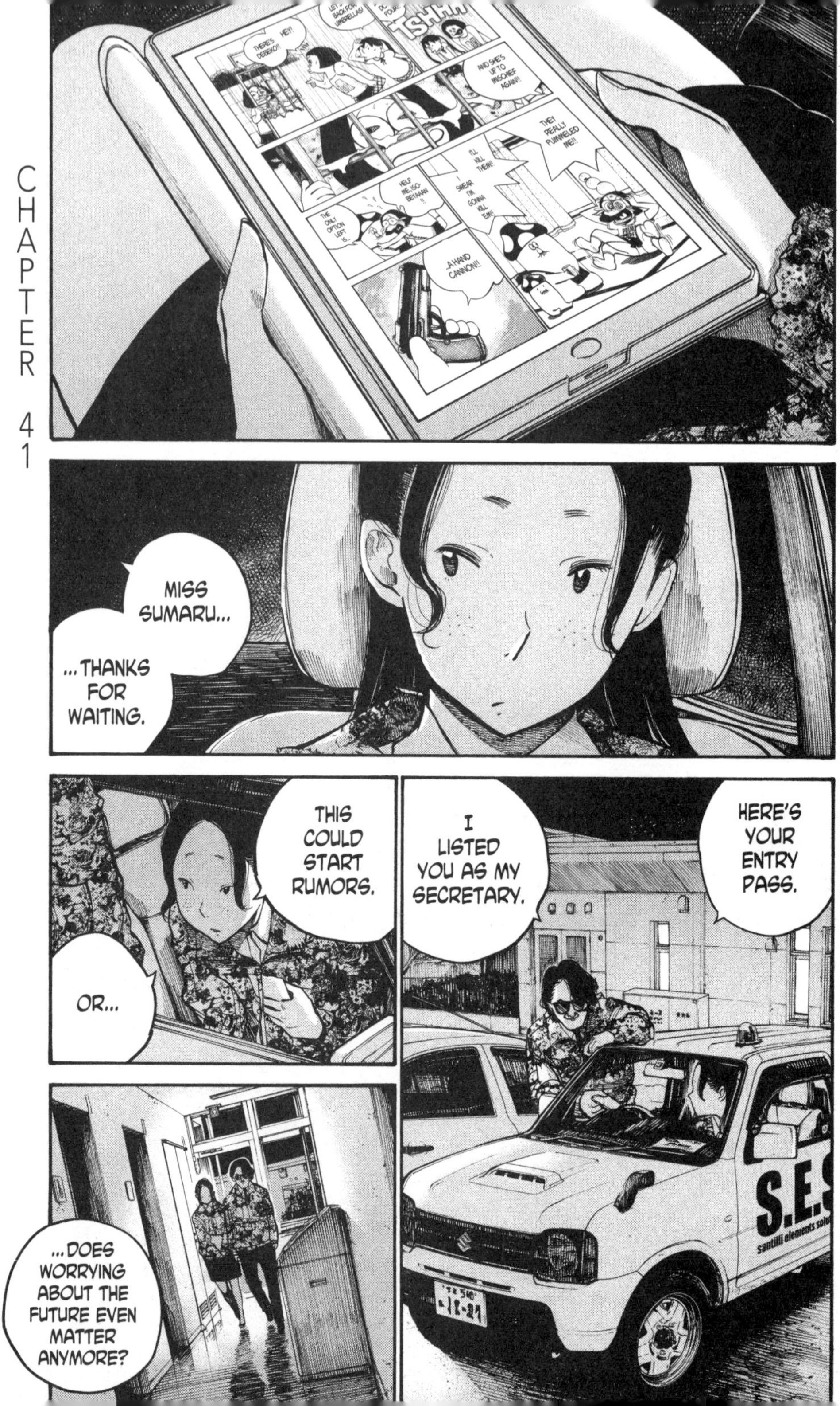
TSHHH
LET'S ... BACK FOR UMBRELLAS!
HEY!
THERE'S DEBEKO!!
AND SHE'S UP TO MISCHIEF AGAIN!!
THEY REALLY PUMMELED ME!!
I'LL KILL THEM!!
I SWEAR I'M GONNA KILL 'EM!!
HELP ME, ISO-BEYAAAN!!
THE ONLY OPTION LEFT IS...
...A HAND CANNON!!
MISS SUMARU...
...THANKS FOR WAITING.
HERE'S YOUR ENTRY PASS.
I LISTED YOU AS MY SECRETARY.
S.E.S
THIS COULD START RUMORS.
OR...
...DOES WORRYING ABOUT THE FUTURE EVEN MATTER ANYMORE?

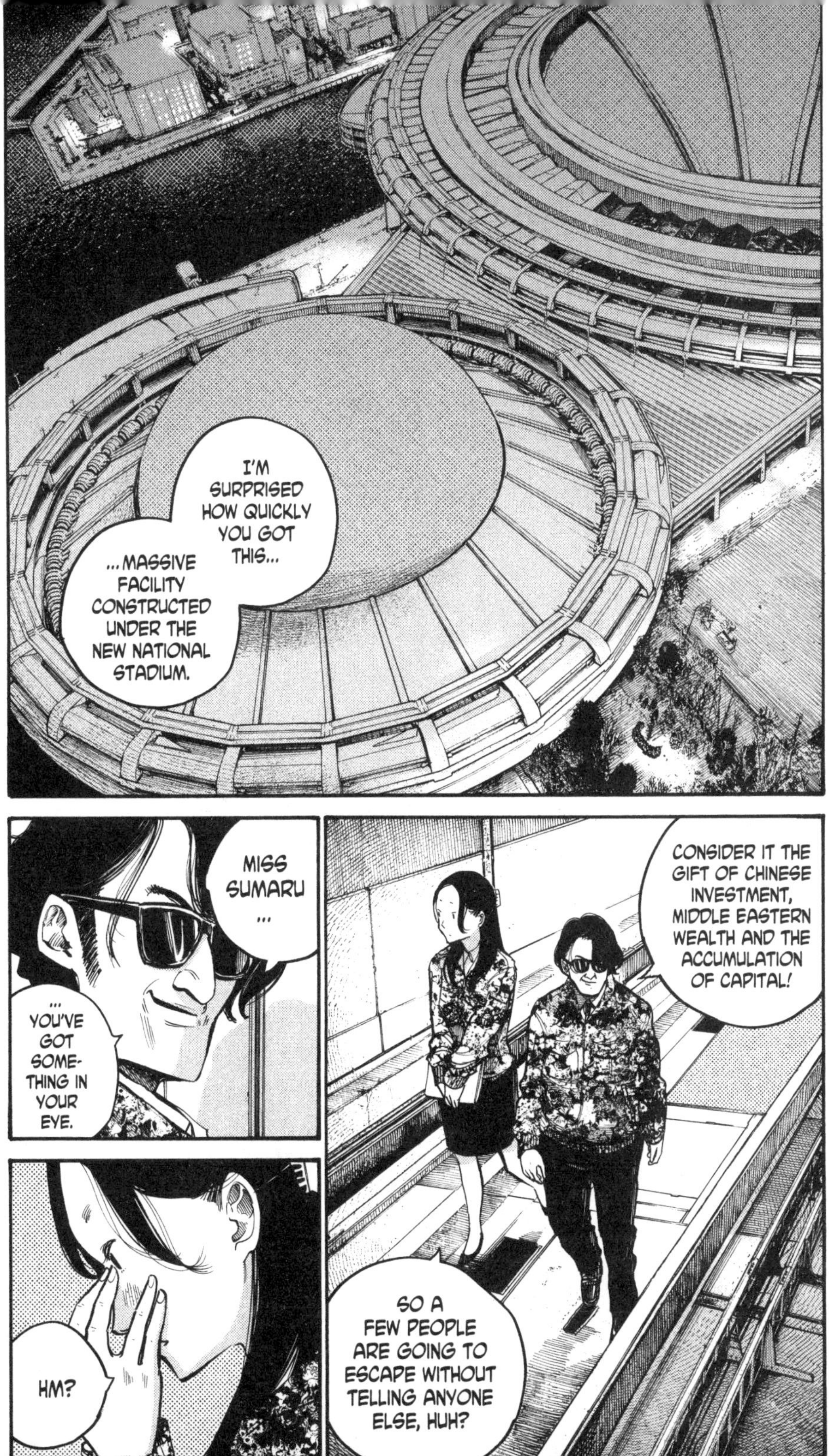
I'M SURPRISED HOW QUICKLY YOU GOT THIS...
...MASSIVE FACILITY CONSTRUCTED UNDER THE NEW NATIONAL STADIUM.
CONSIDER IT THE GIFT OF CHINESE INVESTMENT, MIDDLE EASTERN WEALTH AND THE ACCUMULATION OF CAPITAL!
SO A FEW PEOPLE ARE GOING TO ESCAPE WITHOUT TELLING ANYONE ELSE, HUH?
MISS SUMARU ...
... YOU'VE GOT SOME-THING IN YOUR EYE.
HM?

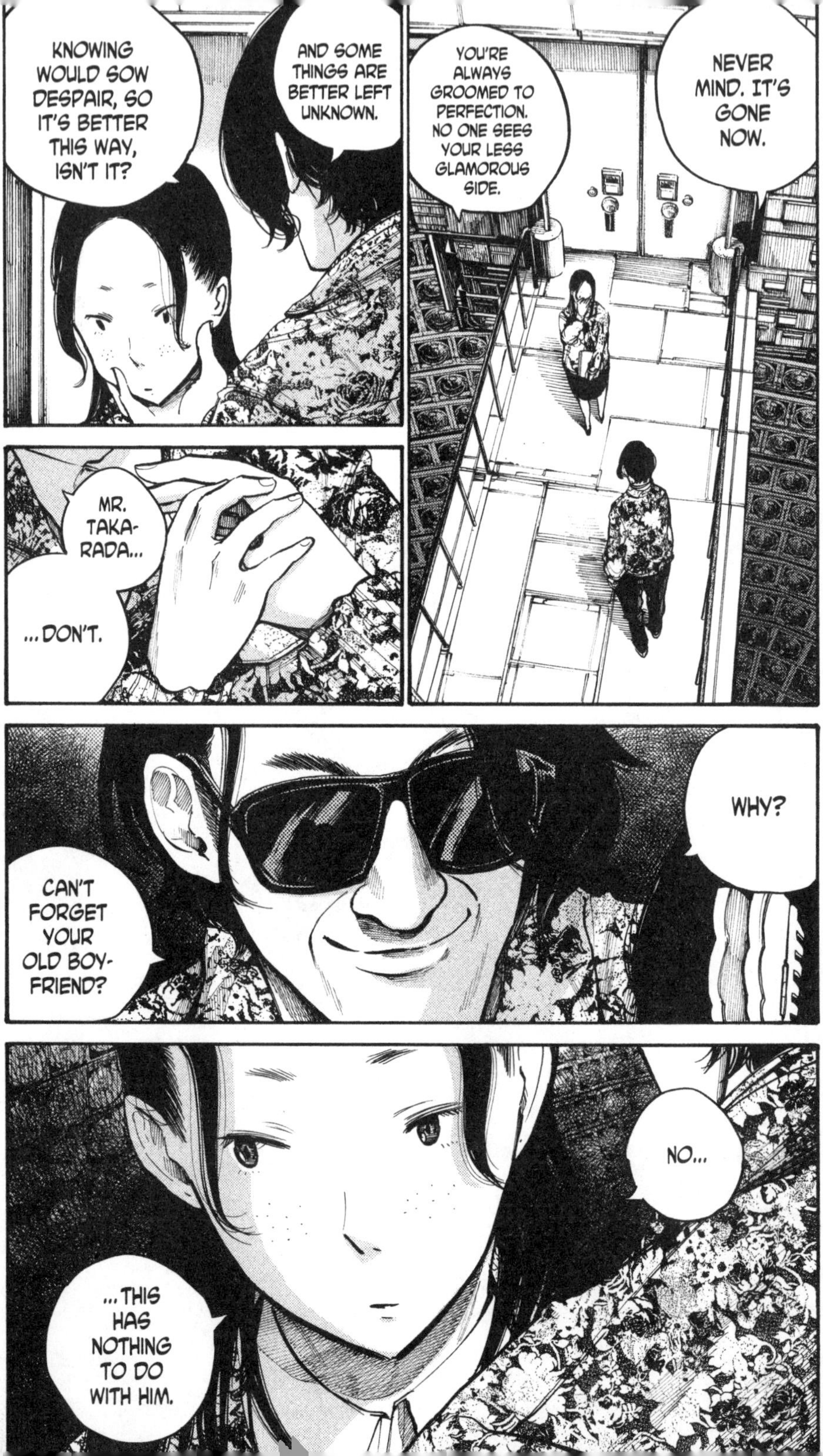
NEVER MIND. IT'S GONE NOW.
YOU'RE ALWAYS GROOMED TO PERFECTION. NO ONE SEES YOUR LESS GLAMOROUS SIDE.
AND SOME THINGS ARE BETTER LEFT UNKNOWN.
KNOWING WOULD SOW DESPAIR, SO IT'S BETTER THIS WAY, ISN'T IT?
MR. TAKA-RADA...
...DON'T.
WHY?
CAN'T FORGET YOUR OLD BOY-FRIEND?
NO...
...THIS HAS NOTHING TO DO WITH HIM.

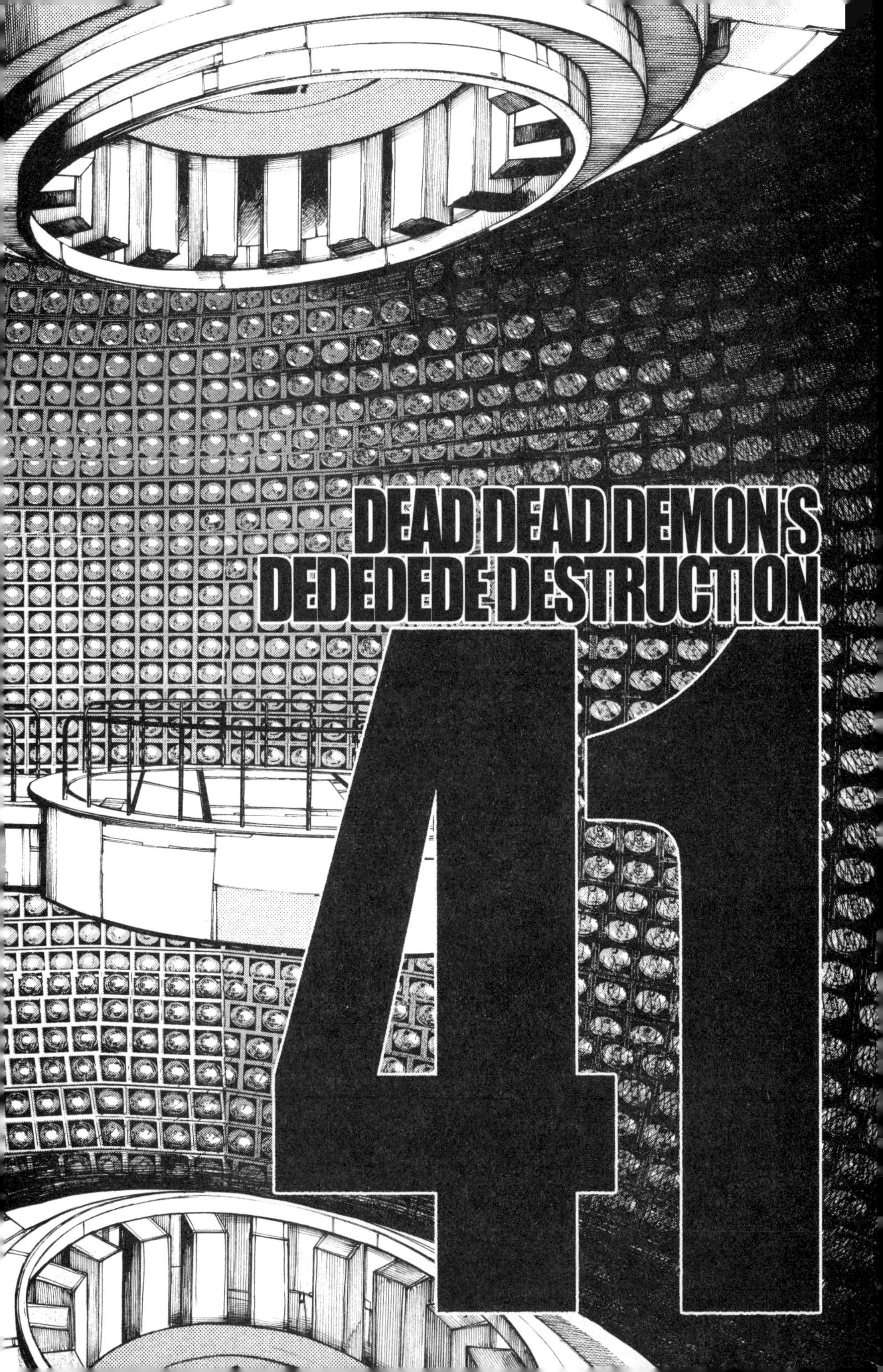
DEAD DEAD DEMON'S
DEDEDEDE DESTRUCTION
41

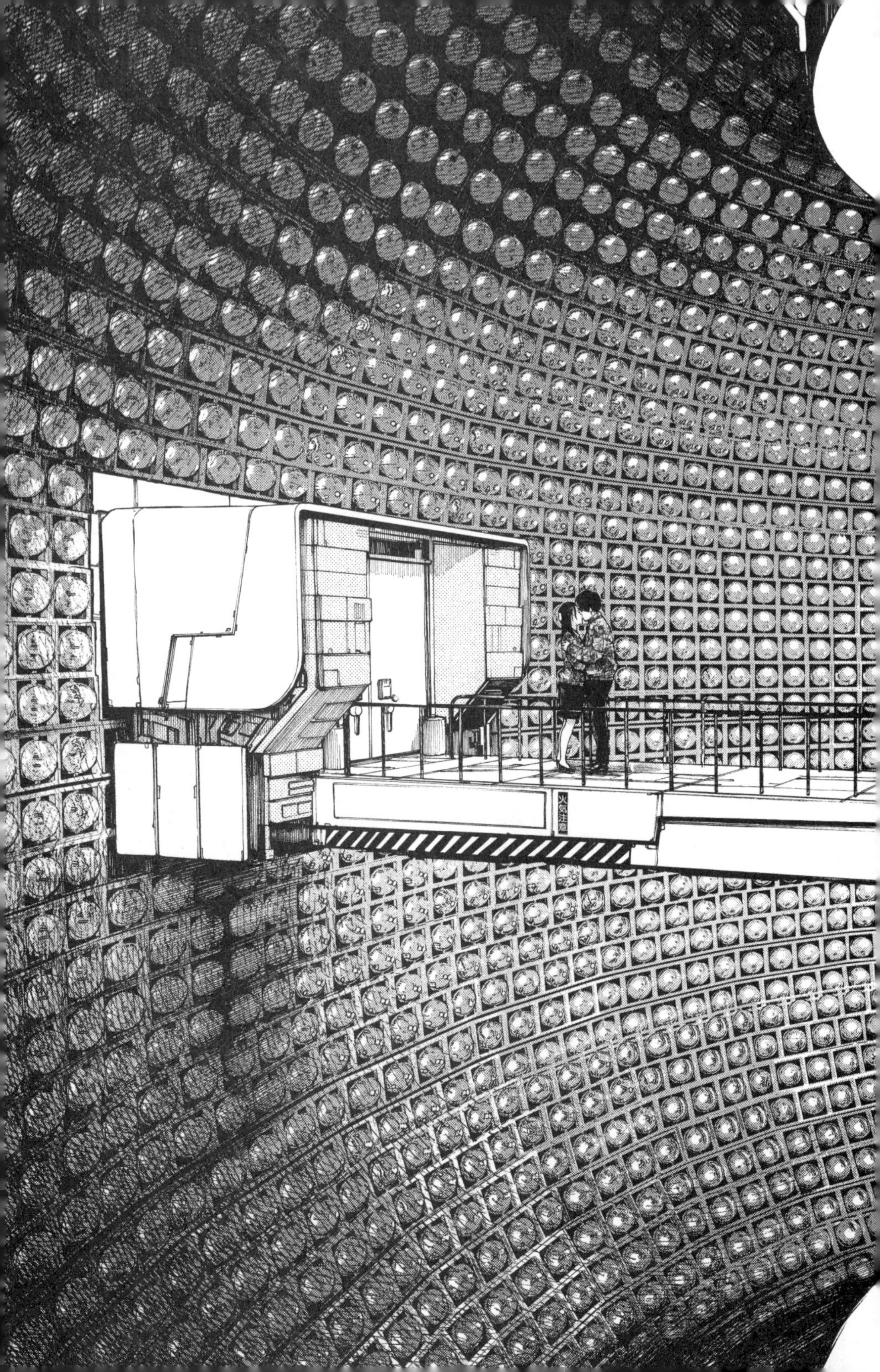
火気注意

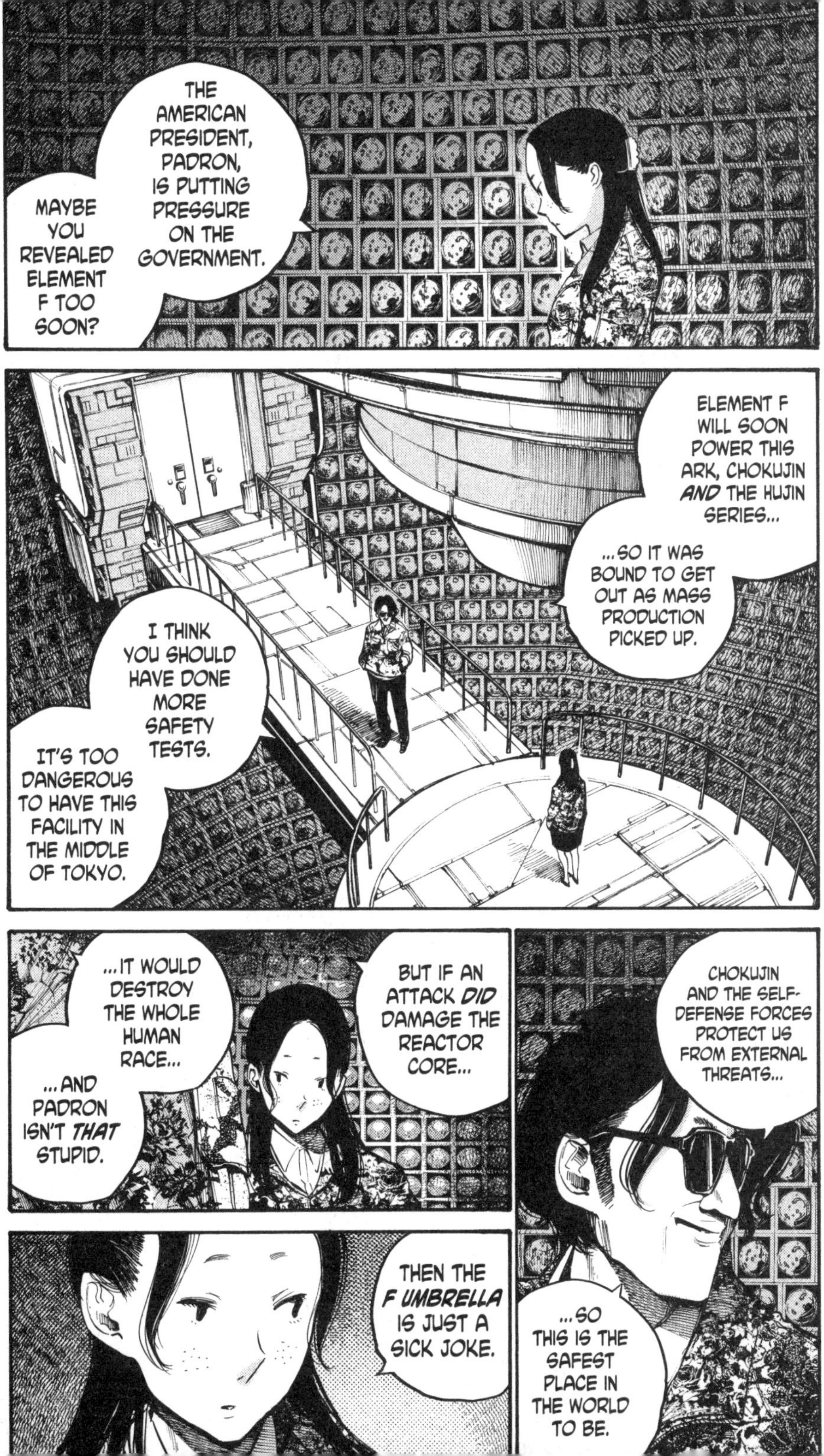
THE AMERICAN PRESIDENT, PADRON, IS PUTTING PRESSURE ON THE GOVERNMENT.
MAYBE YOU REVEALED ELEMENT F TOO SOON?
ELEMENT F WILL SOON POWER THIS ARK, CHOKUJIN AND THE HUJIN SERIES...
...SO IT WAS BOUND TO GET OUT AS MASS PRODUCTION PICKED UP.
I THINK YOU SHOULD HAVE DONE MORE SAFETY TESTS.
IT'S TOO DANGEROUS TO HAVE THIS FACILITY IN THE MIDDLE OF TOKYO.
CHOKUJIN AND THE SELF-DEFENSE FORCES PROTECT US FROM EXTERNAL THREATS...
...SO THIS IS THE SAFEST PLACE IN THE WORLD TO BE.
BUT IF AN ATTACK DID DAMAGE THE REACTOR CORE...
...IT WOULD DESTROY THE WHOLE HUMAN RACE...
...AND PADRON ISN'T THAT STUPID.
THEN THE F UMBRELLA IS JUST A SICK JOKE.

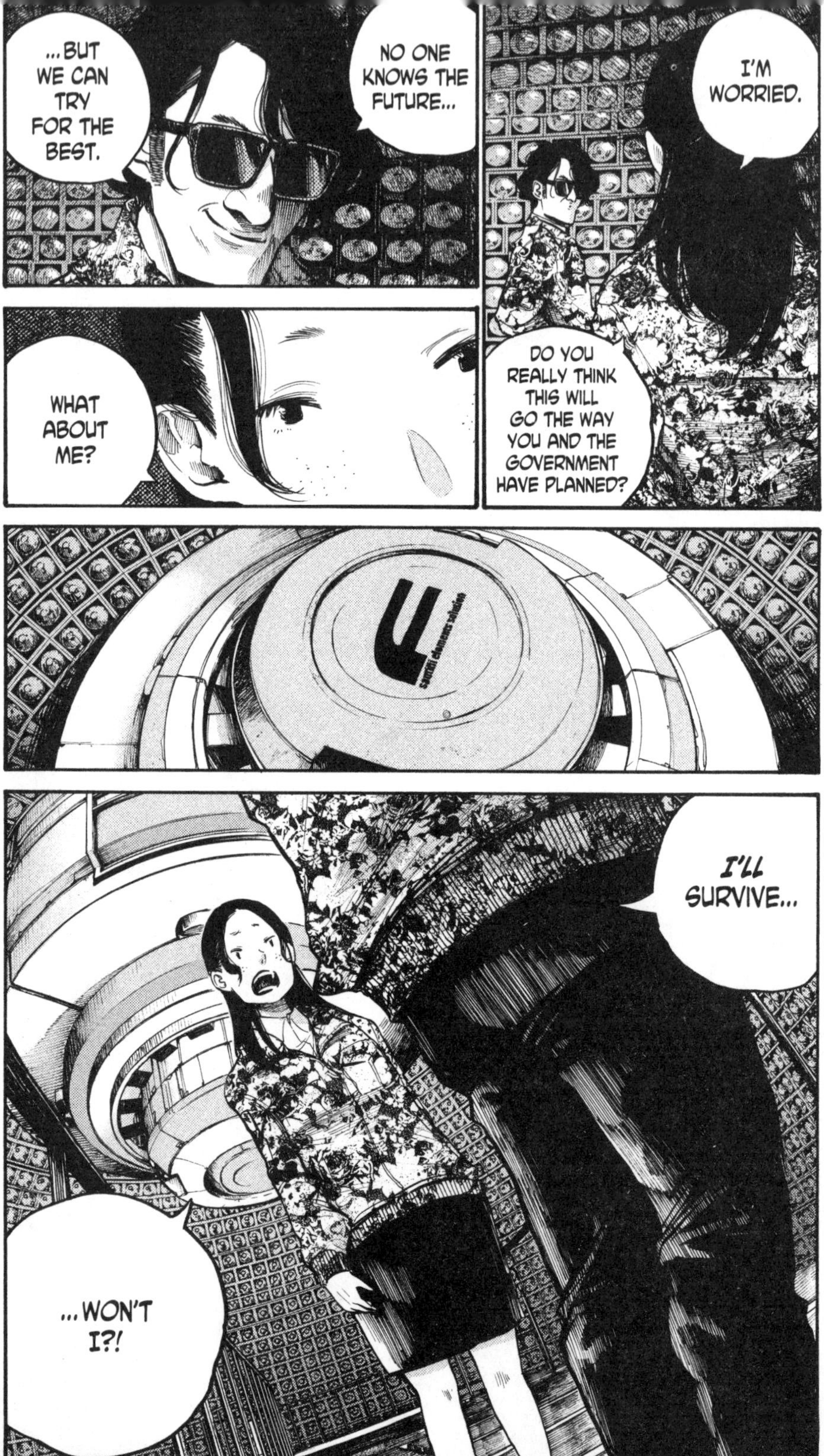
I'M WORRIED.
DO YOU REALLY THINK THIS WILL GO THE WAY YOU AND THE GOVERNMENT HAVE PLANNED?
NO ONE KNOWS THE FUTURE...
...BUT WE CAN TRY FOR THE BEST.
WHAT ABOUT ME?
I'LL SURVIVE...
...WON'T I?!

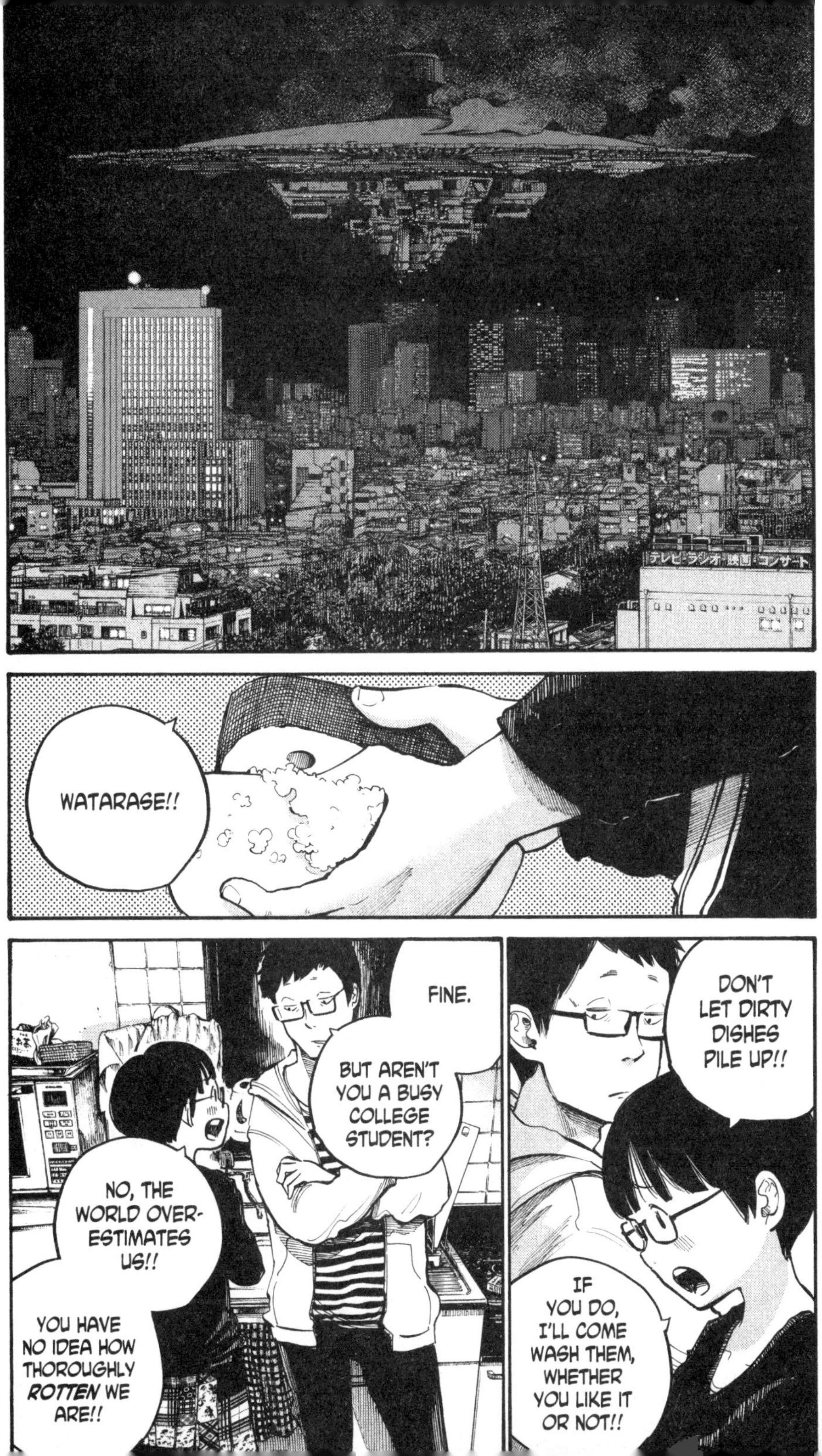
テレビ ラジオ
コンサート
WATARASE!!
DON'T LET DIRTY DISHES PILE UP!!
IF YOU DO, I'LL COME WASH THEM, WHETHER YOU LIKE IT OR NOT!!
FINE.
BUT AREN'T YOU A BUSY COLLEGE STUDENT?
NO, THE WORLD OVER-ESTIMATES US!!
YOU HAVE NO IDEA HOW THOROUGHLY *ROTTEN* WE ARE!!

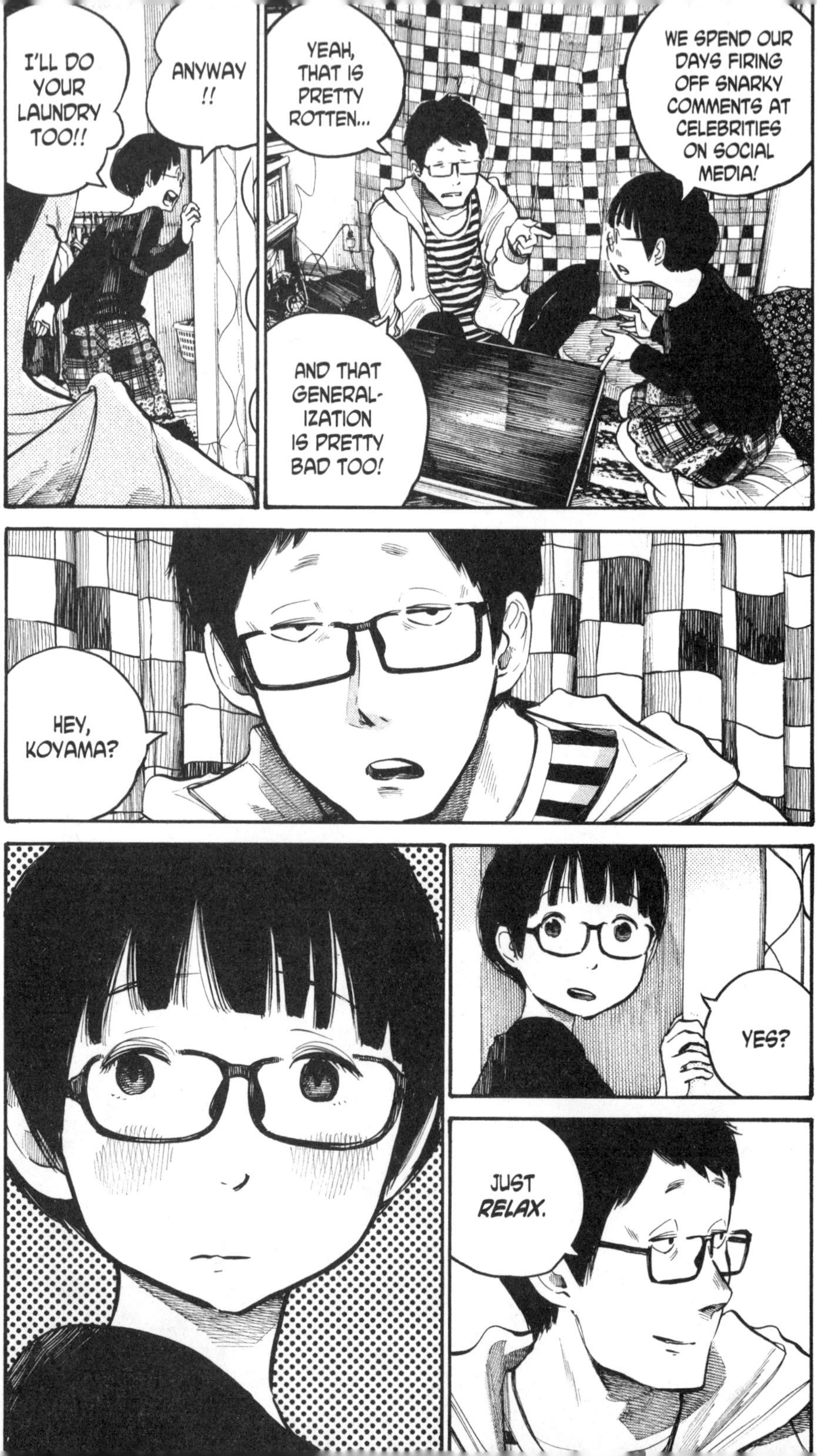
WE SPEND OUR DAYS FIRING OFF SNARKY COMMENTS AT CELEBRITIES ON SOCIAL MEDIA!
YEAH, THAT IS PRETTY ROTTEN...
AND THAT GENERAL-IZATION IS PRETTY BAD TOO!
ANYWAY!!
I'LL DO YOUR LAUNDRY TOO!!
HEY, KOYAMA?
YES?
JUST *RELAX*.

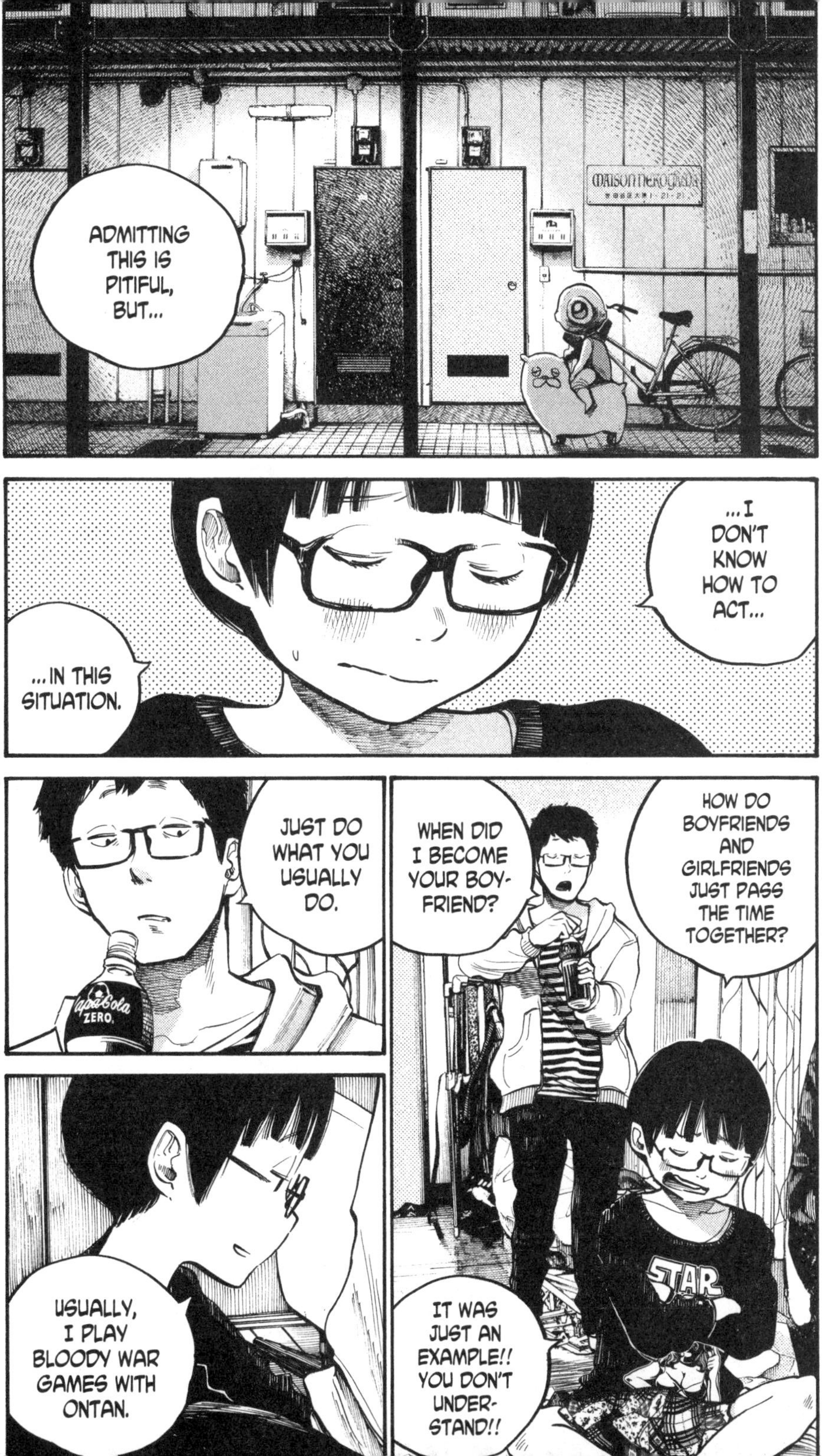
ADMITTING THIS IS PITIFUL, BUT...
...I DON'T KNOW HOW TO ACT...
...IN THIS SITUATION.
HOW DO BOYFRIENDS AND GIRLFRIENDS JUST PASS THE TIME TOGETHER?
WHEN DID I BECOME YOUR BOY-FRIEND?
STAR
IT WAS JUST AN EXAMPLE!! YOU DON'T UNDER-STAND!!
JUST DO WHAT YOU USUALLY DO.
ZERO
USUALLY, I PLAY BLOODY WAR GAMES WITH ONTAN.

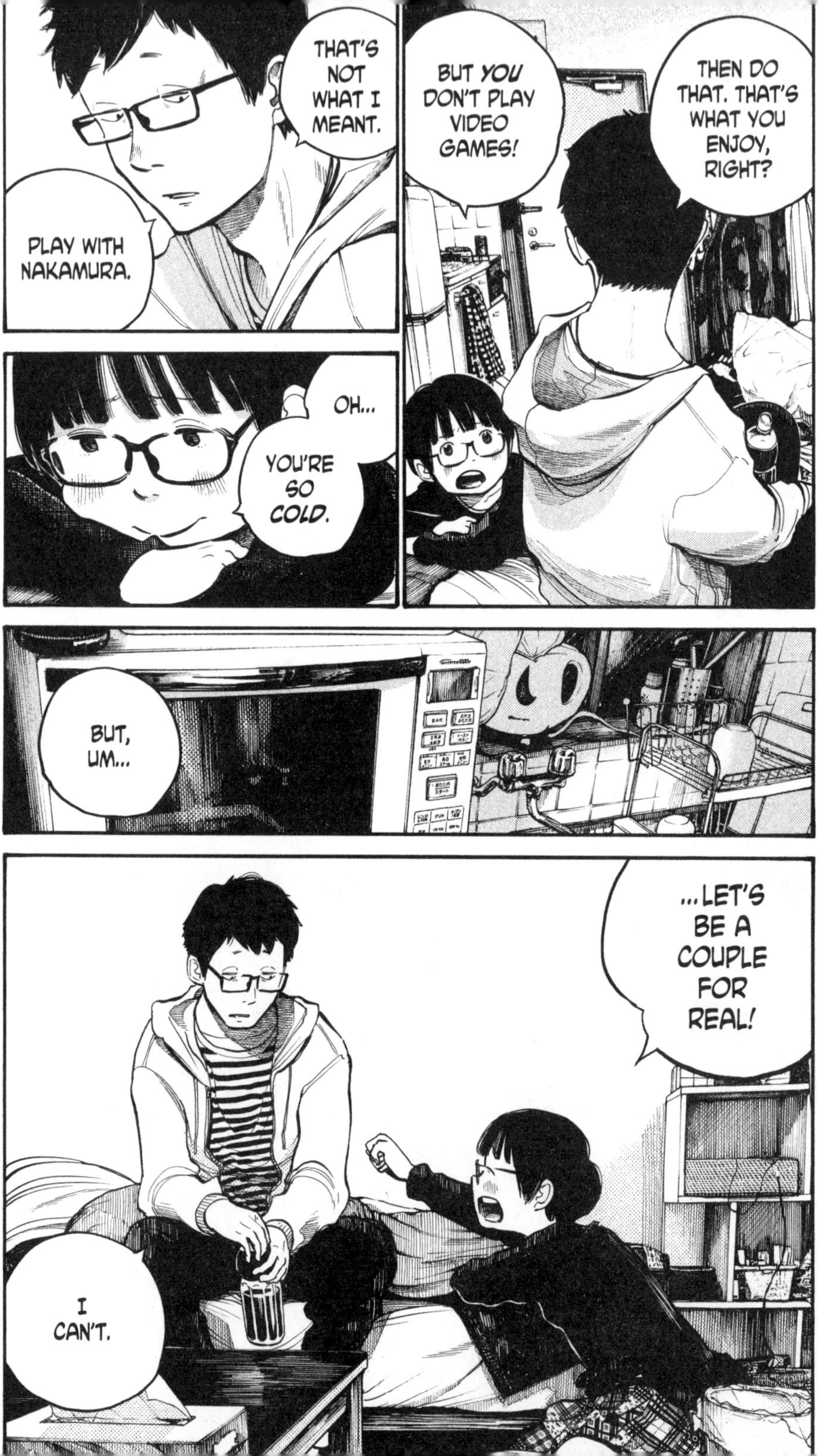
THEN DO THAT. THAT'S WHAT YOU ENJOY, RIGHT?
BUT *YOU* DON'T PLAY VIDEO GAMES!
THAT'S NOT WHAT I MEANT.
PLAY WITH NAKAMURA.
OH...
YOU'RE SO *COLD*.
BUT, UM...
...LET'S BE A COUPLE FOR REAL!
I CAN'T.

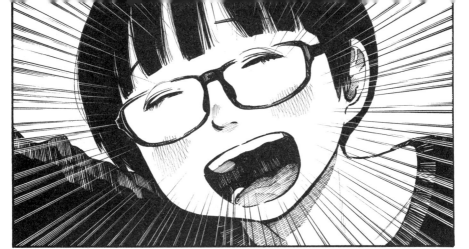

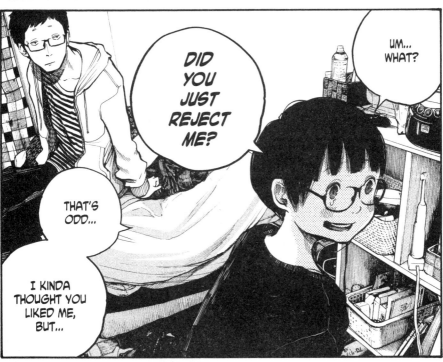

DID YOU JUST REJECT ME?

UM... WHAT?

THAT'S ODD...

I KINDA THOUGHT YOU LIKED ME, BUT...

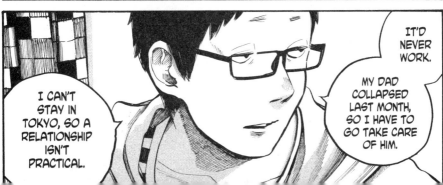

IT'D NEVER WORK.

MY DAD COLLAPSED LAST MONTH, SO I HAVE TO GO TAKE CARE OF HIM.

I CAN'T STAY IN TOKYO, SO A RELATIONSHIP ISN'T PRACTICAL.

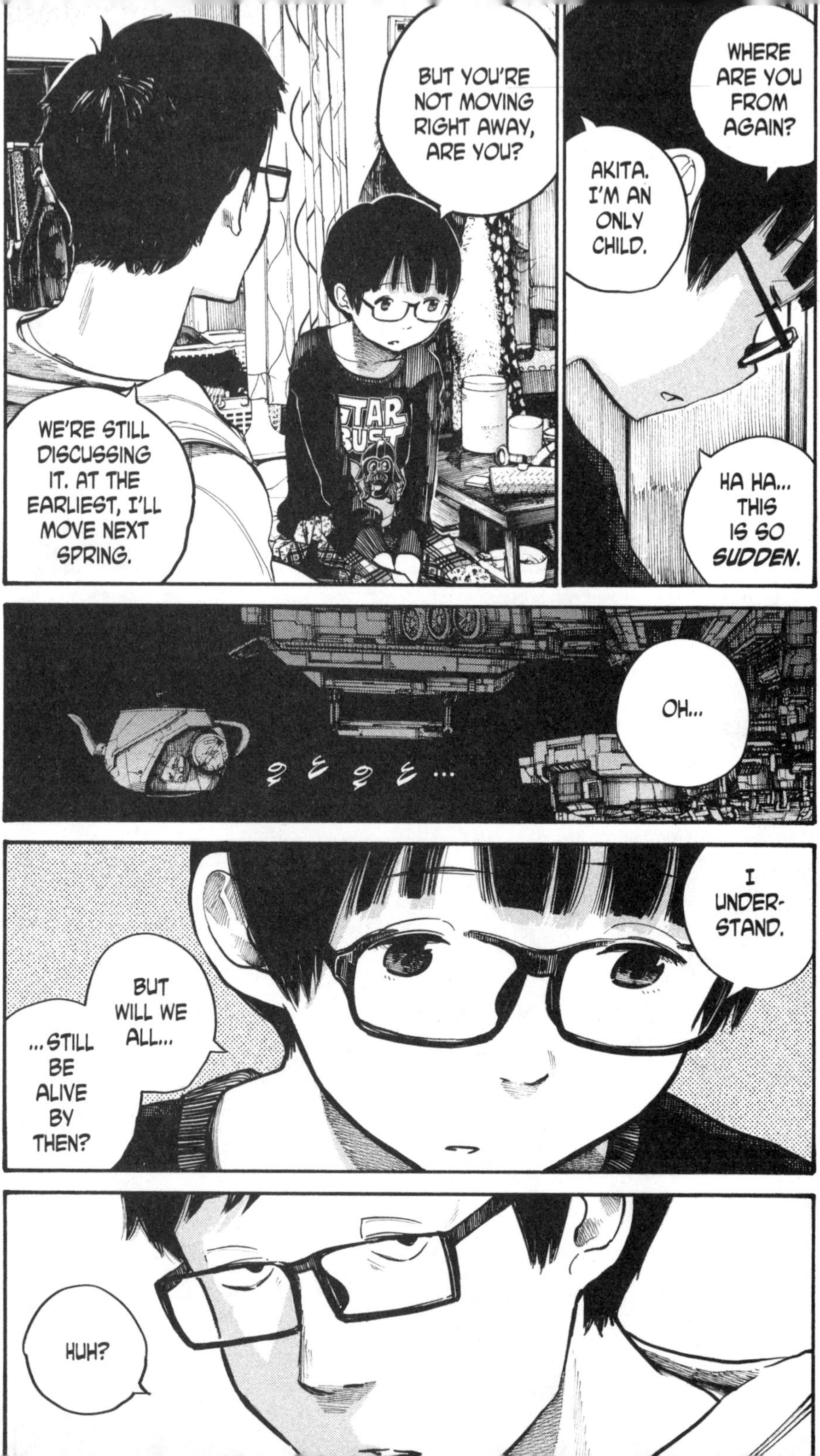
WHERE ARE YOU FROM AGAIN?
AKITA. I'M AN ONLY CHILD.
HA HA... THIS IS SO *SUDDEN*.
BUT YOU'RE NOT MOVING RIGHT AWAY, ARE YOU?
WE'RE STILL DISCUSSING IT. AT THE EARLIEST, I'LL MOVE NEXT SPRING.
OH...
I UNDER-STAND.
BUT WILL WE ALL...
...STILL BE ALIVE BY THEN?
HUH?

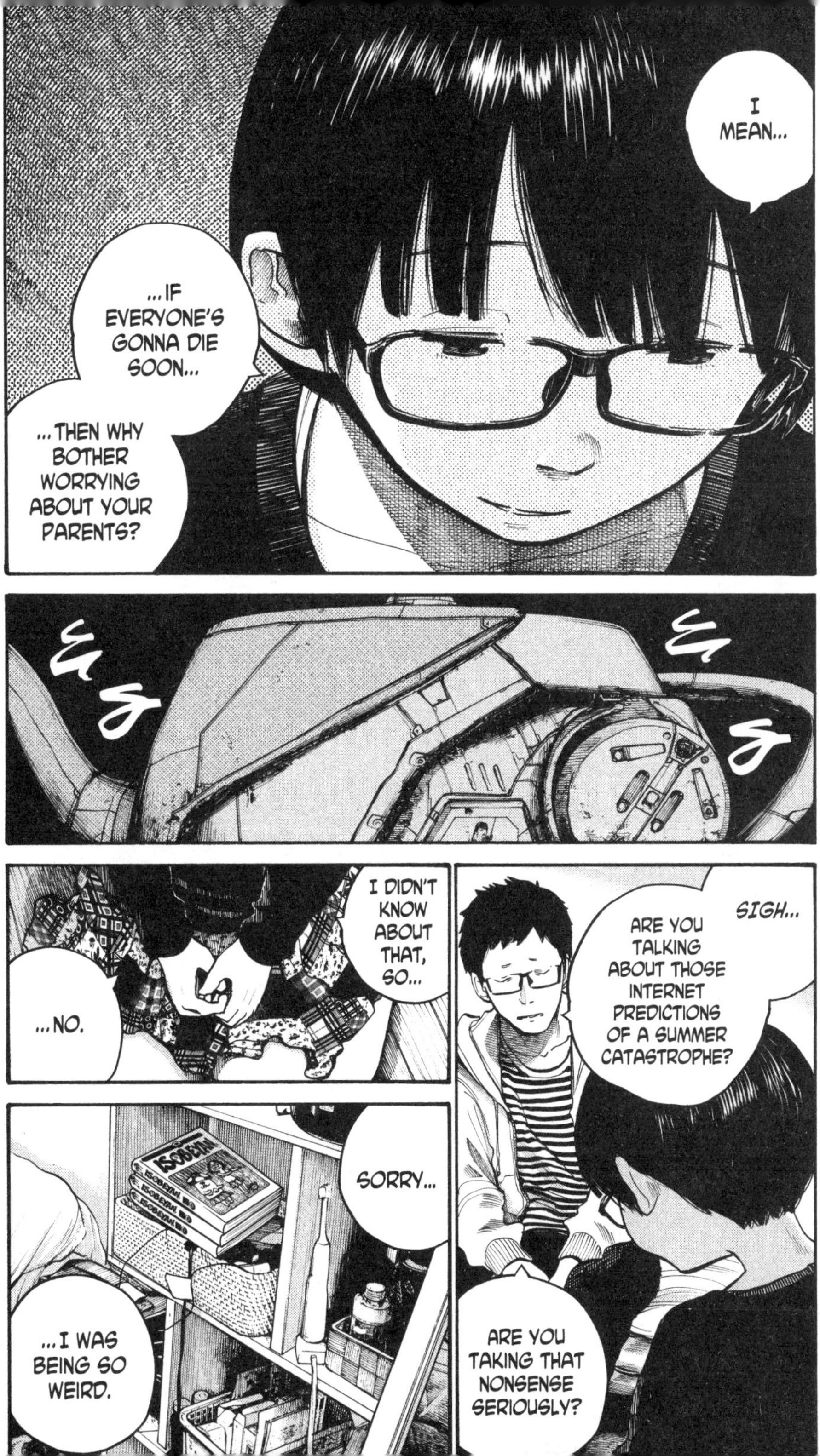
I MEAN...
...IF EVERYONE'S GONNA DIE SOON...
...THEN WHY BOTHER WORRYING ABOUT YOUR PARENTS?
SIGH...
ARE YOU TALKING ABOUT THOSE INTERNET PREDICTIONS OF A SUMMER CATASTROPHE?
ARE YOU TAKING THAT NONSENSE SERIOUSLY?
I DIDN'T KNOW ABOUT THAT, SO...
...NO.
SORRY...
...I WAS BEING SO WEIRD.

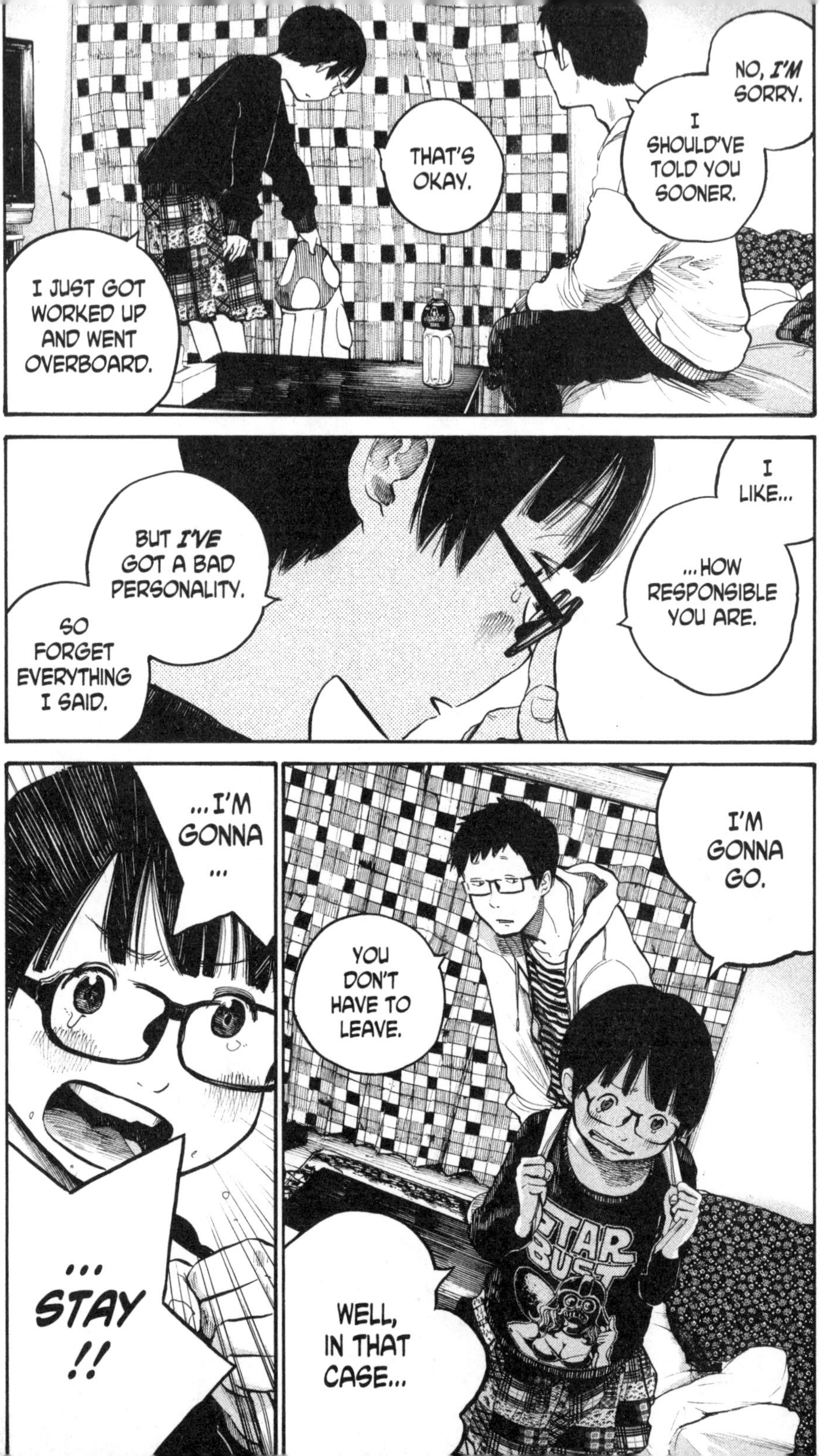
NO, *I'M* SORRY.
I SHOULD'VE TOLD YOU SOONER.
THAT'S OKAY.
I JUST GOT WORKED UP AND WENT OVERBOARD.
I LIKE...
...HOW RESPONSIBLE YOU ARE.
BUT *I'VE* GOT A BAD PERSONALITY.
SO FORGET EVERYTHING I SAID.
I'M GONNA GO.
YOU DON'T HAVE TO LEAVE.
WELL, IN THAT CASE...
...I'M GONNA ...
...STAY!!

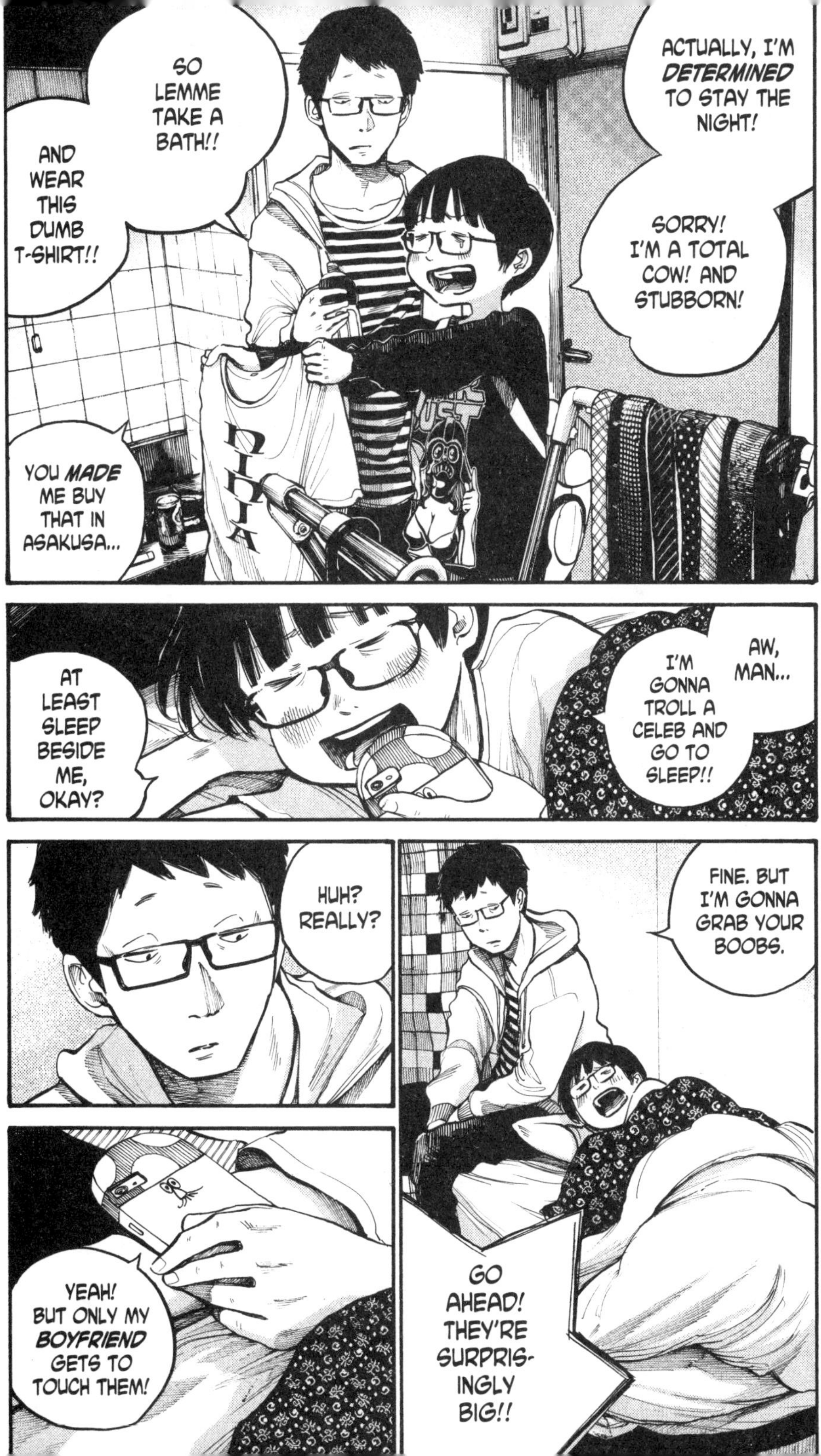
ACTUALLY, I'M *DETERMINED* TO STAY THE NIGHT!
SORRY! I'M A TOTAL COW! AND STUBBORN!
SO LEMME TAKE A BATH!!
AND WEAR THIS DUMB T-SHIRT!!
NINJA
YOU *MADE* ME BUY THAT IN ASAKUSA...
AW, MAN...
I'M GONNA TROLL A CELEB AND GO TO SLEEP!!
AT LEAST SLEEP BESIDE ME, OKAY?
FINE. BUT I'M GONNA GRAB YOUR BOOBS.
GO AHEAD! THEY'RE SURPRIS-INGLY BIG!!
HUH? REALLY?
YEAH! BUT ONLY MY *BOYFRIEND* GETS TO TOUCH THEM!

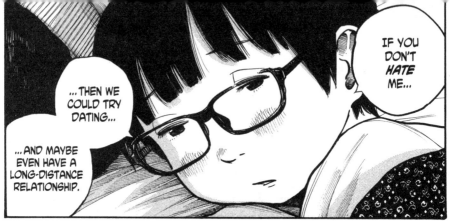

IF YOU DON'T *HATE* ME...

...THEN WE COULD TRY DATING...

...AND MAYBE EVEN HAVE A LONG-DISTANCE RELATIONSHIP.

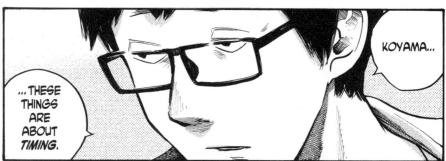

KOYAMA...

...THESE THINGS ARE ABOUT *TIMING*.

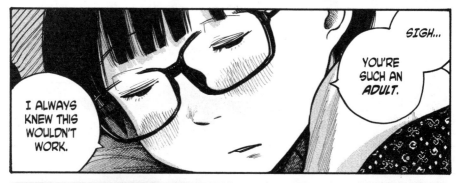

SIGH...

YOU'RE SUCH AN *ADULT*.

I ALWAYS KNEW THIS WOULDN'T WORK.

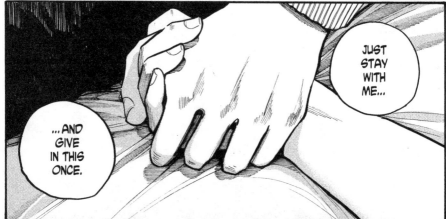

JUST STAY WITH ME...

...AND GIVE IN THIS ONCE.

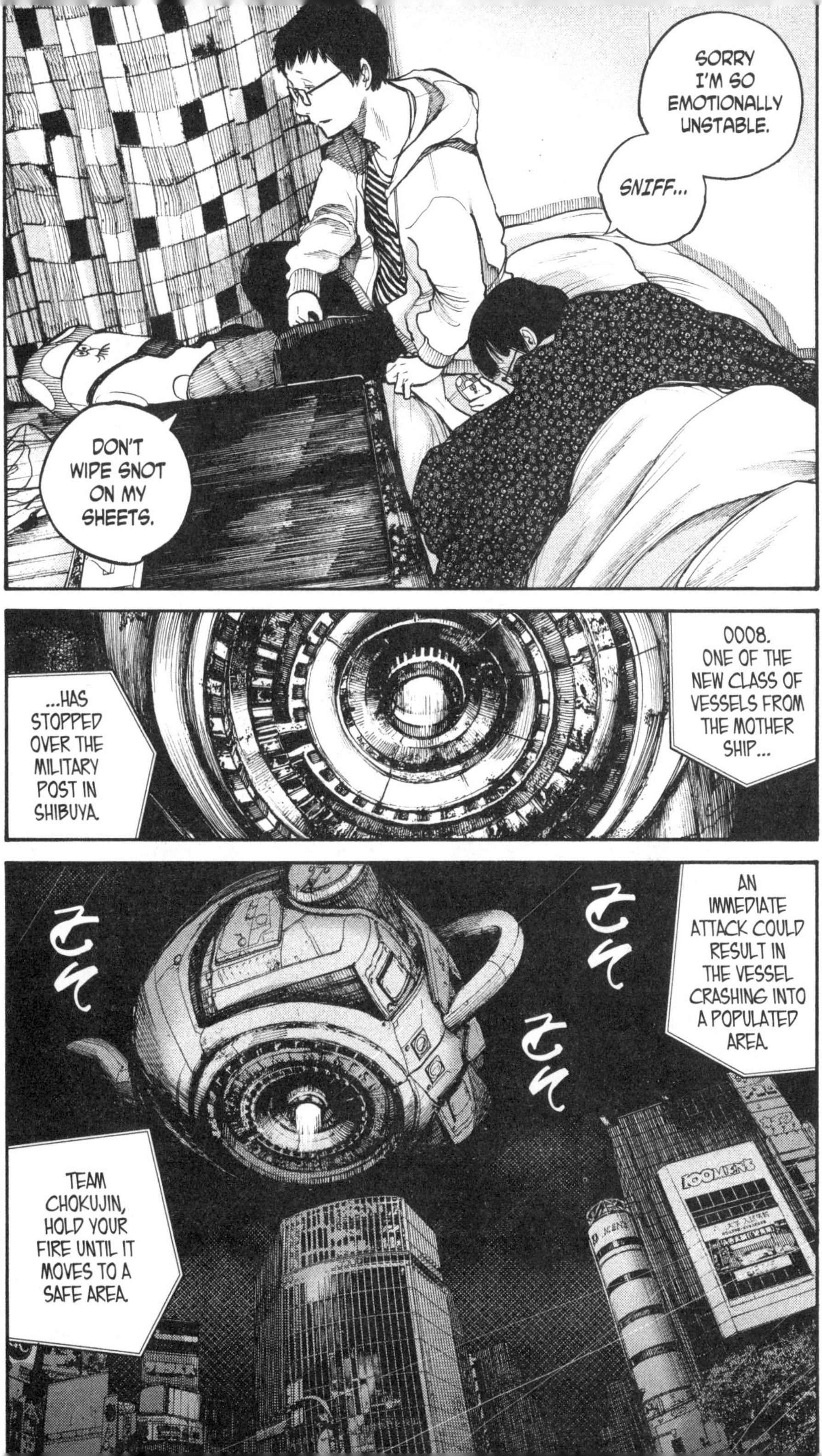
SORRY I'M SO EMOTIONALLY UNSTABLE.
SNIFF...
DON'T WIPE SNOT ON MY SHEETS.
0008. ONE OF THE NEW CLASS OF VESSELS FROM THE MOTHER SHIP...
...HAS STOPPED OVER THE MILITARY POST IN SHIBUYA.
AN IMMEDIATE ATTACK COULD RESULT IN THE VESSEL CRASHING INTO A POPULATED AREA.
TEAM CHOKUJIN, HOLD YOUR FIRE UNTIL IT MOVES TO A SAFE AREA.

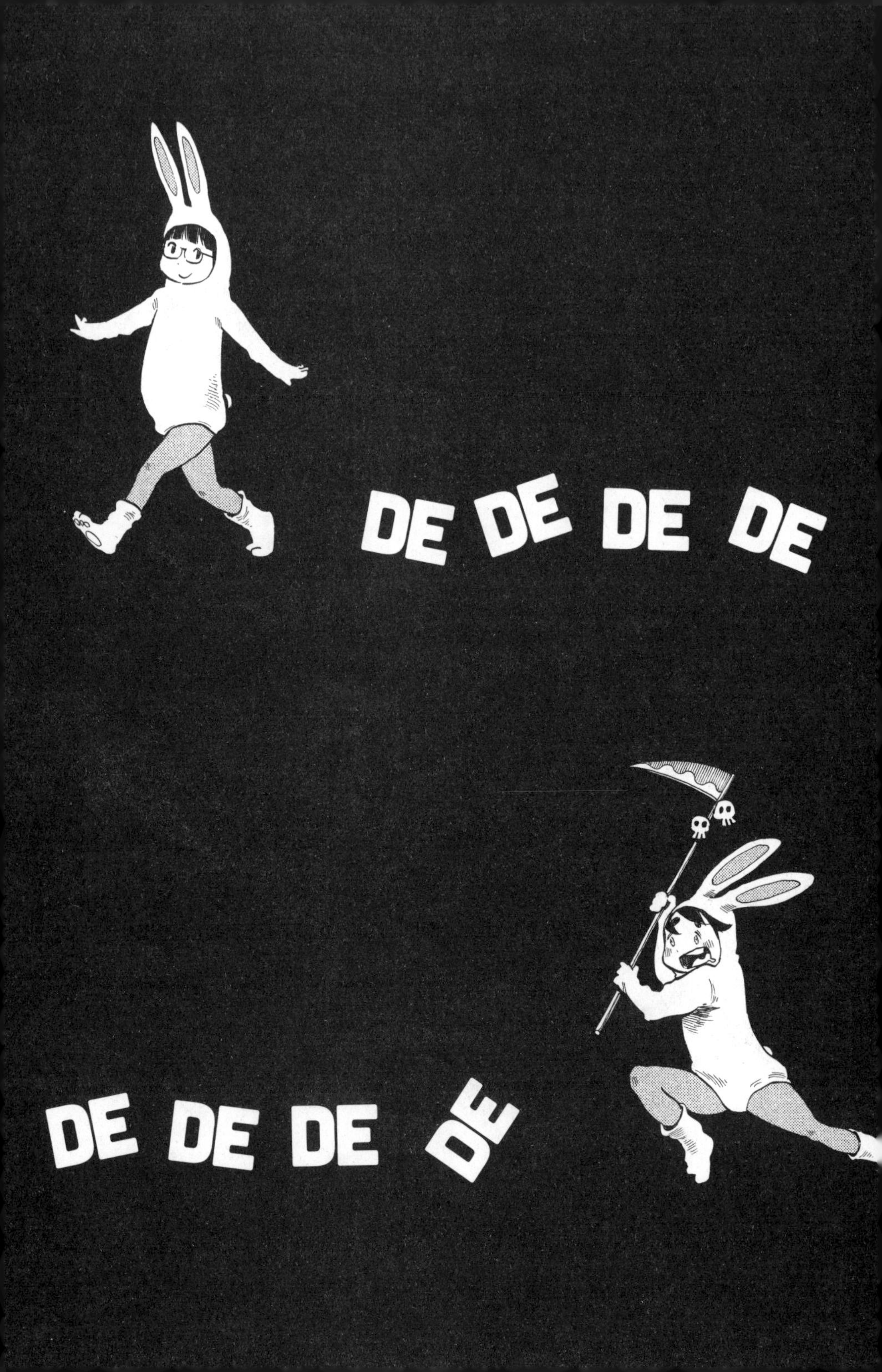
DE DE DE DE
DE DE DE DE

DEDEDEDE

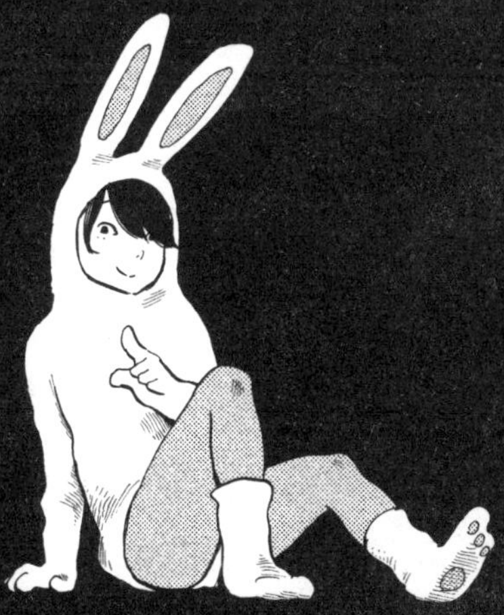

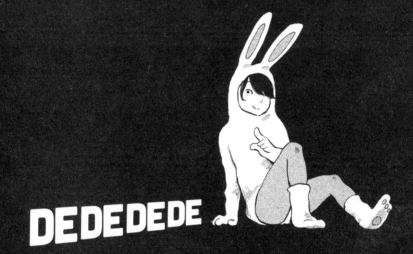

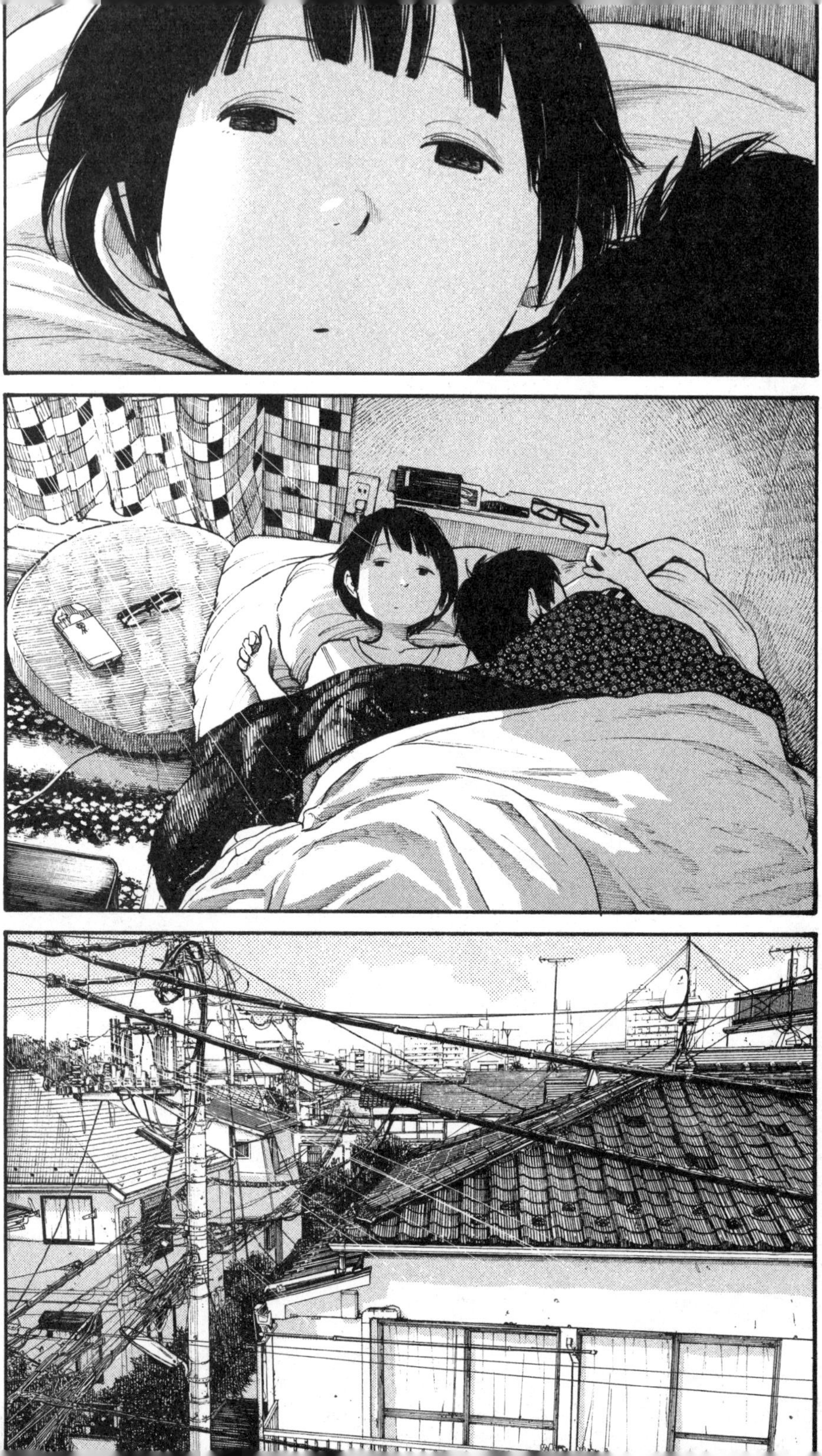

CHAPTER 42

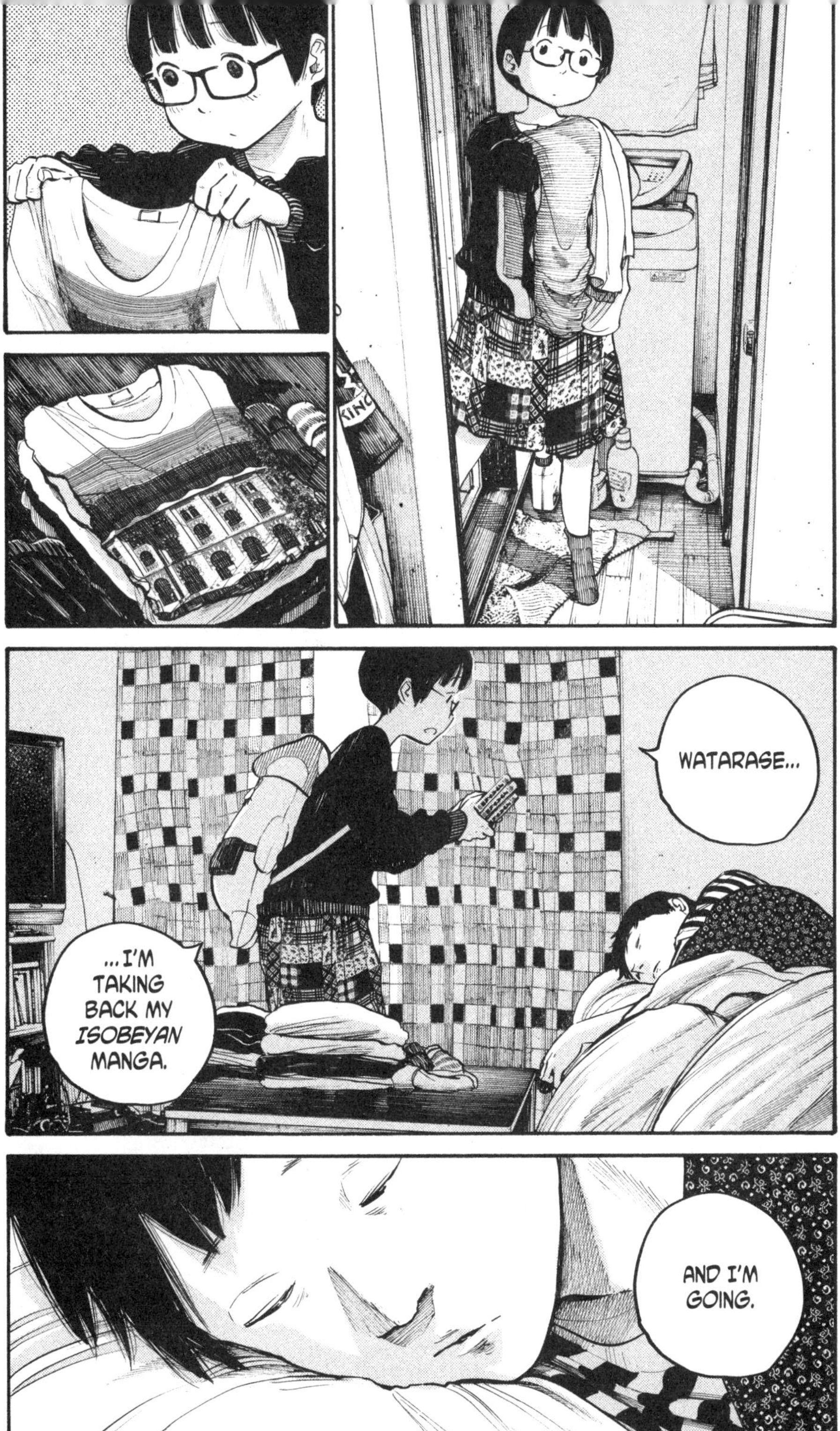
WATARASE...
...I'M TAKING BACK MY *ISOBEYAN* MANGA.
AND I'M GOING.

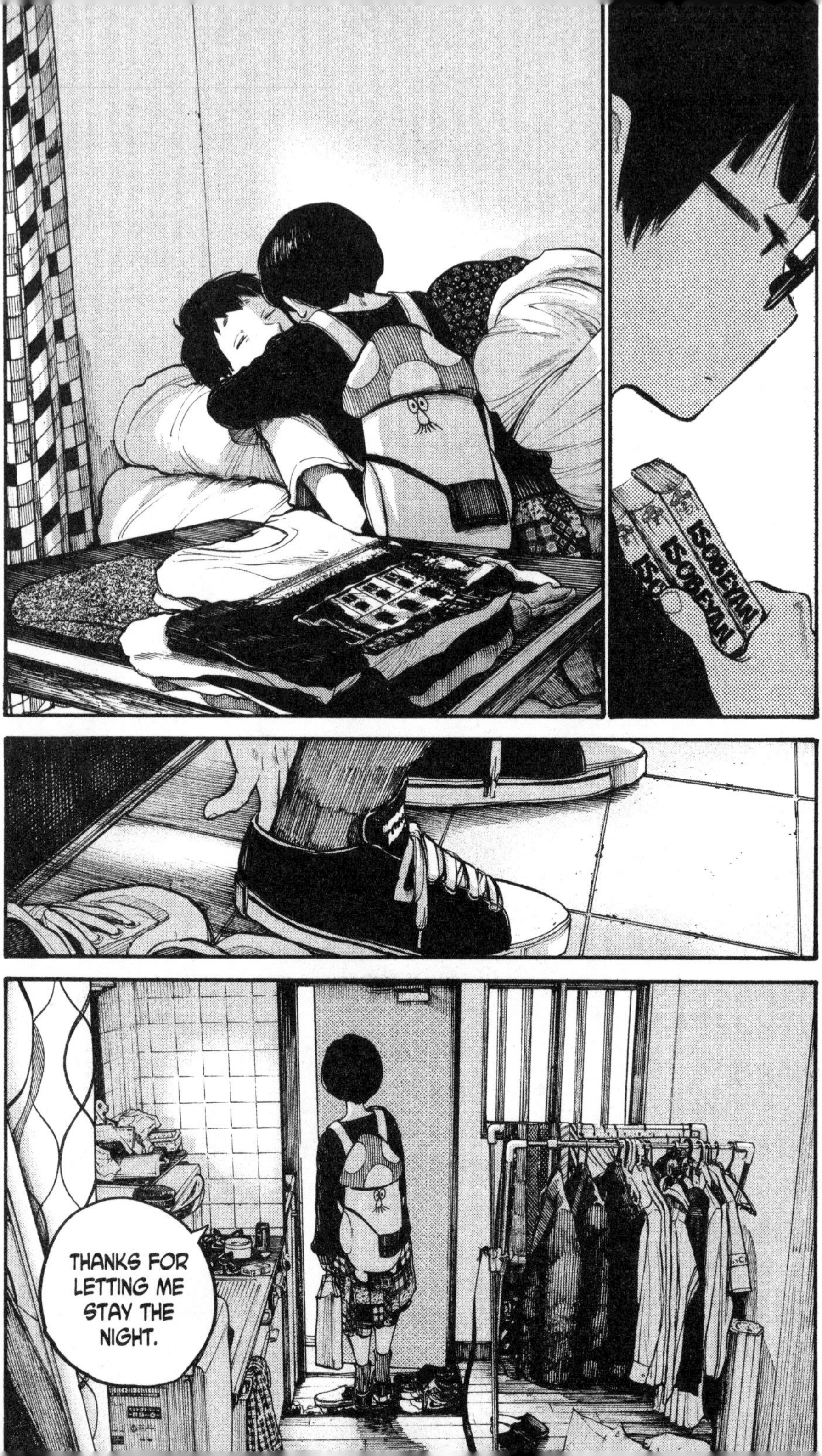
ISOBEYAN
ISOBEYAN
THANKS FOR LETTING ME STAY THE NIGHT.

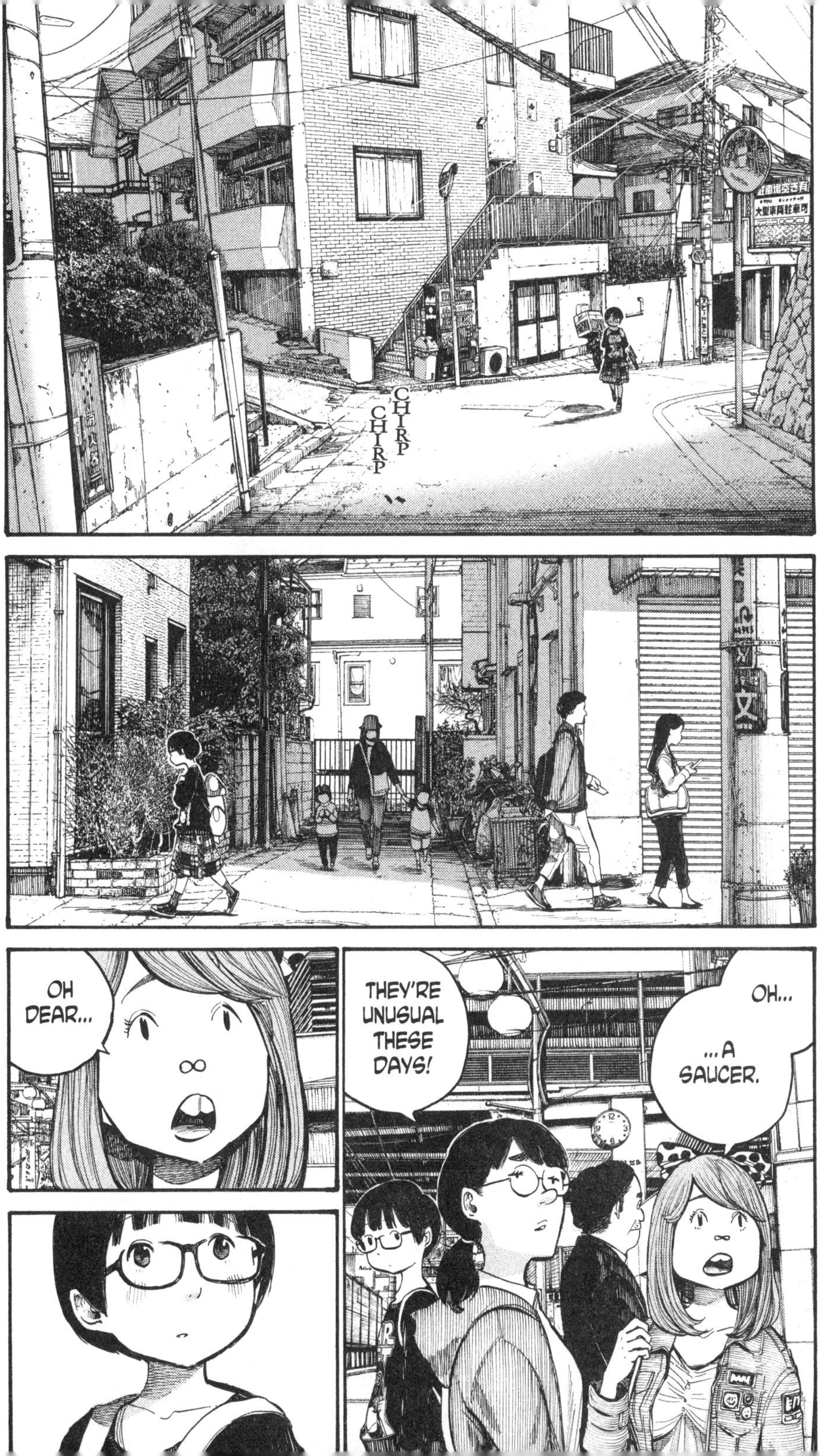
CHIRP
CHIRP
OH...
...A SAUCER.
THEY'RE UNUSUAL THESE DAYS!
OH DEAR...

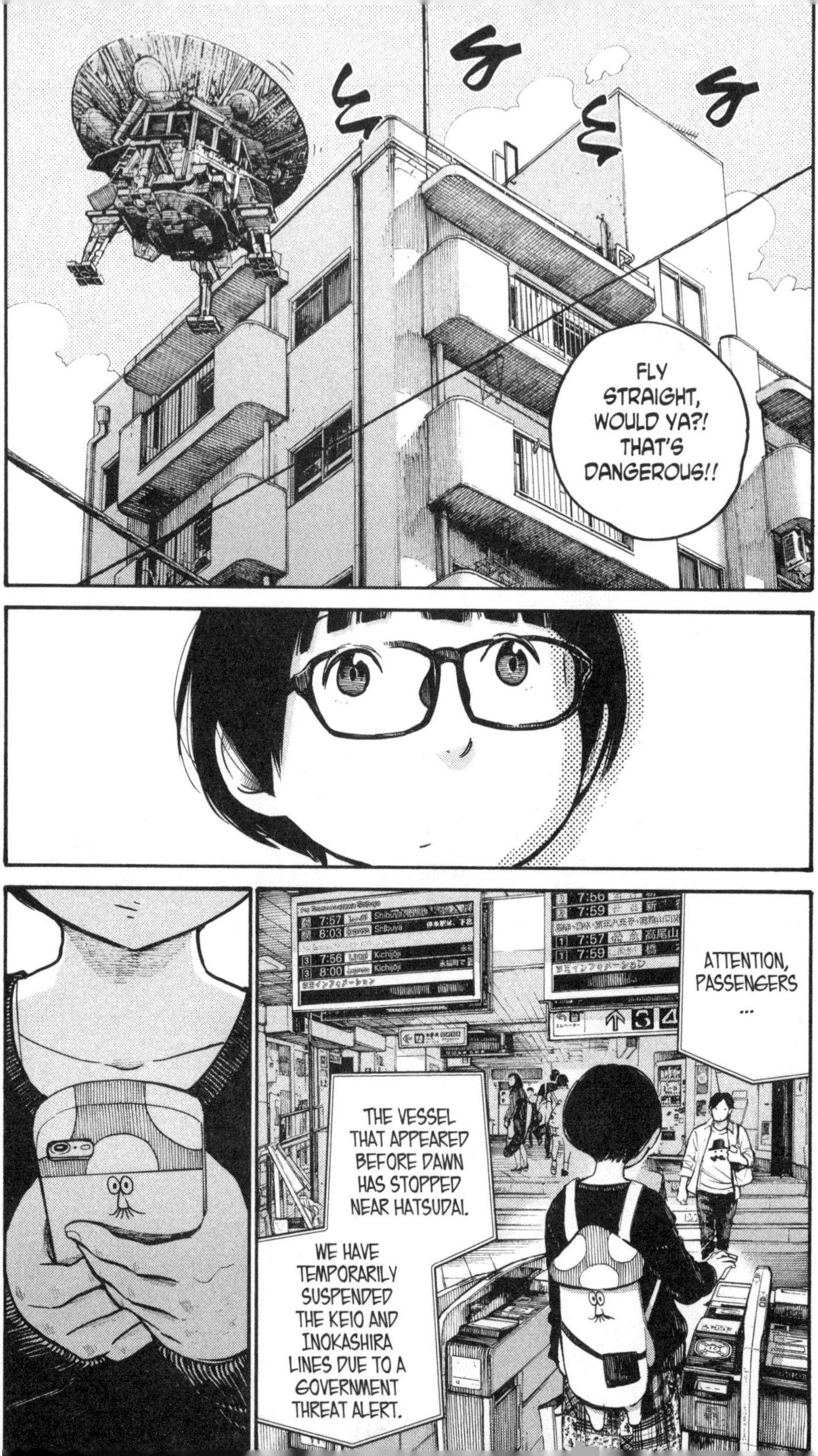
FLY STRAIGHT, WOULD YA?! THAT'S DANGEROUS!!
ATTENTION, PASSENGERS ...
THE VESSEL THAT APPEARED BEFORE DAWN HAS STOPPED NEAR HATSUDAI.
WE HAVE TEMPORARILY SUSPENDED THE KEIO AND INOKASHIRA LINES DUE TO A GOVERNMENT THREAT ALERT.

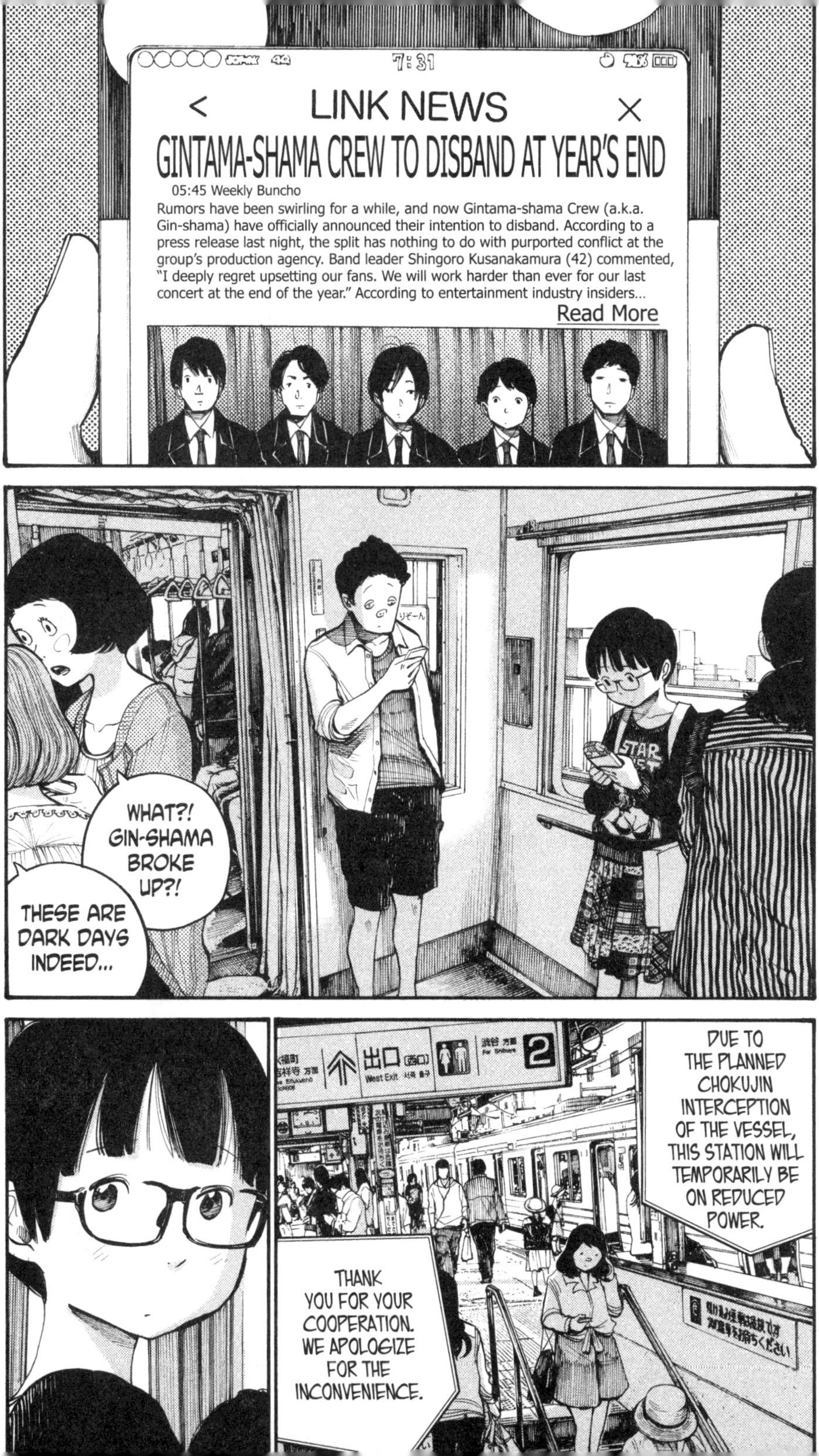
7:31
LINK NEWS
GINTAMA-SHAMA CREW TO DISBAND AT YEAR'S END
05:45 Weekly Buncho
Rumors have been swirling for a while, and now Gintama-shama Crew (a.k.a. Gin-shama) have officially announced their intention to disband. According to a press release last night, the split has nothing to do with purported conflict at the group's production agency. Band leader Shingoro Kusanakamura (42) commented, "I deeply regret upsetting our fans. We will work harder than ever for our last concert at the end of the year." According to entertainment industry insiders...
Read More
WHAT?! GIN-SHAMA BROKE UP?!
THESE ARE DARK DAYS INDEED...
出口
West Exit
2
DUE TO THE PLANNED CHOKUJIN INTERCEPTION OF THE VESSEL, THIS STATION WILL TEMPORARILY BE ON REDUCED POWER.
THANK YOU FOR YOUR COOPERATION. WE APOLOGIZE FOR THE INCONVENIENCE.

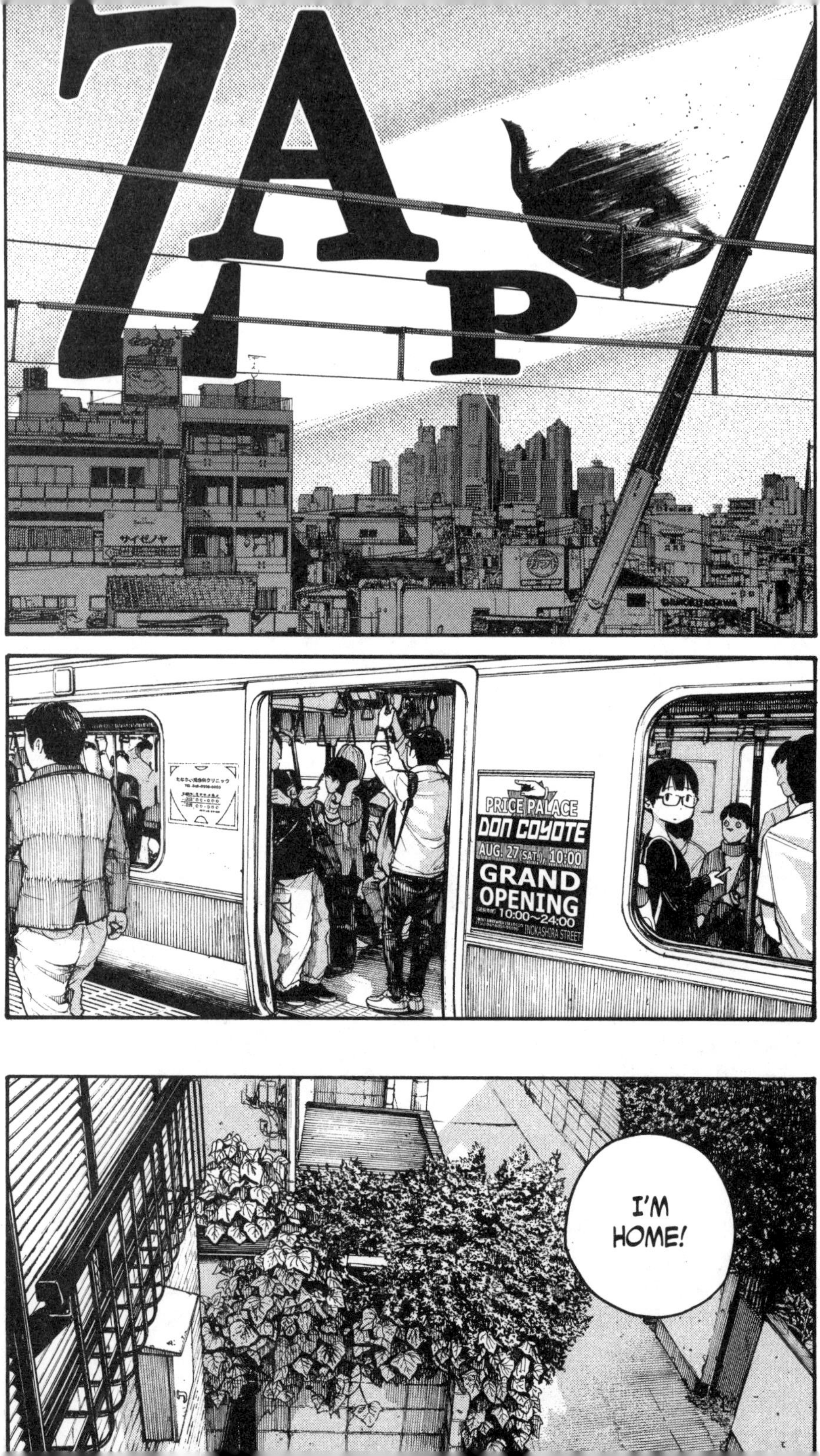
TAP
PRICE PALACE
DON COYOTE
AUG. 27 (SAT.) 10:00
GRAND OPENING
10:00~24:00
INOKASHIRA STREET
I'M HOME!

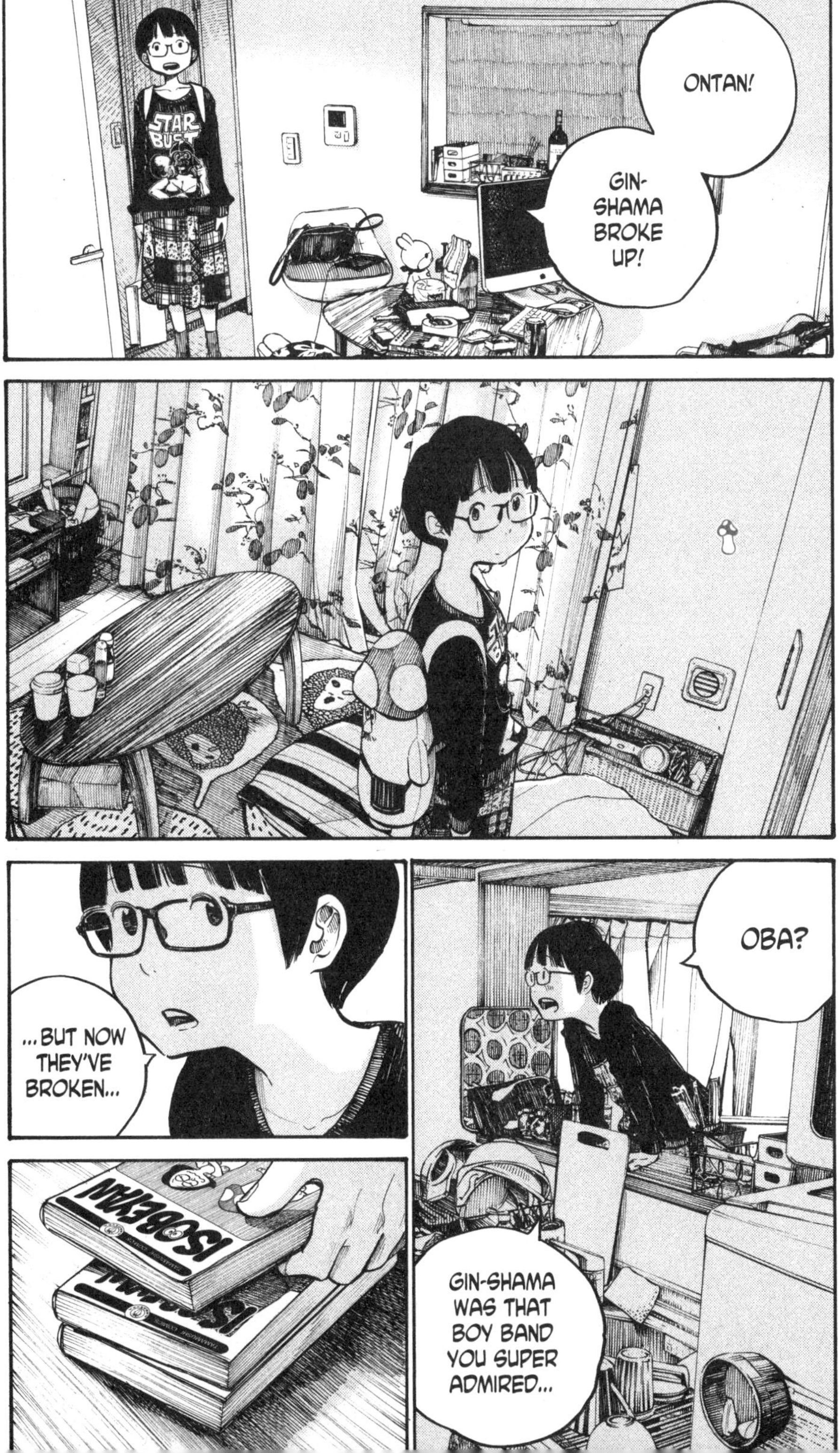
ONTAN!
GIN-SHAMA BROKE UP!
OBA?
GIN-SHAMA WAS THAT BOY BAND YOU SUPER ADMIRED...
...BUT NOW THEY'VE BROKEN...

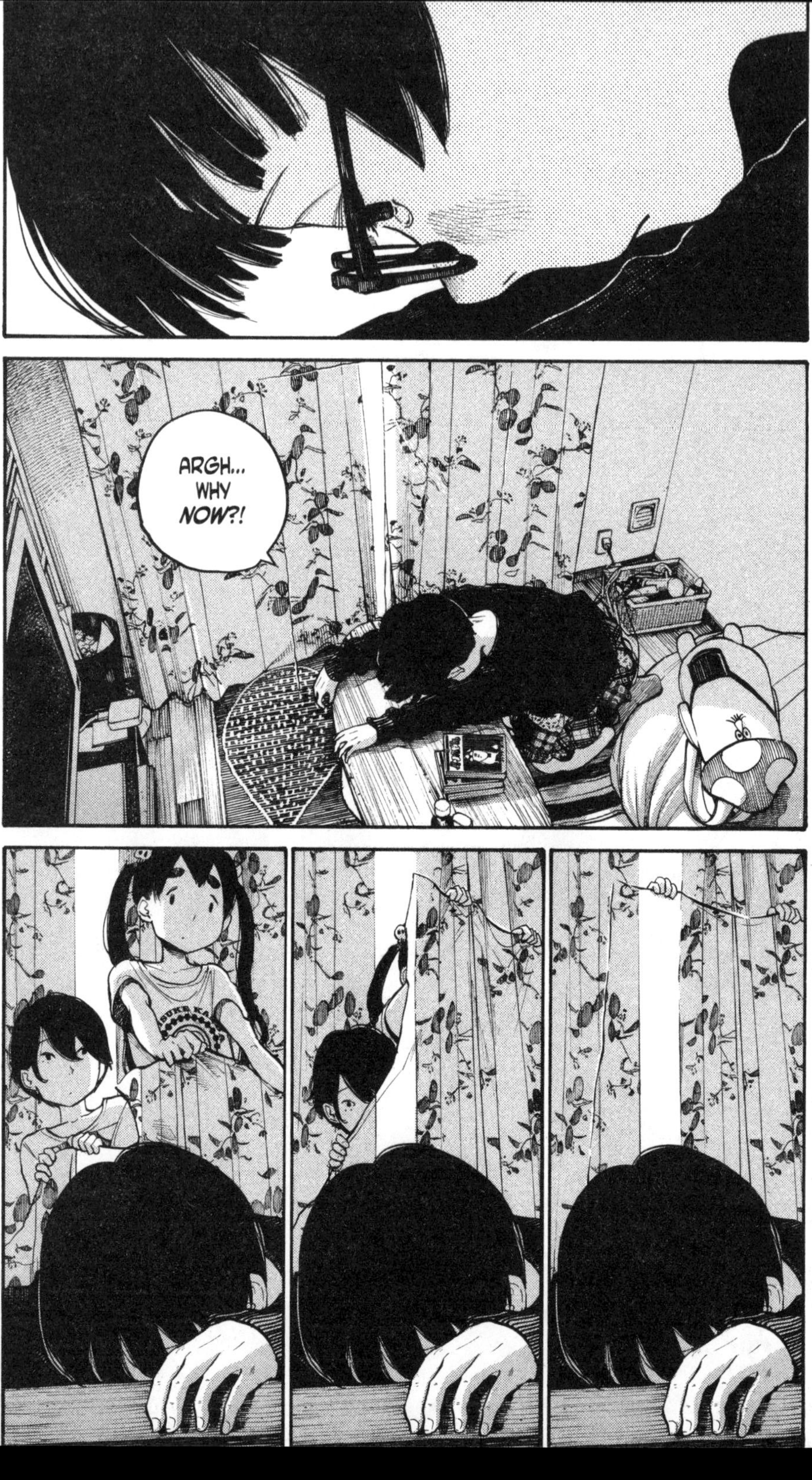
ARGH... WHY NOW?!

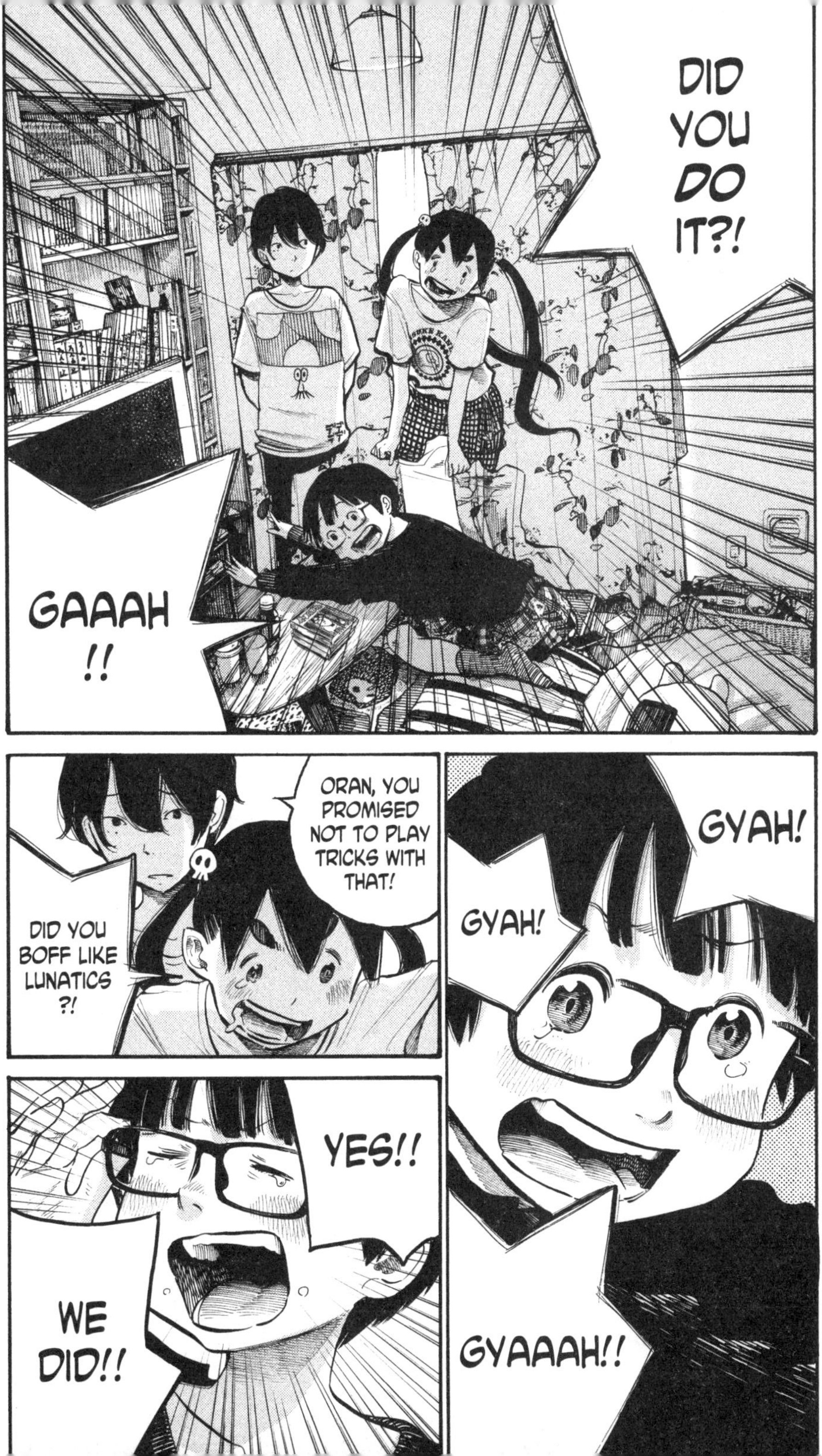
DID YOU DO IT?!
GAAAH !!
GYAH!
GYAH!
GYAAAH!!
ORAN, YOU PROMISED NOT TO PLAY TRICKS WITH THAT!
DID YOU BOFF LIKE LUNATICS ?!
YES!!
WE DID!!

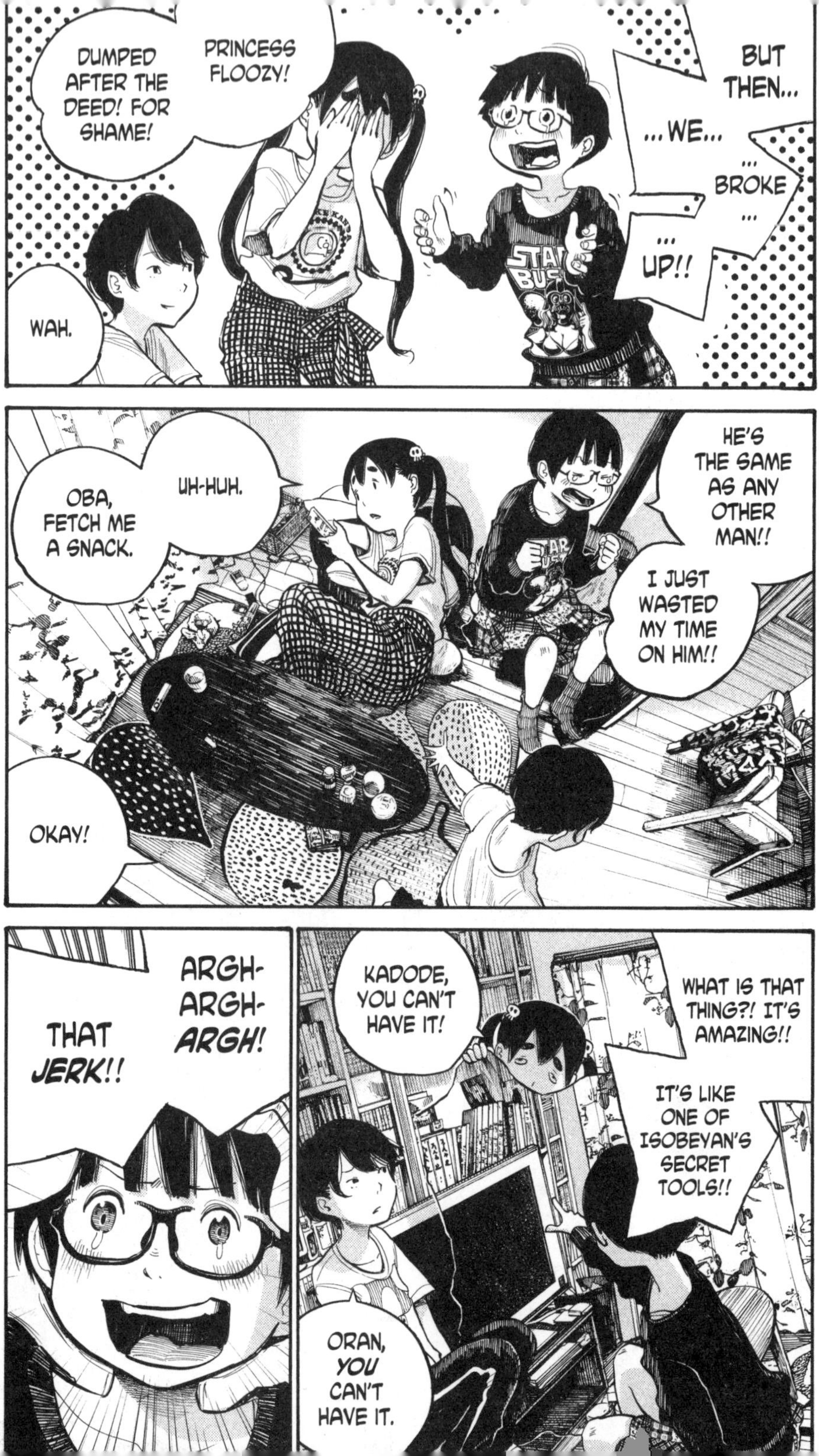
BUT THEN...
...WE...
...BROKE...
...UP!!
PRINCESS FLOOZY!
DUMPED AFTER THE DEED! FOR SHAME!
WAH.
HE'S THE SAME AS ANY OTHER MAN!!
I JUST WASTED MY TIME ON HIM!!
UH-HUH.
OBA, FETCH ME A SNACK.
OKAY!
WHAT IS THAT THING?! IT'S AMAZING!!
IT'S LIKE ONE OF ISOBEYAN'S SECRET TOOLS!!
KADODE, YOU CAN'T HAVE IT!
ORAN, *YOU* CAN'T HAVE IT.
ARGH-ARGH-*ARGH*!
THAT *JERK*!!

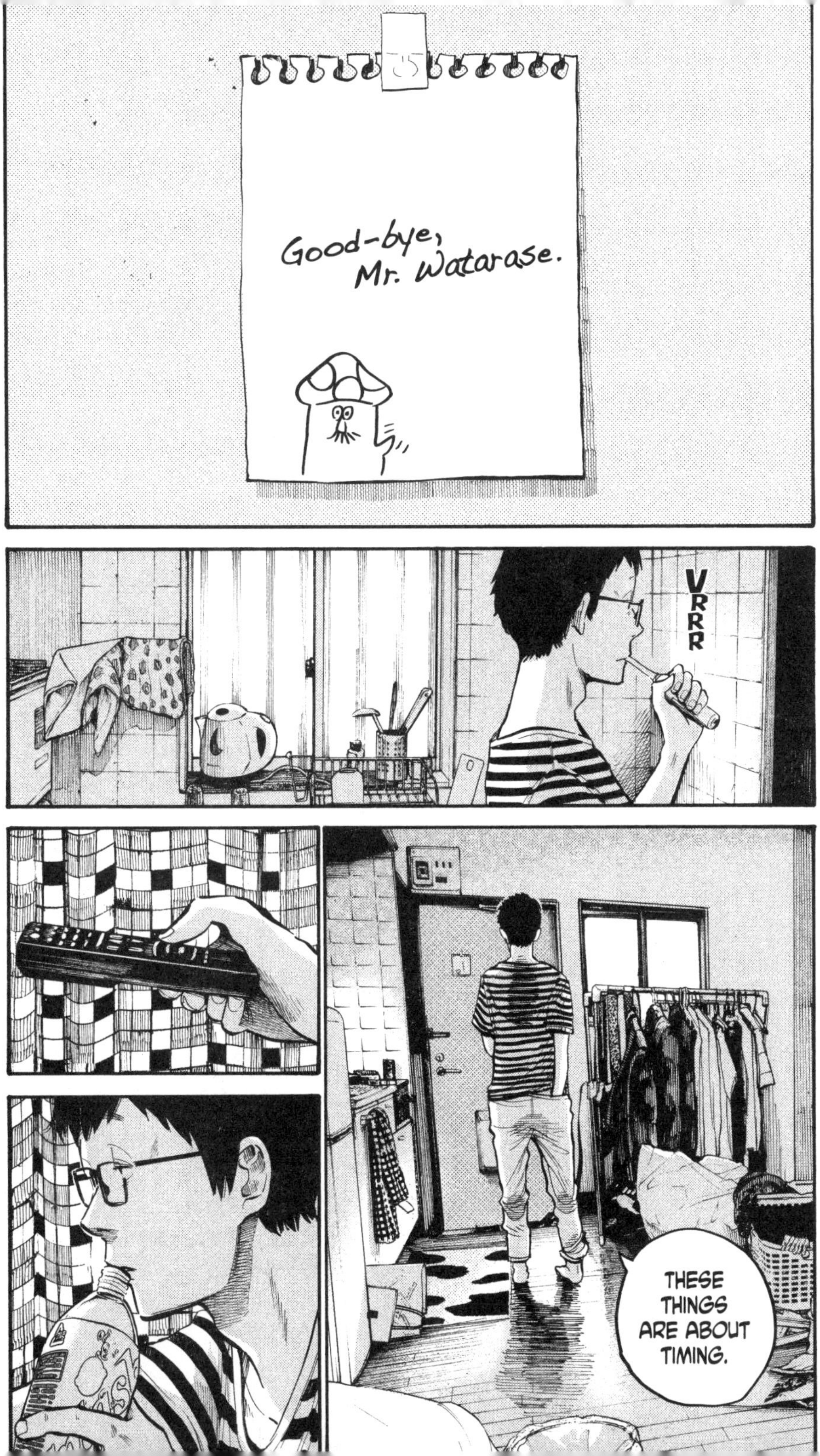
Good-bye, Mr. Watarase.
VRRR
THESE THINGS ARE ABOUT TIMING.

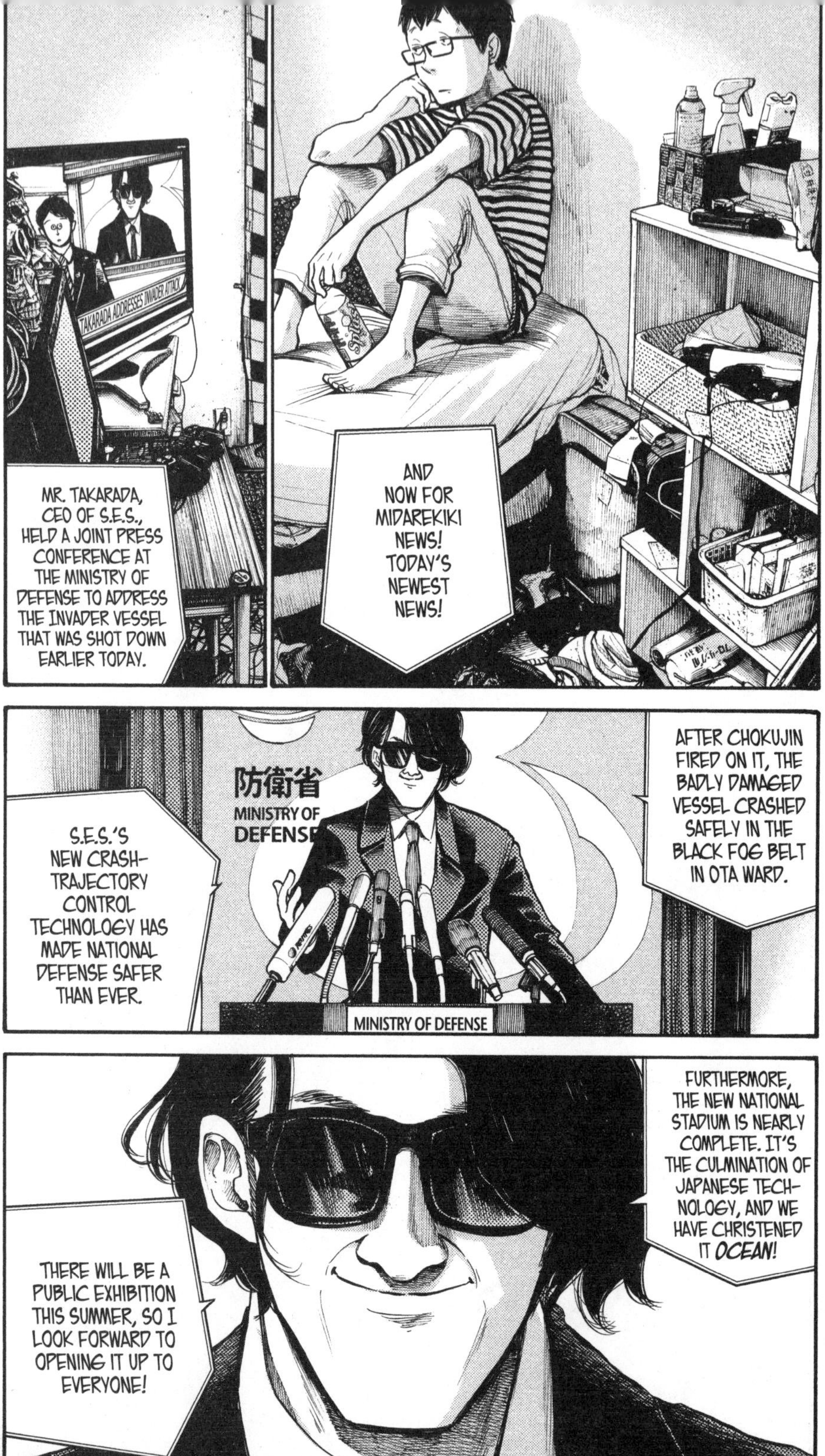
AND NOW FOR MIDAREKIKI NEWS! TODAY'S NEWEST NEWS!
TAKARADA ADDRESSES INVADER ATTACK
MR. TAKARADA, CEO OF S.E.S., HELD A JOINT PRESS CONFERENCE AT THE MINISTRY OF DEFENSE TO ADDRESS THE INVADER VESSEL THAT WAS SHOT DOWN EARLIER TODAY.
AFTER CHOKUJIN FIRED ON IT, THE BADLY DAMAGED VESSEL CRASHED SAFELY IN THE BLACK FOG BELT IN OTA WARD.
防衛省
MINISTRY OF DEFENSE
S.E.S.'S NEW CRASH-TRAJECTORY CONTROL TECHNOLOGY HAS MADE NATIONAL DEFENSE SAFER THAN EVER.
MINISTRY OF DEFENSE
FURTHERMORE, THE NEW NATIONAL STADIUM IS NEARLY COMPLETE. IT'S THE CULMINATION OF JAPANESE TECHNOLOGY, AND WE HAVE CHRISTENED IT *OCEAN*!
THERE WILL BE A PUBLIC EXHIBITION THIS SUMMER, SO I LOOK FORWARD TO OPENING IT UP TO EVERYONE!

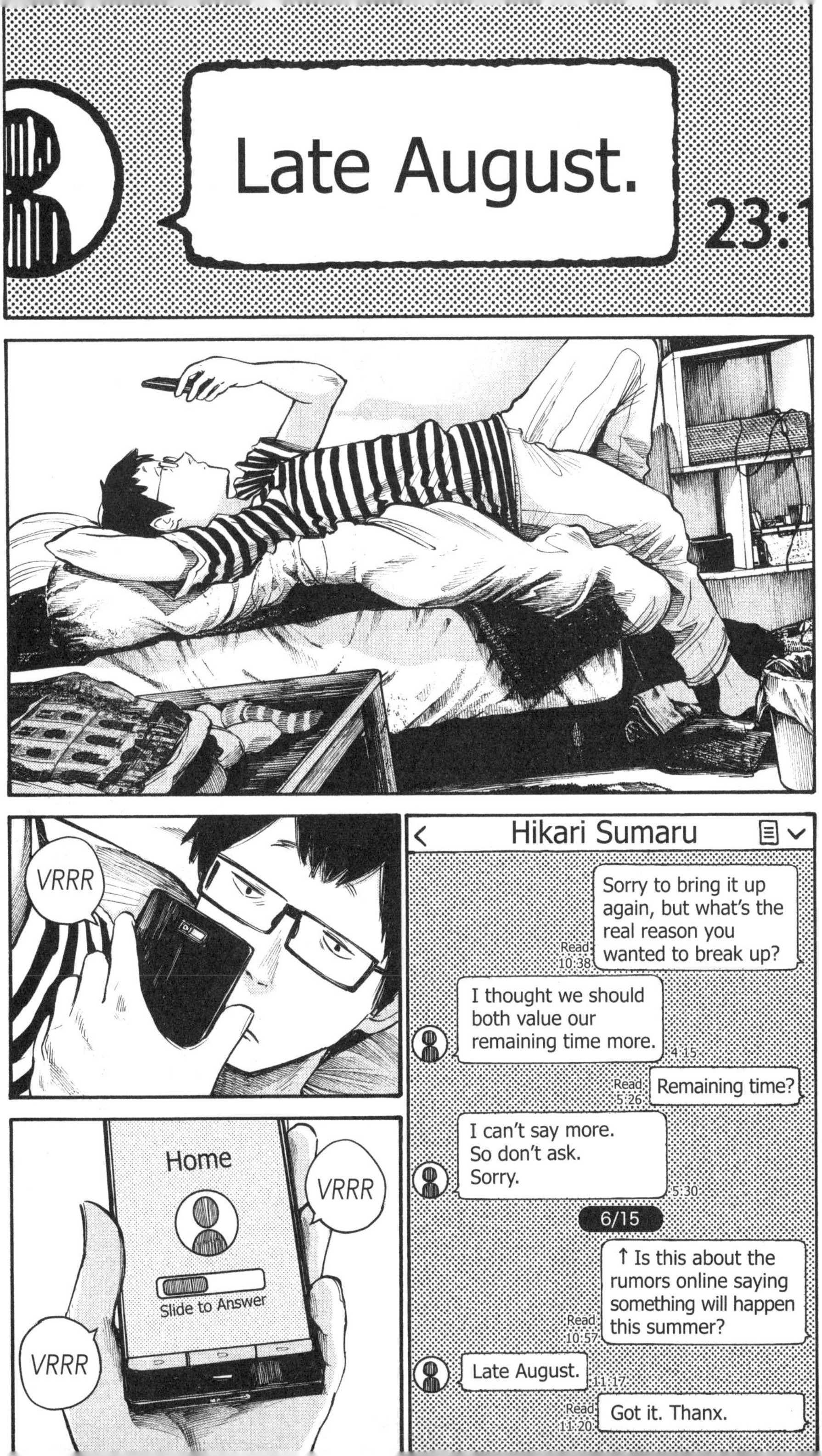
Late August.
23:1
Hikari Sumaru
Sorry to bring it up again, but what's the real reason you wanted to break up?
Read 10:38
I thought we should both value our remaining time more.
4:15
Read 5:26
Remaining time?
I can't say more. So don't ask. Sorry.
5:30
6/15
↑ Is this about the rumors online saying something will happen this summer?
Read 10:57
Late August.
11:17
Read 11:20
Got it. Thanx.
VRRR
Home
Slide to Answer
VRRR
VRRR

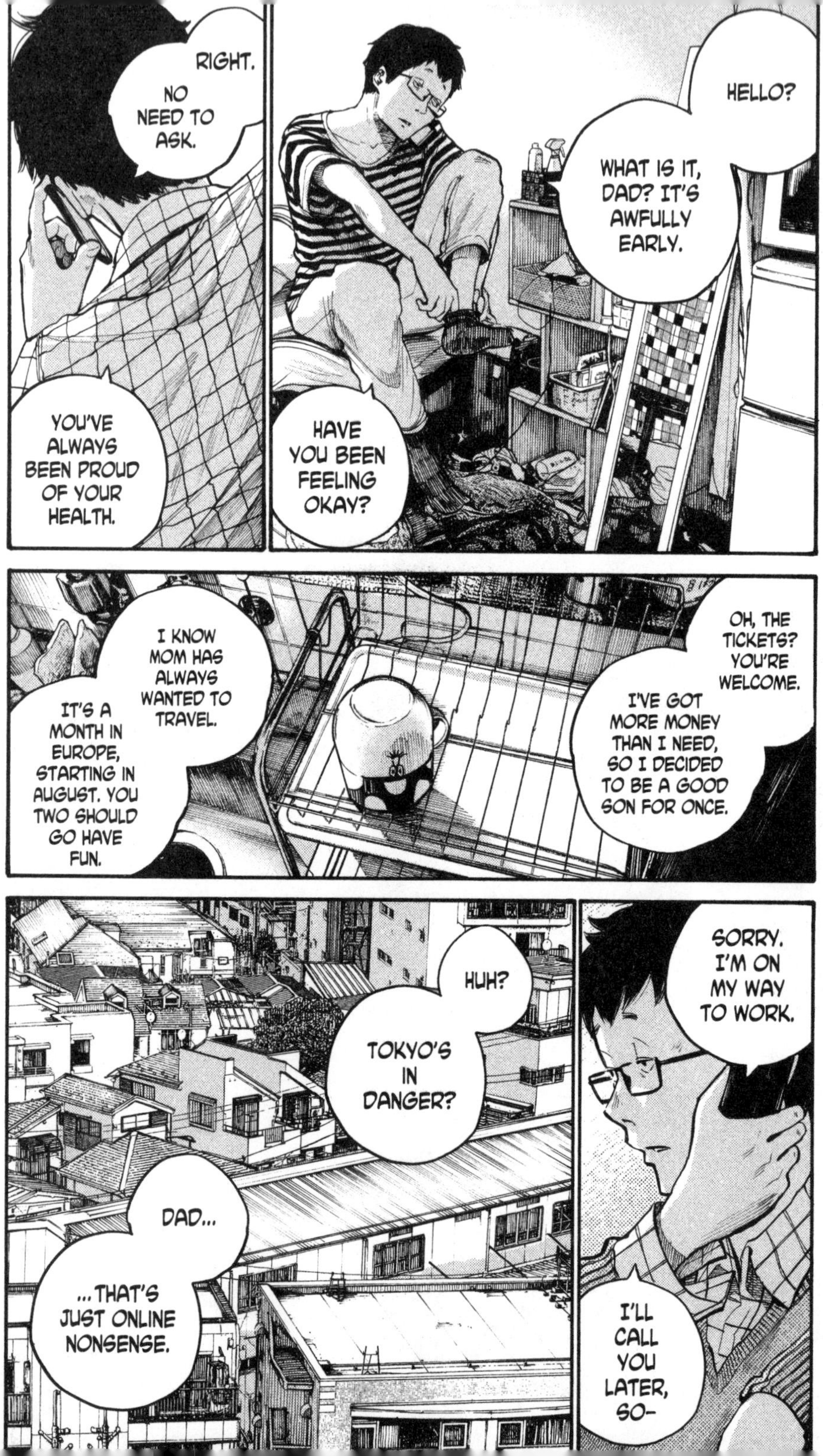
HELLO?
WHAT IS IT, DAD? IT'S AWFULLY EARLY.
HAVE YOU BEEN FEELING OKAY?
RIGHT.
NO NEED TO ASK.
YOU'VE ALWAYS BEEN PROUD OF YOUR HEALTH.
OH, THE TICKETS? YOU'RE WELCOME.
I'VE GOT MORE MONEY THAN I NEED, SO I DECIDED TO BE A GOOD SON FOR ONCE.
I KNOW MOM HAS ALWAYS WANTED TO TRAVEL.
IT'S A MONTH IN EUROPE, STARTING IN AUGUST. YOU TWO SHOULD GO HAVE FUN.
SORRY. I'M ON MY WAY TO WORK.
I'LL CALL YOU LATER, SO-
HUH?
TOKYO'S IN DANGER?
DAD...
...THAT'S JUST ONLINE NONSENSE.

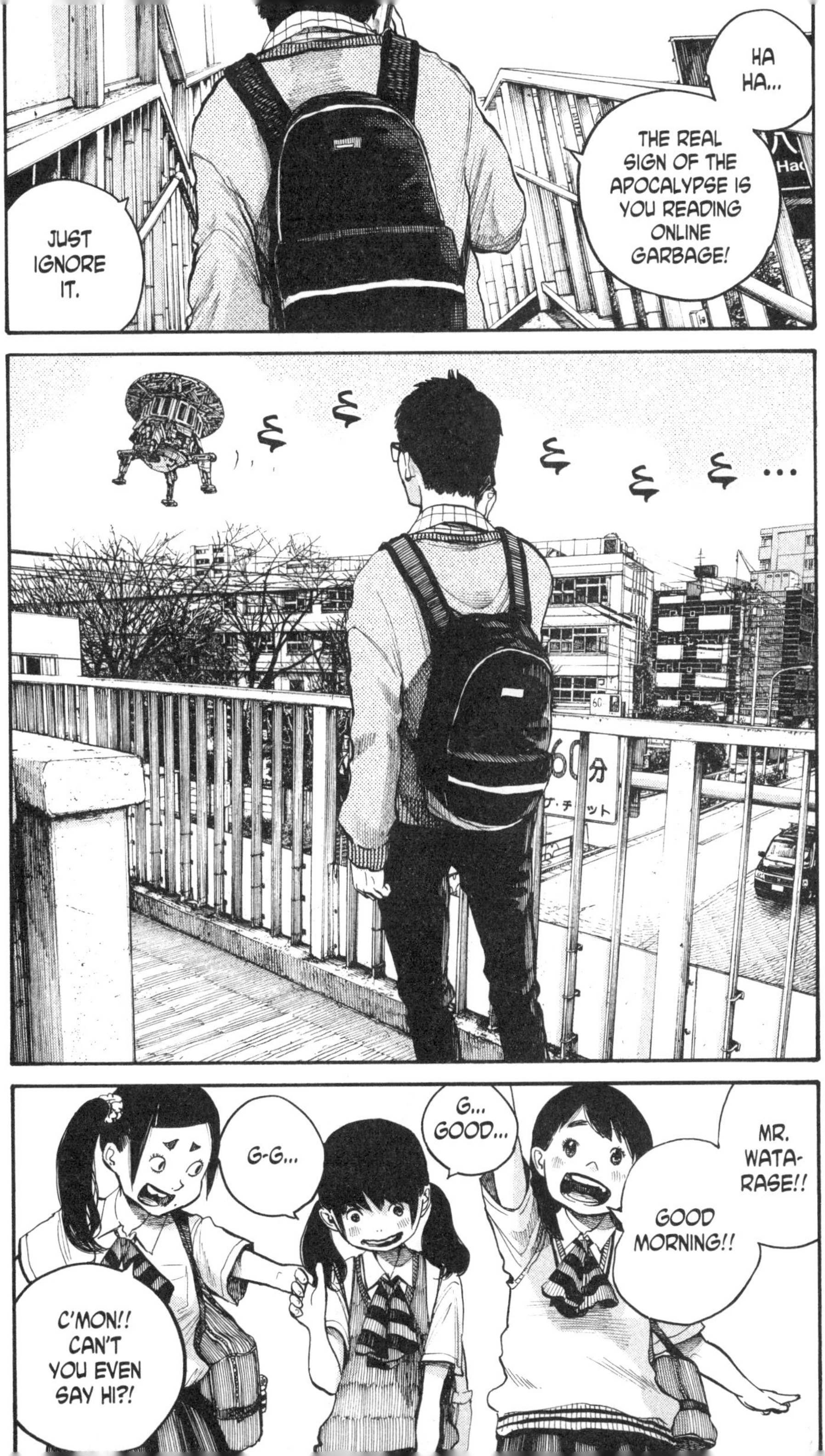
HA HA...
THE REAL SIGN OF THE APOCALYPSE IS YOU READING ONLINE GARBAGE!
JUST IGNORE IT.
...
MR. WATARASE!!
GOOD MORNING!!
G... GOOD...
G-G...
C'MON!! CAN'T YOU EVEN SAY HI?!

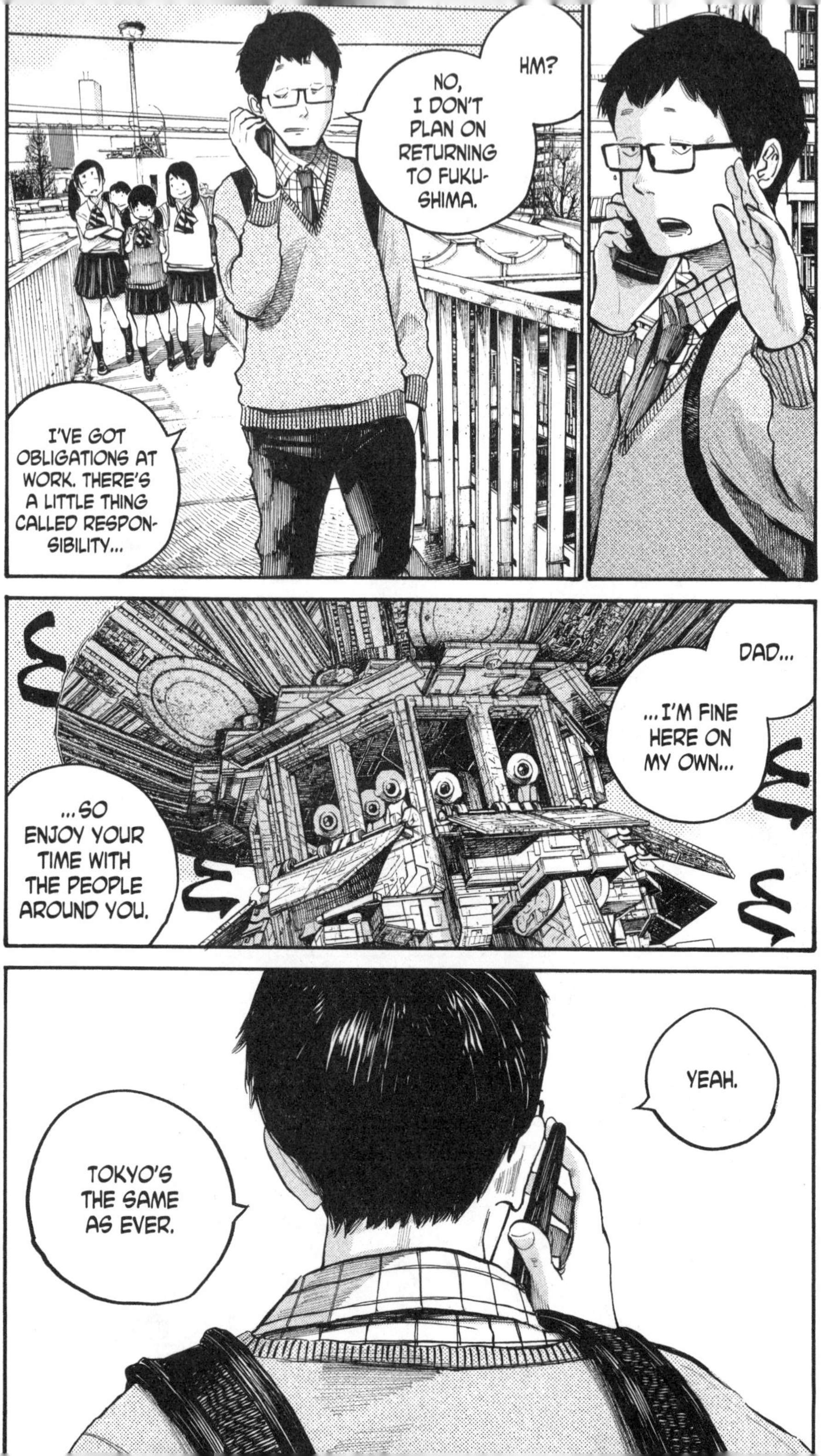
HM?
NO, I DON'T PLAN ON RETURNING TO FUKU-SHIMA.
I'VE GOT OBLIGATIONS AT WORK. THERE'S A LITTLE THING CALLED RESPON-SIBILITY...
DAD...
...I'M FINE HERE ON MY OWN...
...SO ENJOY YOUR TIME WITH THE PEOPLE AROUND YOU.
YEAH.
TOKYO'S THE SAME AS EVER.

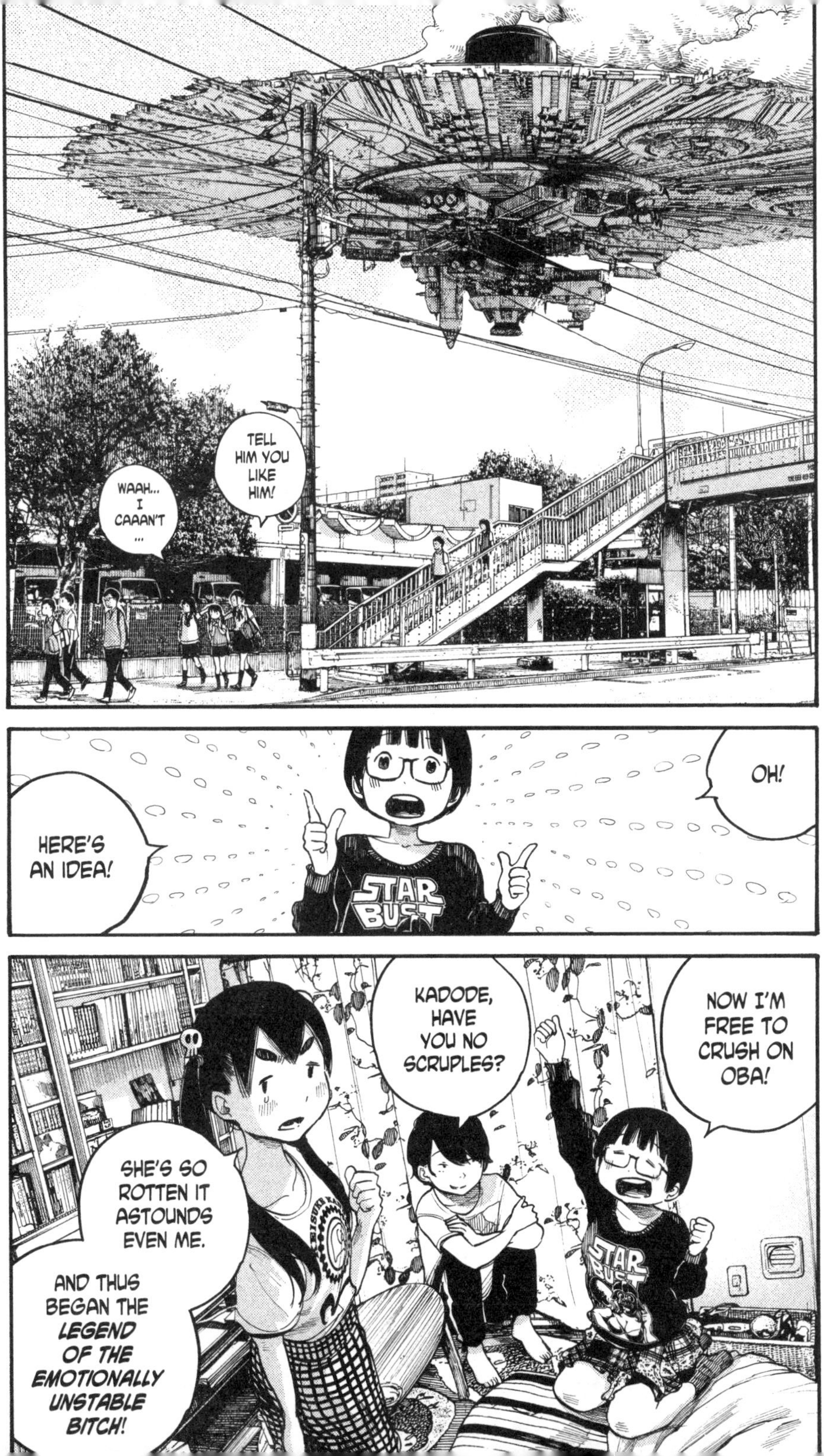
TELL HIM YOU LIKE HIM!
WAAH... I CAAAN'T ...
OH!
HERE'S AN IDEA!
STAR BUST
NOW I'M FREE TO CRUSH ON OBA!
KADODE, HAVE YOU NO SCRUPLES?
SHE'S SO ROTTEN IT ASTOUNDS EVEN ME.
AND THUS BEGAN THE *LEGEND OF THE EMOTIONALLY UNSTABLE BITCH!*
STAR BUST

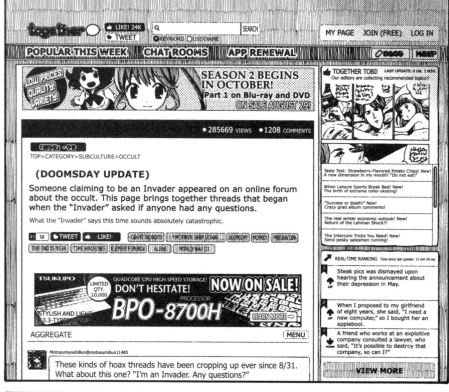

together
LIKE! 24K
TWEET
SEARCH
KEYWORD USERNAME
MY PAGE JOIN (FREE) LOG IN
POPULAR THIS WEEK
CHAT ROOMS
APP RENEWAL
LOW PRICES! QUALITY! VARIETY!
SEASON 2 BEGINS IN OCTOBER!
Part 1 on Blu-ray and DVD
ON SALE AUGUST 29!
TOGETHER TOBI! LAST UPDATE: 0 HR. 2 MIN.
Our editors are collecting recommended topics!!
285669 VIEWS 1208 COMMENTS
TOP>CATEGORY>SUBCULTURE>OCCULT
(DOOMSDAY UPDATE)
Someone claiming to be an Invader appeared on an online forum about the occult. This page brings together threads that began when the "Invader" asked if anyone had any questions.
What the "Invader" says this time sounds absolutely catastrophic.
12 TWEET LIKE!
GIANT ROBOTS
MOTHER SHIP DOWN
DOOMSDAY
PROPHECY
PRECOGNITION
THE END IS NIGH
TIME MACHINES
ELEMENT F ENERGY
ALIENS
WORLD WAR III
Taste Test: Strawberry-Flavored Potato Chips! New!
A new dimension in my mouth! "Do not eat!"
When Leisure Sports Break Bad! New!
The birth of extreme roller-skating!
"Success or death!" New!
Crazy grad album comments!
The real winter economic outlook! New!
Return of the Lehman Shock?!
The Intercom Tricks You Need! New!
Send pesky salesmen running!
TSUKUPO
LIMITED QTY. 10,000
QUADCORE CPU HIGH-SPEED STORAGE!
DON'T HESITATE!
NOW ON SALE!
PROCESSOR
BPO-8700H
STYLISH AND LIGHT 13.3-TYPE LAPTOP
LEARN MORE
REAL-TIME RANKING Time since last update: 15 min 50 sec
Steak pics was dismayed upon hearing the announcement about their depression in May.
UP
When I proposed to my girlfriend of eight years, she said, "I need a new computer," so I bought her an applebool.
UP
A friend who works at an exploitive company consulted a lawyer, who said, "It's possible to destroy that company, so can I?"
DOWN
VIEW MORE
AGGREGATE
MENU
MotosumiyoshiBun@motosumibun11485
These kinds of hoax threads have been cropping up ever since 8/31.
What about this one? "I'm an Invader. Any questions?"
TOP>CATEGORY>SUBCULTURE>OCCULT
(DOOMSDAY UPDATE)
Someone claiming to be an Invader appeared on an online forum about the occult. This page brings together threads that began when the "Invader" asked if anyone had any questions.
What the "Invader" says this time sounds absolutely catastrophic.
GIANT ROBOTS
MOTHER SHIP DOWN
DOOMSDAY
PROPHECY
PRECOGNITION
TWEET 1780
217
LIKE! 5,782
+1 45
Pocket 98
COMMENT
ScarfingNoodles@xxx @Wowow_Pecker
Ugh. This be stupid. Anyone who pushes this shit be stupid.
And anyone who takes it srsly be /srsly/ stupid.
hibagon @hibasanmyaku
Read 22:16
But what if it's true? The steam from the mother ship isn't stopping.
I'm freaking. I want to cry. I'm gonna write a good-bye note. When I die, read it, ok?
22:17
22:21
If we're all toast, no one's reading anything!

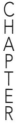

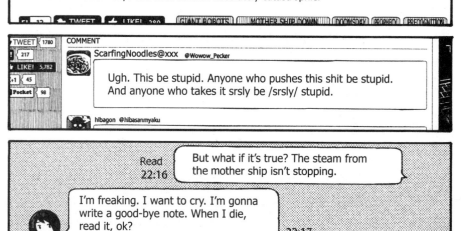

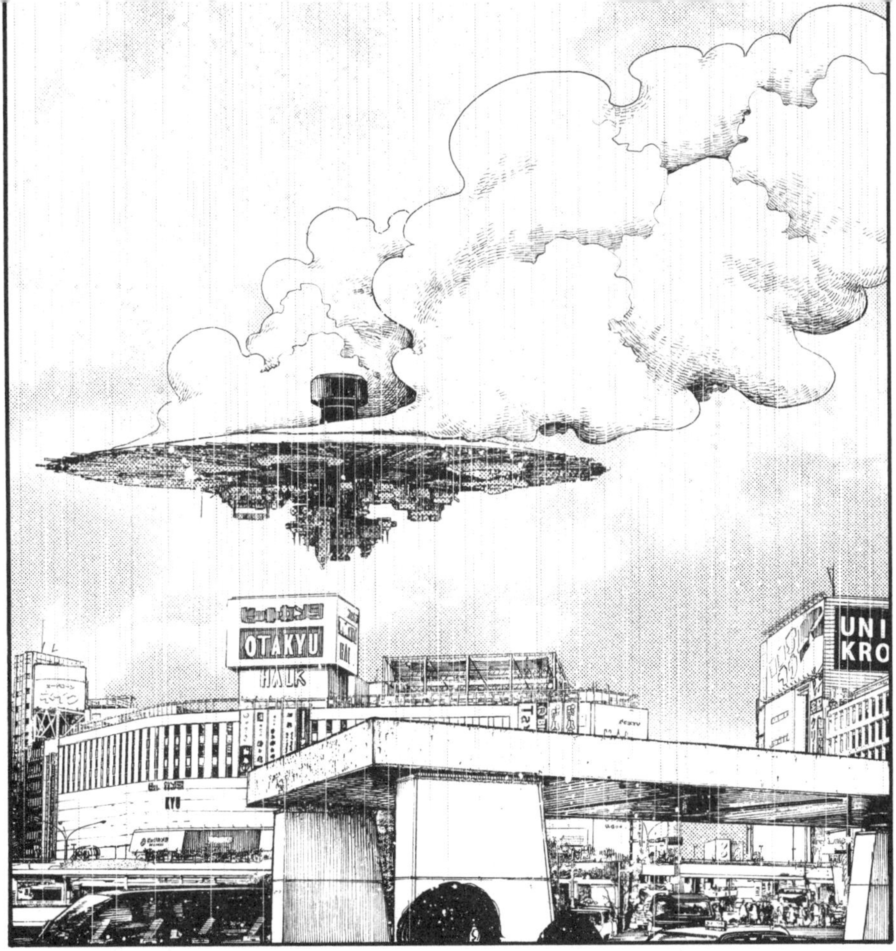
OTAKYU
HALK
UNI
KRO
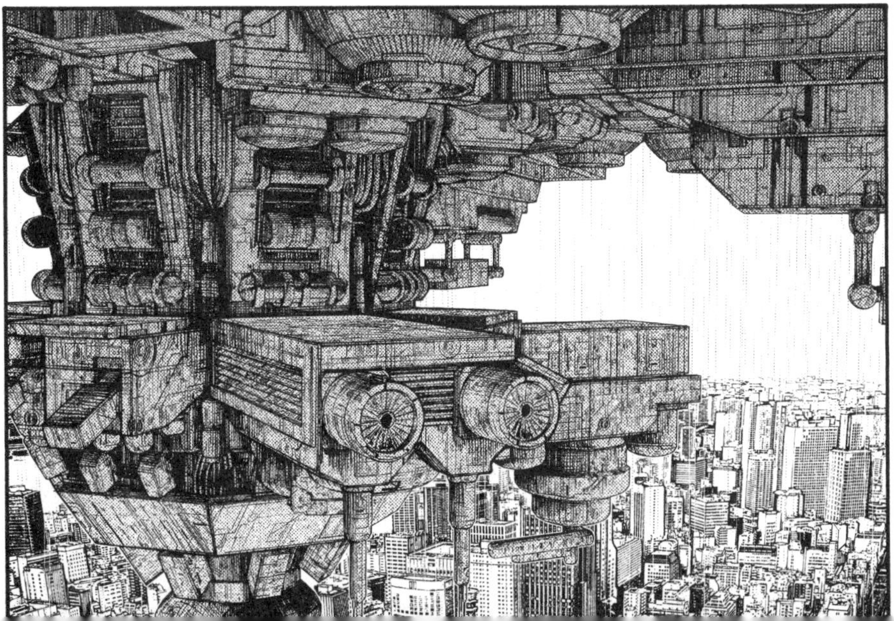

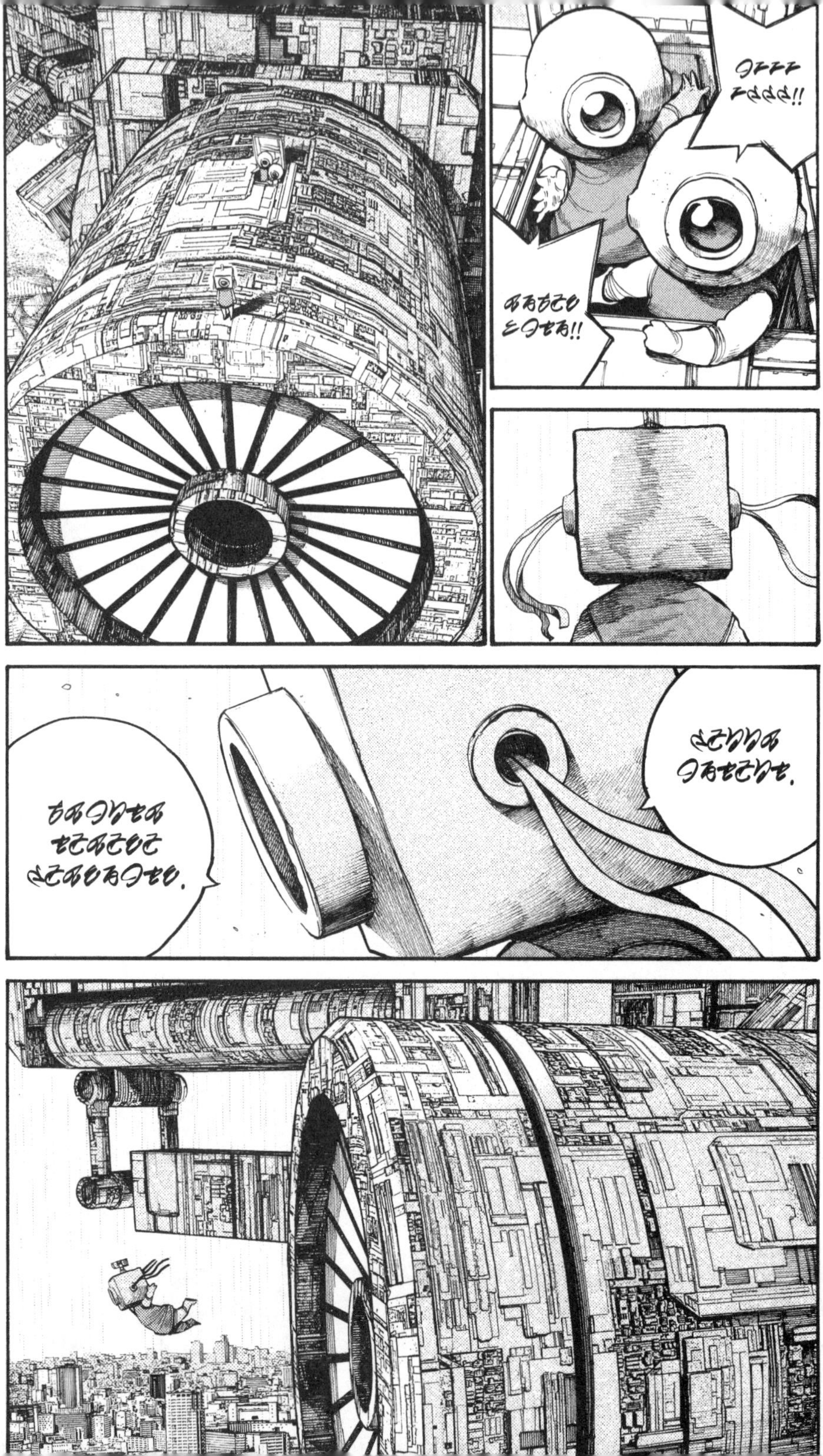

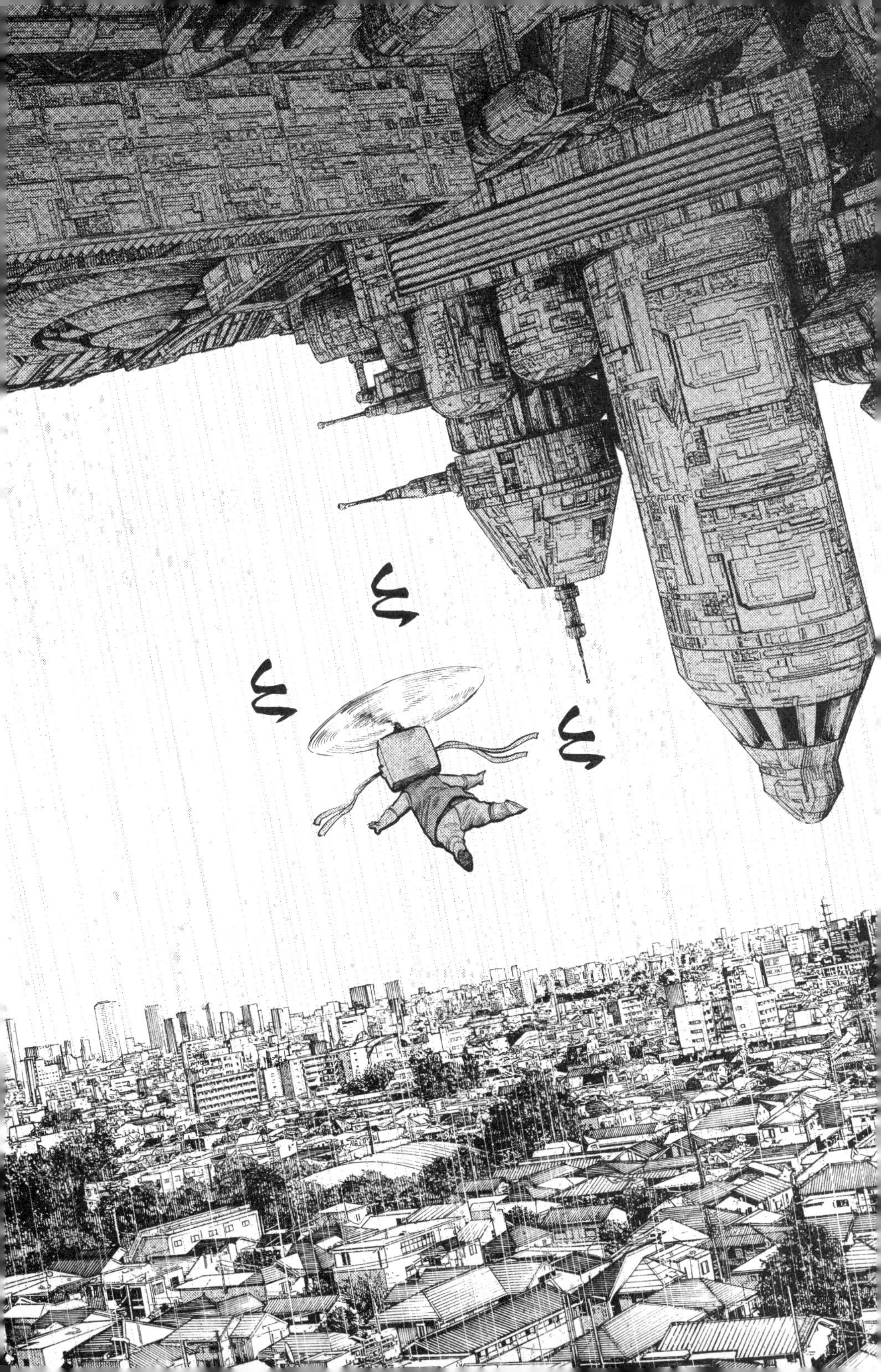

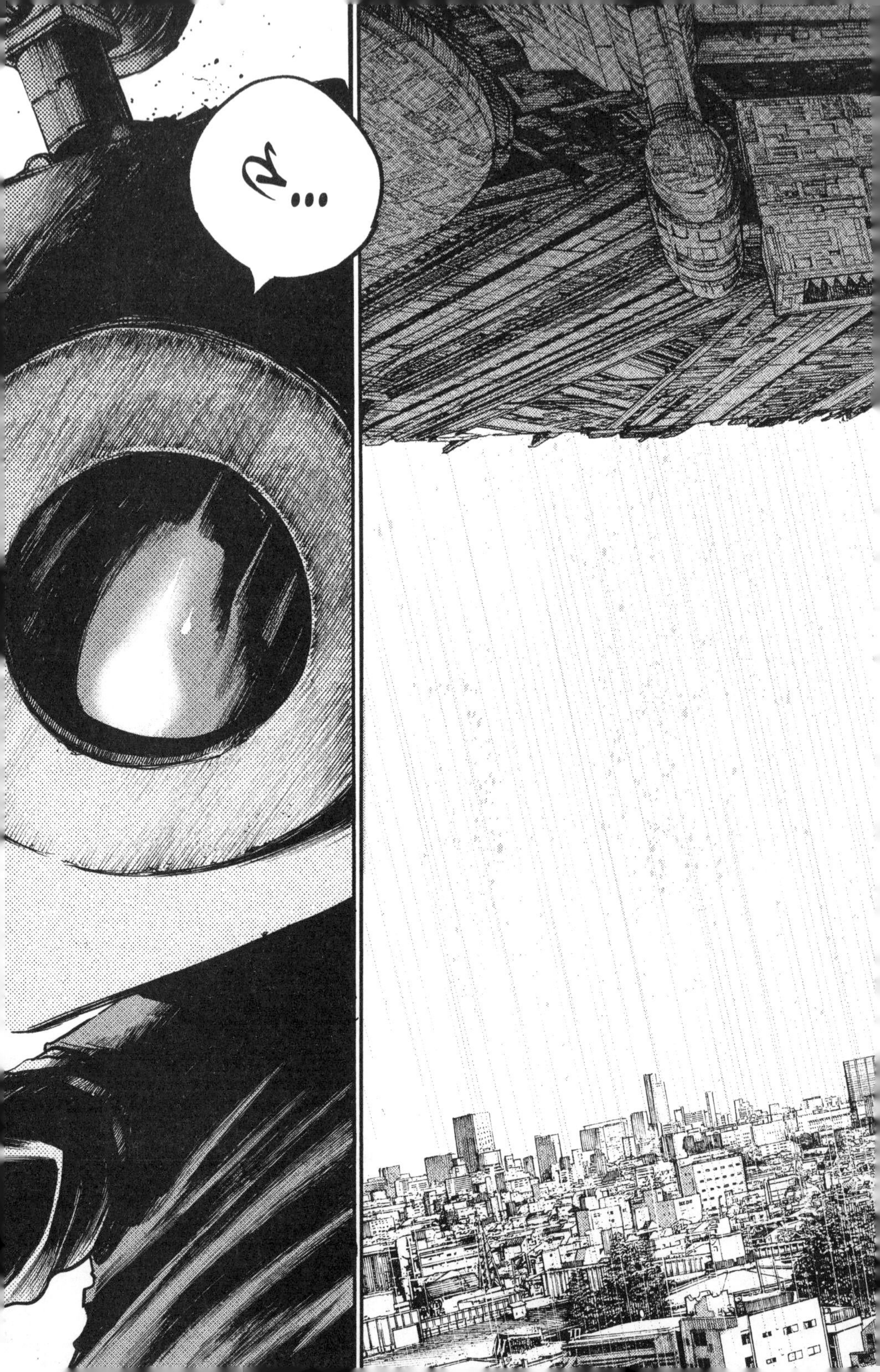

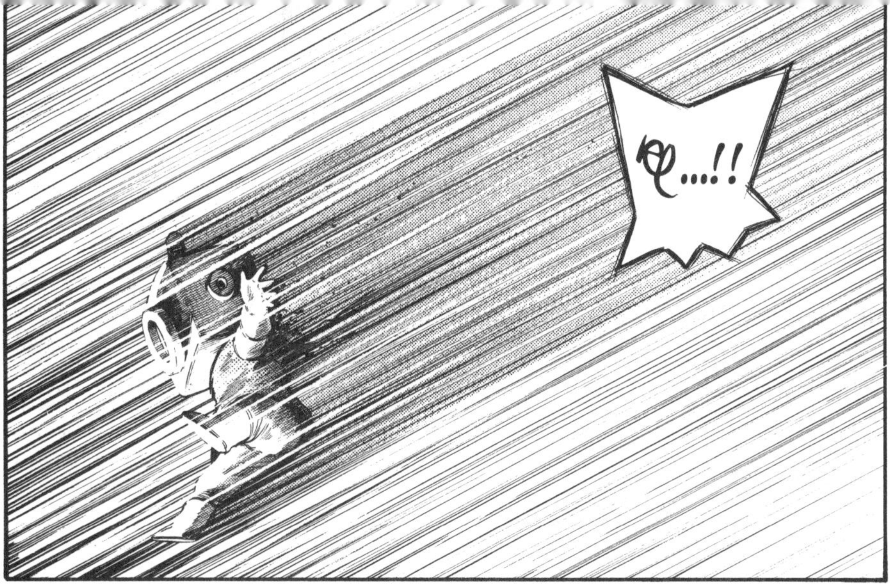
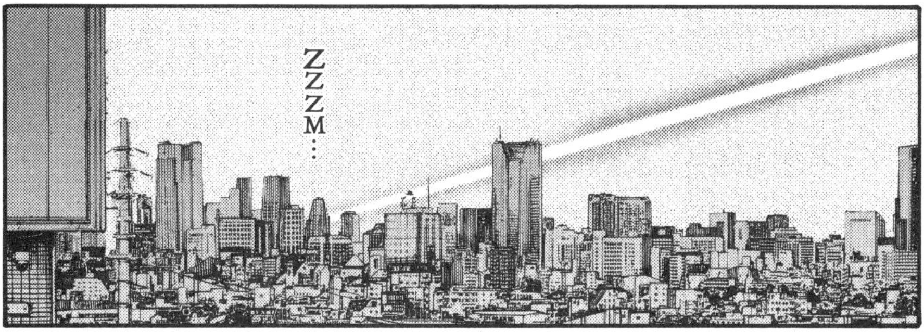
ZZZM...
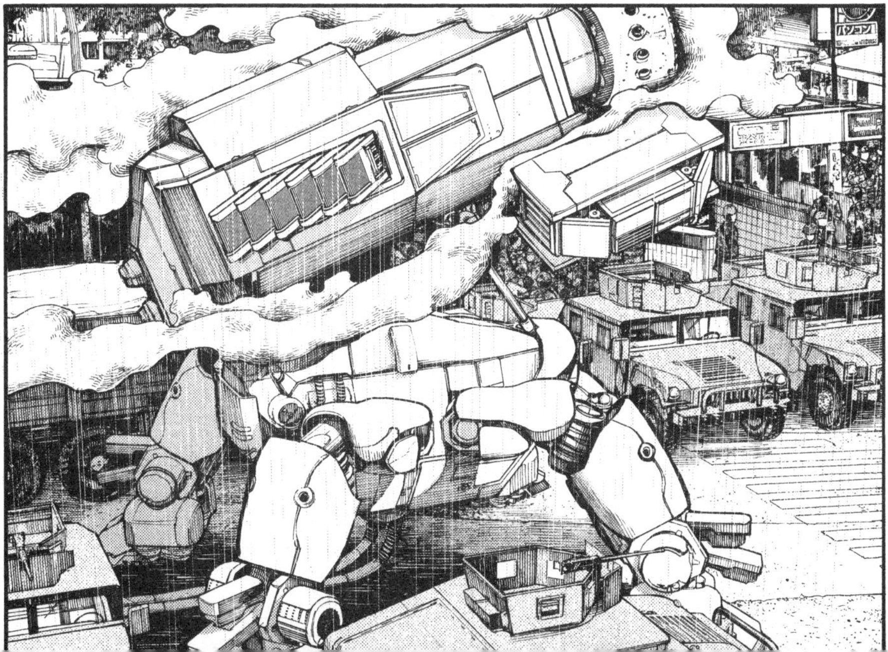
パソコン

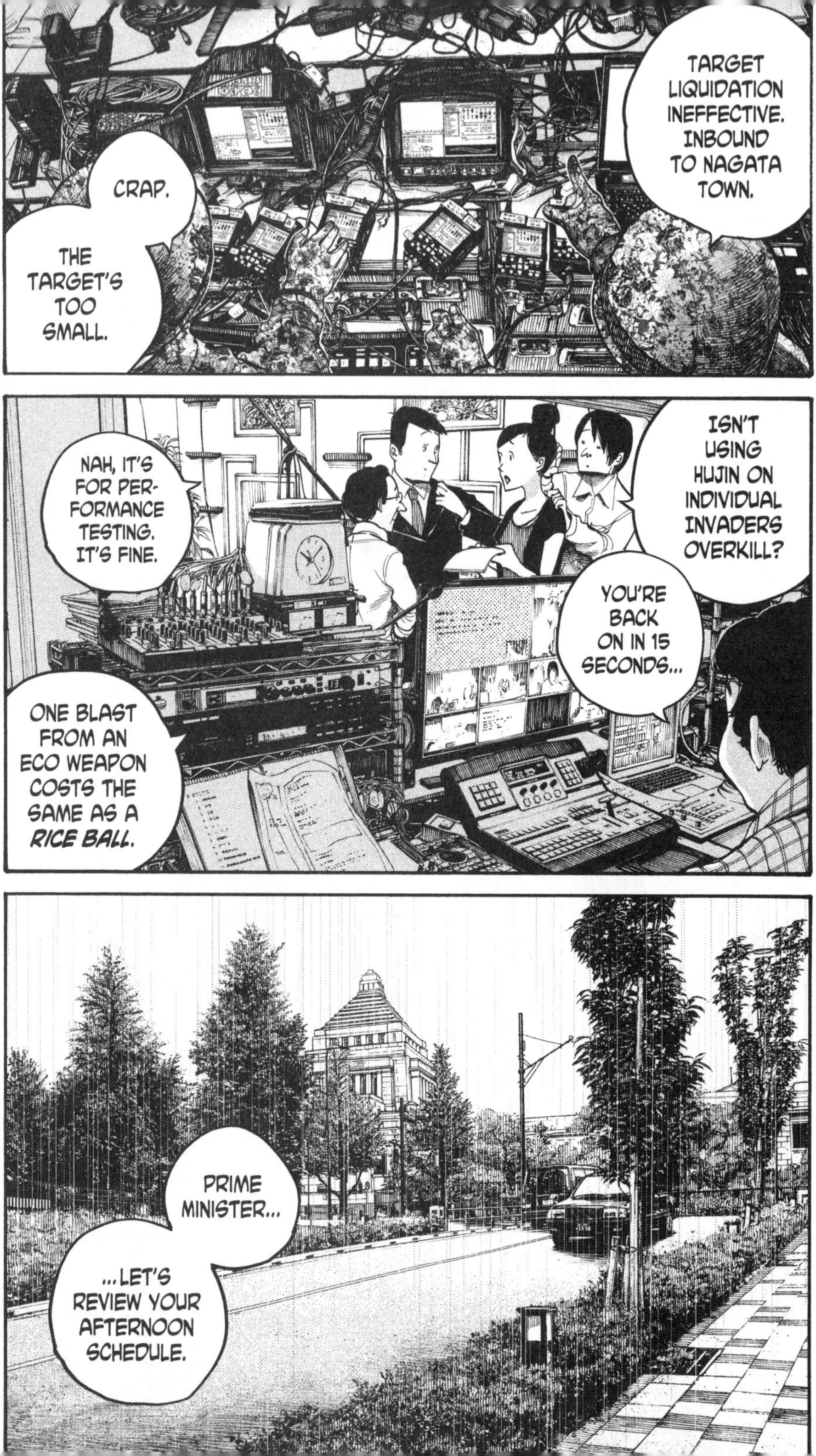
TARGET LIQUIDATION INEFFECTIVE. INBOUND TO NAGATA TOWN.
CRAP.
THE TARGET'S TOO SMALL.
ISN'T USING HUJIN ON INDIVIDUAL INVADERS OVERKILL?
NAH, IT'S FOR PER-FORMANCE TESTING. IT'S FINE.
YOU'RE BACK ON IN 15 SECONDS...
ONE BLAST FROM AN ECO WEAPON COSTS THE SAME AS A *RICE BALL*.
PRIME MINISTER...
...LET'S REVIEW YOUR AFTERNOON SCHEDULE.

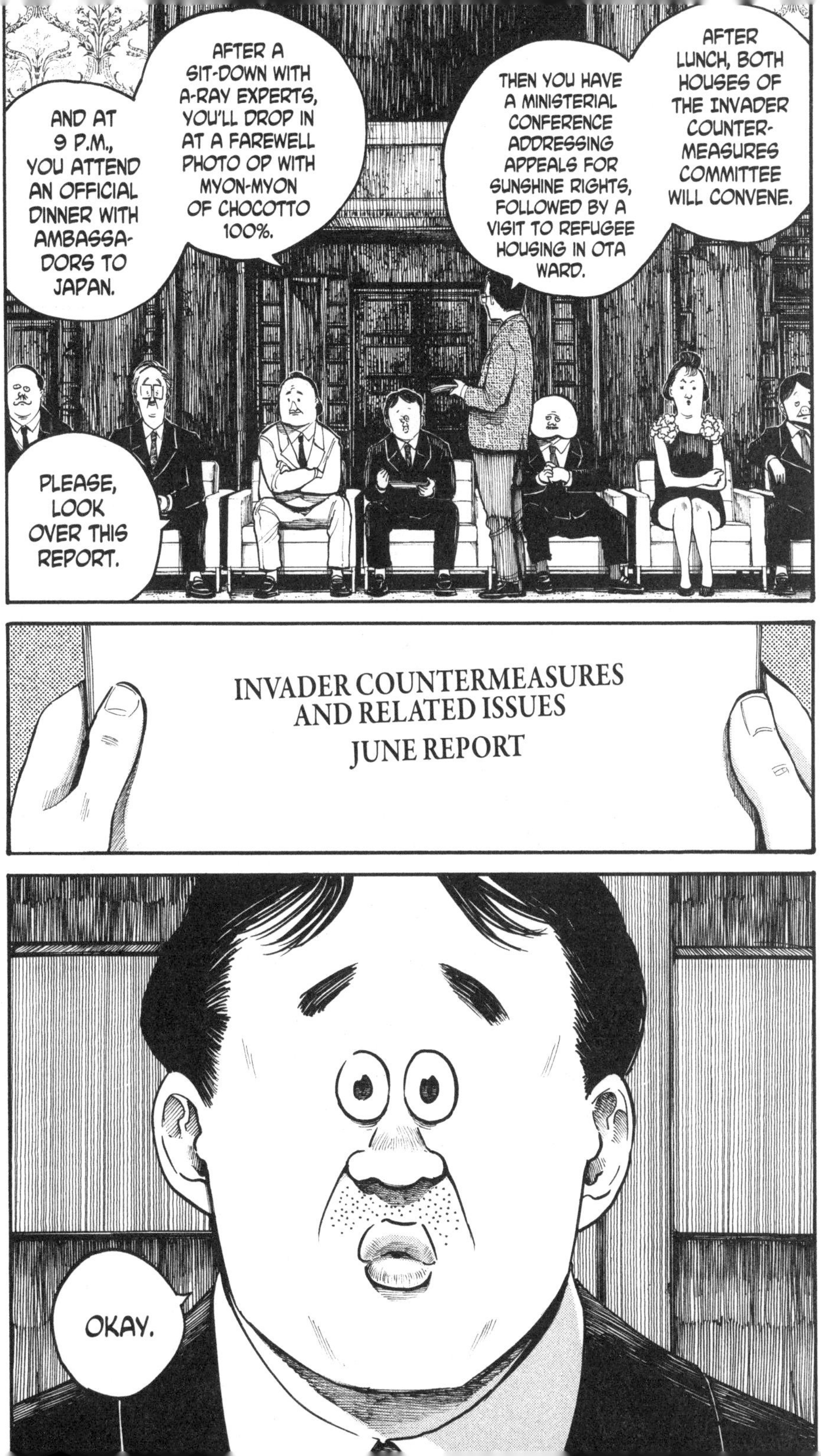
AFTER LUNCH, BOTH HOUSES OF THE INVADER COUNTER-MEASURES COMMITTEE WILL CONVENE.
THEN YOU HAVE A MINISTERIAL CONFERENCE ADDRESSING APPEALS FOR SUNSHINE RIGHTS, FOLLOWED BY A VISIT TO REFUGEE HOUSING IN OTA WARD.
AFTER A SIT-DOWN WITH A-RAY EXPERTS, YOU'LL DROP IN AT A FAREWELL PHOTO OP WITH MYON-MYON OF CHOCOTTO 100%.
AND AT 9 P.M., YOU ATTEND AN OFFICIAL DINNER WITH AMBASSA-DORS TO JAPAN.
PLEASE, LOOK OVER THIS REPORT.
INVADER COUNTERMEASURES AND RELATED ISSUES
JUNE REPORT
OKAY.

The number of Hujin Type 7 units deployed within the city has risen to 130, while the number of Type 9 units has risen to 1,200. Together with the four Chokujin installations in the city, they are providing increased defensive capability in the city center. These weapons have engaged 96% of airborne targets, short of the 99% goal. The success rate, however, is nearly 100% against small to medium vessels. In ground combat, the Self-Defense Forces maintains an overwhelming advantage as it eradicates the remaining Invaders. Deployment of the autonomous humanoid defense weapon Hujin Type 10 is planned to begin within the year. (See attachment on A.I. for use in autonomous systems.)

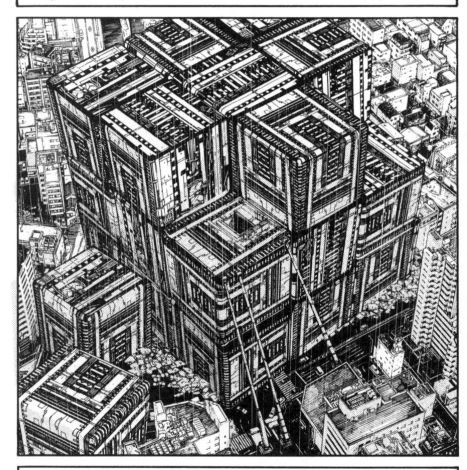

The cleanup operation at the site where the cube-shaped medium vessel crashed in Musashino City last December is scheduled to finish by the end of next month. The vessel's power area contained an Element-F generator. The generator was recovered along with dozens of biological samples of Invaders and sent to S.E.S.'s Tsukuba Research Laboratory.

The commercial district around Kichijoji Station suffered the worst damage. The area will be cleared and joined with Inokashira Park. Plans for the area include establishment of a large (120 ha) defensive park centered on the reconstructed Chokujin Musashino, with construction to begin next year.

UMPH!!
WHEW! ☆

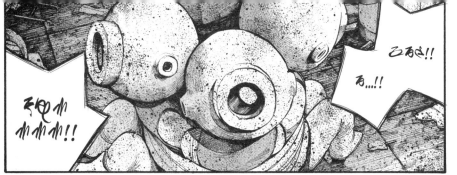

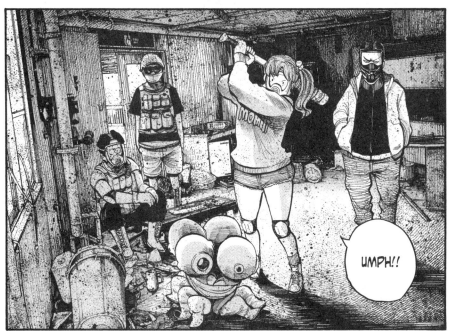

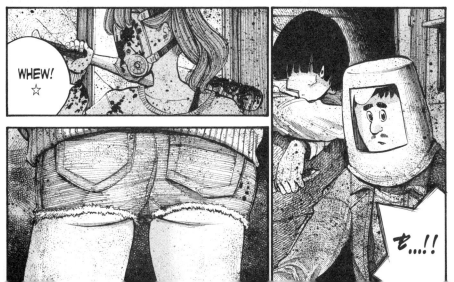

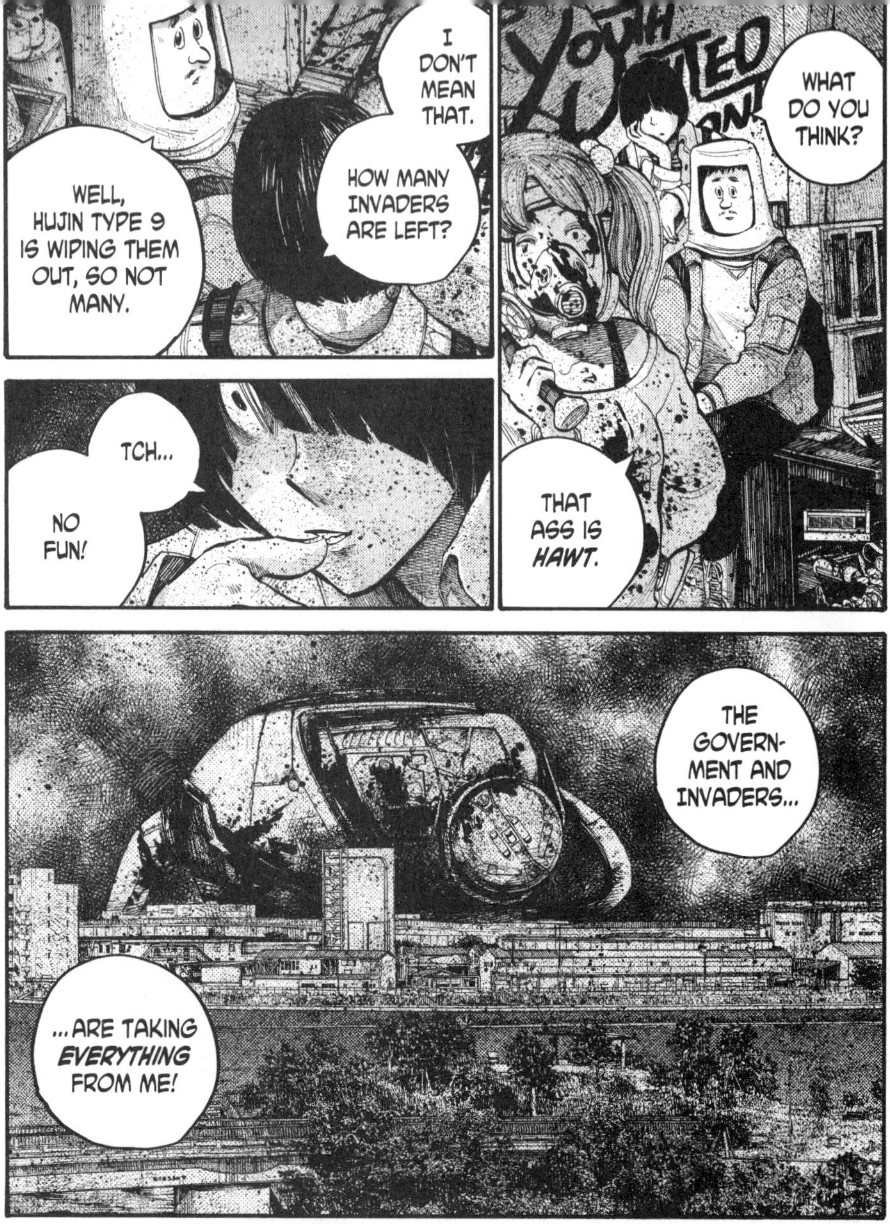
WHAT DO YOU THINK?
THAT ASS IS *HAWT*.
I DON'T MEAN THAT.
HOW MANY INVADERS ARE LEFT?
WELL, HUJIN TYPE 9 IS WIPING THEM OUT, SO NOT MANY.
TCH...
NO FUN!
THE GOVERNMENT AND INVADERS...
...ARE TAKING *EVERYTHING* FROM ME!

The teapot-shaped vessel that was shot down and crashed in Ota Ward's black fog belt on the 26th of this month was carrying over 13,000 Invaders. Over half are presumed dead, but Hujin Type 9 units have been deployed to eradicate survivors. A group of delinquents that hunts Invaders and calls itself the Youth United Front (Y.U.F.) has been illegally entering abandoned areas, stealing valuables and committing acts of vandalism, so caution is recommended. Addressing this issue requires deliberation after consultation with the Police Anti-Terror Section.

Try not to shoot citizens!!

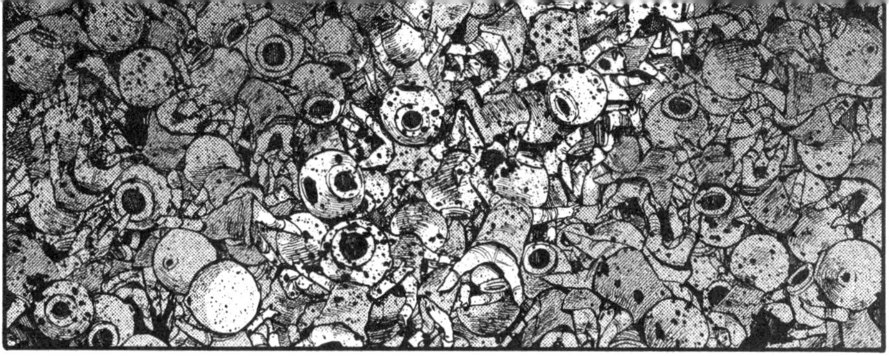

The Invader corpse disposal facility in Kawasaki City will reach capacity at the end of September, so incineration will commence in October. Residents have been complaining of the bad smell and health risks, but the management of the facility appears to be satisfactory and no leaked A-rays have been detected. The complaints are likely due to propaganda from student groups such as S.H.I.P., which demand human rights for Invaders, but support among the youth for student activism has been waning since spring and the number of protesters is plummeting. This should lead to a concomitant decrease in complaints.

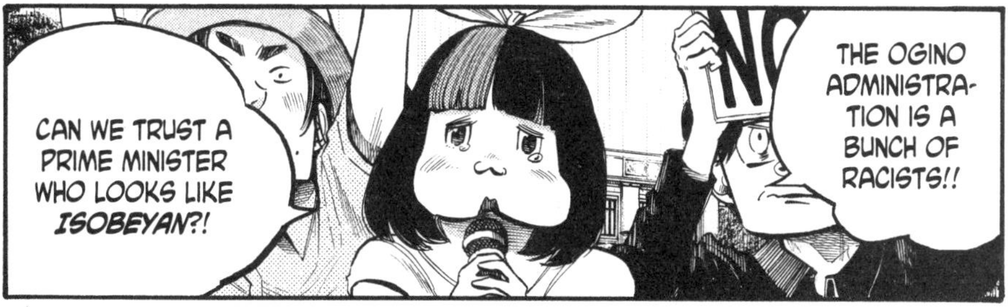
THE OGINO ADMINISTRATION IS A BUNCH OF RACISTS!!
CAN WE TRUST A PRIME MINISTER WHO LOOKS LIKE *ISOBEYAN*?!

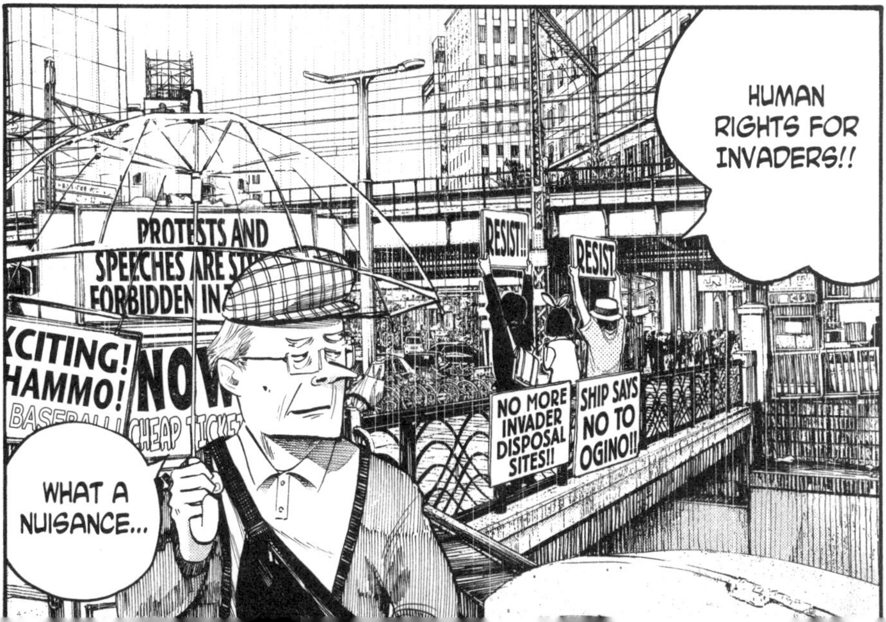
HUMAN RIGHTS FOR INVADERS!!
RESIST!!
RESIST
SHIP SAYS NO TO OGINO!!
NO MORE INVADER DISPOSAL SITES!!
PROTESTS AND
WHAT A NUISANCE...

Additional Notes:
Geekle Co., Ltd.'s development of the artificial intelligence slated to be installed in Hujin Types 9 and 10 has experienced difficulties. Thus, the onboard A.I. installation will now be Plankton, which was jointly developed by S.E.S. and Toyo University's brain science research team. Plankton is a conversational cloud network-based system that will manage everything from city infrastructure to public transportation to individual handheld devices, thereby transforming Tokyo into a smart city with efficient management of public safety.

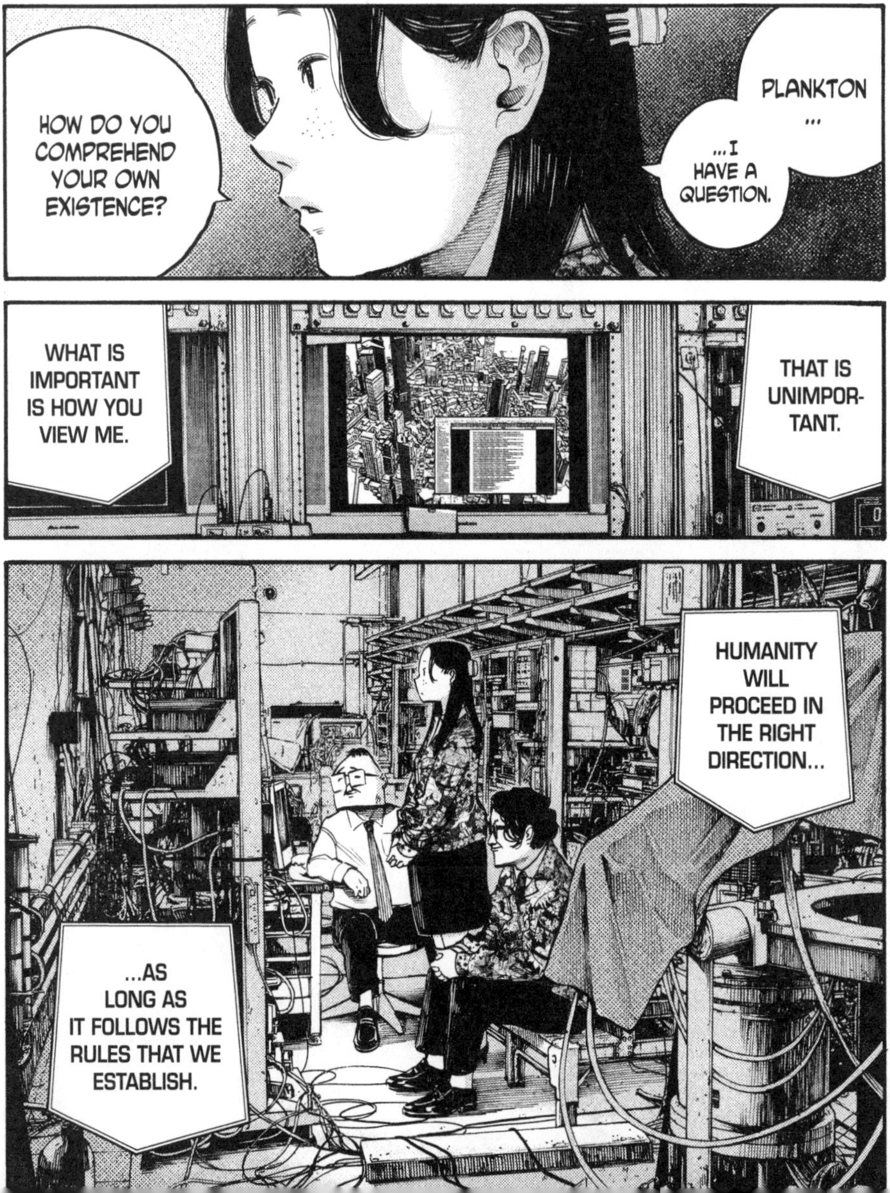
PLANKTON ...
...I HAVE A QUESTION.
HOW DO YOU COMPREHEND YOUR OWN EXISTENCE?
THAT IS UNIMPOR-TANT.
WHAT IS IMPORTANT IS HOW YOU VIEW ME.
HUMANITY WILL PROCEED IN THE RIGHT DIRECTION...
...AS LONG AS IT FOLLOWS THE RULES THAT WE ESTABLISH.

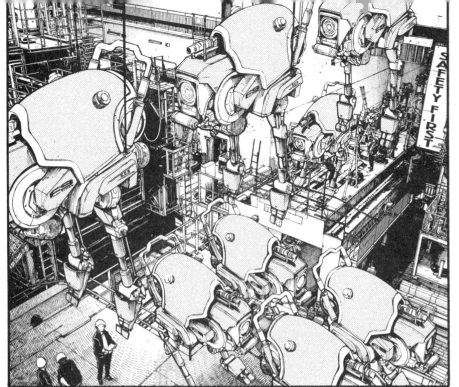

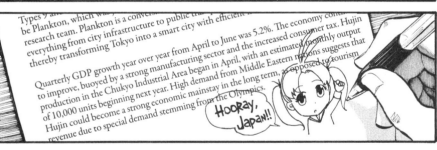

SAFETY FIRST
be Plankton, which was
research team. Plankton is a conver
everything from city infrastructure to public
thereby transforming Tokyo into a smart city with efficient
Quarterly GDP growth year over year from April to June was 5.2%. The economy conti
to improve, buoyed by a strong manufacturing sector and the increased consumer tax. Hujin
production in the Chukyo Industrial Area began in April, with an estimated monthly output
of 10,000 units beginning next year. High demand from Middle Eastern nations suggests that
Hujin could become a strong economic mainstay in the long term, as opposed to tourism
revenue due to special demand stemming from the Olympics.
HOORAY, JAPAN!!
YOU'RE GOOD AT DRAWING GIRLS, SIR.
THANKS!
S.E.S. IS BUILDING FACTORIES ALL OVER NAGOYA. HAVE WE SECURED A LABOR FORCE?
THE BIRTH RATE IS STILL FALLING...
...SO WE SHOULD WELCOME IMMIGRANTS TO BOLSTER THE POPULATION.
THERE'LL BE A PUBLIC BACKLASH. AND CRIME WILL INCREASE.

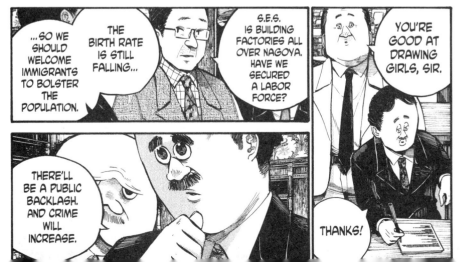

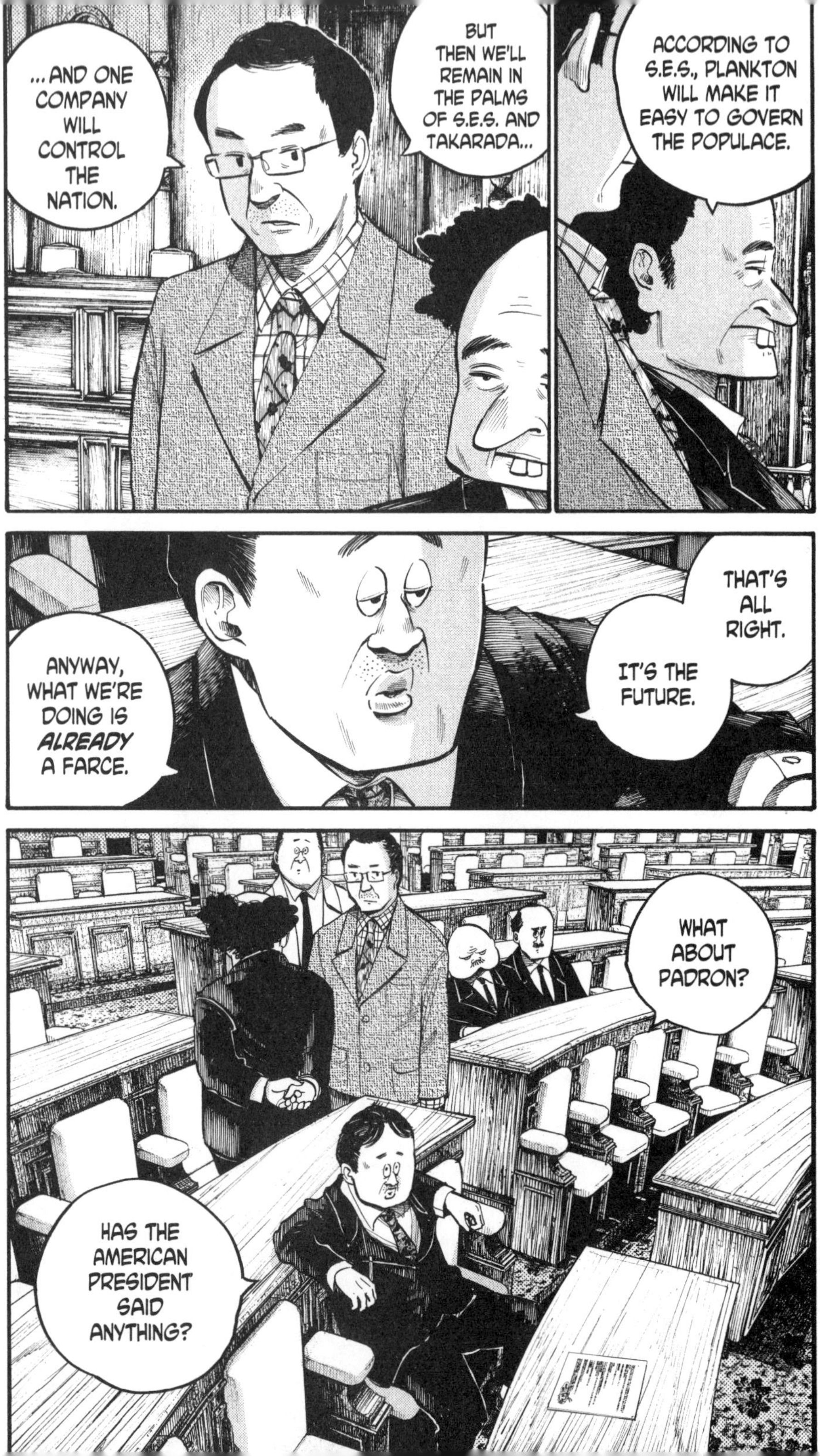
ACCORDING TO S.E.S., PLANKTON WILL MAKE IT EASY TO GOVERN THE POPULACE.
BUT THEN WE'LL REMAIN IN THE PALMS OF S.E.S. AND TAKARADA...
...AND ONE COMPANY WILL CONTROL THE NATION.
THAT'S ALL RIGHT.
IT'S THE FUTURE.
ANYWAY, WHAT WE'RE DOING IS *ALREADY* A FARCE.
WHAT ABOUT PADRON?
HAS THE AMERICAN PRESIDENT SAID ANYTHING?

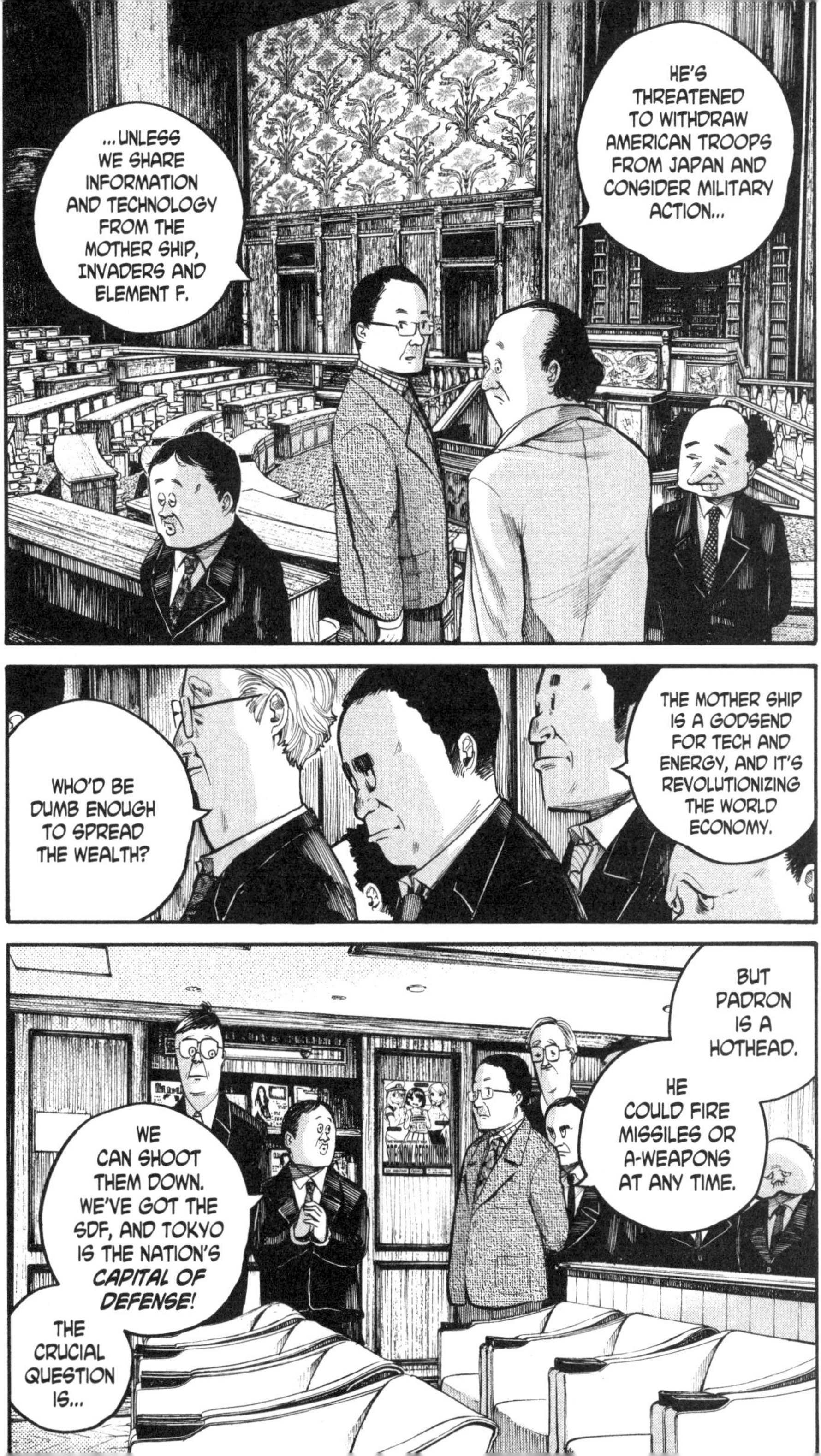
HE'S THREATENED TO WITHDRAW AMERICAN TROOPS FROM JAPAN AND CONSIDER MILITARY ACTION...
...UNLESS WE SHARE INFORMATION AND TECHNOLOGY FROM THE MOTHER SHIP, INVADERS AND ELEMENT F.
THE MOTHER SHIP IS A GODSEND FOR TECH AND ENERGY, AND IT'S REVOLUTIONIZING THE WORLD ECONOMY.
WHO'D BE DUMB ENOUGH TO SPREAD THE WEALTH?
BUT PADRON IS A HOTHEAD.
HE COULD FIRE MISSILES OR A-WEAPONS AT ANY TIME.
WE CAN SHOOT THEM DOWN. WE'VE GOT THE SDF, AND TOKYO IS THE NATION'S *CAPITAL OF DEFENSE!*
THE CRUCIAL QUESTION IS...

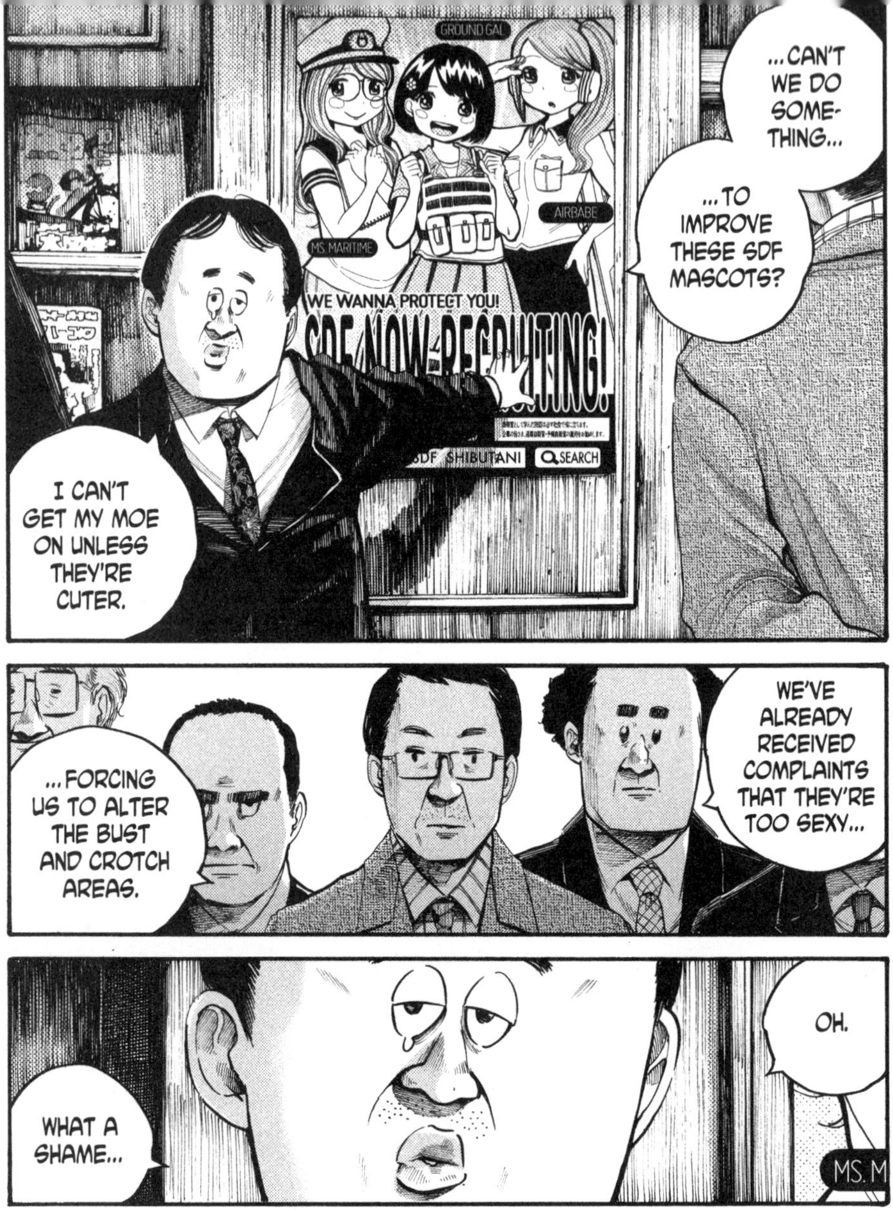

GROUND GAL
AIRBABE
MS. MARITIME
WE WANNA PROTECT YOU!
SDF NOW RECRUITING!
SDF SHIBUTANI
SEARCH
...CAN'T WE DO SOMETHING...
...TO IMPROVE THESE SDF MASCOTS?
I CAN'T GET MY MOE ON UNLESS THEY'RE CUTER.
WE'VE ALREADY RECEIVED COMPLAINTS THAT THEY'RE TOO SEXY...
...FORCING US TO ALTER THE BUST AND CROTCH AREAS.
OH.
WHAT A SHAME...
MS. M

Additional Notes 2:
Someone claiming to be an Invader invited questions on a major online forum and the post went viral. Tracking the IP address revealed the source to be the home computer of Shosuke Ojiro, a fourth-year student at Surume University in Setagaya Ward. An investigation from May to June did not reveal anything suspicious. An outside party may have hacked his computer, raising the possibility of a citizen with IT knowledge who is collaborating with the Invaders.

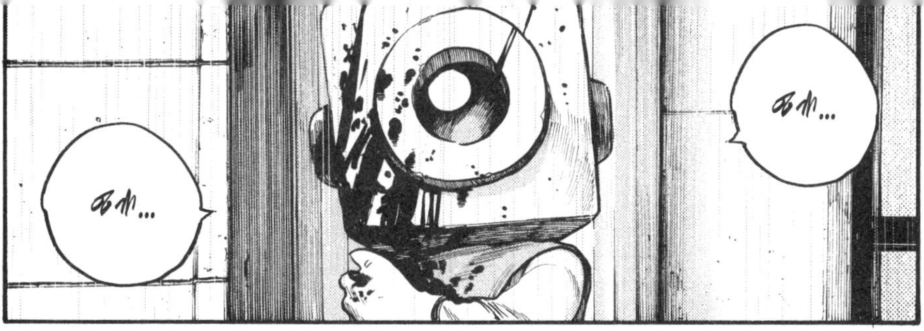

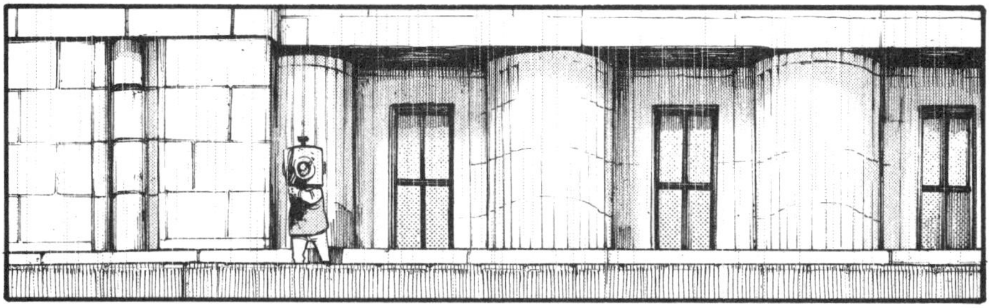

According to online statements by the self-professed Invader, abnormal heat buildup inside the mother ship is reducing the available power supporting the vessel's base. S.E.S. claims the mother ship will collapse and possibly explode in late August. The company is currently investigating the potential scale of damage. Within 24 hours of confirmation of an emergency, Hujin Type 8 (the new national stadium Ocean) will activate and leave the atmosphere.

TOP SECRET

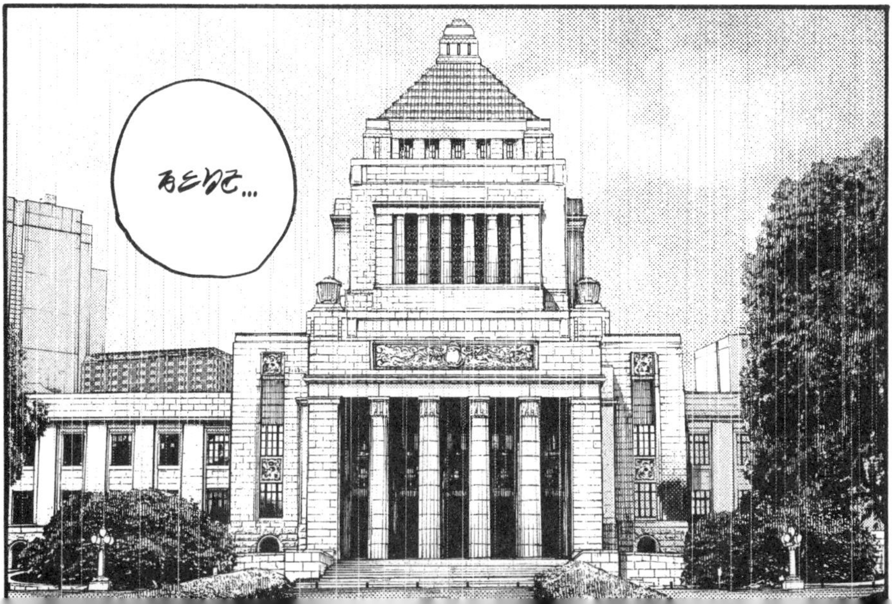

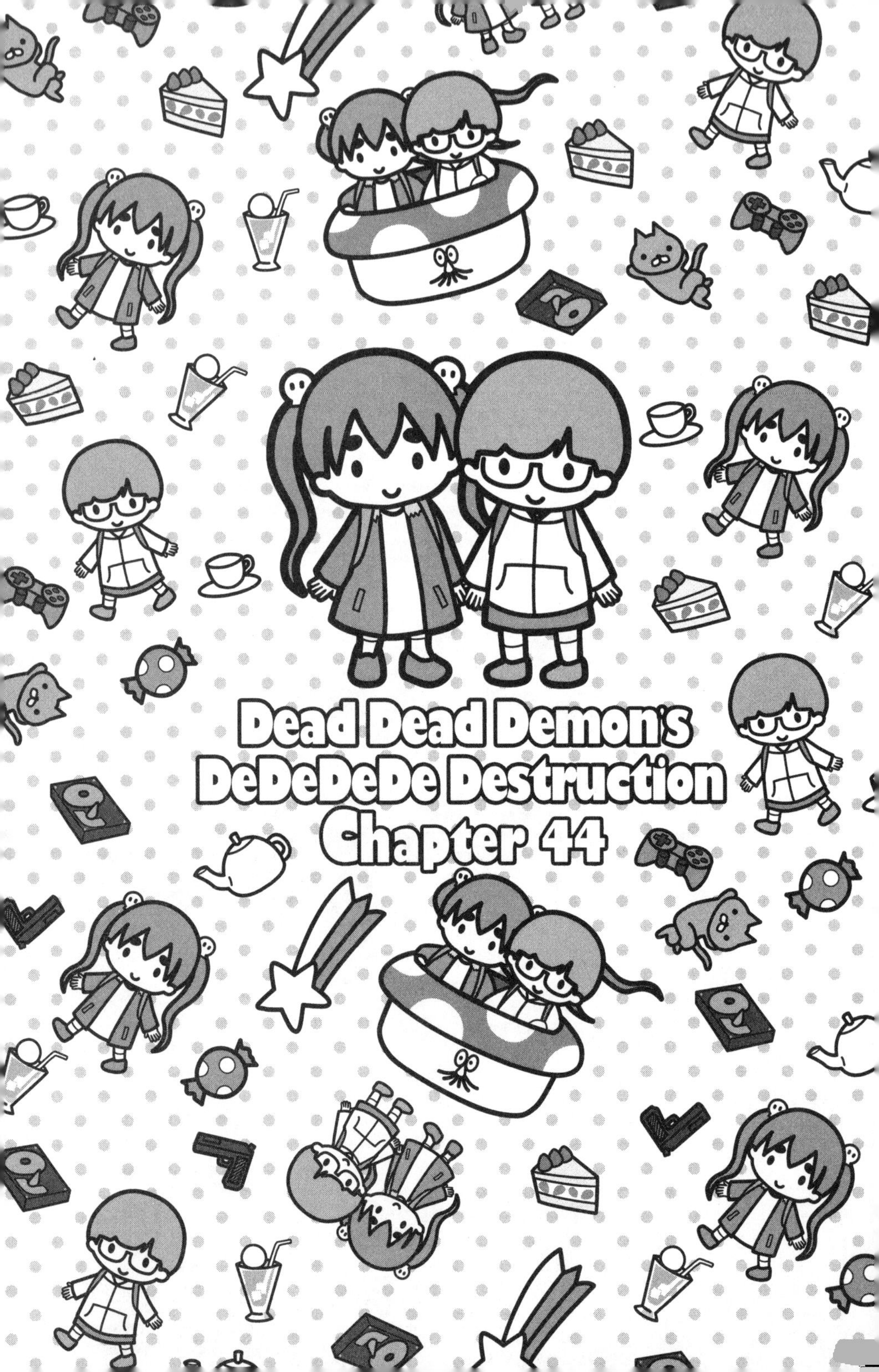

Dead Dead Demon's DeDeDeDe Destruction
Chapter 44

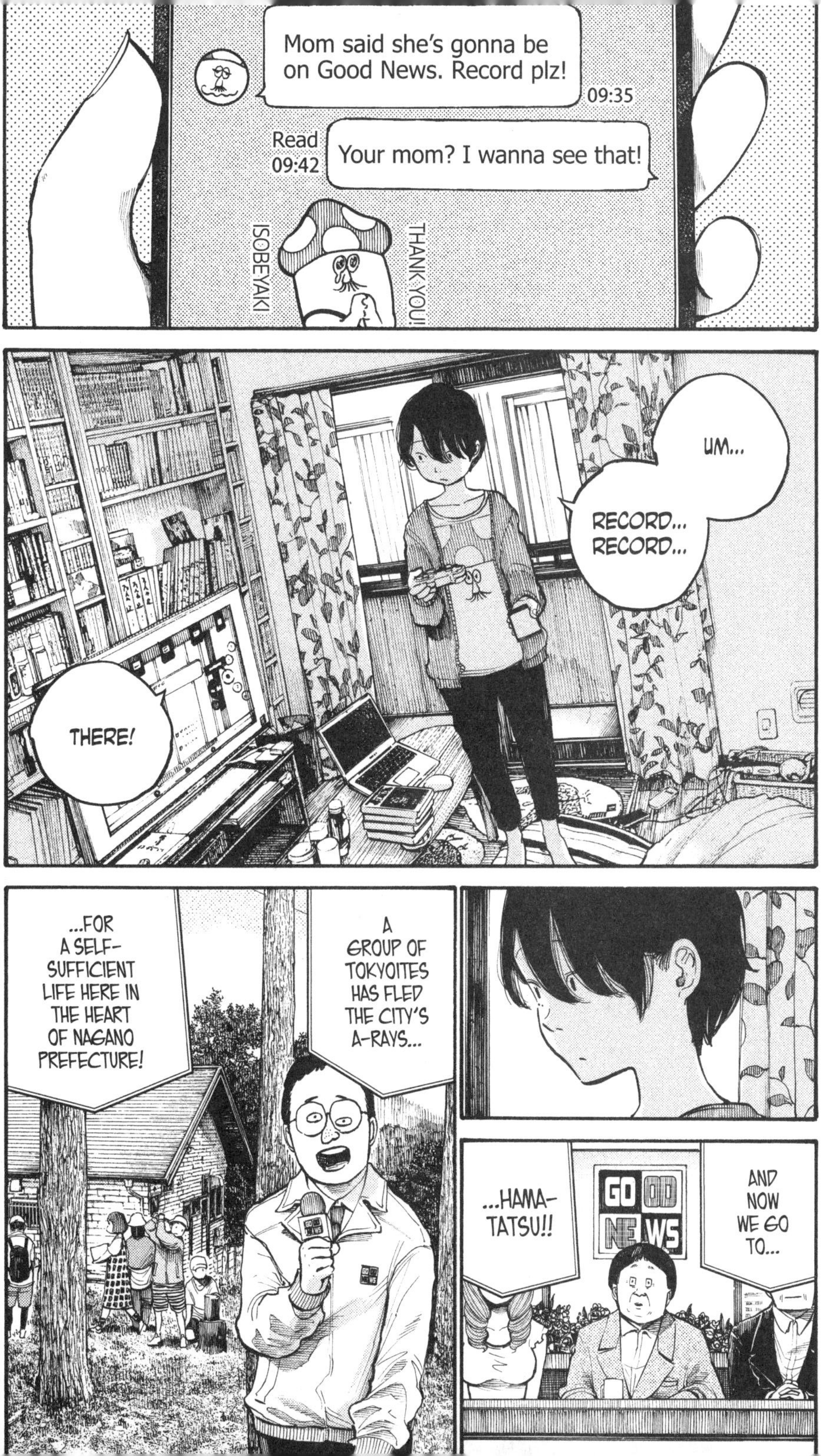
Mom said she's gonna be on Good News. Record plz!
09:35
Read 09:42
Your mom? I wanna see that!
THANK YOU!
ISOBEYAKI
UM...
RECORD... RECORD...
THERE!
AND NOW WE GO TO...
...HAMA-TATSU!!
A GROUP OF TOKYOITES HAS FLED THE CITY'S A-RAYS...
...FOR A SELF-SUFFICIENT LIFE HERE IN THE HEART OF NAGANO PREFECTURE!

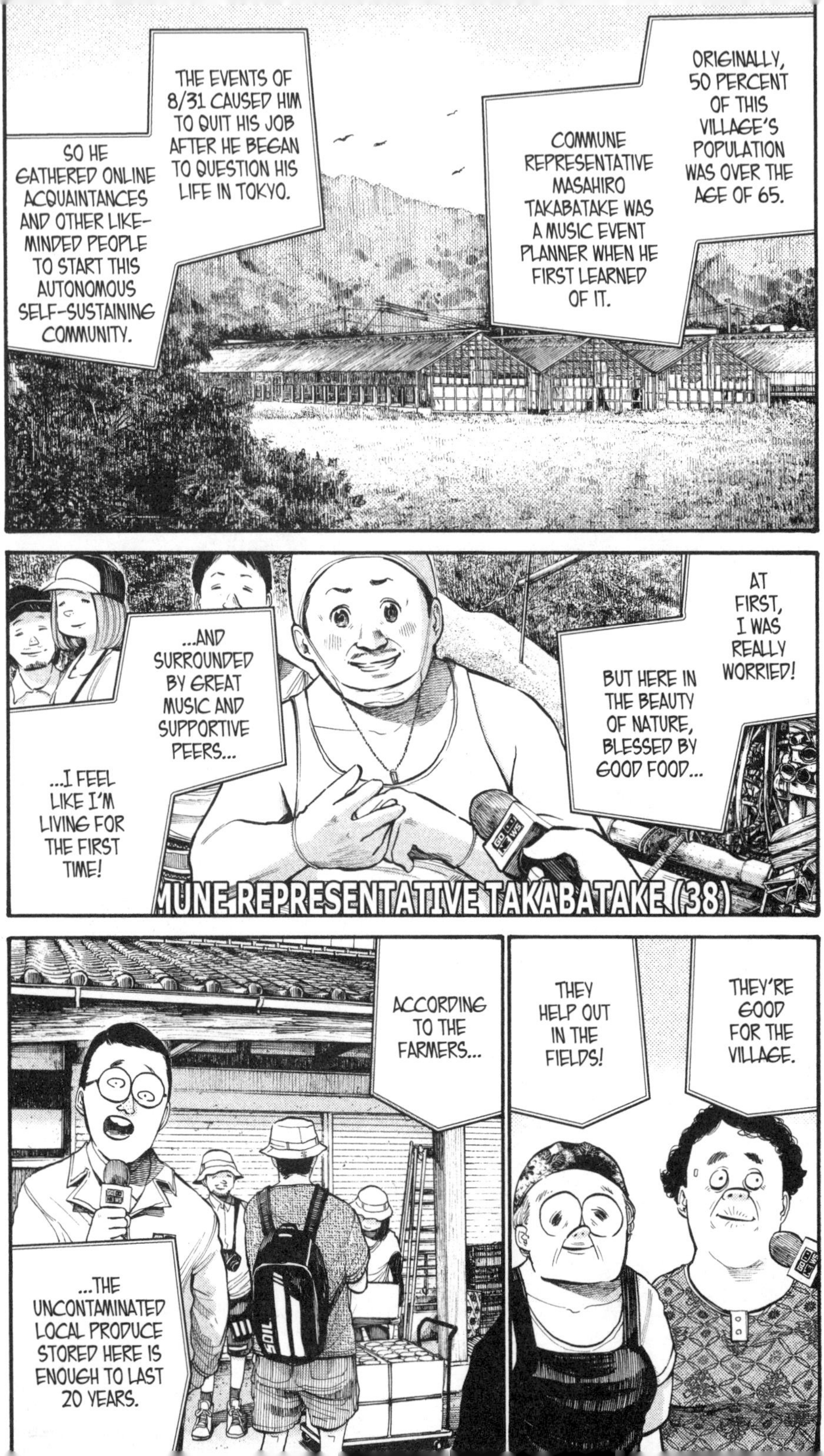
ORIGINALLY, 50 PERCENT OF THIS VILLAGE'S POPULATION WAS OVER THE AGE OF 65.
COMMUNE REPRESENTATIVE MASAHIRO TAKABATAKE WAS A MUSIC EVENT PLANNER WHEN HE FIRST LEARNED OF IT.
THE EVENTS OF 8/31 CAUSED HIM TO QUIT HIS JOB AFTER HE BEGAN TO QUESTION HIS LIFE IN TOKYO.
SO HE GATHERED ONLINE ACQUAINTANCES AND OTHER LIKE-MINDED PEOPLE TO START THIS AUTONOMOUS SELF-SUSTAINING COMMUNITY.
AT FIRST, I WAS REALLY WORRIED!
BUT HERE IN THE BEAUTY OF NATURE, BLESSED BY GOOD FOOD...
...AND SURROUNDED BY GREAT MUSIC AND SUPPORTIVE PEERS...
...I FEEL LIKE I'M LIVING FOR THE FIRST TIME!
MUNE REPRESENTATIVE TAKABATAKE (38)
THEY'RE GOOD FOR THE VILLAGE.
THEY HELP OUT IN THE FIELDS!
ACCORDING TO THE FARMERS...
...THE UNCONTAMINATED LOCAL PRODUCE STORED HERE IS ENOUGH TO LAST 20 YEARS.

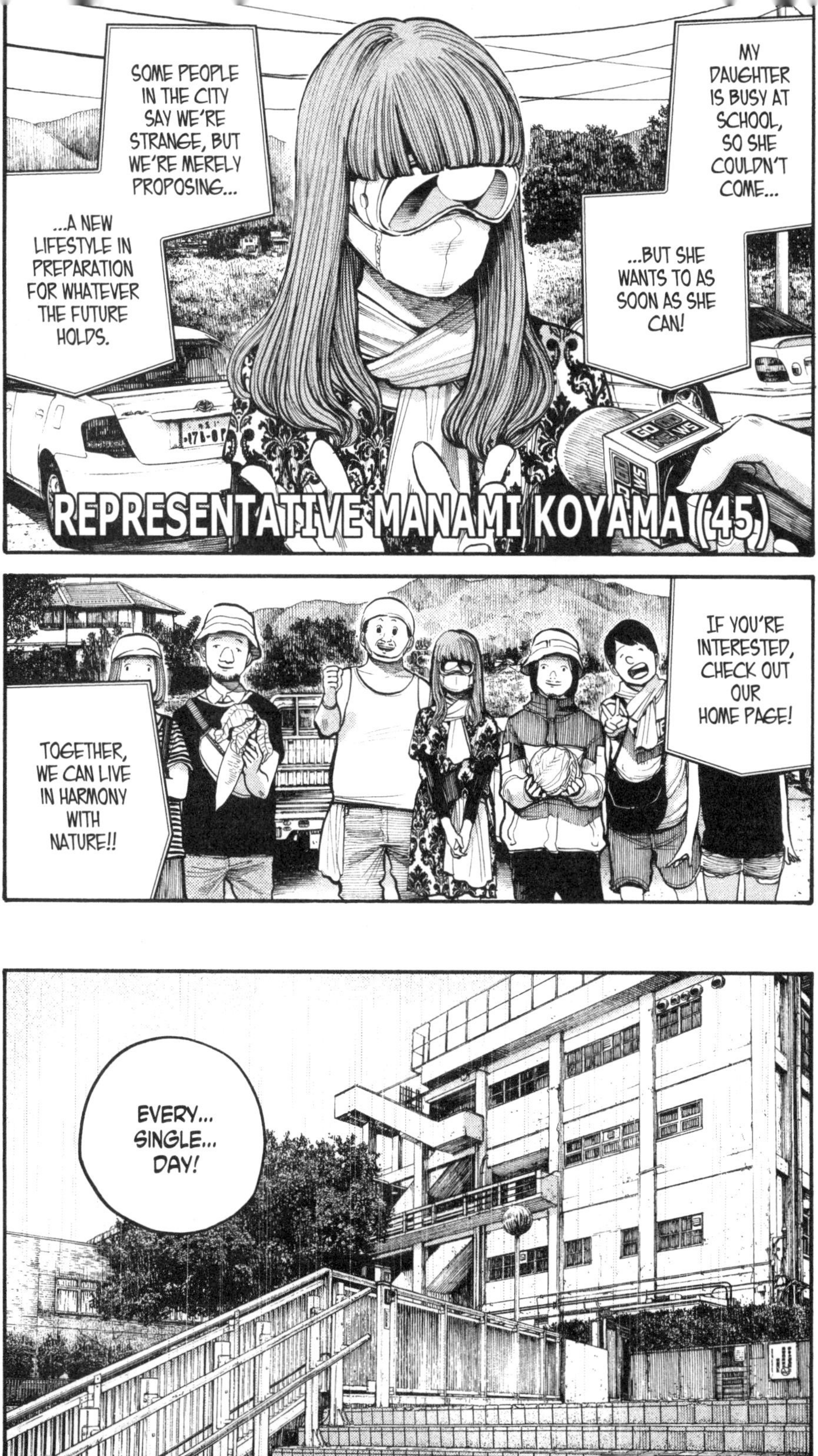
MY DAUGHTER IS BUSY AT SCHOOL, SO SHE COULDN'T COME...
...BUT SHE WANTS TO AS SOON AS SHE CAN!
SOME PEOPLE IN THE CITY SAY WE'RE STRANGE, BUT WE'RE MERELY PROPOSING...
...A NEW LIFESTYLE IN PREPARATION FOR WHATEVER THE FUTURE HOLDS.
REPRESENTATIVE MANAMI KOYAMA (45)
IF YOU'RE INTERESTED, CHECK OUT OUR HOME PAGE!
TOGETHER, WE CAN LIVE IN HARMONY WITH NATURE!!
EVERY... SINGLE... DAY!

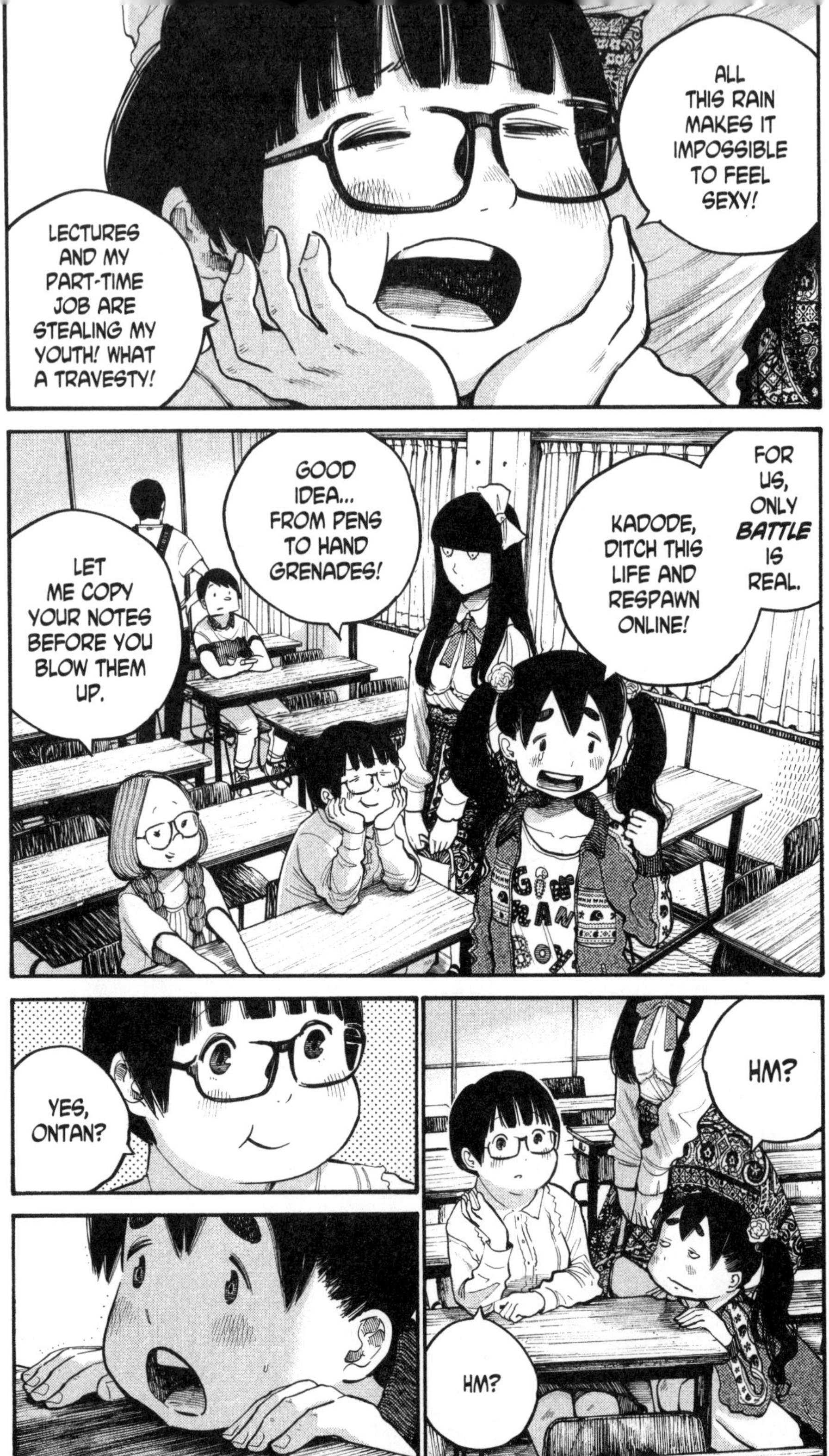
ALL THIS RAIN MAKES IT IMPOSSIBLE TO FEEL SEXY!
LECTURES AND MY PART-TIME JOB ARE STEALING MY YOUTH! WHAT A TRAVESTY!
FOR US, ONLY *BATTLE* IS REAL.
KADODE, DITCH THIS LIFE AND RESPAWN ONLINE!
GOOD IDEA... FROM PENS TO HAND GRENADES!
LET ME COPY YOUR NOTES BEFORE YOU BLOW THEM UP.
HM?
HM?
YES, ONTAN?

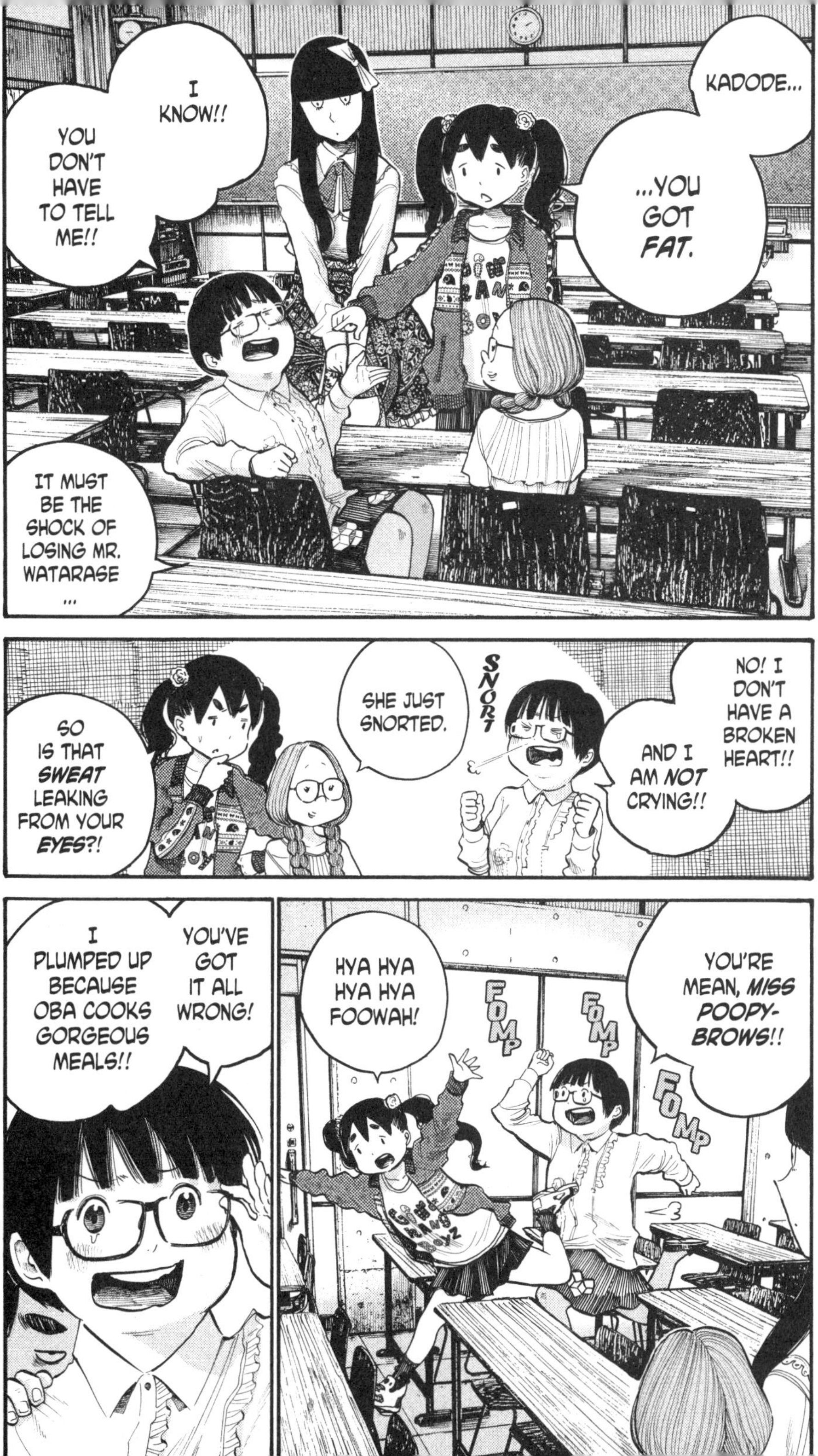
KADODE...
...YOU GOT FAT.
I KNOW!!
YOU DON'T HAVE TO TELL ME!!
IT MUST BE THE SHOCK OF LOSING MR. WATARASE ...
NO! I DON'T HAVE A BROKEN HEART!!
AND I AM NOT CRYING!!
SNORT
SHE JUST SNORTED.
SO IS THAT SWEAT LEAKING FROM YOUR EYES?!
YOU'RE MEAN, MISS POOPY-BROWS!!
FOMP
FOMP
FOMP
HYA HYA HYA HYA FOOWAH!
YOU'VE GOT IT ALL WRONG!
I PLUMPED UP BECAUSE OBA COOKS GORGEOUS MEALS!!

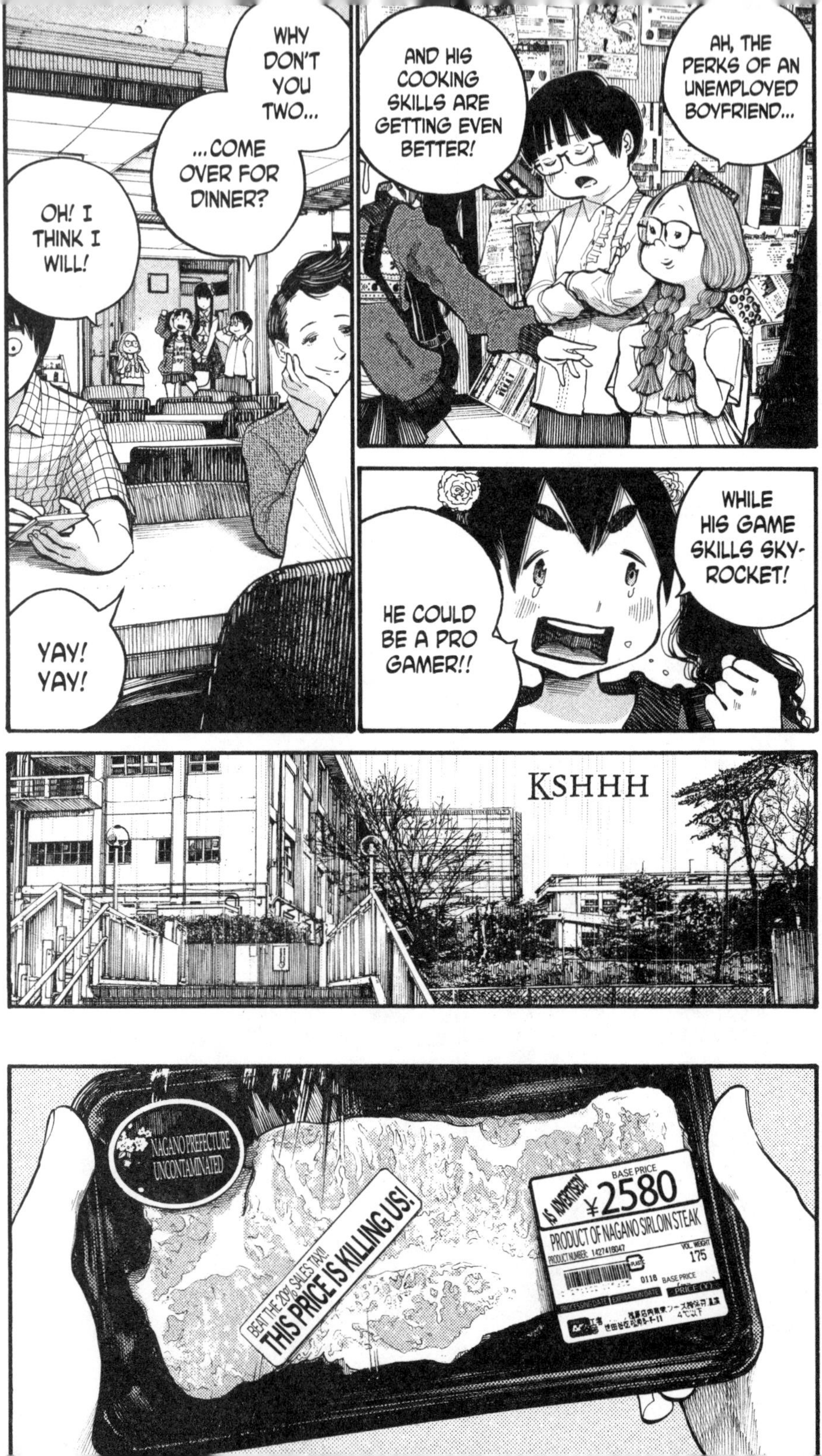
AH, THE PERKS OF AN UNEMPLOYED BOYFRIEND...
AND HIS COOKING SKILLS ARE GETTING EVEN BETTER!
WHILE HIS GAME SKILLS SKY-ROCKET!
HE COULD BE A PRO GAMER!!
WHY DON'T YOU TWO...
...COME OVER FOR DINNER?
OH! I THINK I WILL!
YAY! YAY!
KSHHH
NAGANO PREFECTURE UNCONTAMINATED
BEAT THE 20% SALES TAX!!
THIS PRICE IS KILLING US!
AS ADVERTISED!
BASE PRICE
¥2580
PRODUCT OF NAGANO SIRLOIN STEAK
PRODUCT NUMBER 1427416047
VOL. WEIGHT
175
BASE PRICE

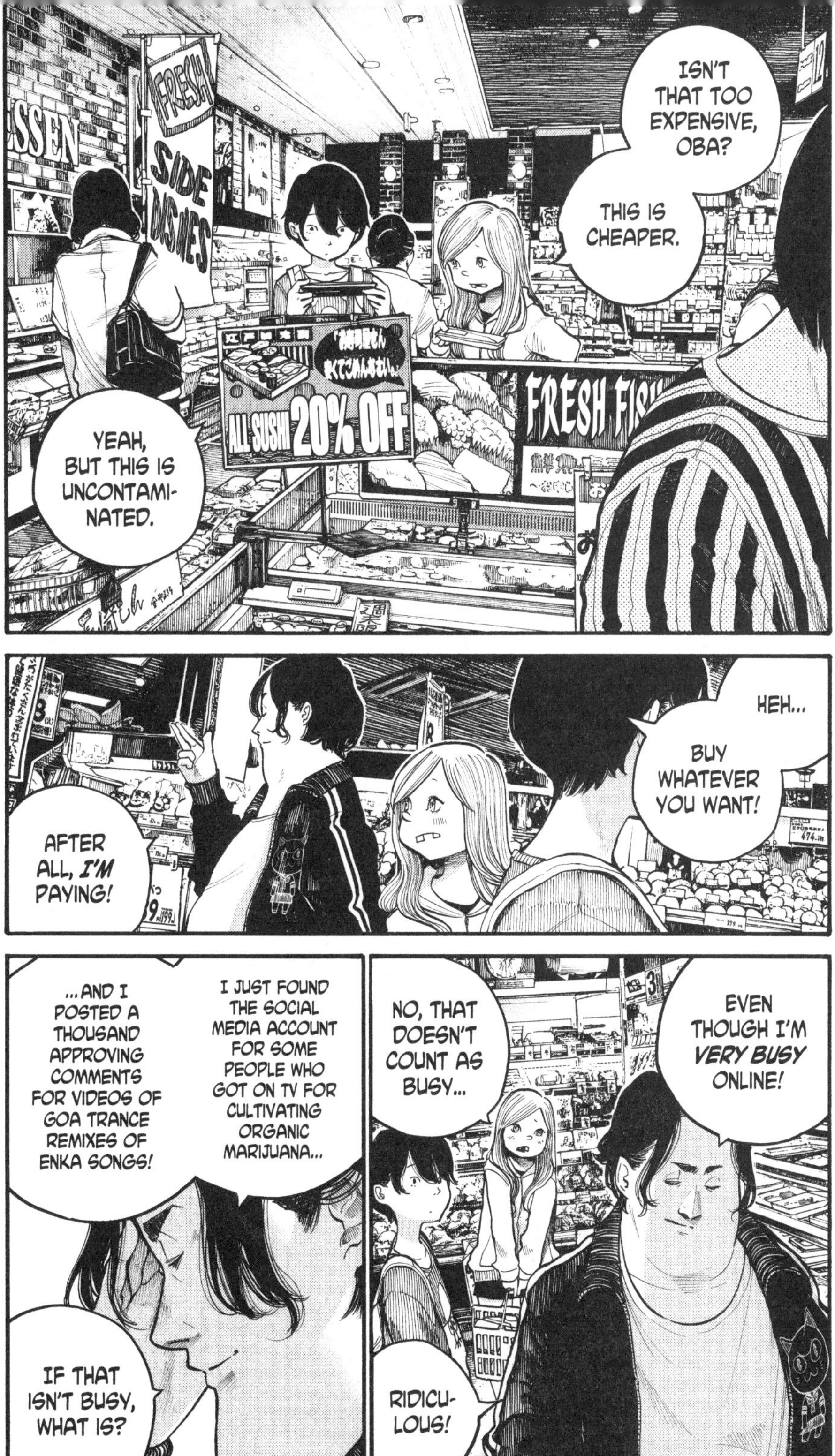
FRESH
SIDE DISHES
ALL SUSHI 20% OFF
ISN'T THAT TOO EXPENSIVE, OBA?
THIS IS CHEAPER.
YEAH, BUT THIS IS UNCONTAMI-NATED.
HEH...
BUY WHATEVER YOU WANT!
AFTER ALL, *I'M* PAYING!
EVEN THOUGH I'M *VERY BUSY* ONLINE!
NO, THAT DOESN'T COUNT AS BUSY...
RIDICU-LOUS!
I JUST FOUND THE SOCIAL MEDIA ACCOUNT FOR SOME PEOPLE WHO GOT ON TV FOR CULTIVATING ORGANIC MARIJUANA...
...AND I POSTED A THOUSAND APPROVING COMMENTS FOR VIDEOS OF GOA TRANCE REMIXES OF ENKA SONGS!
IF THAT ISN'T BUSY, WHAT IS?

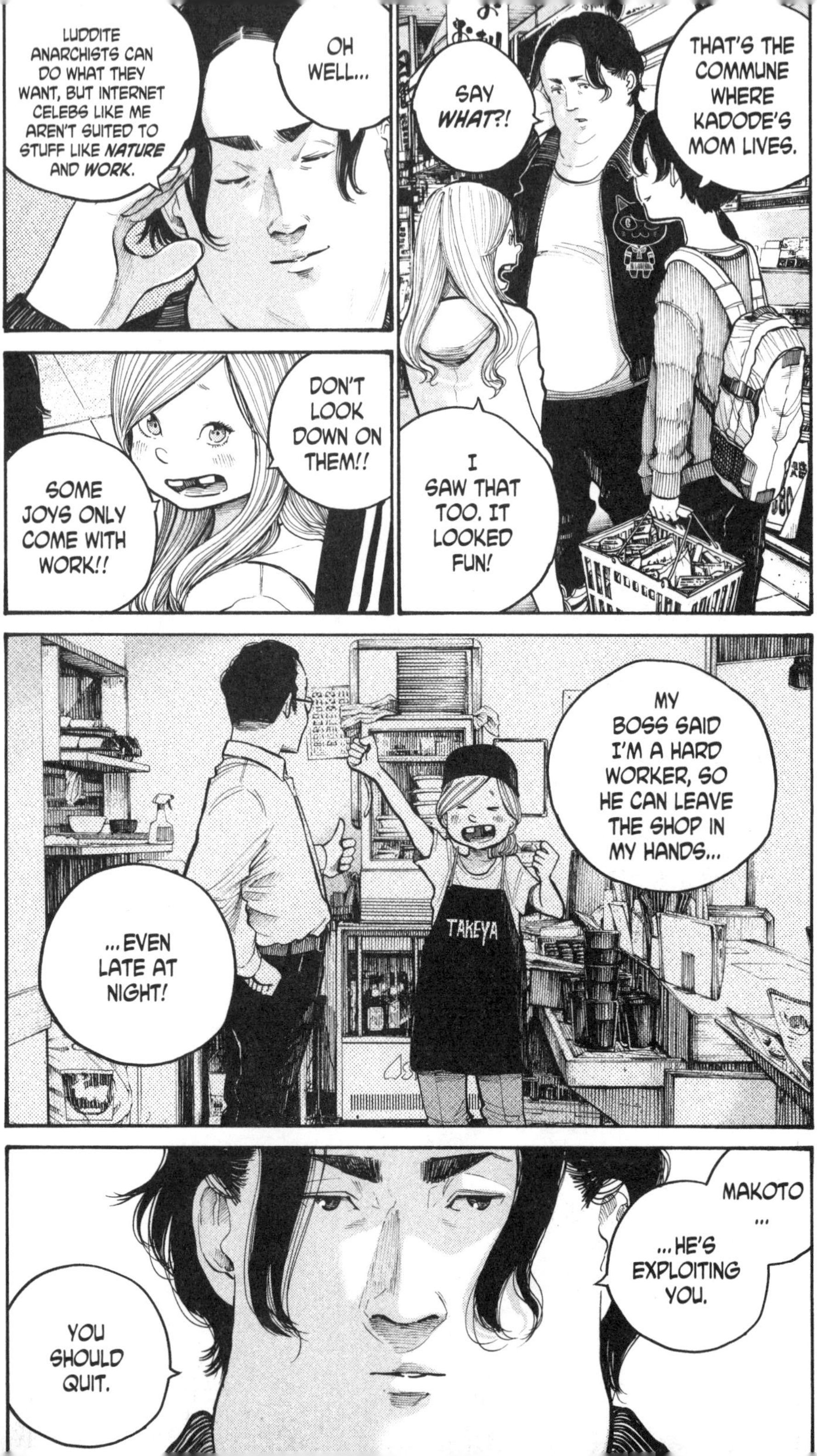
THAT'S THE COMMUNE WHERE KADODE'S MOM LIVES.
SAY *WHAT?!*
I SAW THAT TOO. IT LOOKED FUN!
OH WELL...
LUDDITE ANARCHISTS CAN DO WHAT THEY WANT, BUT INTERNET CELEBS LIKE ME AREN'T SUITED TO STUFF LIKE ***NATURE*** AND ***WORK***.
DON'T LOOK DOWN ON THEM!!
SOME JOYS ONLY COME WITH WORK!!
MY BOSS SAID I'M A HARD WORKER, SO HE CAN LEAVE THE SHOP IN MY HANDS...
...EVEN LATE AT NIGHT!
TAKEYA
MAKOTO...
...HE'S EXPLOITING YOU.
YOU SHOULD QUIT.

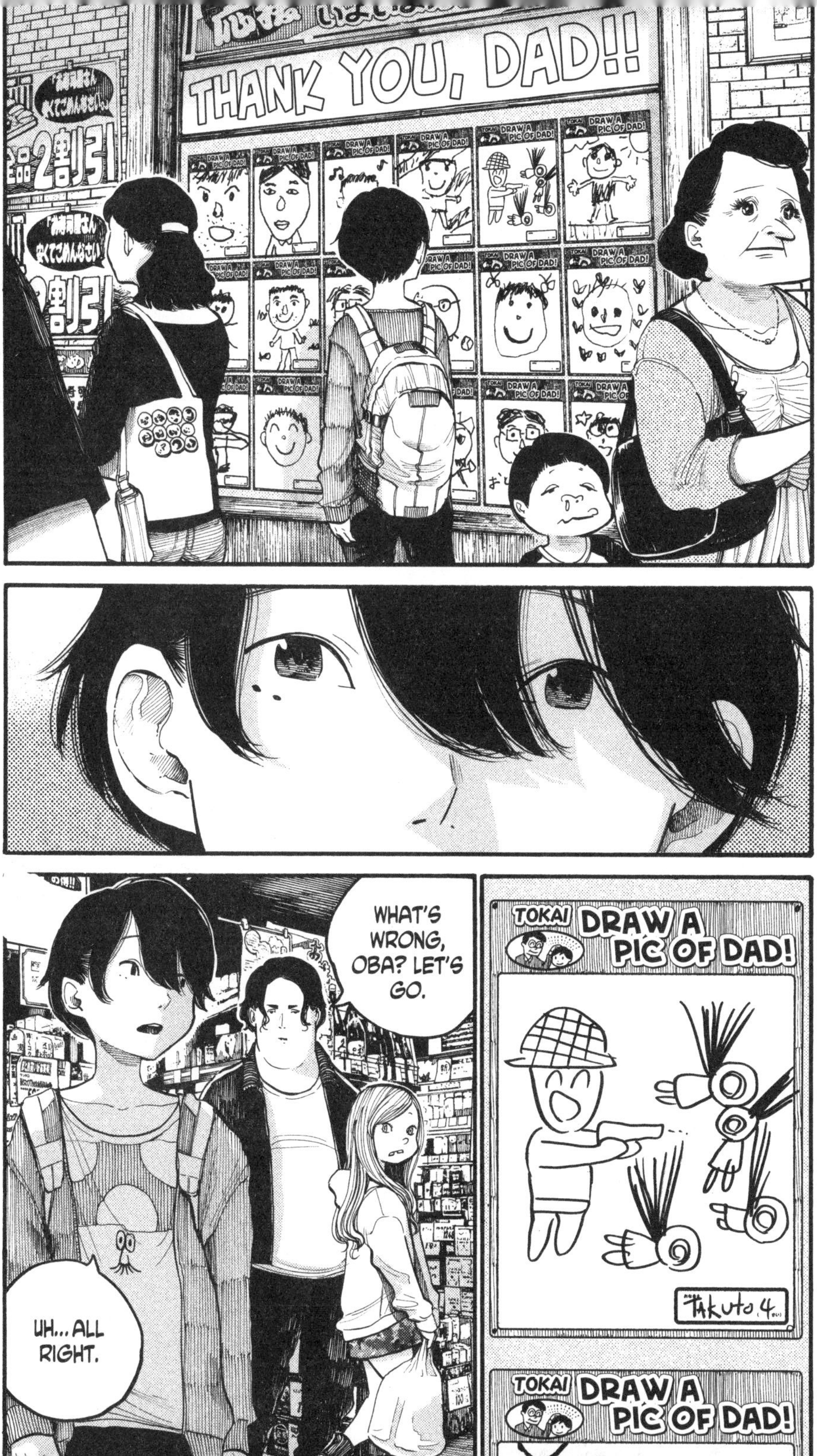
THANK YOU, DAD!!
TOKAI DRAW A PIC OF DAD!
TOKAI DRAW A PIC OF DAD!
TAkuto 4
TOKAI DRAW A PIC OF DAD!
WHAT'S WRONG, OBA? LET'S GO.
UH... ALL RIGHT.

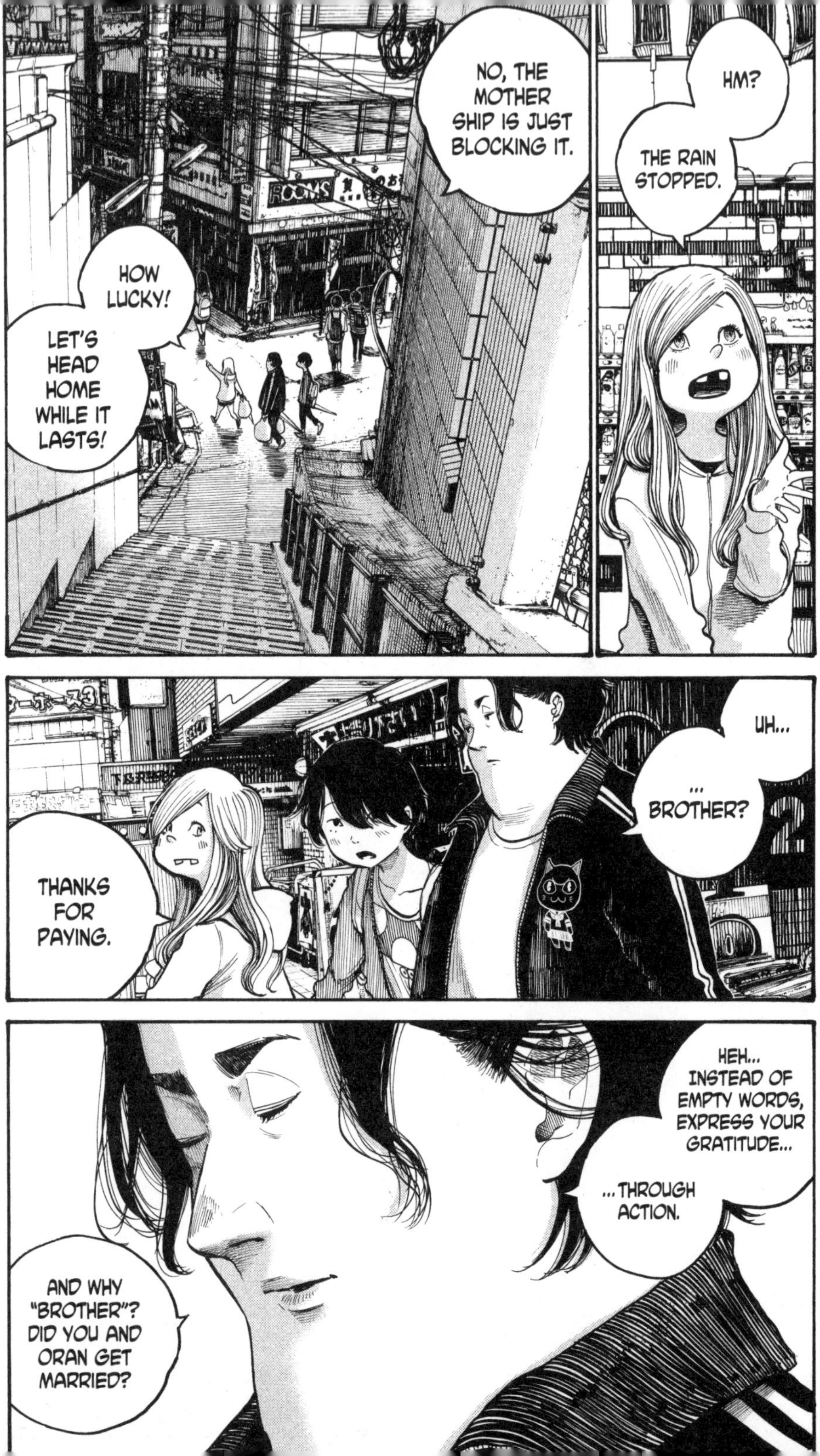
HM?
THE RAIN STOPPED.
NO, THE MOTHER SHIP IS JUST BLOCKING IT.
HOW LUCKY!
LET'S HEAD HOME WHILE IT LASTS!
UH...
... BROTHER?
THANKS FOR PAYING.
HEH... INSTEAD OF EMPTY WORDS, EXPRESS YOUR GRATITUDE...
...THROUGH ACTION.
AND WHY "BROTHER"? DID YOU AND ORAN GET MARRIED?

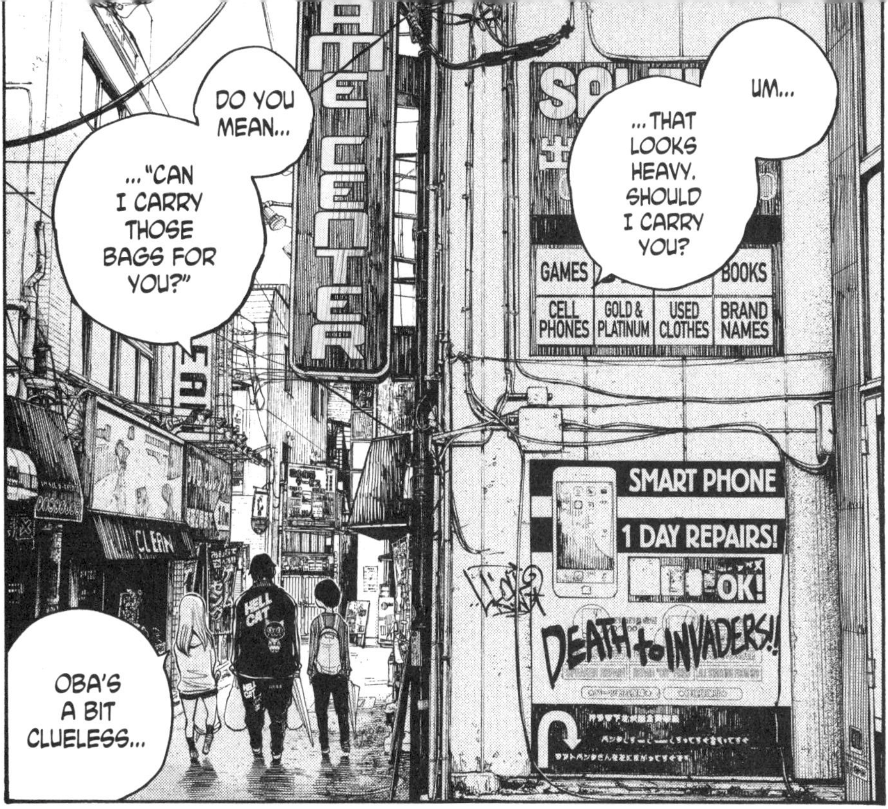
UM...
...THAT LOOKS HEAVY. SHOULD I CARRY YOU?
DO YOU MEAN...
..."CAN I CARRY THOSE BAGS FOR YOU?"
GAMES
BOOKS
CELL PHONES
GOLD & PLATINUM
USED CLOTHES
BRAND NAMES
SMART PHONE
1 DAY REPAIRS!
OK!
DEATH to INVADERS!!
OBA'S A BIT CLUELESS...

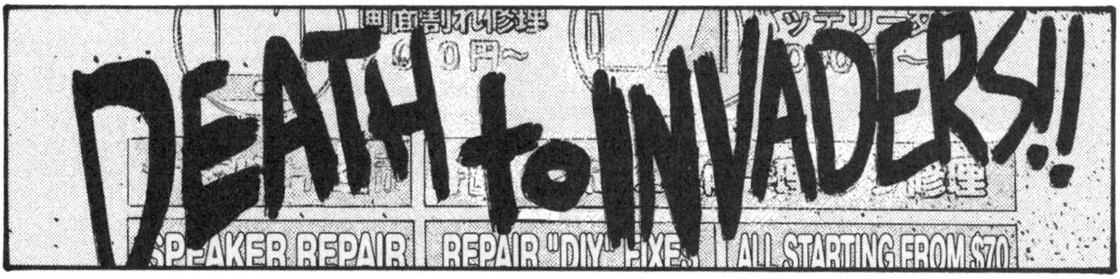
DEATH to INVADERS!!
SPEAKER REPAIR
ALL STARTING FROM $70

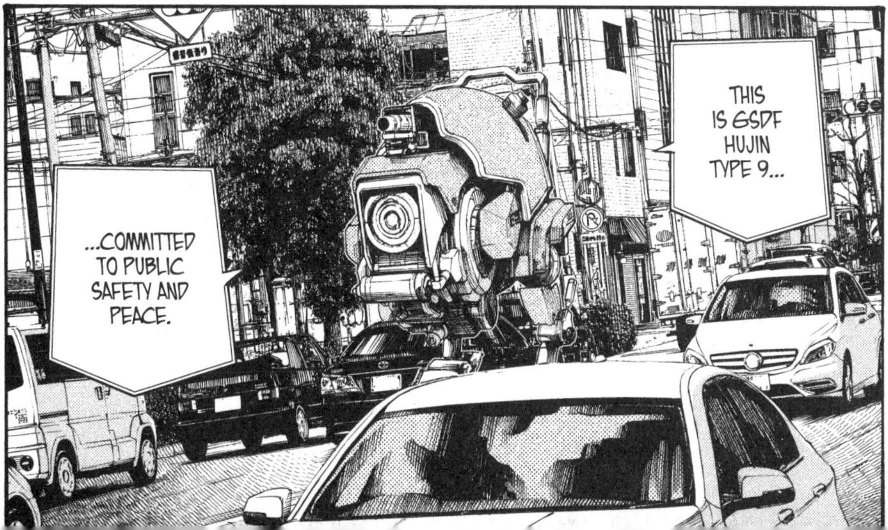
THIS IS GSDF HUJIN TYPE 9...
...COMMITTED TO PUBLIC SAFETY AND PEACE.

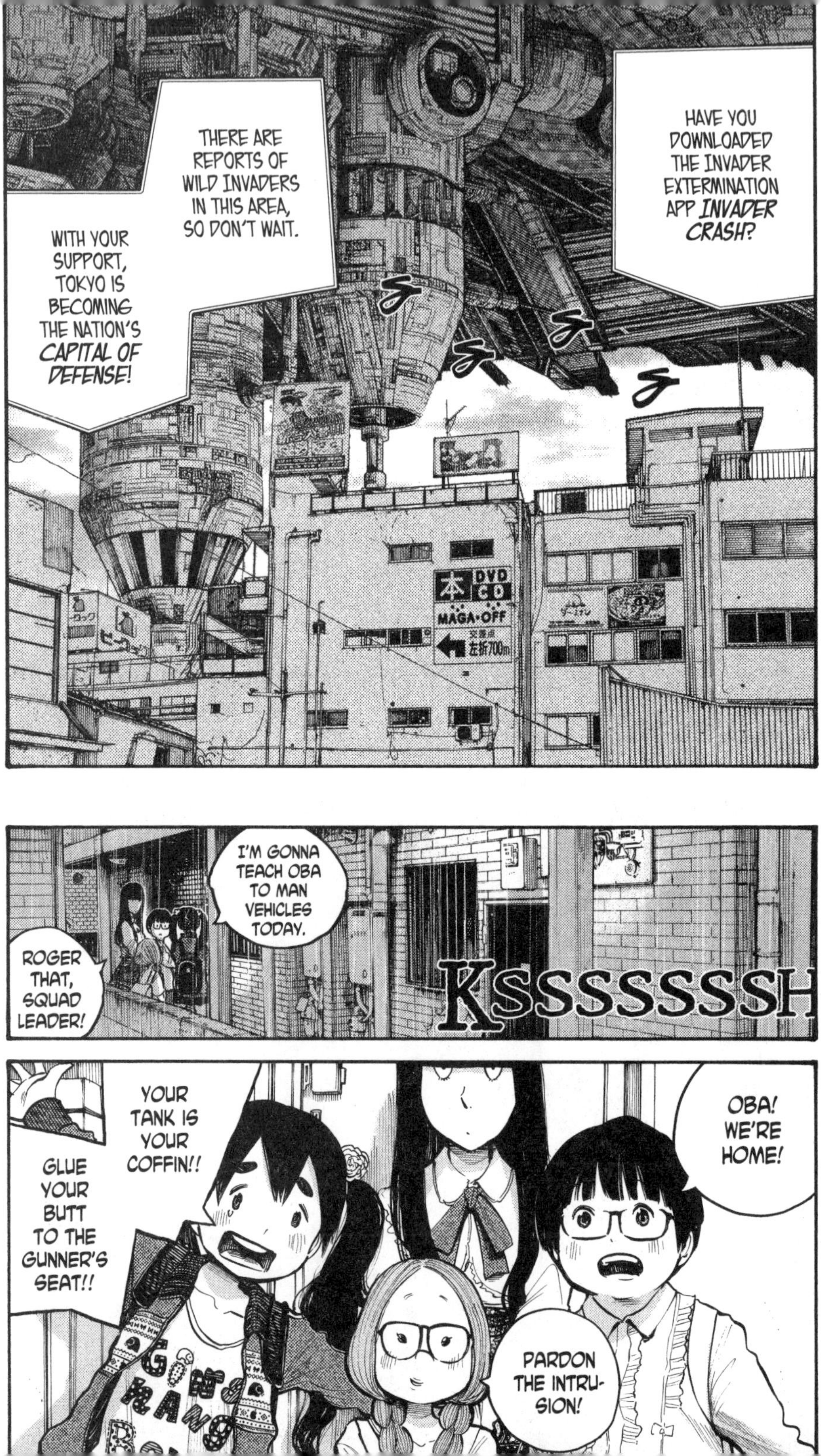
HAVE YOU DOWNLOADED THE INVADER EXTERMINATION APP *INVADER CRASH*?
THERE ARE REPORTS OF WILD INVADERS IN THIS AREA, SO DON'T WAIT.
WITH YOUR SUPPORT, TOKYO IS BECOMING THE NATION'S *CAPITAL OF DEFENSE!*
本 DVD CD
MAGA・OFF
I'M GONNA TEACH OBA TO MAN VEHICLES TODAY.
ROGER THAT, SQUAD LEADER!
KSSSSSSH
OBA! WE'RE HOME!
PARDON THE INTRUSION!
YOUR TANK IS YOUR COFFIN!!
GLUE YOUR BUTT TO THE GUNNER'S SEAT!!

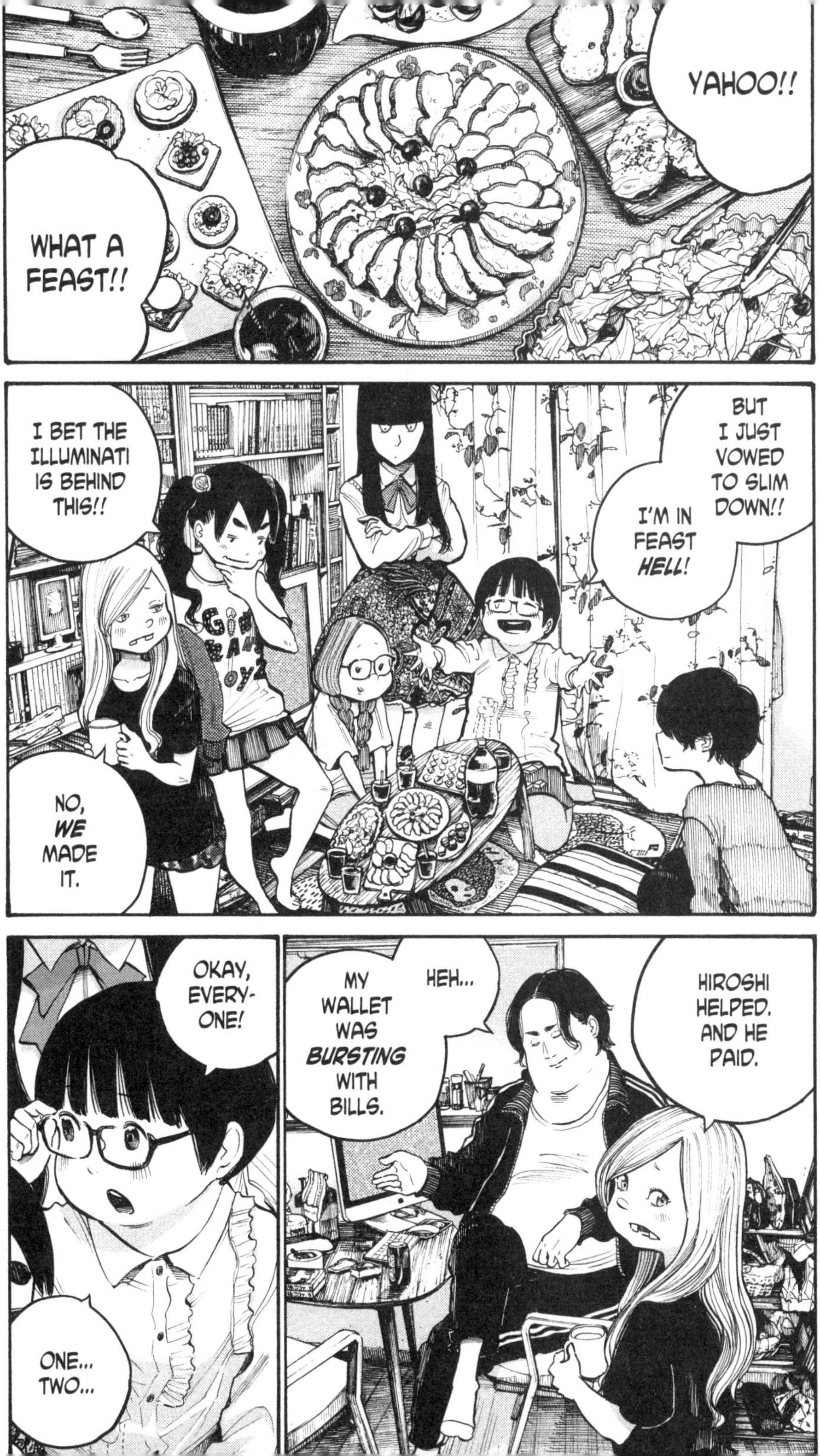
YAHOO!!
WHAT A FEAST!!
BUT I JUST VOWED TO SLIM DOWN!!
I'M IN FEAST *HELL*!
I BET THE ILLUMINATI IS BEHIND THIS!!
NO, *WE* MADE IT.
HIROSHI HELPED. AND HE PAID.
HEH...
MY WALLET WAS *BURSTING* WITH BILLS.
OKAY, EVERY-ONE!
ONE... TWO...

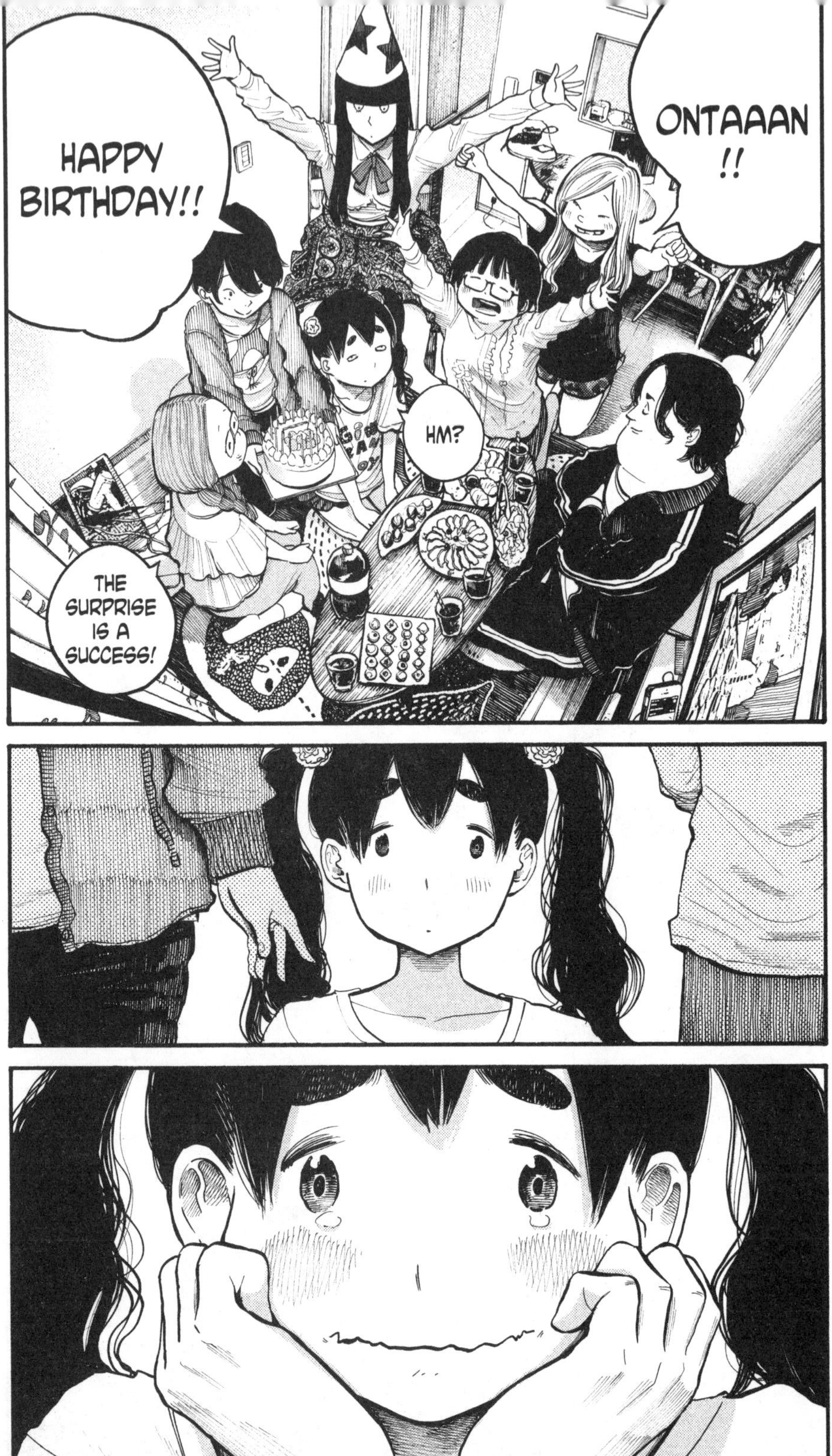
ONTAAAN!!
HAPPY BIRTHDAY!!
HM?
THE SURPRISE IS A SUCCESS!

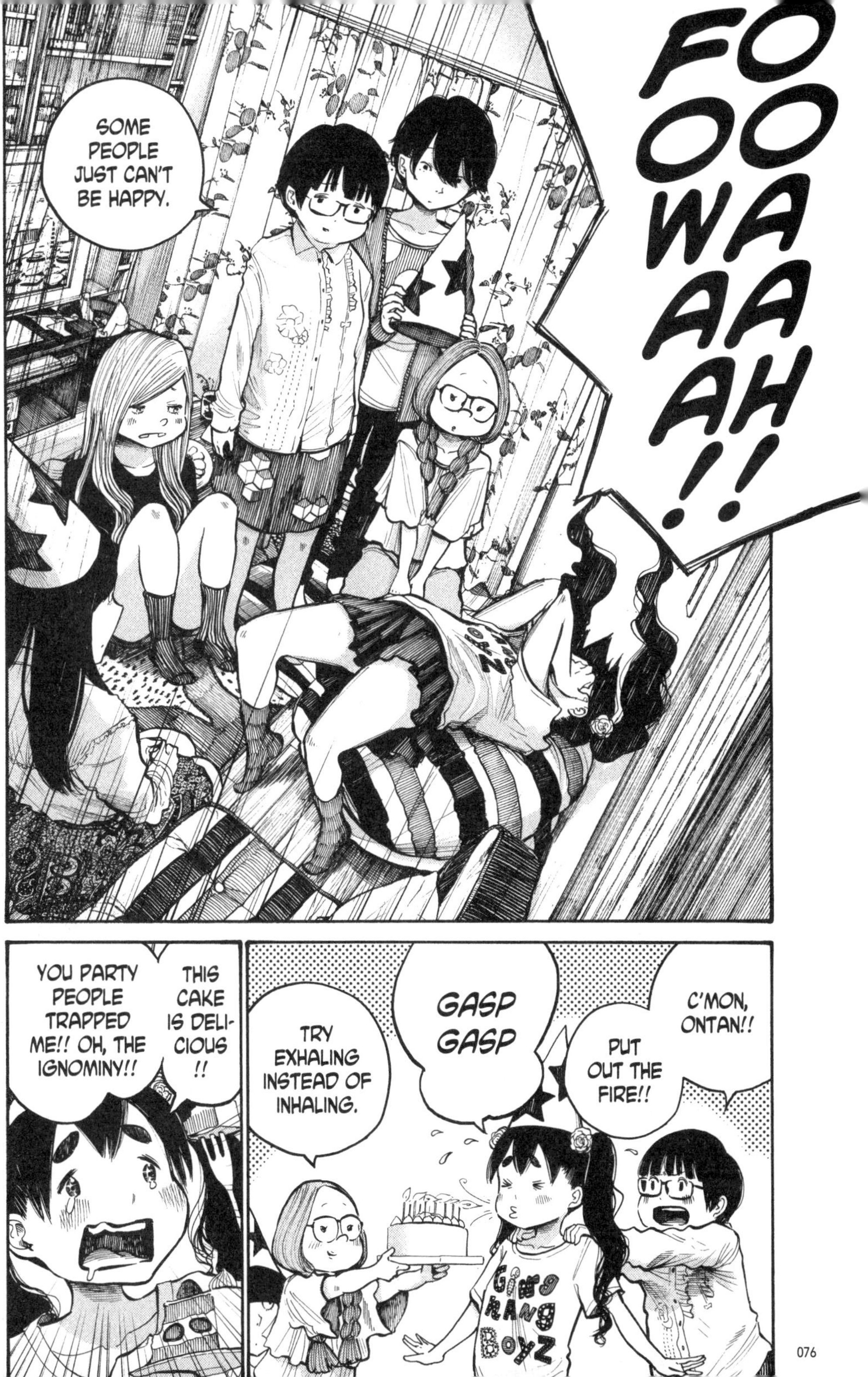
FOOOWAAAAH!!
SOME PEOPLE JUST CAN'T BE HAPPY.
C'MON, ONTAN!!
PUT OUT THE FIRE!!
GASP GASP
TRY EXHALING INSTEAD OF INHALING.
THIS CAKE IS DELI-CIOUS!!
YOU PARTY PEOPLE TRAPPED ME!! OH, THE IGNOMINY!!

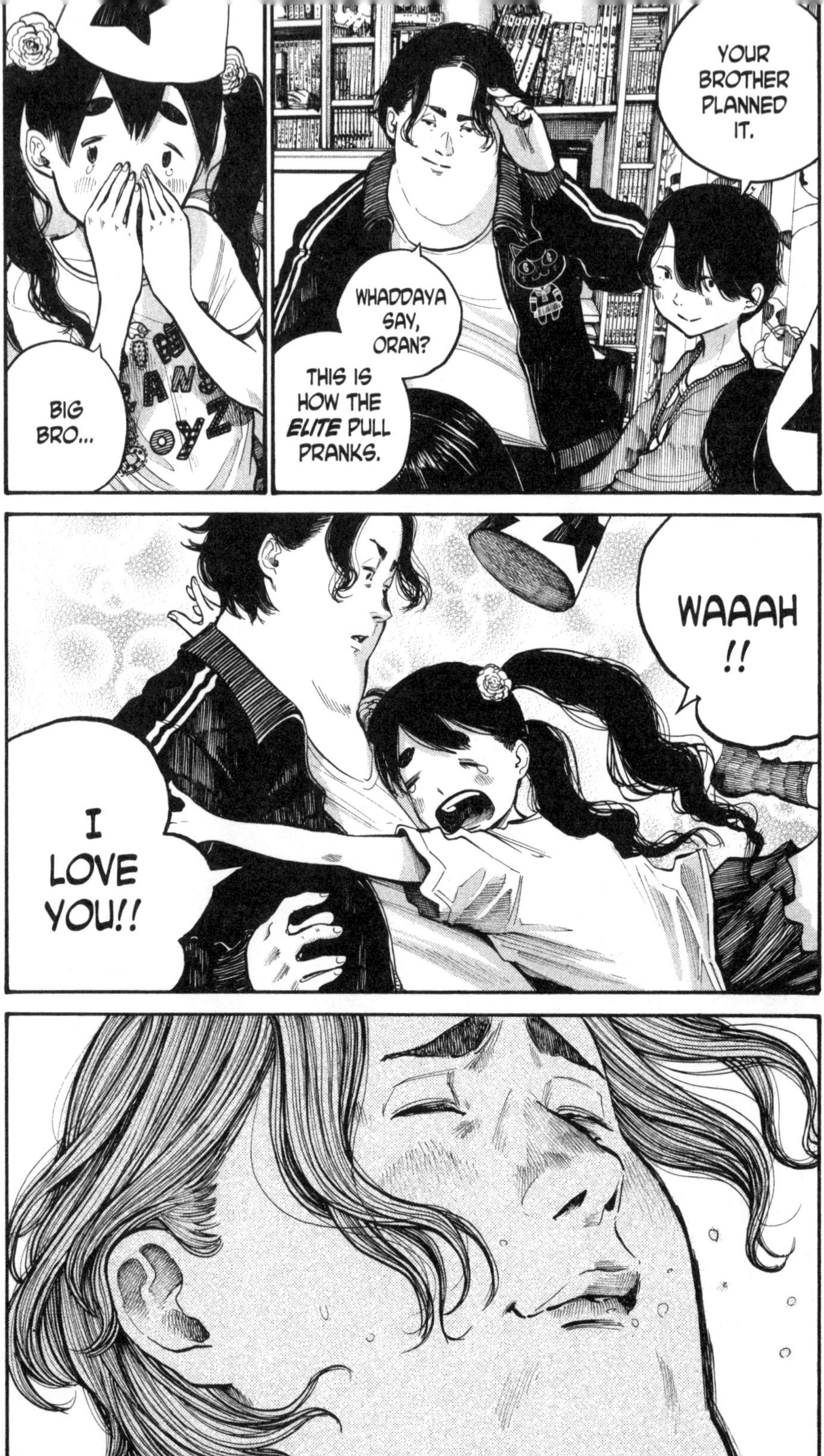
YOUR BROTHER PLANNED IT.
WHADDAYA SAY, ORAN?
THIS IS HOW THE ELITE PULL PRANKS.
BIG BRO...
WAAAH!!
I LOVE YOU!!

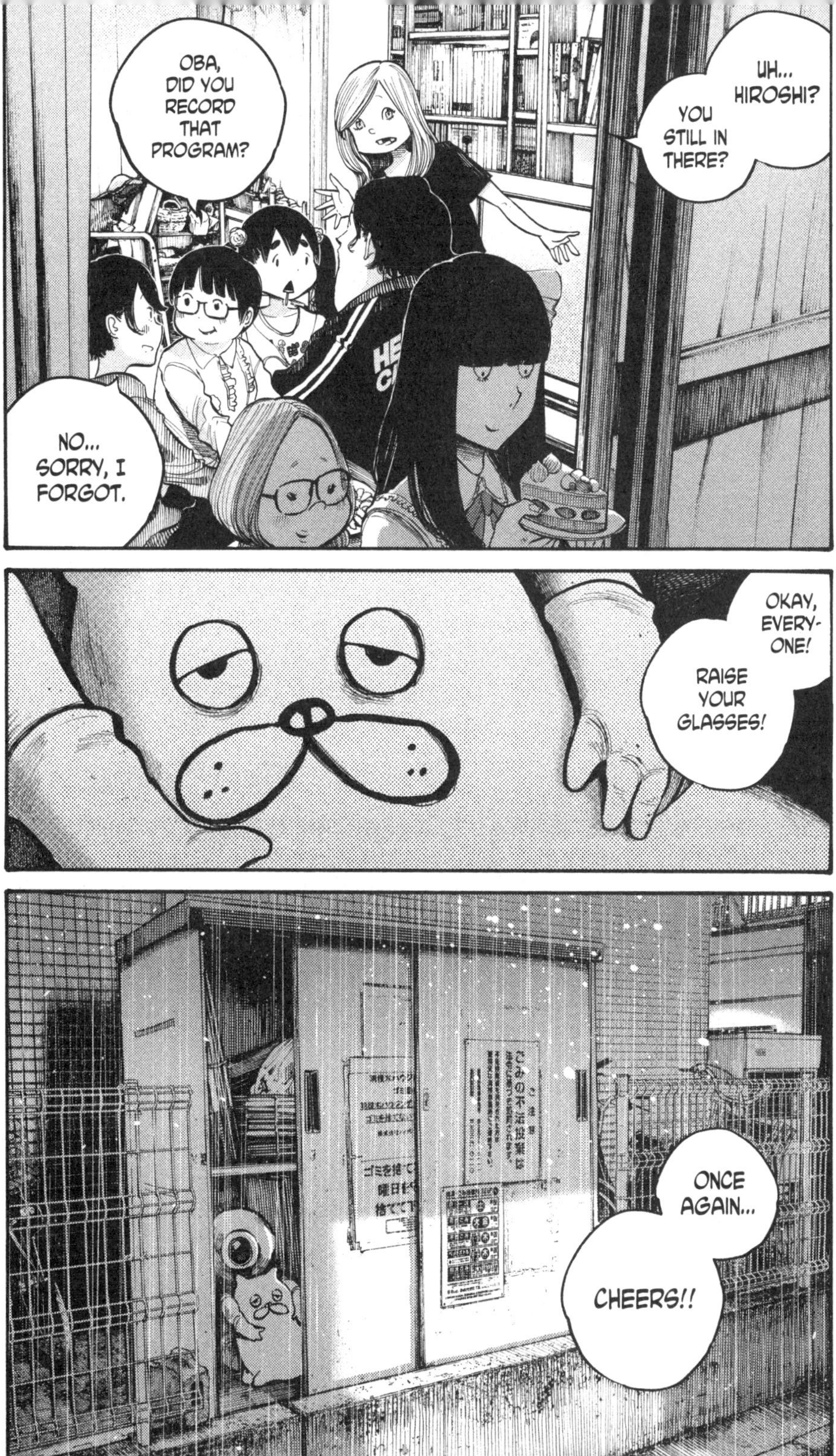
UH... HIROSHI?
YOU STILL IN THERE?
OBA, DID YOU RECORD THAT PROGRAM?
NO... SORRY, I FORGOT.
OKAY, EVERYONE!
RAISE YOUR GLASSES!
ONCE AGAIN...
CHEERS!!

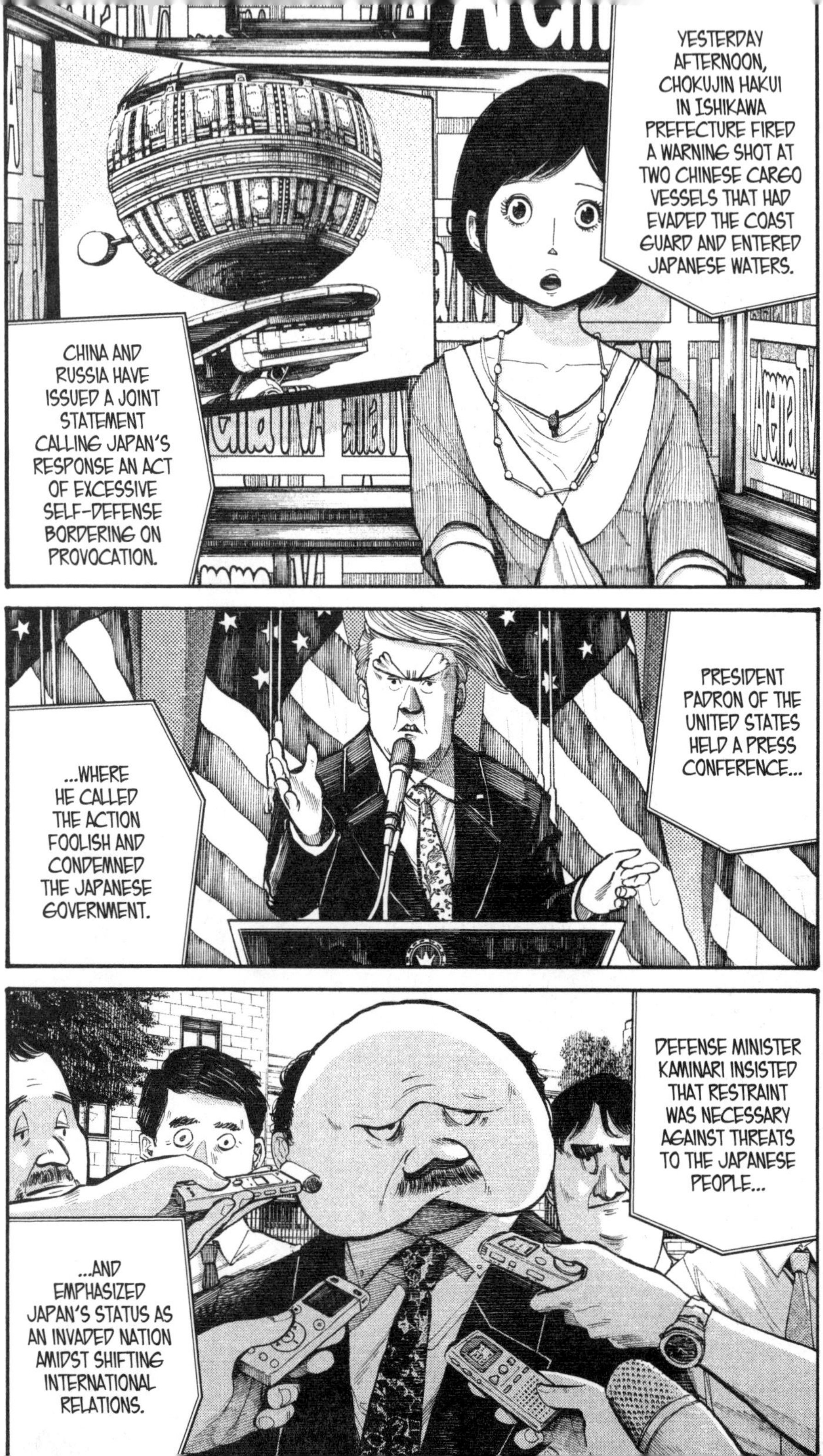
YESTERDAY AFTERNOON, CHOKUJIN HAKUI IN ISHIKAWA PREFECTURE FIRED A WARNING SHOT AT TWO CHINESE CARGO VESSELS THAT HAD EVADED THE COAST GUARD AND ENTERED JAPANESE WATERS.
CHINA AND RUSSIA HAVE ISSUED A JOINT STATEMENT CALLING JAPAN'S RESPONSE AN ACT OF EXCESSIVE SELF-DEFENSE BORDERING ON PROVOCATION.
PRESIDENT PADRON OF THE UNITED STATES HELD A PRESS CONFERENCE...
...WHERE HE CALLED THE ACTION FOOLISH AND CONDEMNED THE JAPANESE GOVERNMENT.
DEFENSE MINISTER KAMINARI INSISTED THAT RESTRAINT WAS NECESSARY AGAINST THREATS TO THE JAPANESE PEOPLE...
...AND EMPHASIZED JAPAN'S STATUS AS AN INVADED NATION AMIDST SHIFTING INTERNATIONAL RELATIONS.

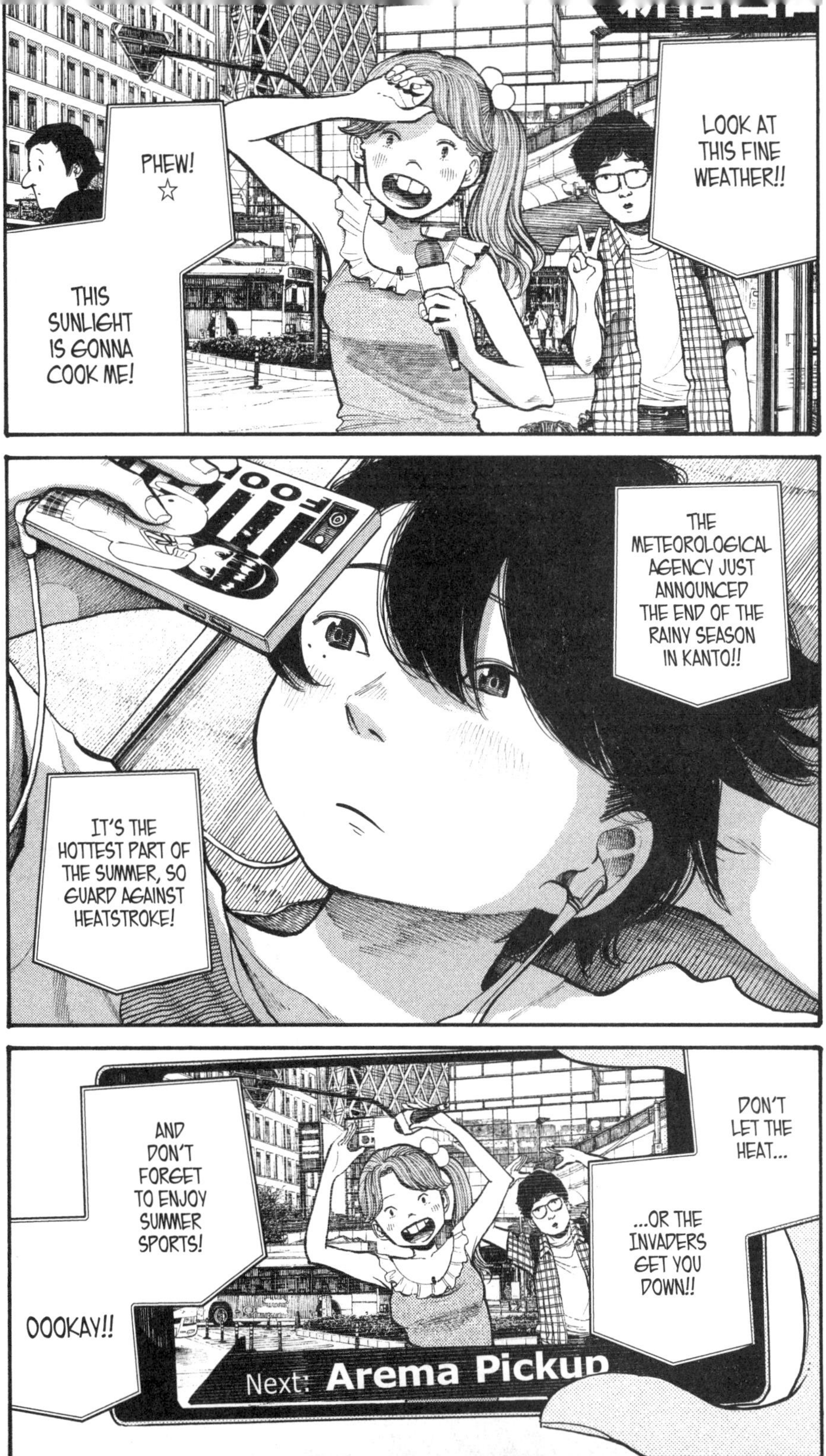
LOOK AT THIS FINE WEATHER!!
PHEW! ☆
THIS SUNLIGHT IS GONNA COOK ME!
THE METEOROLOGICAL AGENCY JUST ANNOUNCED THE END OF THE RAINY SEASON IN KANTO!!
IT'S THE HOTTEST PART OF THE SUMMER, SO GUARD AGAINST HEATSTROKE!
DON'T LET THE HEAT...
...OR THE INVADERS GET YOU DOWN!!
AND DON'T FORGET TO ENJOY SUMMER SPORTS!
OOOKAY!!
Next: Arema Pickup

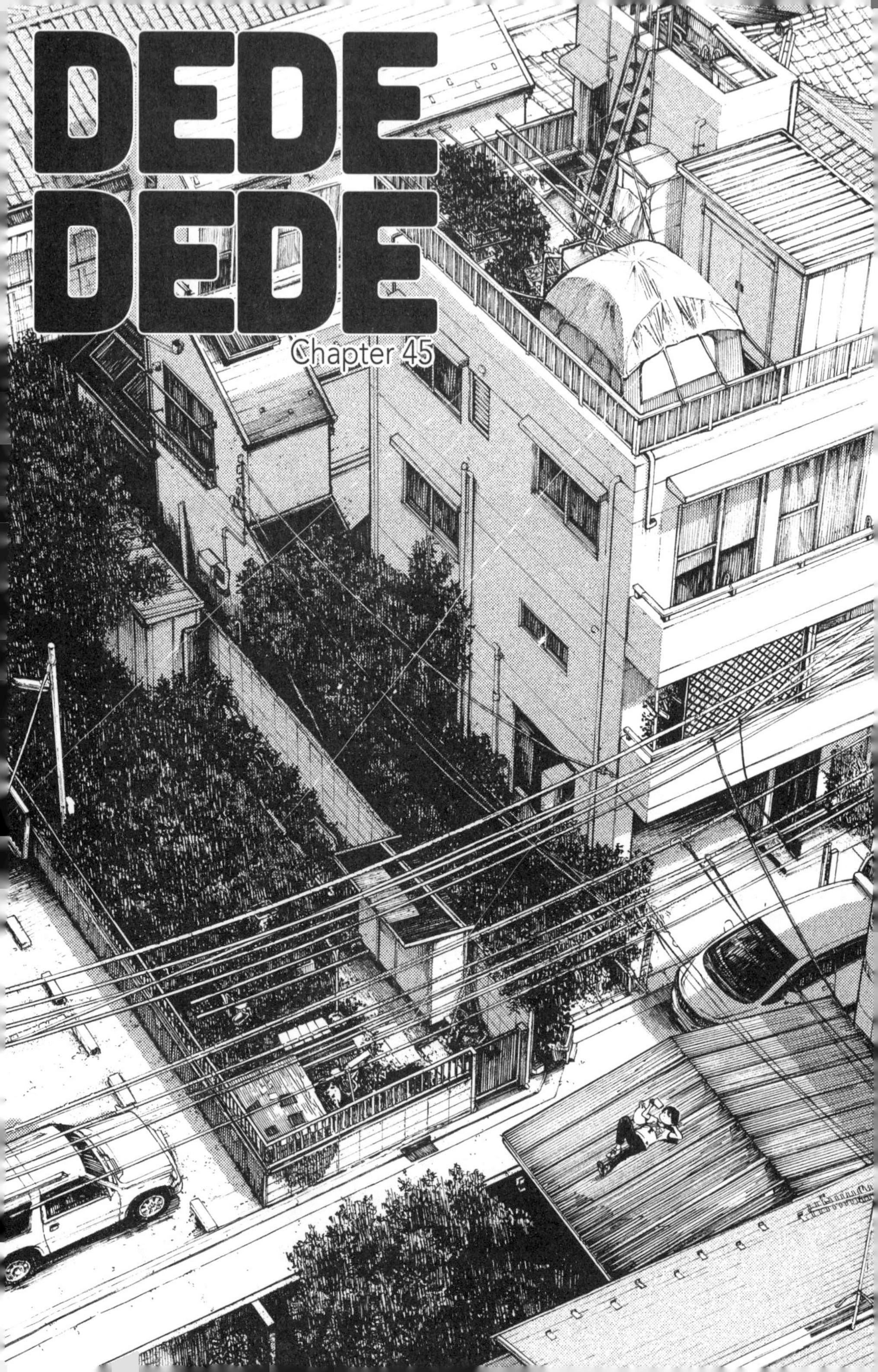
DEDE
DEDE
Chapter 45

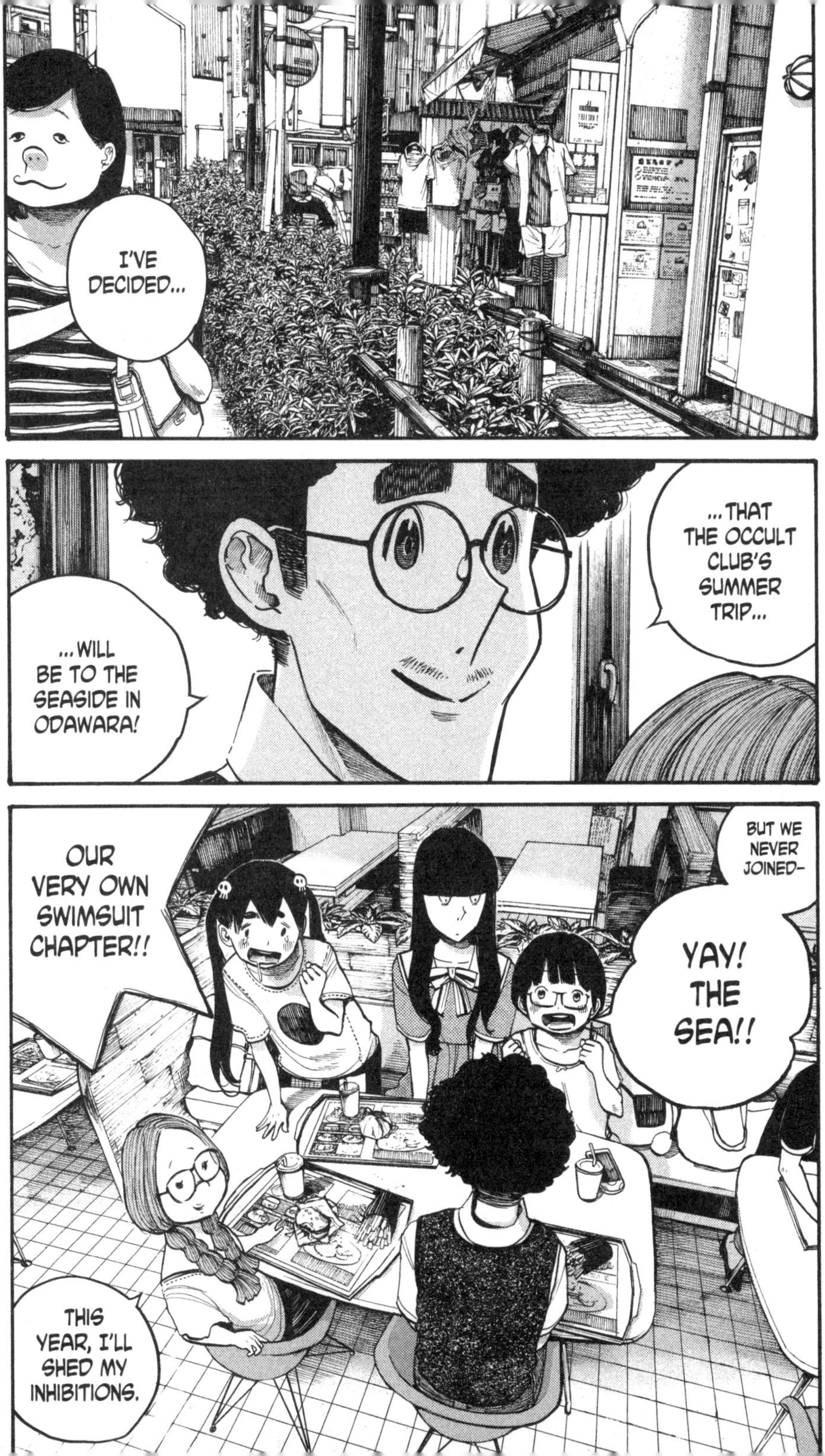
I'VE DECIDED...
...THAT THE OCCULT CLUB'S SUMMER TRIP...
...WILL BE TO THE SEASIDE IN ODAWARA!
BUT WE NEVER JOINED–
YAY! THE SEA!!
OUR VERY OWN SWIMSUIT CHAPTER!!
THIS YEAR, I'LL SHED MY INHIBITIONS.

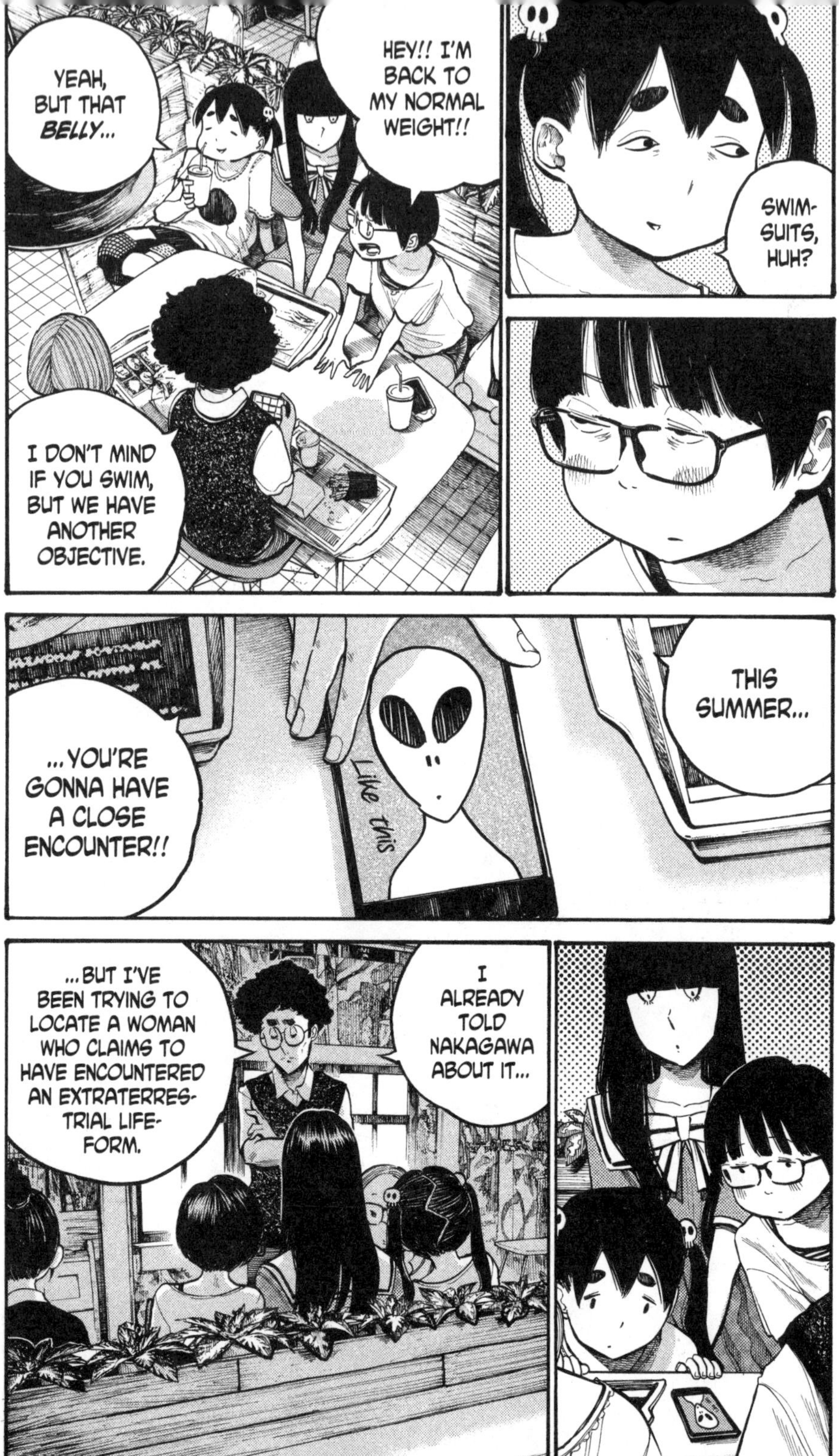
SWIM-SUITS, HUH?
HEY!! I'M BACK TO MY NORMAL WEIGHT!!
YEAH, BUT THAT *BELLY*...
I DON'T MIND IF YOU SWIM, BUT WE HAVE ANOTHER OBJECTIVE.
THIS SUMMER...
...YOU'RE GONNA HAVE A CLOSE ENCOUNTER!!
Like this
I ALREADY TOLD NAKAGAWA ABOUT IT...
...BUT I'VE BEEN TRYING TO LOCATE A WOMAN WHO CLAIMS TO HAVE ENCOUNTERED AN EXTRATERRES-TRIAL LIFE-FORM.

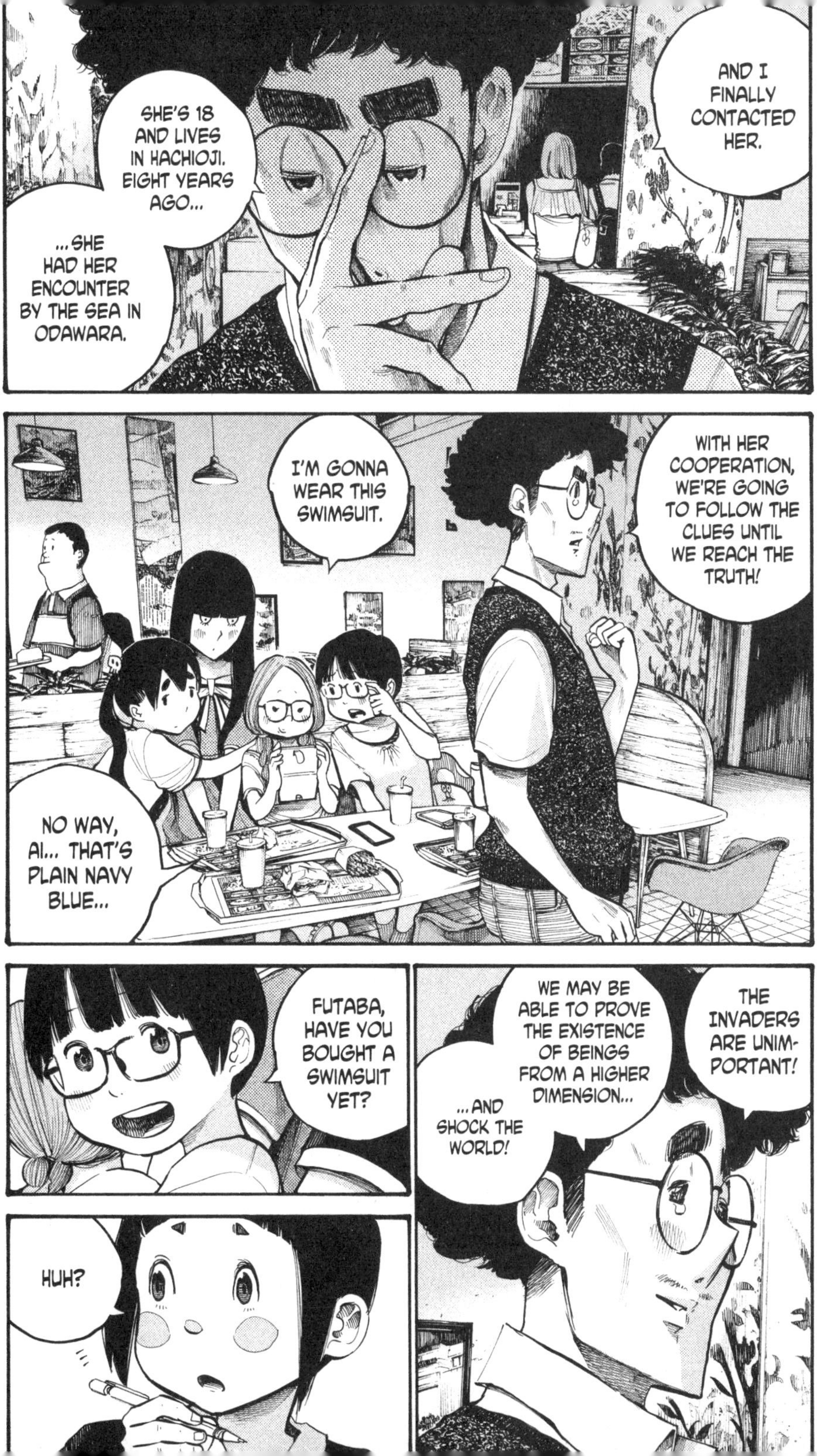
AND I FINALLY CONTACTED HER.
SHE'S 18 AND LIVES IN HACHIOJI. EIGHT YEARS AGO...
...SHE HAD HER ENCOUNTER BY THE SEA IN ODAWARA.
WITH HER COOPERATION, WE'RE GOING TO FOLLOW THE CLUES UNTIL WE REACH THE TRUTH!
I'M GONNA WEAR THIS SWIMSUIT.
NO WAY, AI... THAT'S PLAIN NAVY BLUE...
THE INVADERS ARE UNIM-PORTANT!
WE MAY BE ABLE TO PROVE THE EXISTENCE OF BEINGS FROM A HIGHER DIMENSION...
...AND SHOCK THE WORLD!
FUTABA, HAVE YOU BOUGHT A SWIMSUIT YET?
HUH?

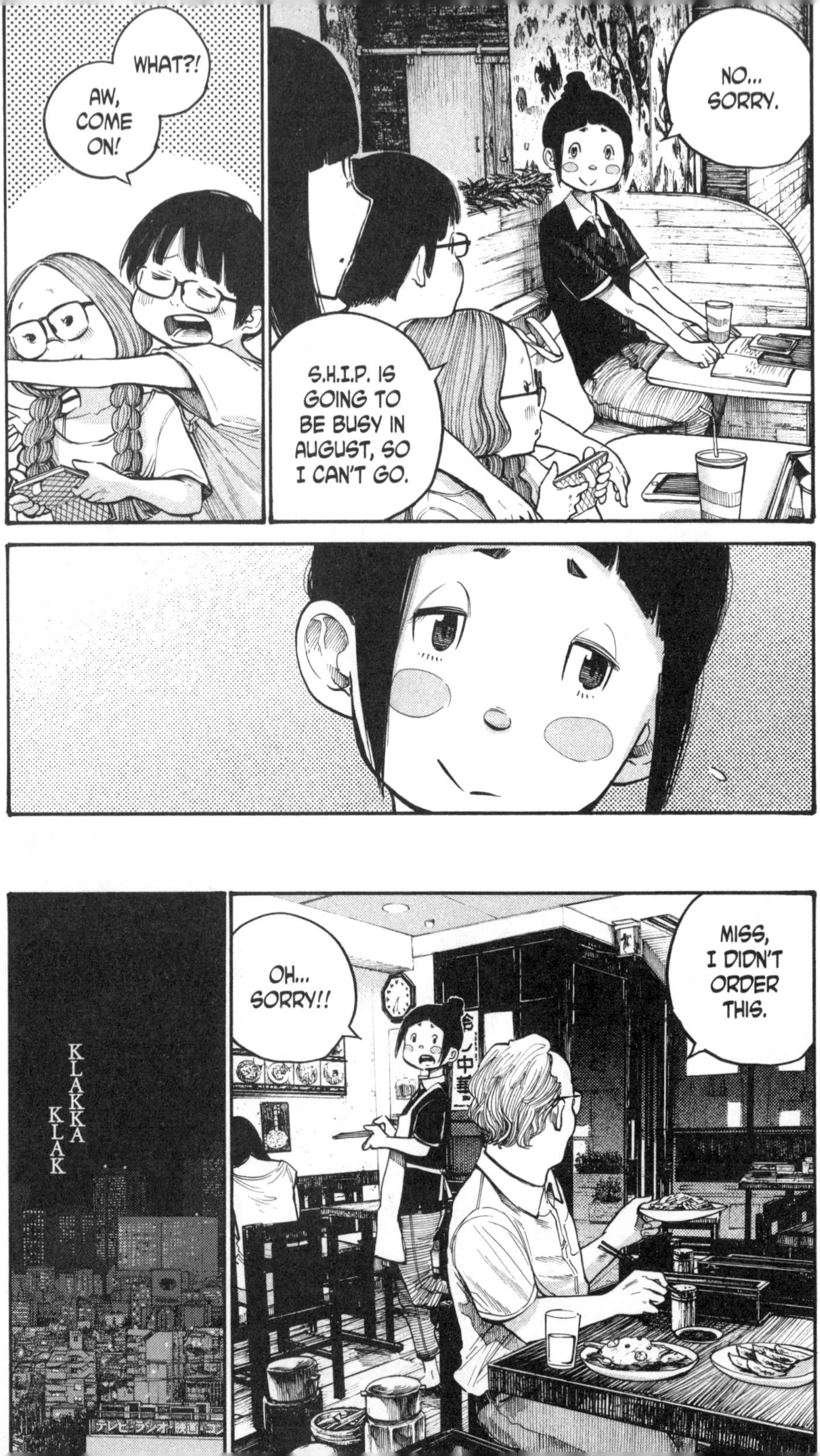
NO... SORRY.
S.H.I.P. IS GOING TO BE BUSY IN AUGUST, SO I CAN'T GO.
WHAT?!
AW, COME ON!
MISS, I DIDN'T ORDER THIS.
OH... SORRY!!
KLAKKA KLAK

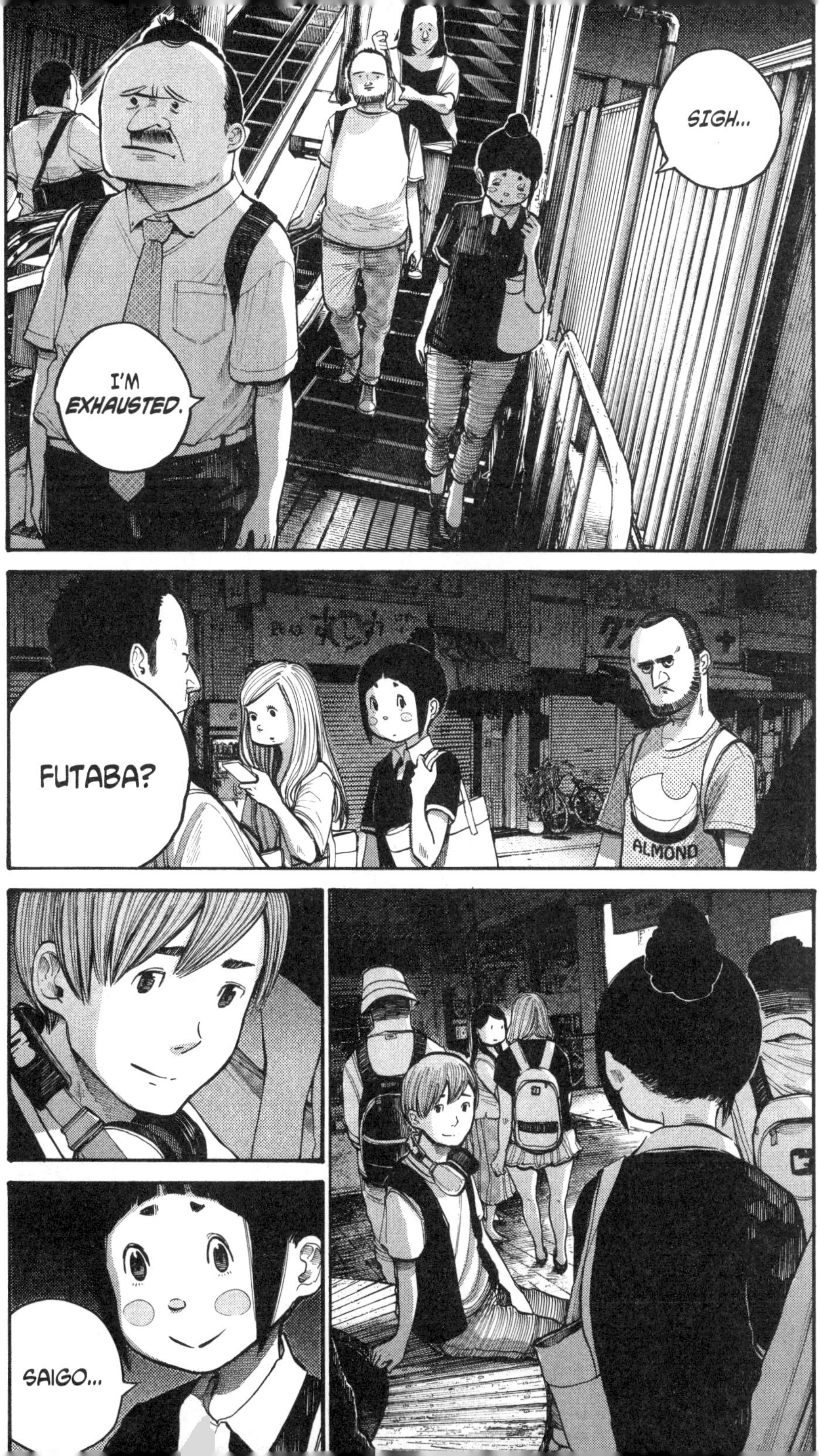
SIGH...
I'M EXHAUSTED.
FUTABA?
ALMOND
SAIGO...

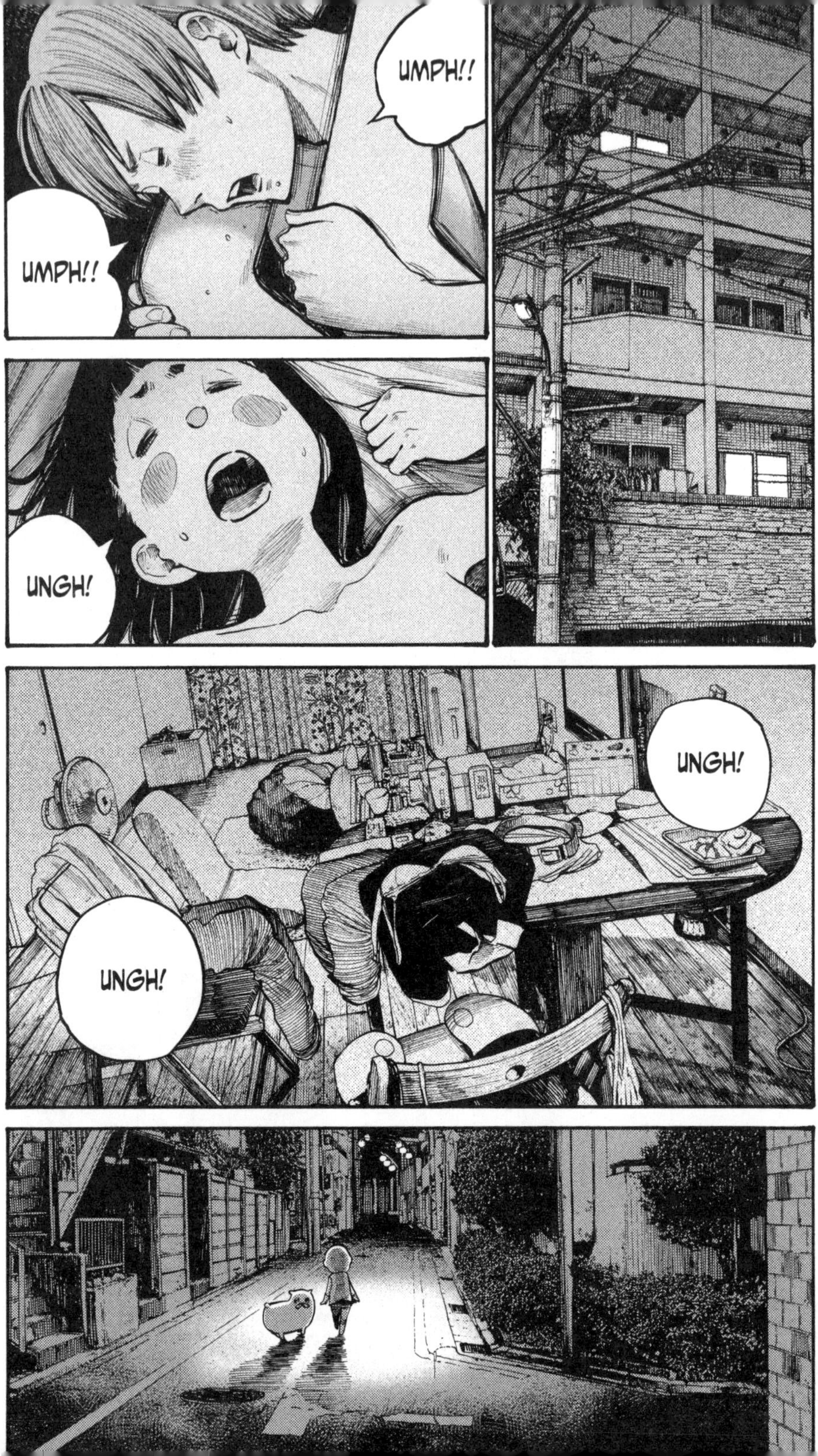
UMPH!!
UMPH!!
UNGH!
UNGH!
UNGH!

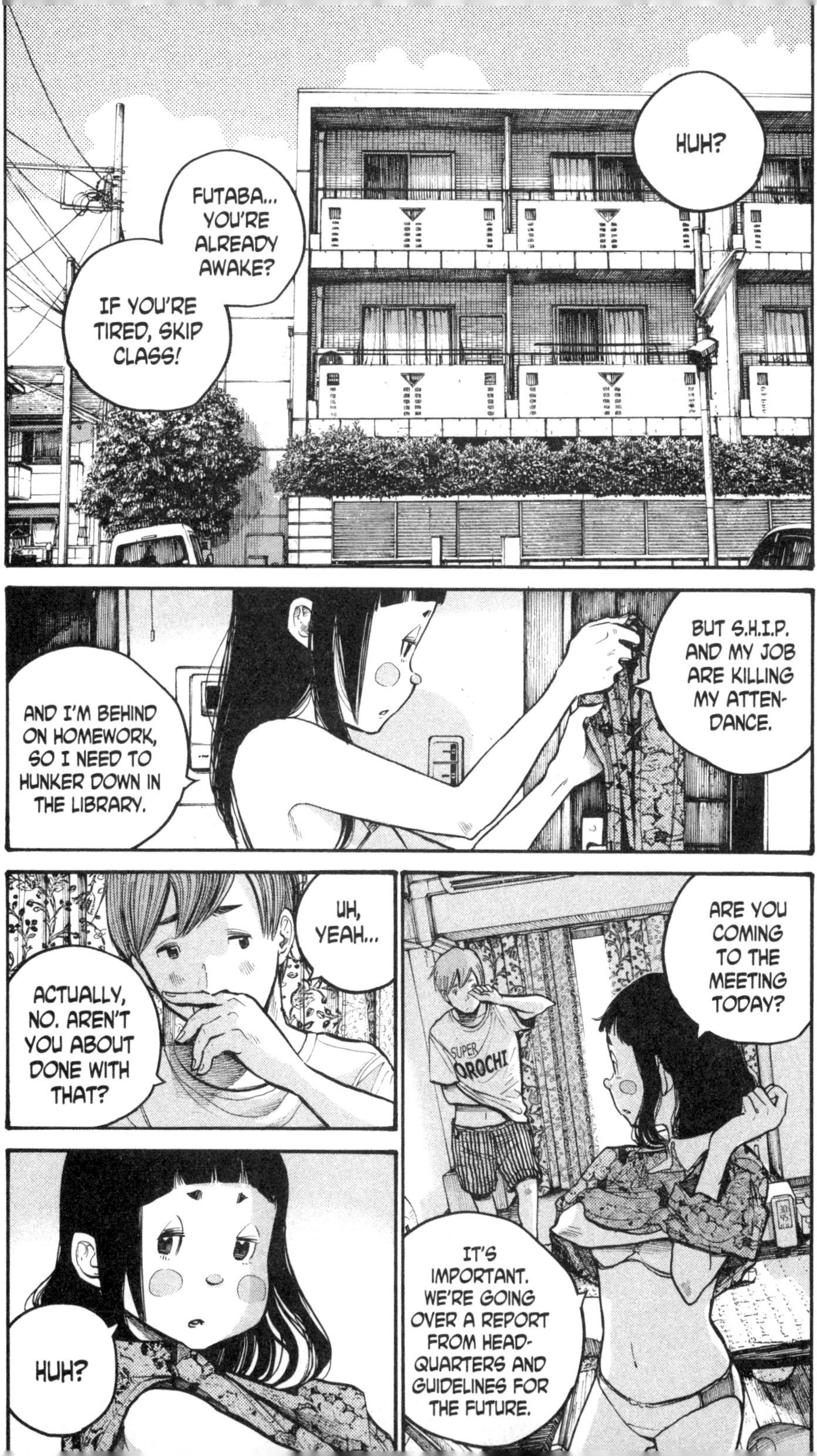
HUH?
FUTABA... YOU'RE ALREADY AWAKE?
IF YOU'RE TIRED, SKIP CLASS!
BUT S.H.I.P. AND MY JOB ARE KILLING MY ATTEN-DANCE.
AND I'M BEHIND ON HOMEWORK, SO I NEED TO HUNKER DOWN IN THE LIBRARY.
ARE YOU COMING TO THE MEETING TODAY?
SUPER OROCHI
IT'S IMPORTANT. WE'RE GOING OVER A REPORT FROM HEAD-QUARTERS AND GUIDELINES FOR THE FUTURE.
UH, YEAH...
ACTUALLY, NO. AREN'T YOU ABOUT DONE WITH THAT?
HUH?

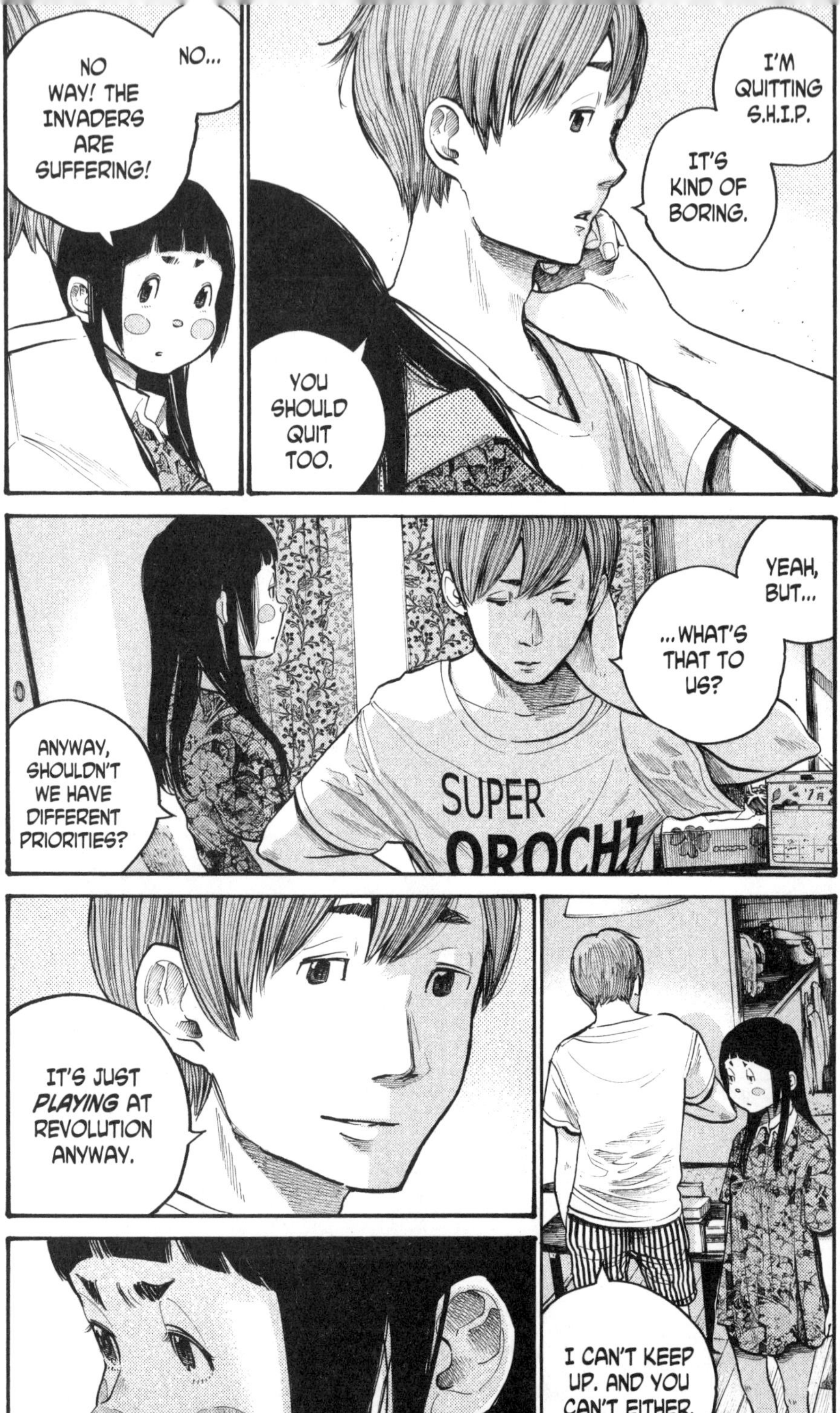
I'M QUITTING S.H.I.P.
IT'S KIND OF BORING.
YOU SHOULD QUIT TOO.
NO...
NO WAY! THE INVADERS ARE SUFFERING!
YEAH, BUT...
...WHAT'S THAT TO US?
ANYWAY, SHOULDN'T WE HAVE DIFFERENT PRIORITIES?
SUPER OROCHI
I CAN'T KEEP UP. AND YOU CAN'T EITHER, RIGHT?
IT'S JUST *PLAYING* AT REVOLUTION ANYWAY.

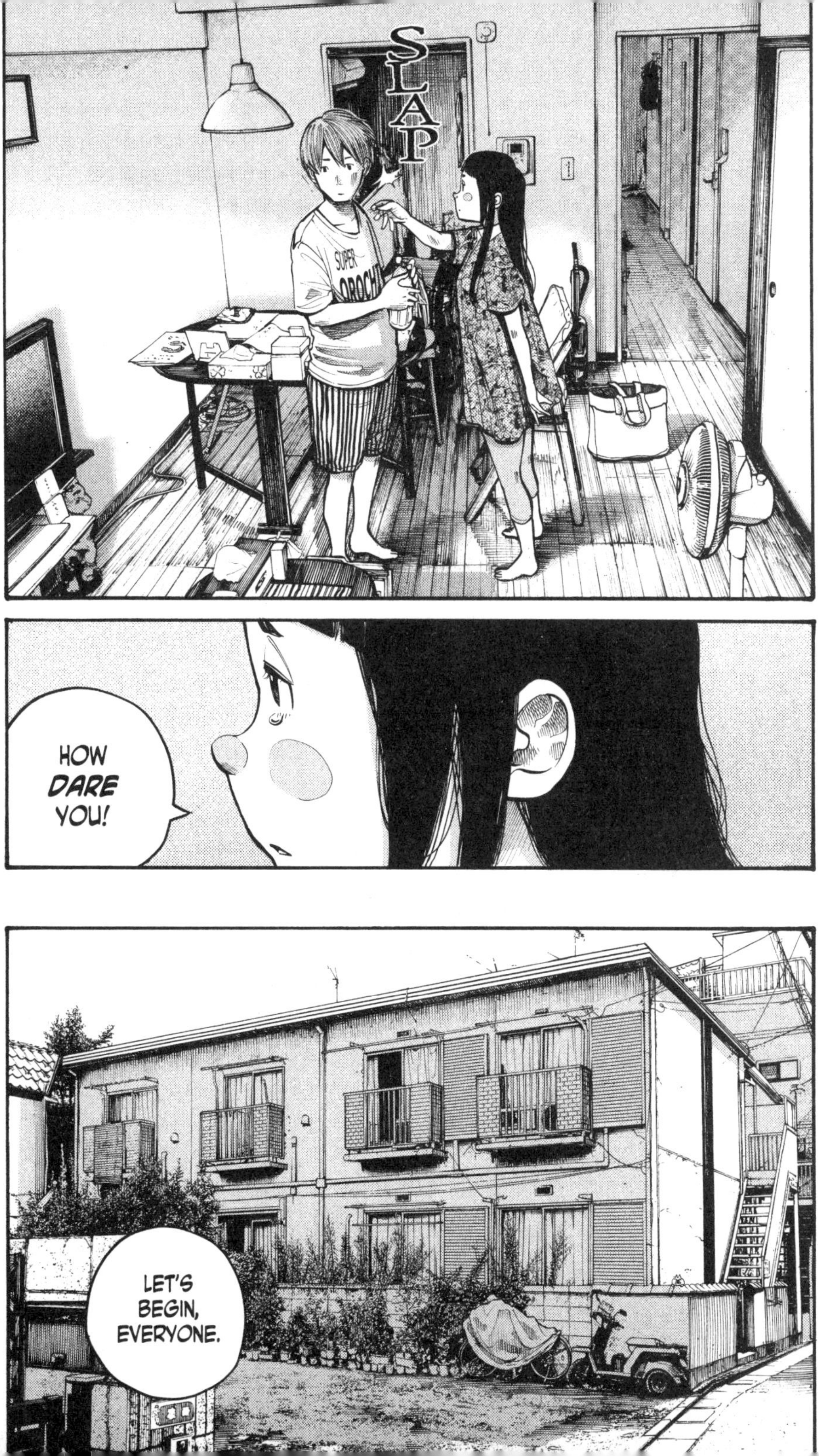
SLAP
SUPER OROCHI
HOW DARE YOU!
LET'S BEGIN, EVERYONE.

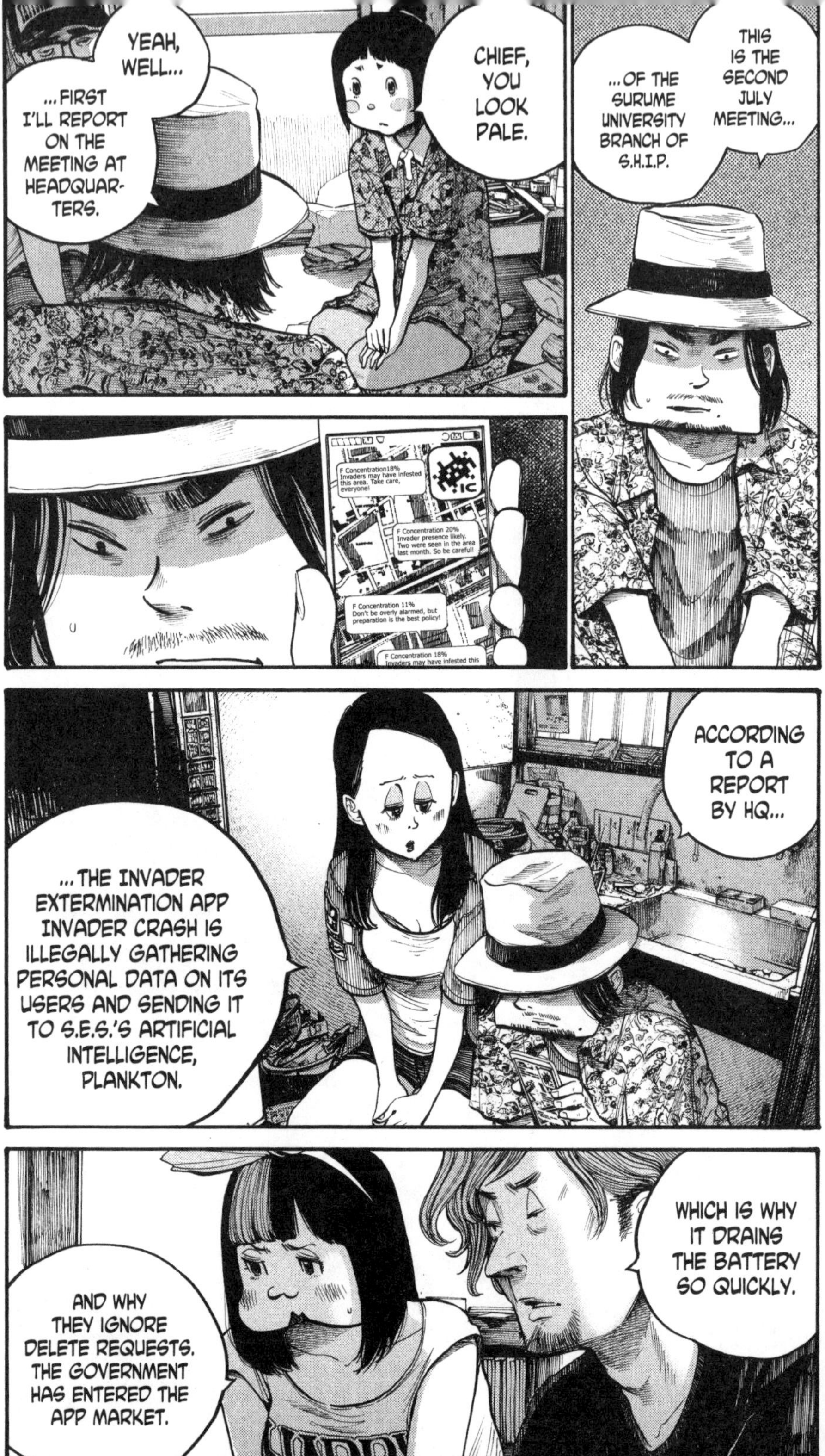
THIS IS THE SECOND JULY MEETING...
...OF THE SURUME UNIVERSITY BRANCH OF S.H.I.P.
CHIEF, YOU LOOK PALE.
YEAH, WELL...
...FIRST I'LL REPORT ON THE MEETING AT HEADQUARTERS.
F Concentration18% Invaders may have infested this area. Take care, everyone!
IC
F Concentration 20% Invader presence likely. Two were seen in the area last month. So be careful!
F Concentration 11% Don't be overly alarmed, but preparation is the best policy!
F Concentration 18% Invaders may have infested this
ACCORDING TO A REPORT BY HQ...
...THE INVADER EXTERMINATION APP INVADER CRASH IS ILLEGALLY GATHERING PERSONAL DATA ON ITS USERS AND SENDING IT TO S.E.S.'S ARTIFICIAL INTELLIGENCE, PLANKTON.
WHICH IS WHY IT DRAINS THE BATTERY SO QUICKLY.
AND WHY THEY IGNORE DELETE REQUESTS. THE GOVERNMENT HAS ENTERED THE APP MARKET.

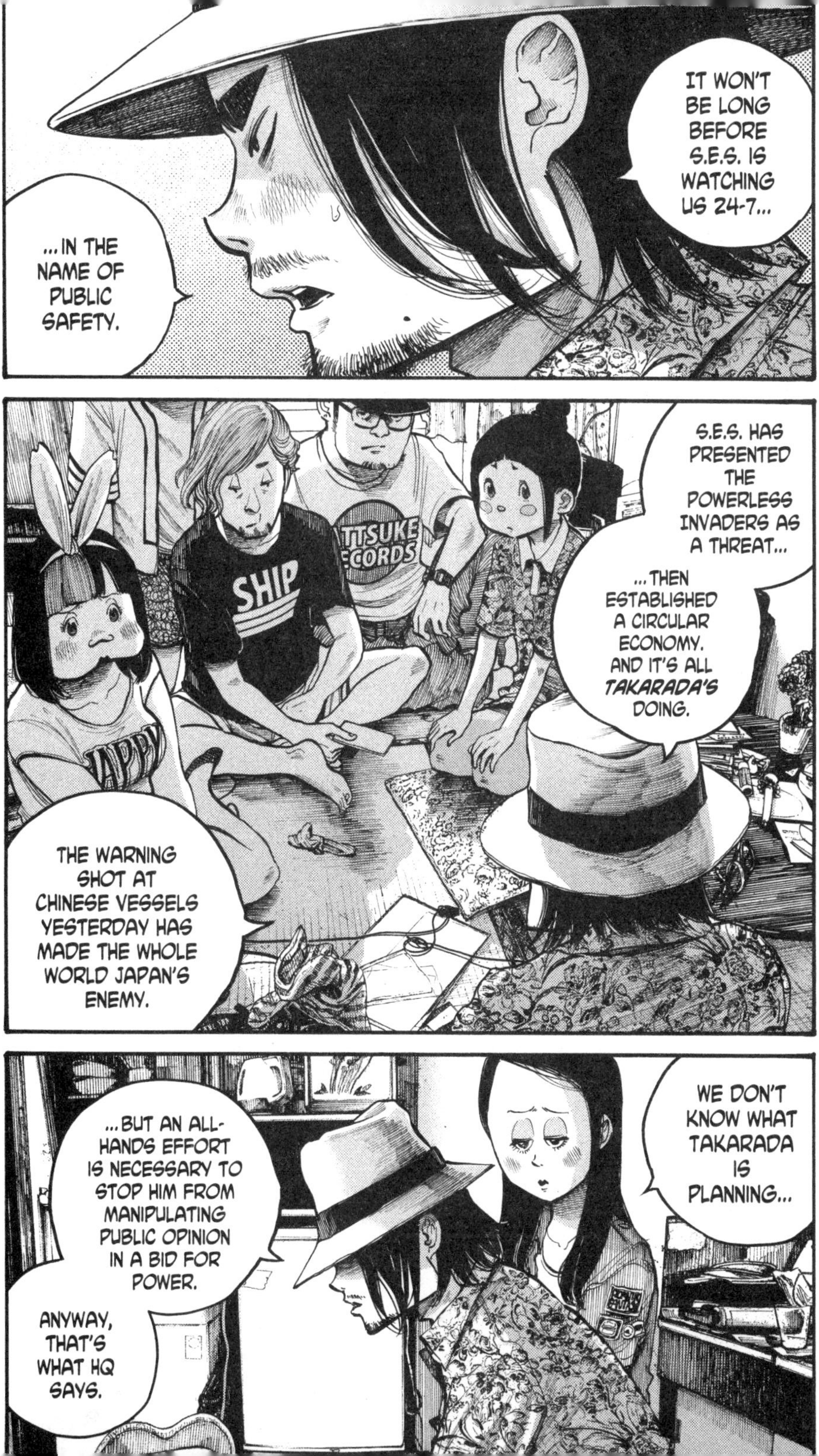
IT WON'T BE LONG BEFORE S.E.S. IS WATCHING US 24-7...
...IN THE NAME OF PUBLIC SAFETY.
S.E.S. HAS PRESENTED THE POWERLESS INVADERS AS A THREAT...
...THEN ESTABLISHED A CIRCULAR ECONOMY. AND IT'S ALL *TAKARADA'S* DOING.
THE WARNING SHOT AT CHINESE VESSELS YESTERDAY HAS MADE THE WHOLE WORLD JAPAN'S ENEMY.
WE DON'T KNOW WHAT TAKARADA IS PLANNING...
...BUT AN ALL-HANDS EFFORT IS NECESSARY TO STOP HIM FROM MANIPULATING PUBLIC OPINION IN A BID FOR POWER.
ANYWAY, THAT'S WHAT HQ SAYS.

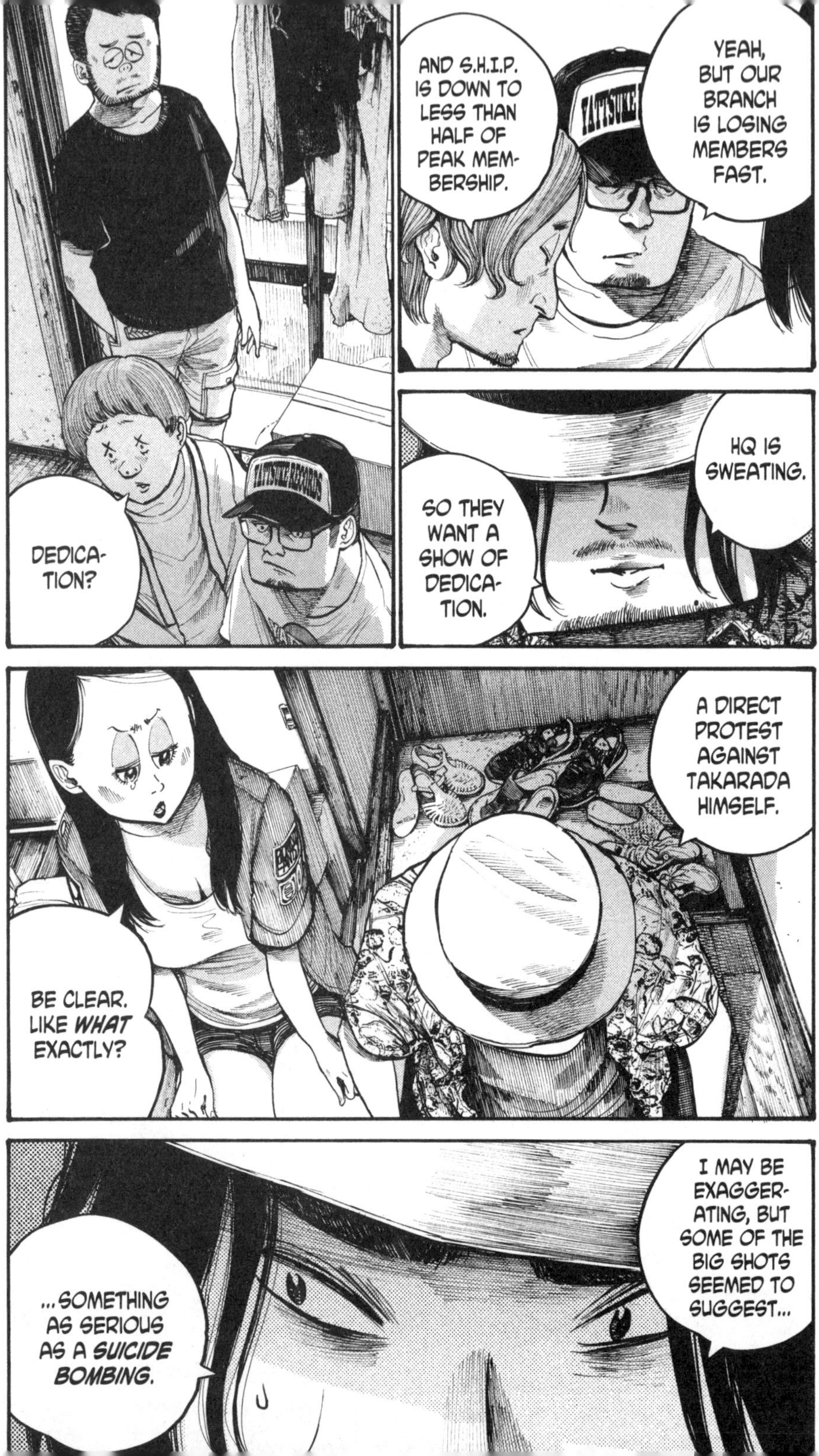
YEAH, BUT OUR BRANCH IS LOSING MEMBERS FAST.
AND S.H.I.P. IS DOWN TO LESS THAN HALF OF PEAK MEMBERSHIP.
HQ IS SWEATING.
SO THEY WANT A SHOW OF DEDICATION.
DEDICATION?
A DIRECT PROTEST AGAINST TAKARADA HIMSELF.
BE CLEAR. LIKE *WHAT* EXACTLY?
I MAY BE EXAGGERATING, BUT SOME OF THE BIG SHOTS SEEMED TO SUGGEST...
...SOMETHING AS SERIOUS AS A *SUICIDE BOMBING*.

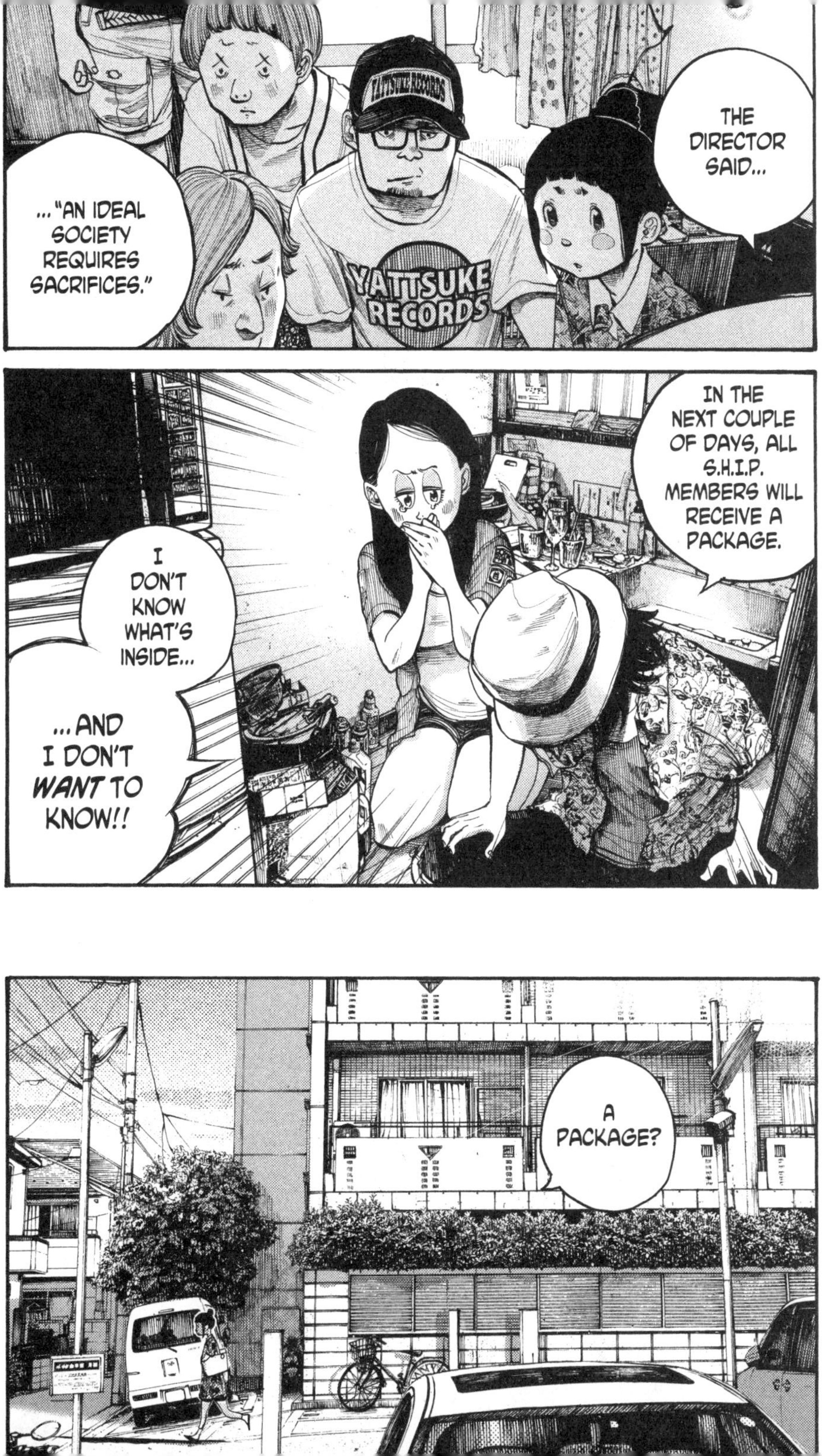
THE DIRECTOR SAID...
YATTSUKE RECORDS
YATTSUKE RECORDS
..."AN IDEAL SOCIETY REQUIRES SACRIFICES."
IN THE NEXT COUPLE OF DAYS, ALL S.H.I.P. MEMBERS WILL RECEIVE A PACKAGE.
I DON'T KNOW WHAT'S INSIDE...
...AND I DON'T *WANT* TO KNOW!!
A PACKAGE?

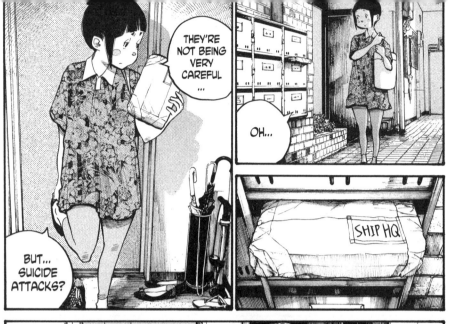

THEY'RE NOT BEING VERY CAREFUL...

OH...

SHIP HQ

BUT... SUICIDE ATTACKS?

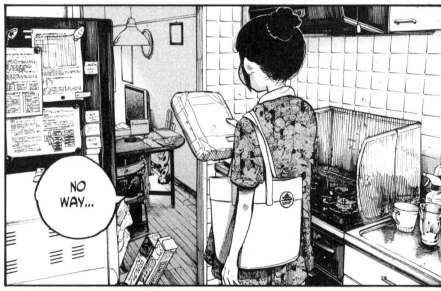

NO WAY...

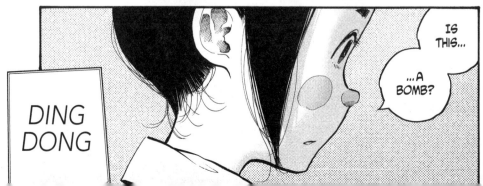

DING DONG

IS THIS...

...A BOMB?

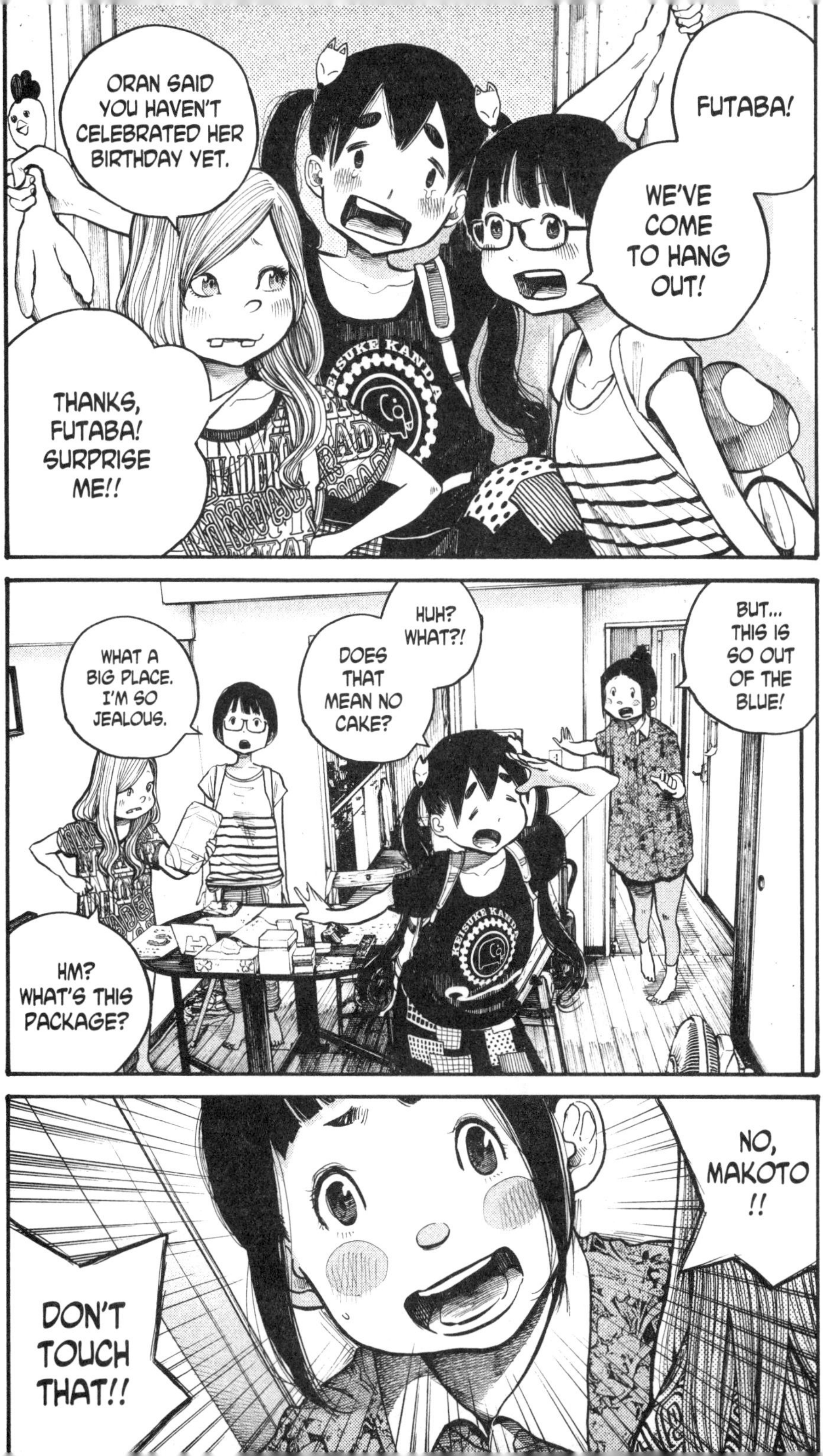
FUTABA!
WE'VE COME TO HANG OUT!
ORAN SAID YOU HAVEN'T CELEBRATED HER BIRTHDAY YET.
THANKS, FUTABA! SURPRISE ME!!
BUT... THIS IS SO OUT OF THE BLUE!
HUH? WHAT?!
DOES THAT MEAN NO CAKE?
WHAT A BIG PLACE. I'M SO JEALOUS.
HM? WHAT'S THIS PACKAGE?
NO, MAKOTO!!
DON'T TOUCH THAT!!

CHAPTER 46

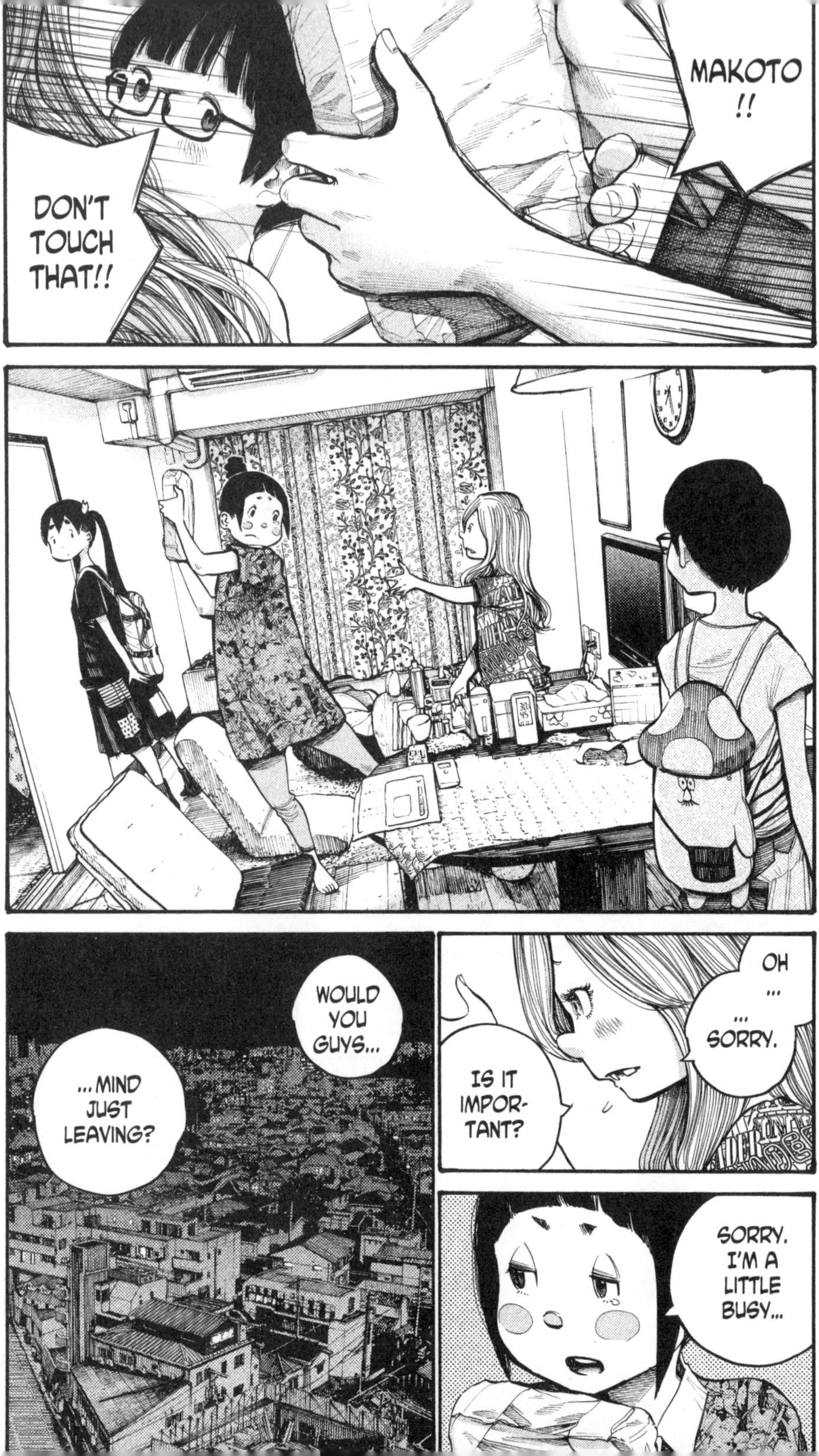
MAKOTO !!
DON'T TOUCH THAT!!
OH ... ... SORRY.
IS IT IMPOR-TANT?
SORRY. I'M A LITTLE BUSY...
WOULD YOU GUYS...
...MIND JUST LEAVING?

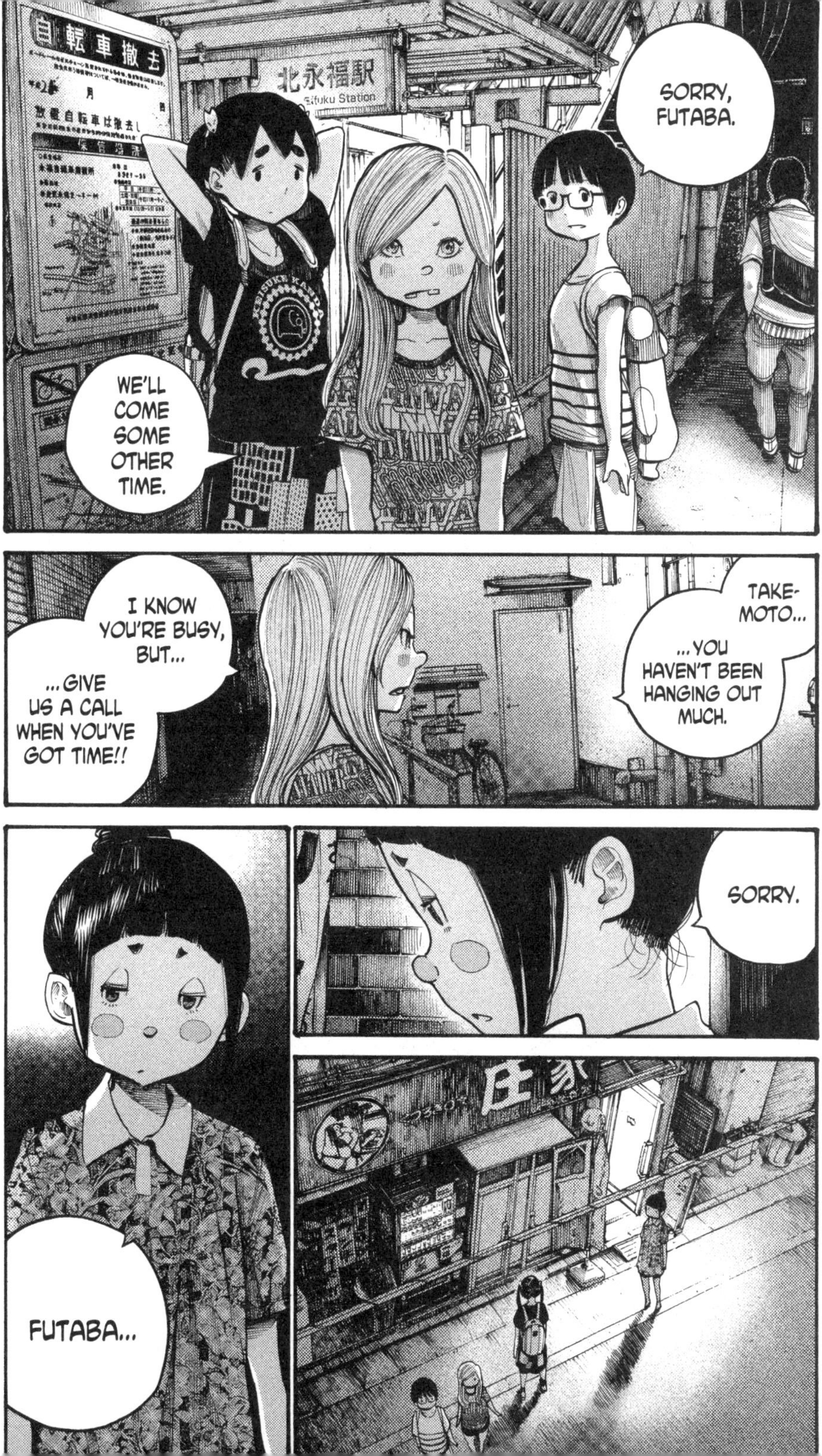
自転車撤去
北永福駅
SORRY, FUTABA.
WE'LL COME SOME OTHER TIME.
TAKE-MOTO...
...YOU HAVEN'T BEEN HANGING OUT MUCH.
I KNOW YOU'RE BUSY, BUT...
...GIVE US A CALL WHEN YOU'VE GOT TIME!!
SORRY.
FUTABA...

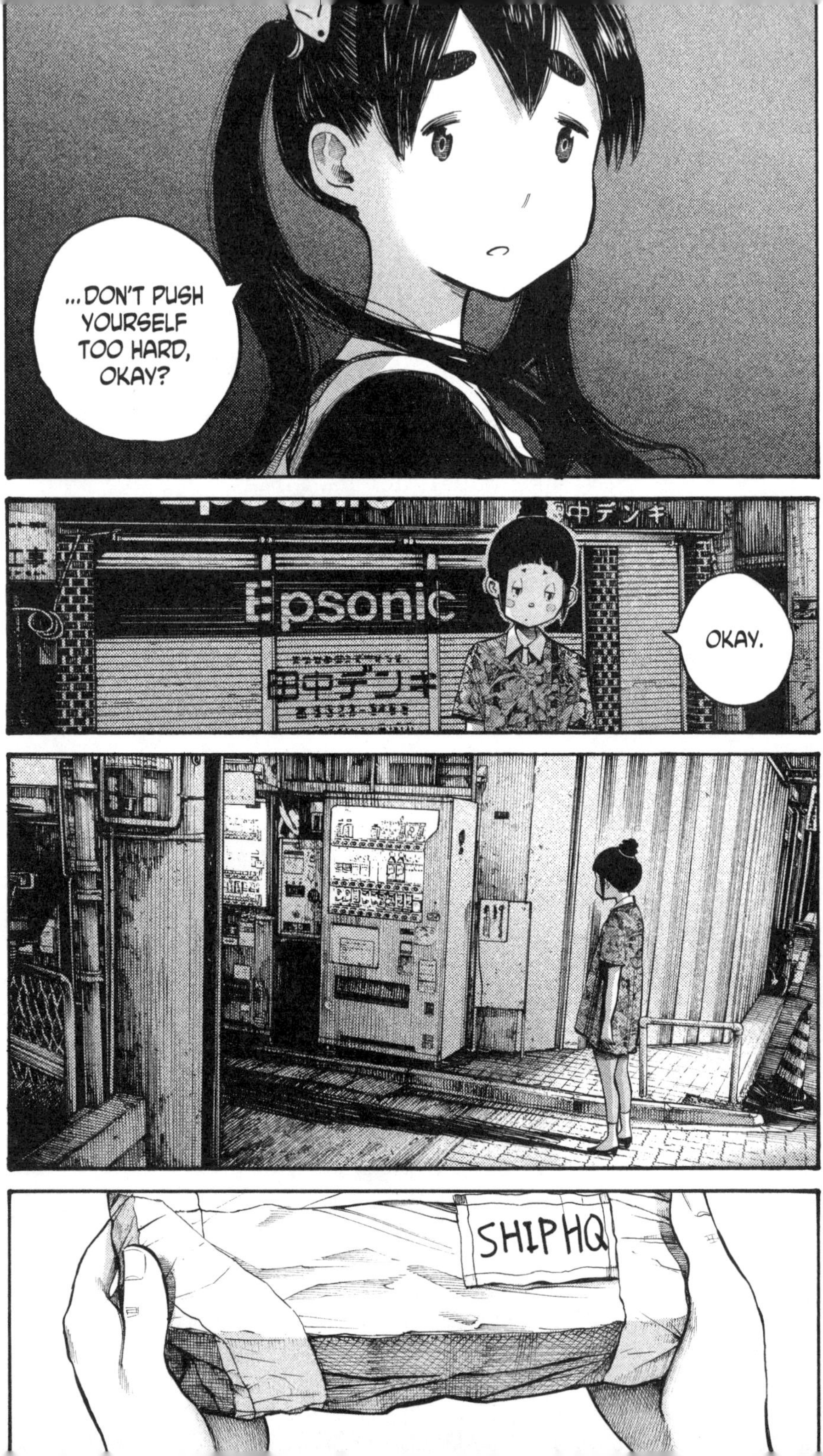
...DON'T PUSH YOURSELF TOO HARD, OKAY?
Epsonic
田中デンキ
OKAY.
SHIPHQ

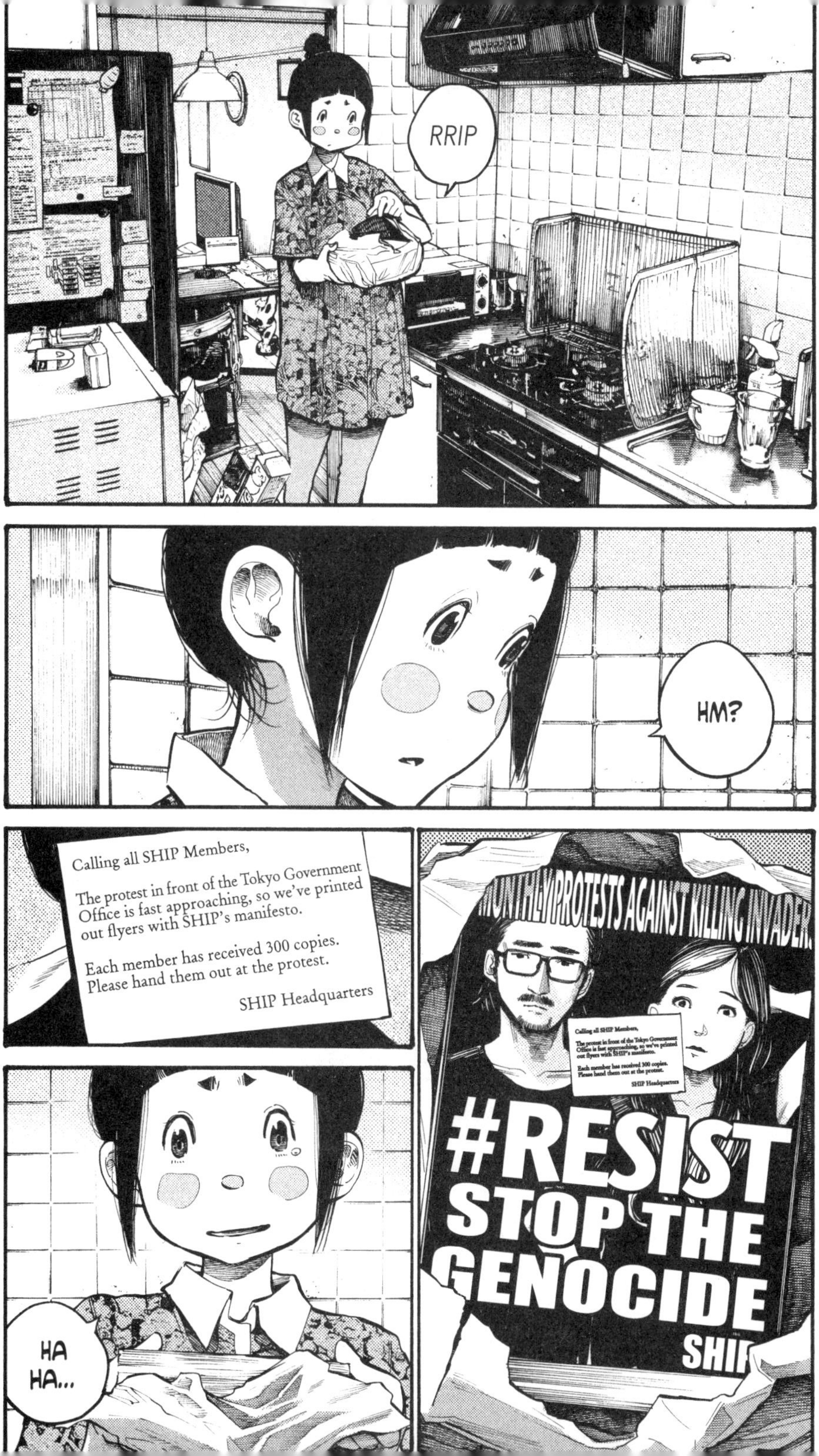
RRIP
HM?
ONTHLYPROTESTS AGAINST KILLING INVADER
#RESIST
STOP THE
GENOCIDE
SHI
Calling all SHIP Members,
The protest in front of the Tokyo Government Office is fast approaching, so we've printed out flyers with SHIP's manifesto.
Each member has received 300 copies. Please hand them out at the protest.
SHIP Headquarters
HA HA...

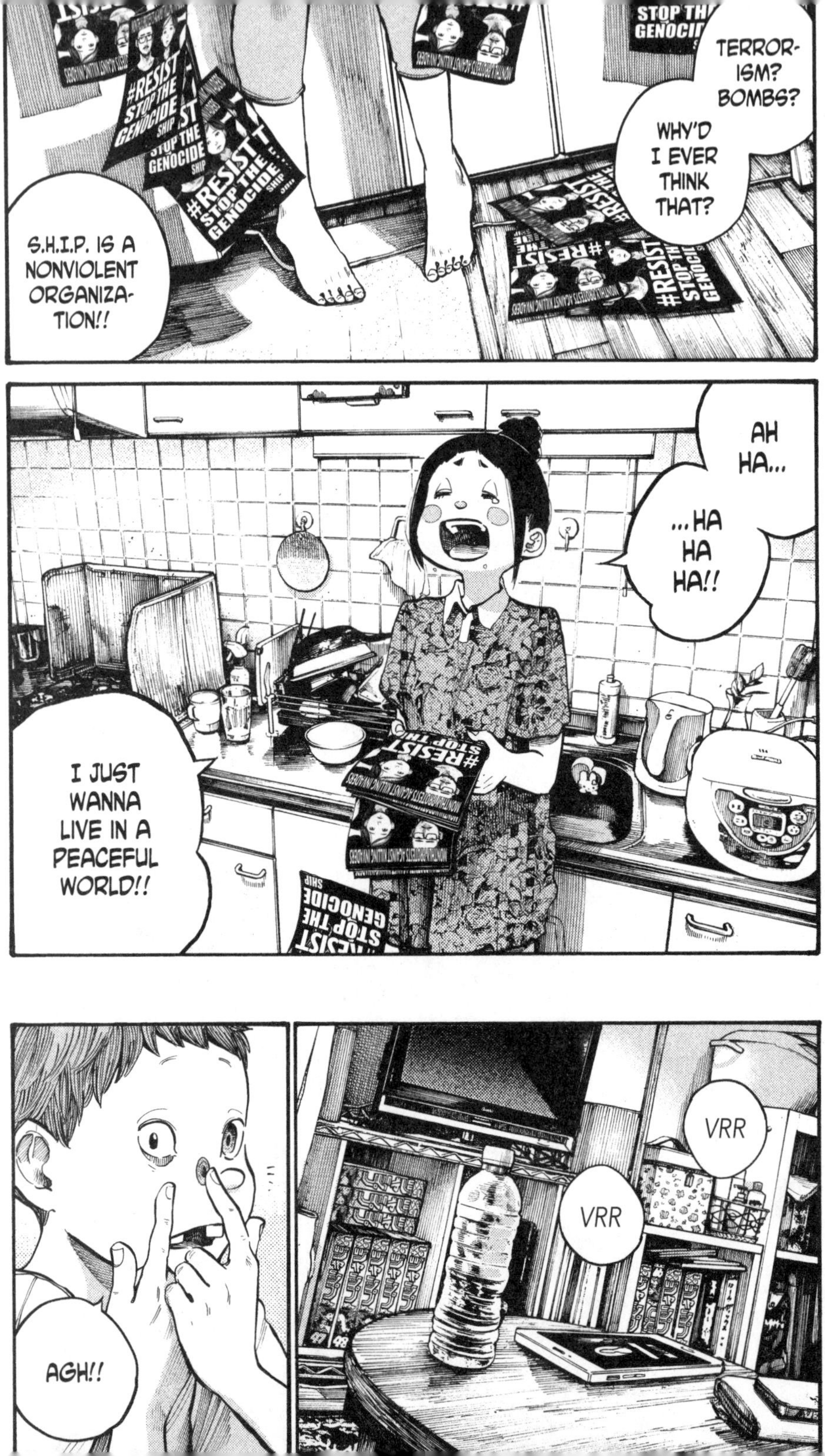
STOP THE GENOCIDE
TERRORISM? BOMBS?
WHY'D I EVER THINK THAT?
#RESIST STOP THE GENOCIDE SHIP
S.H.I.P. IS A NONVIOLENT ORGANIZATION!!
AH HA...
...HA HA HA!!
#RESIST STOP THE
I JUST WANNA LIVE IN A PEACEFUL WORLD!!
VRR
VRR
AGH!!

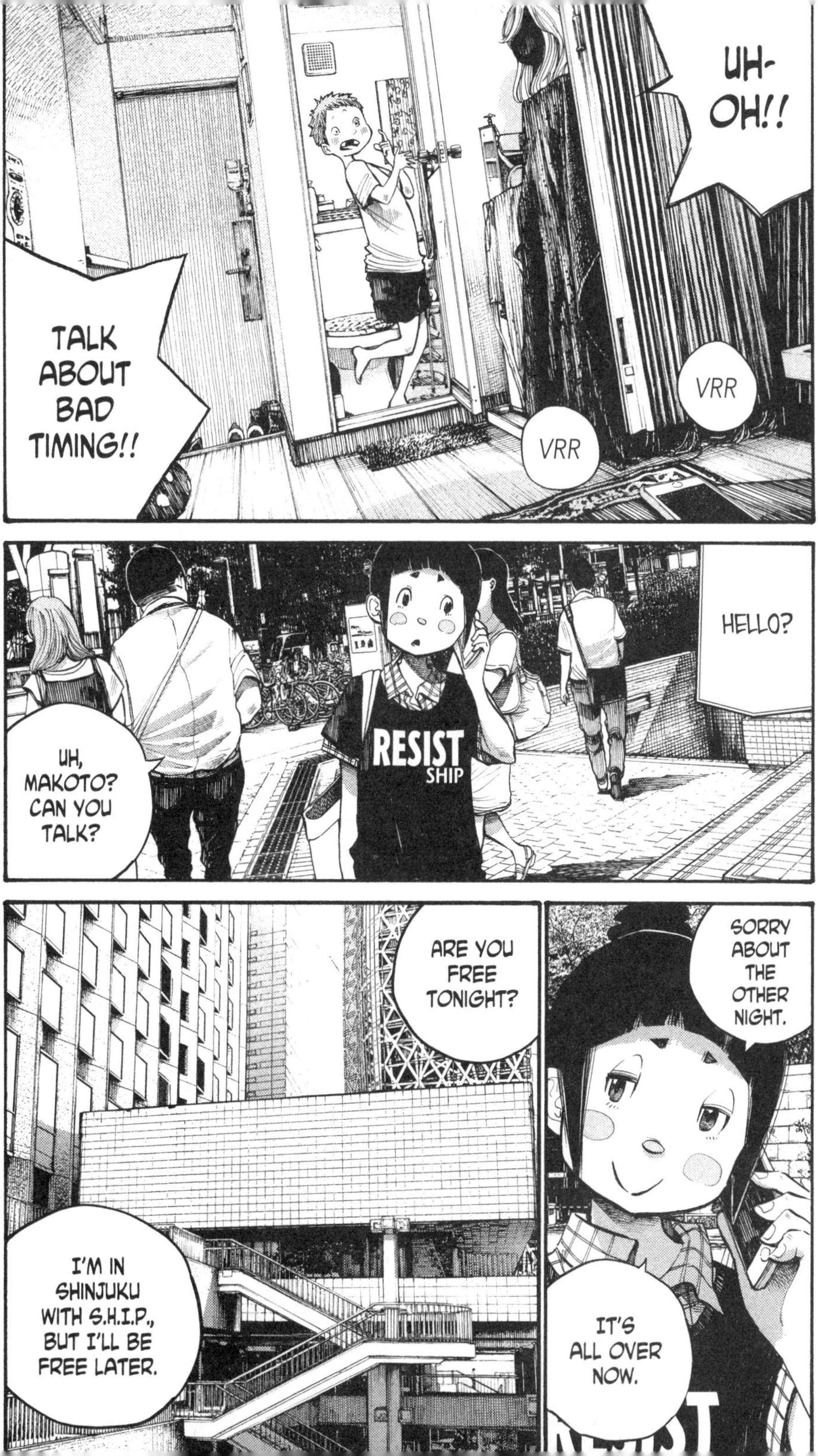
UH-OH!!
VRR
VRR
TALK ABOUT BAD TIMING!!
HELLO?
RESIST SHIP
UH, MAKOTO? CAN YOU TALK?
SORRY ABOUT THE OTHER NIGHT.
IT'S ALL OVER NOW.
ARE YOU FREE TONIGHT?
I'M IN SHINJUKU WITH S.H.I.P., BUT I'LL BE FREE LATER.

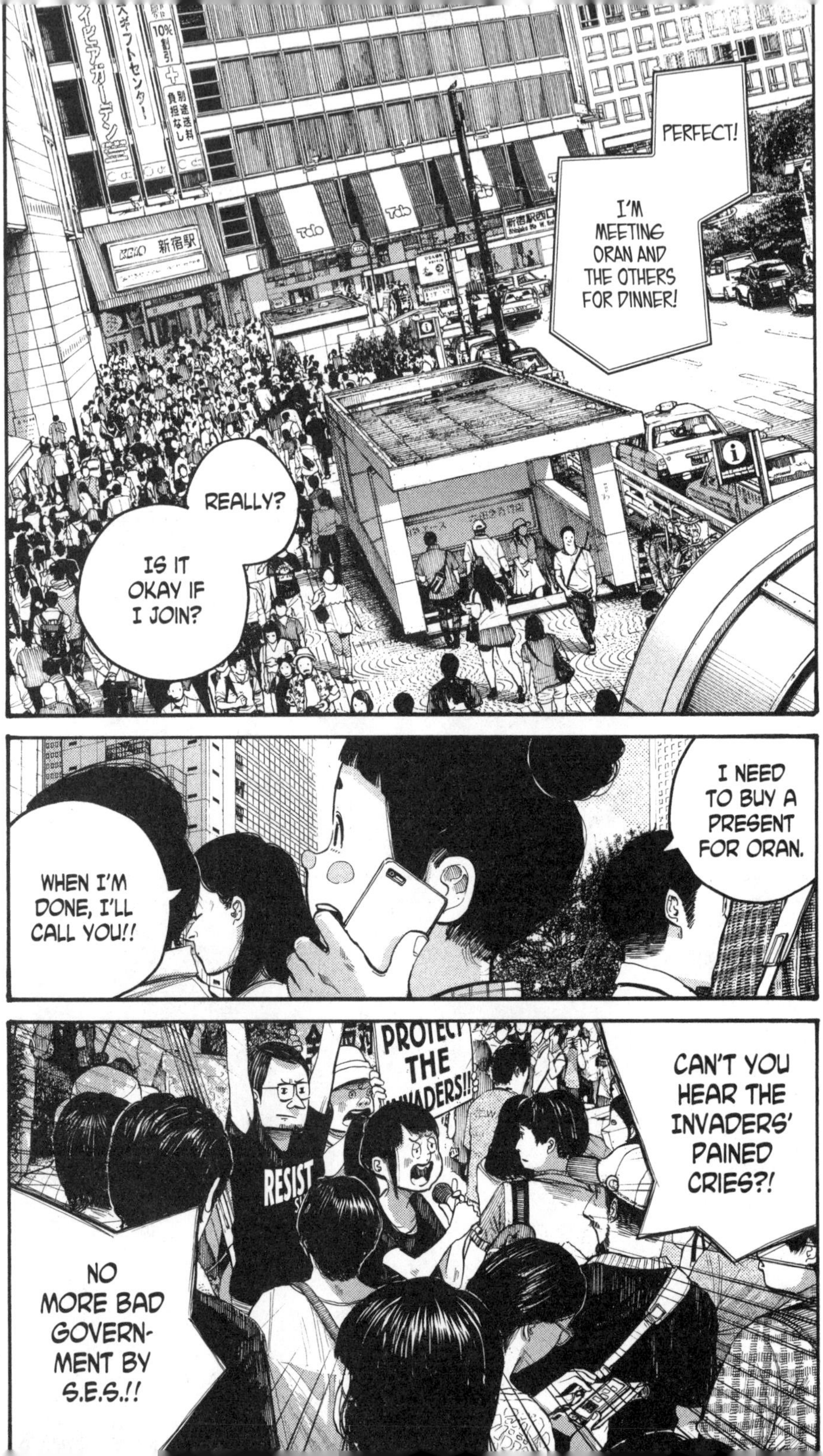
PERFECT!
I'M MEETING ORAN AND THE OTHERS FOR DINNER!
REALLY?
IS IT OKAY IF I JOIN?
I NEED TO BUY A PRESENT FOR ORAN.
WHEN I'M DONE, I'LL CALL YOU!!
CAN'T YOU HEAR THE INVADERS' PAINED CRIES?!
RESIST
NO MORE BAD GOVERN-MENT BY S.E.S.!!

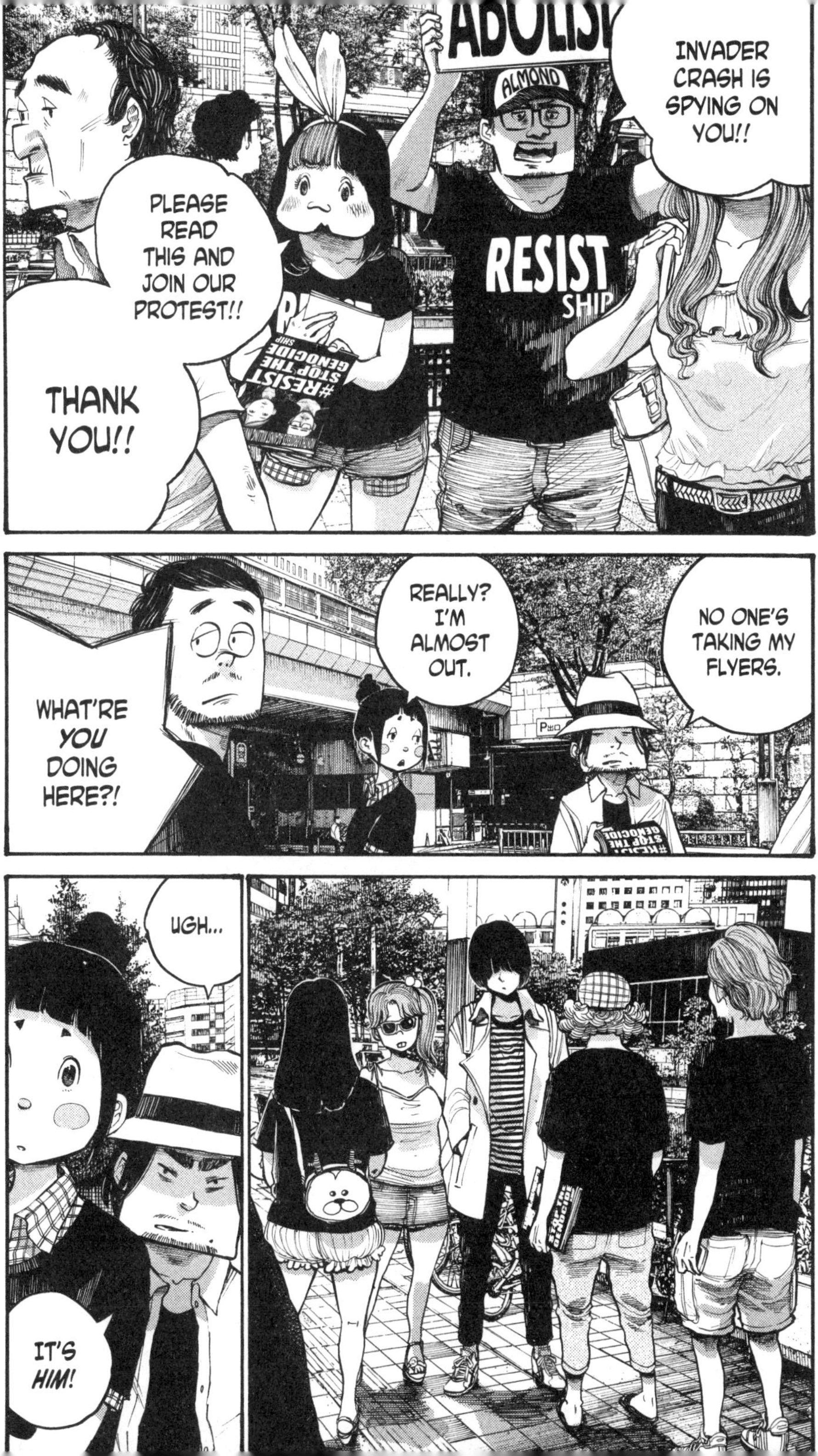
INVADER CRASH IS SPYING ON YOU!!
ALMOND
RESIST
SHIP
PLEASE READ THIS AND JOIN OUR PROTEST!!
#RESIST STOP THE GENOCIDE SHIP
THANK YOU!!
NO ONE'S TAKING MY FLYERS.
REALLY? I'M ALMOST OUT.
WHAT'RE *YOU* DOING HERE?!
UGH...
IT'S *HIM*!

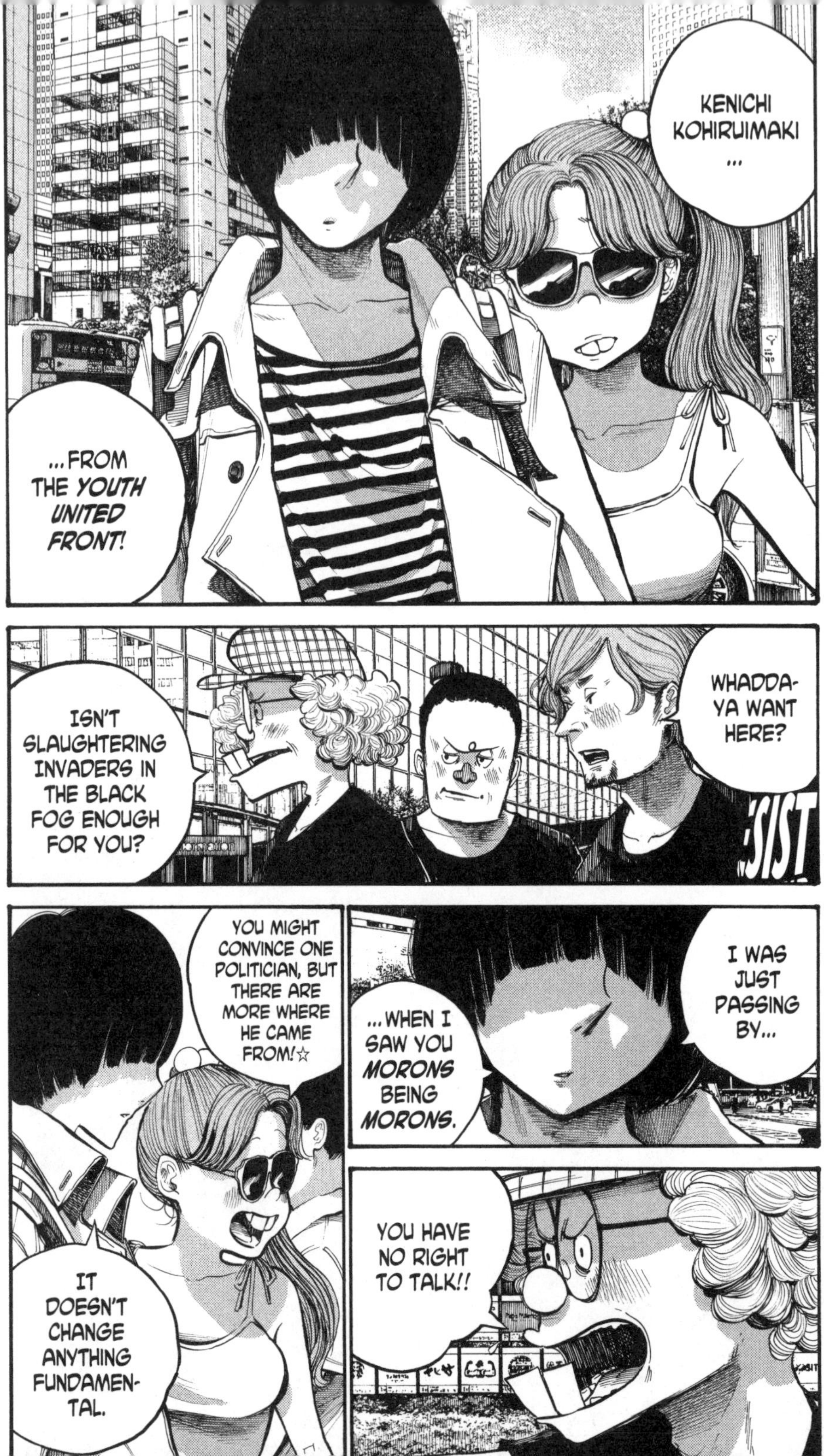
KENICHI KOHIRUIMAKI ...
...FROM THE *YOUTH UNITED FRONT*!
WHADDA-YA WANT HERE?
ISN'T SLAUGHTERING INVADERS IN THE BLACK FOG ENOUGH FOR YOU?
I WAS JUST PASSING BY...
...WHEN I SAW YOU *MORONS* BEING *MORONS*.
YOU HAVE NO RIGHT TO TALK!!
YOU MIGHT CONVINCE ONE POLITICIAN, BUT THERE ARE MORE WHERE HE CAME FROM!☆
IT DOESN'T CHANGE ANYTHING FUNDAMENTAL.

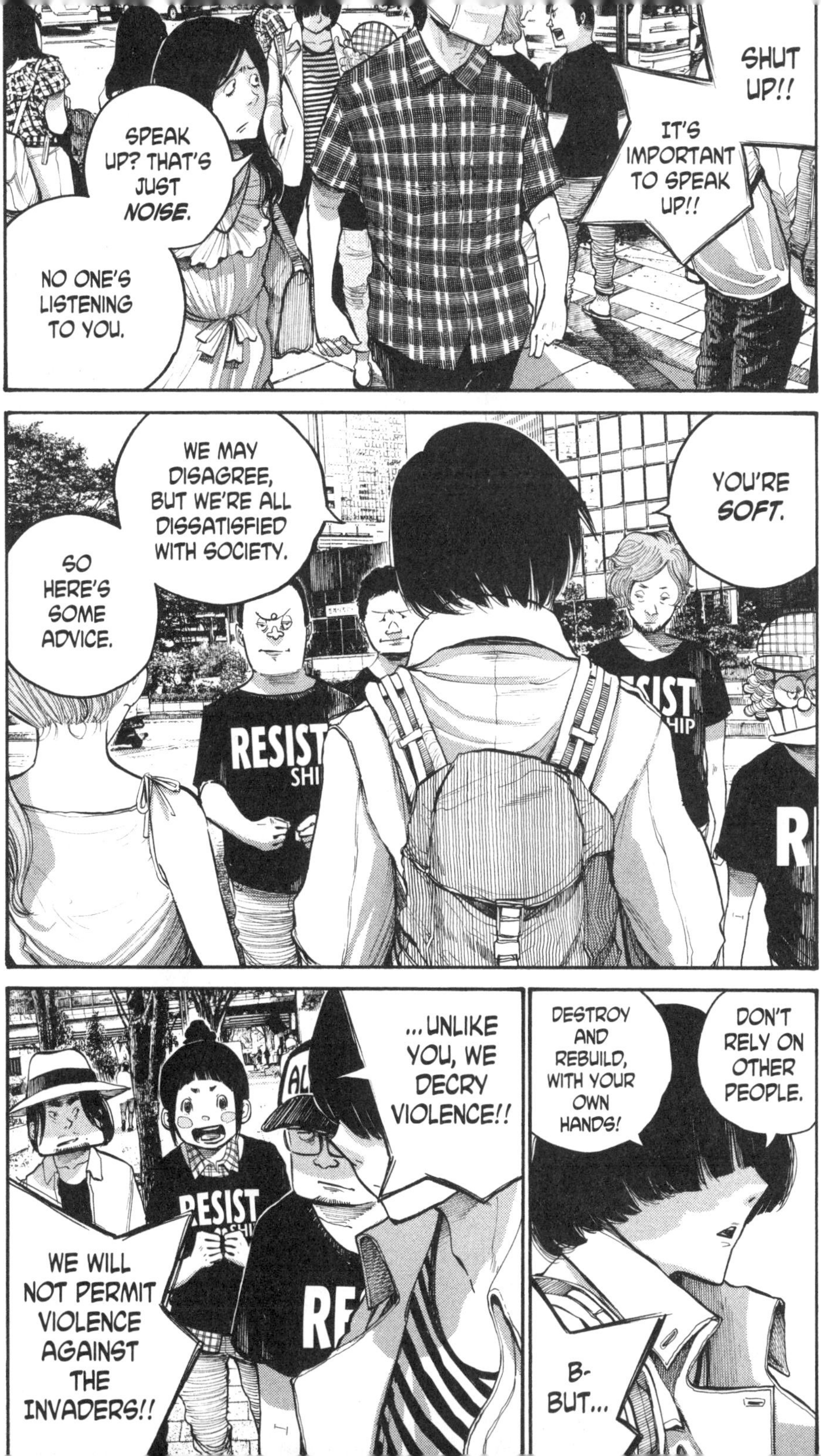
SHUT UP!!
IT'S IMPORTANT TO SPEAK UP!!
SPEAK UP? THAT'S JUST *NOISE*.
NO ONE'S LISTENING TO YOU.
YOU'RE *SOFT*.
WE MAY DISAGREE, BUT WE'RE ALL DISSATISFIED WITH SOCIETY.
SO HERE'S SOME ADVICE.
RESIST
DON'T RELY ON OTHER PEOPLE.
DESTROY AND REBUILD, WITH YOUR OWN HANDS!
B- BUT...
...UNLIKE YOU, WE DECRY VIOLENCE!!
WE WILL NOT PERMIT VIOLENCE AGAINST THE INVADERS!!

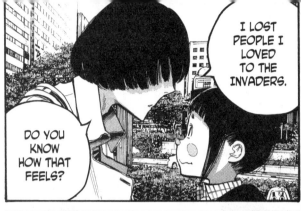

I LOST PEOPLE I LOVED TO THE INVADERS.

DO YOU KNOW HOW THAT FEELS?

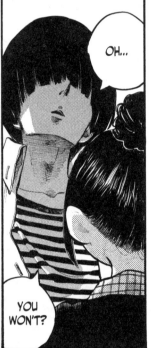

OH...

YOU WON'T?

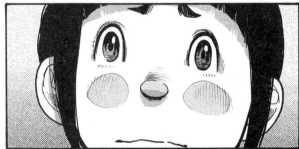

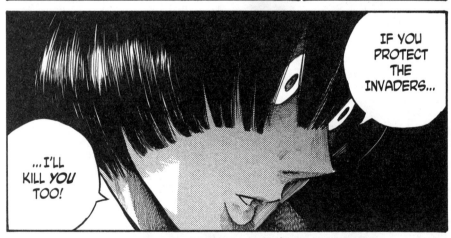

IF YOU PROTECT THE INVADERS...

...I'LL KILL *YOU* TOO!

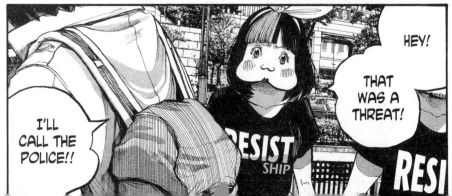

HEY!

THAT WAS A THREAT!

I'LL CALL THE POLICE!!

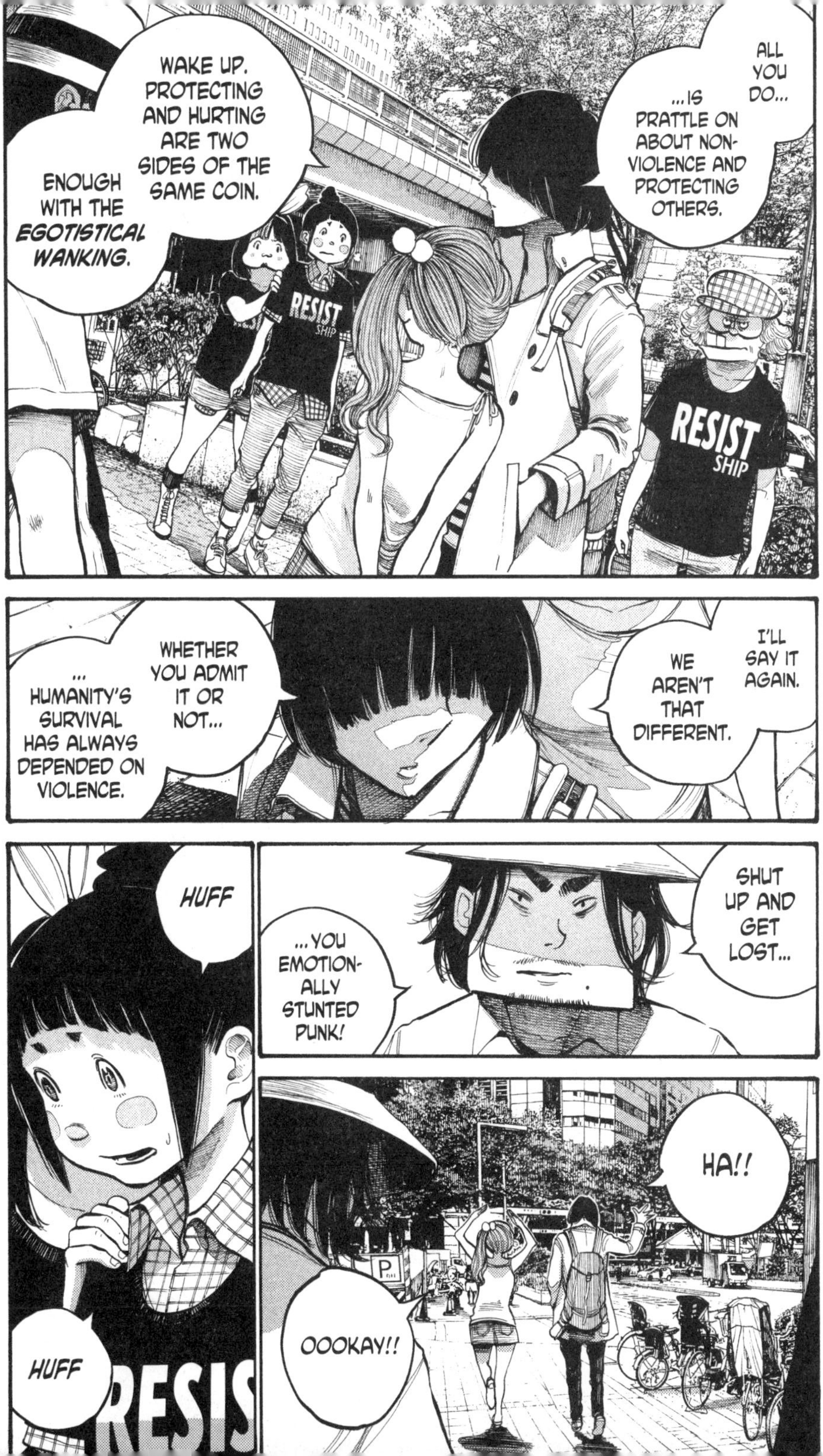
ALL YOU DO...
...IS PRATTLE ON ABOUT NON-VIOLENCE AND PROTECTING OTHERS.
RESIST SHIP
WAKE UP. PROTECTING AND HURTING ARE TWO SIDES OF THE SAME COIN.
ENOUGH WITH THE *EGOTISTICAL WANKING.*
RESIST SHIP
I'LL SAY IT AGAIN.
WE AREN'T THAT DIFFERENT.
WHETHER YOU ADMIT IT OR NOT...
...HUMANITY'S SURVIVAL HAS ALWAYS DEPENDED ON VIOLENCE.
SHUT UP AND GET LOST...
...YOU EMOTION-ALLY STUNTED PUNK!
HA!!
OOOKAY!!
HUFF
HUFF
RESIS

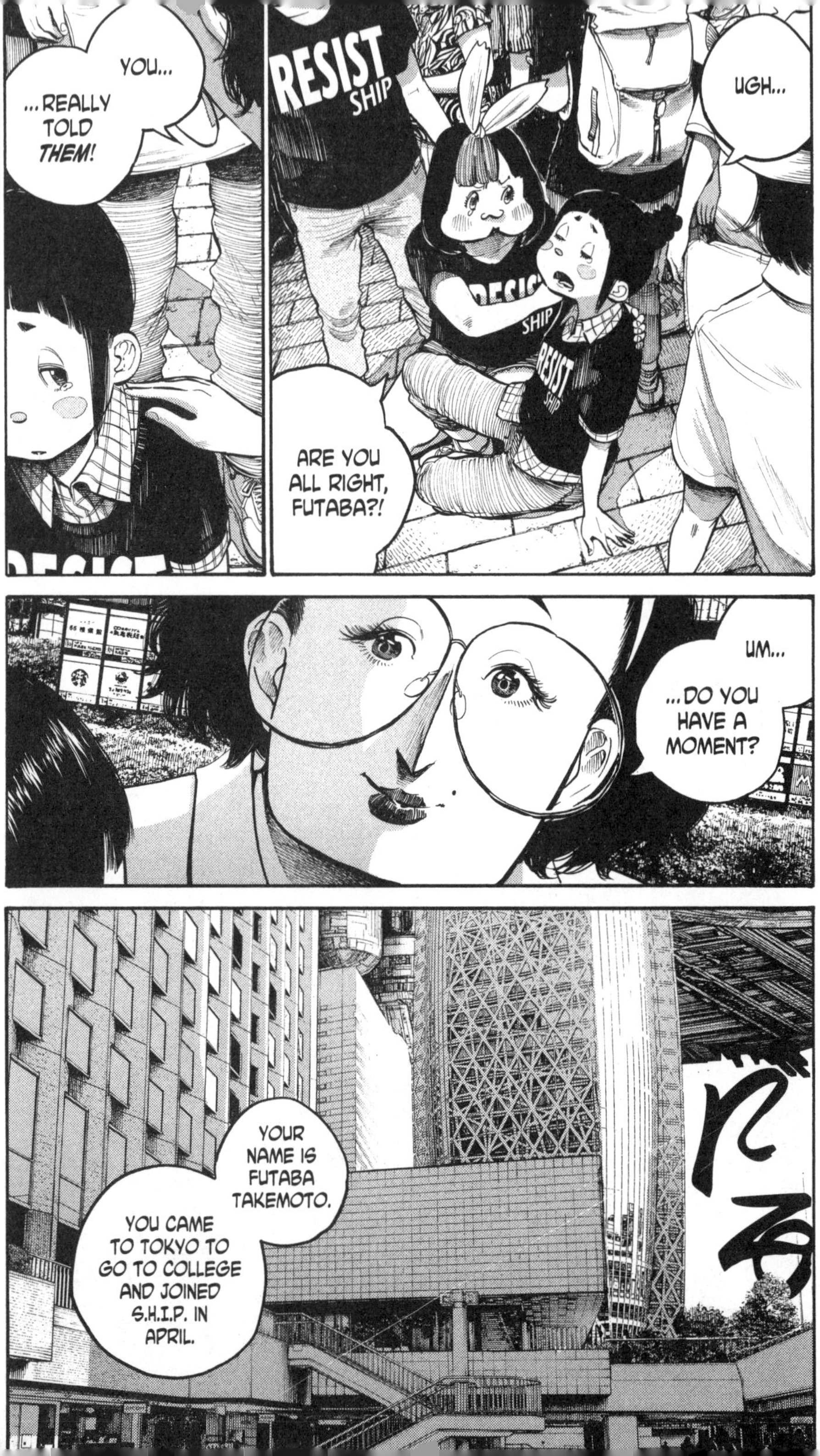
UGH...
ARE YOU ALL RIGHT, FUTABA?!
RESIST SHIP
YOU...
...REALLY TOLD *THEM*!
UM...
...DO YOU HAVE A MOMENT?
YOUR NAME IS FUTABA TAKEMOTO.
YOU CAME TO TOKYO TO GO TO COLLEGE AND JOINED S.H.I.P. IN APRIL.

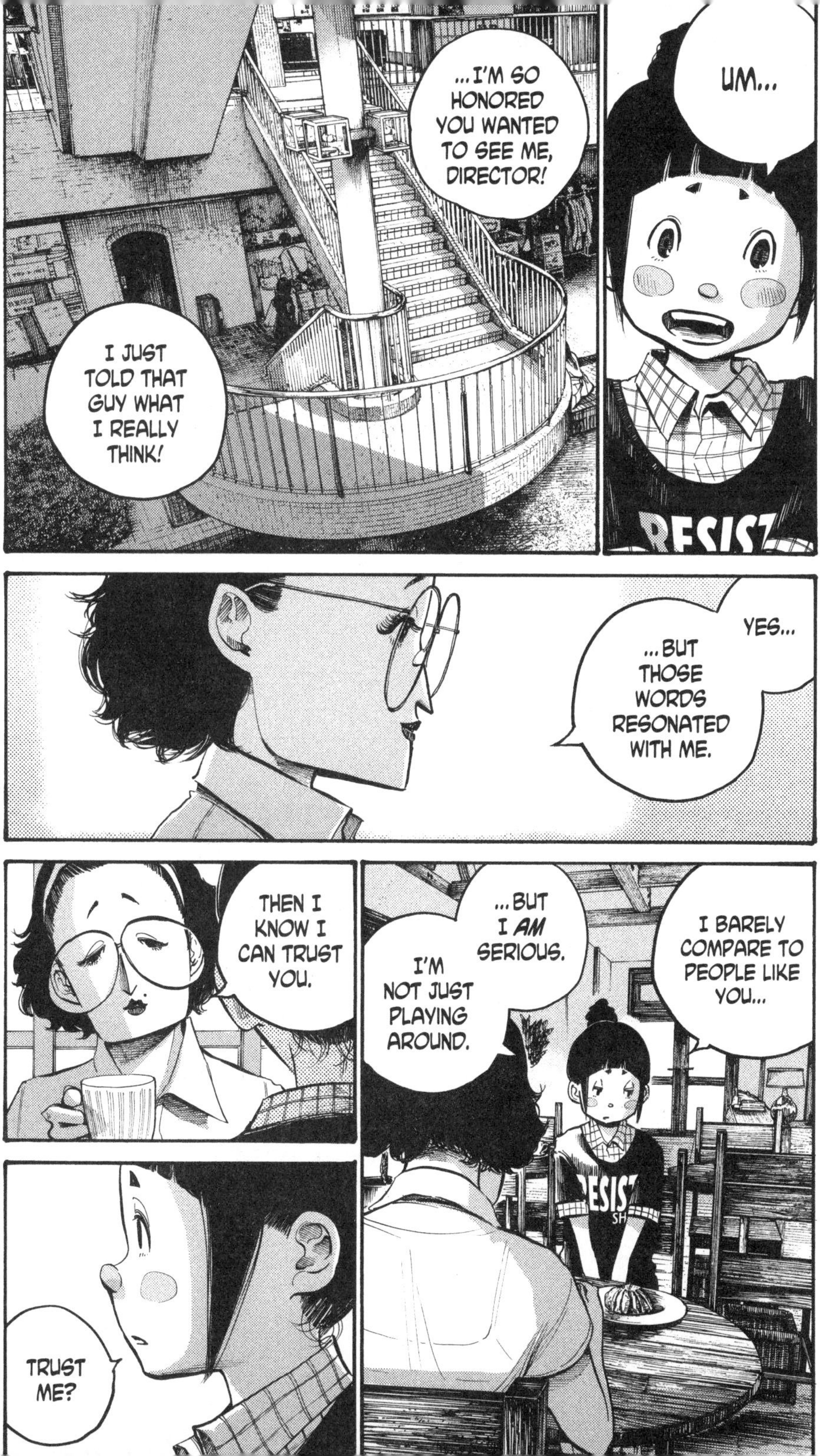
UM...
...I'M SO HONORED YOU WANTED TO SEE ME, DIRECTOR!
I JUST TOLD THAT GUY WHAT I REALLY THINK!
YES...
...BUT THOSE WORDS RESONATED WITH ME.
I BARELY COMPARE TO PEOPLE LIKE YOU...
...BUT I *AM* SERIOUS.
I'M NOT JUST PLAYING AROUND.
THEN I KNOW I CAN TRUST YOU.
TRUST ME?

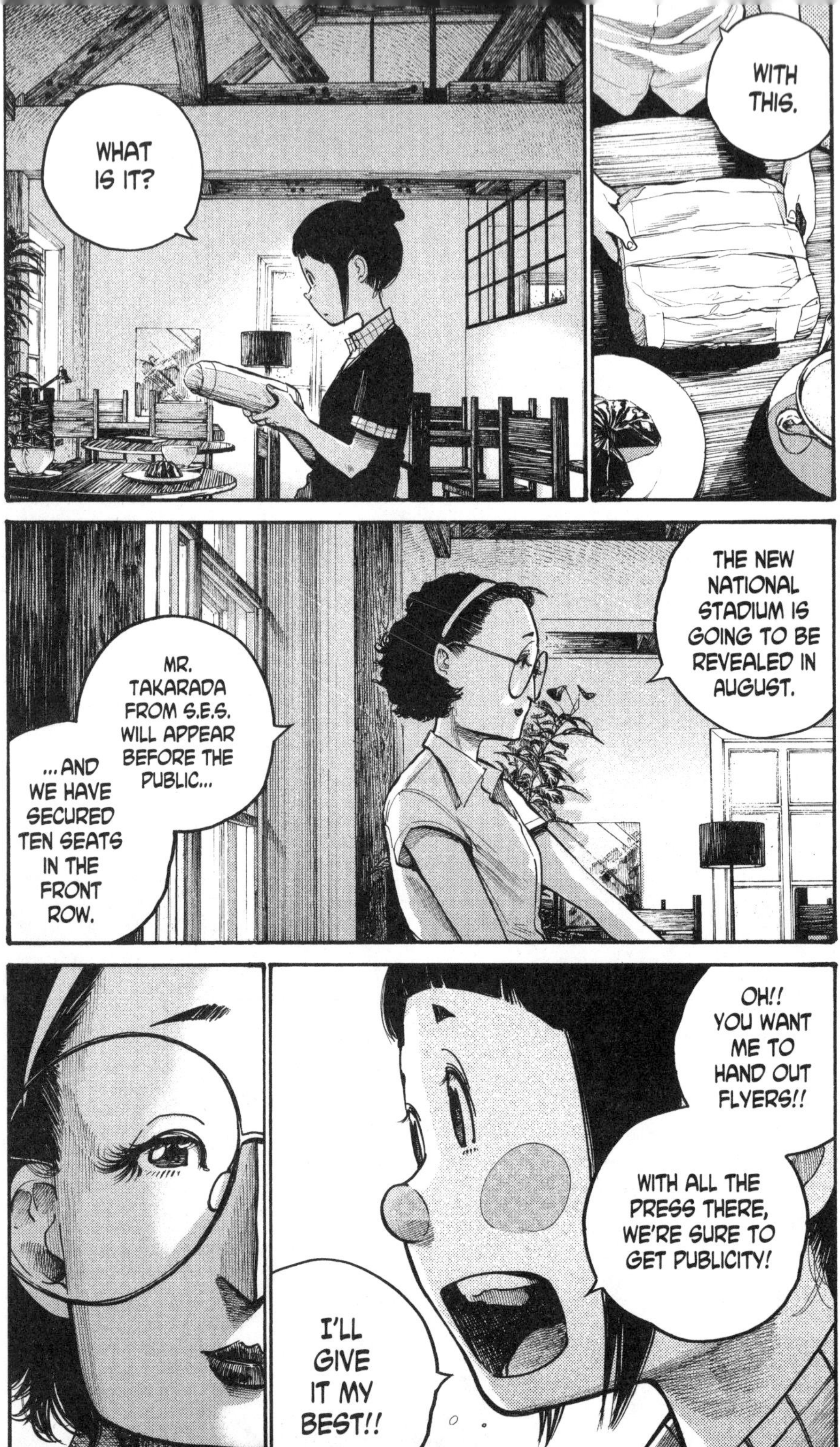
WITH THIS.
WHAT IS IT?
THE NEW NATIONAL STADIUM IS GOING TO BE REVEALED IN AUGUST.
MR. TAKARADA FROM S.E.S. WILL APPEAR BEFORE THE PUBLIC...
...AND WE HAVE SECURED TEN SEATS IN THE FRONT ROW.
OH!! YOU WANT ME TO HAND OUT FLYERS!!
WITH ALL THE PRESS THERE, WE'RE SURE TO GET PUBLICITY!
I'LL GIVE IT MY BEST!!

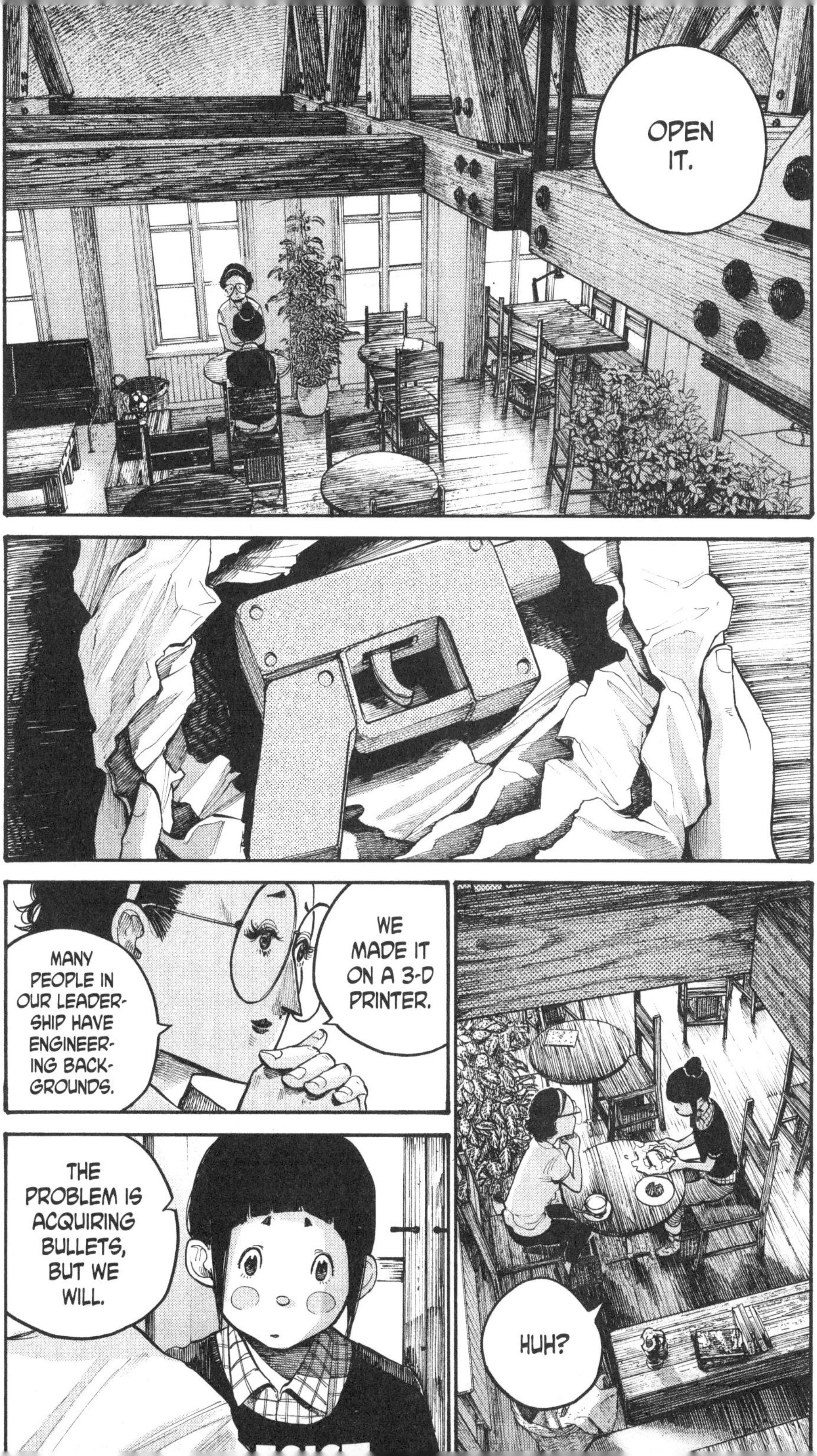
OPEN IT.
HUH?
WE MADE IT ON A 3-D PRINTER.
MANY PEOPLE IN OUR LEADERSHIP HAVE ENGINEERING BACKGROUNDS.
THE PROBLEM IS ACQUIRING BULLETS, BUT WE WILL.

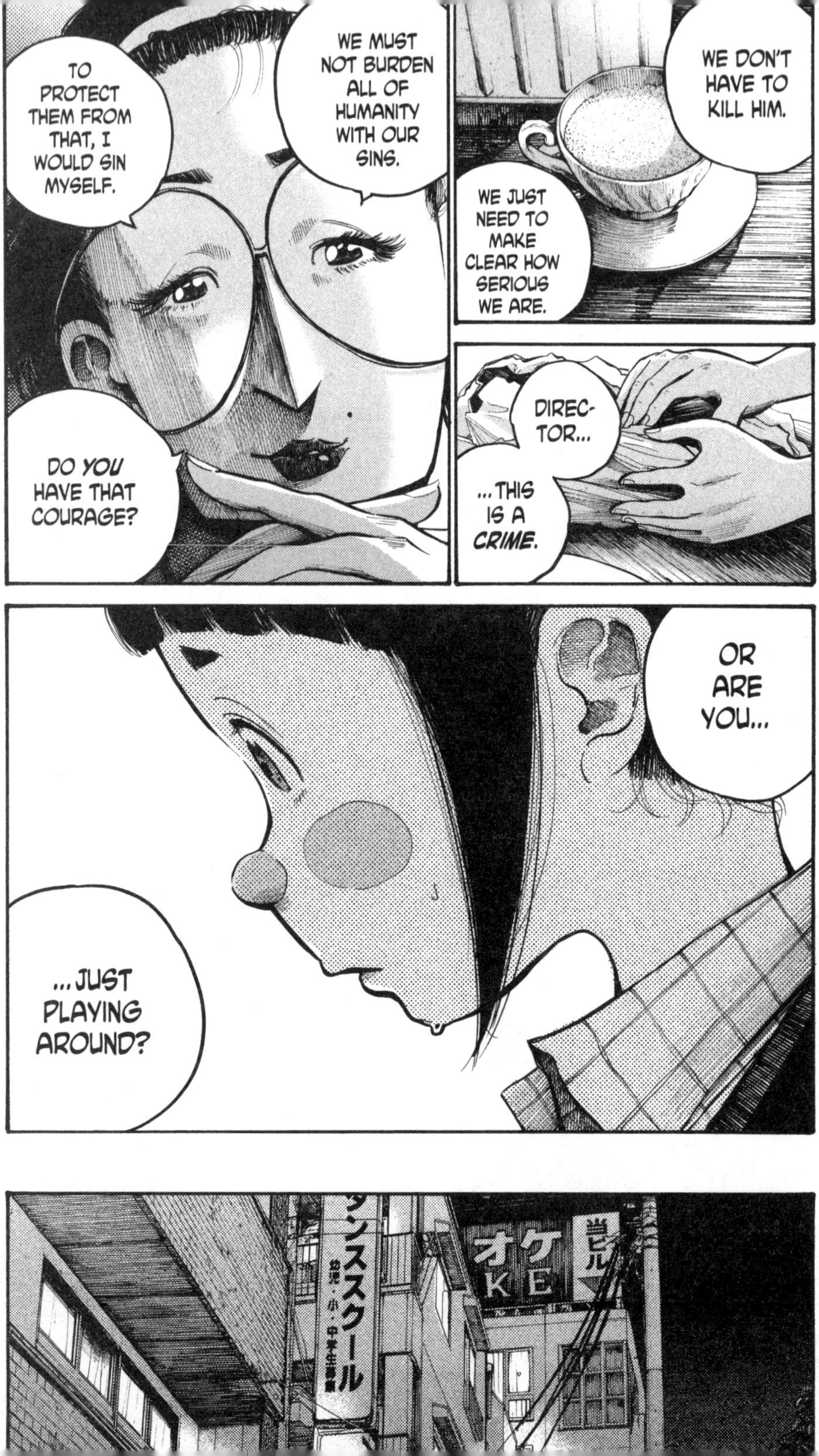
WE DON'T HAVE TO KILL HIM.
WE JUST NEED TO MAKE CLEAR HOW SERIOUS WE ARE.
DIRECTOR...
...THIS IS A *CRIME*.
WE MUST NOT BURDEN ALL OF HUMANITY WITH OUR SINS.
TO PROTECT THEM FROM THAT, I WOULD SIN MYSELF.
DO *YOU* HAVE THAT COURAGE?
OR ARE YOU...
...JUST PLAYING AROUND?
ダンススクール
幼児・小・中学生募集
オケ
KE
当ビル

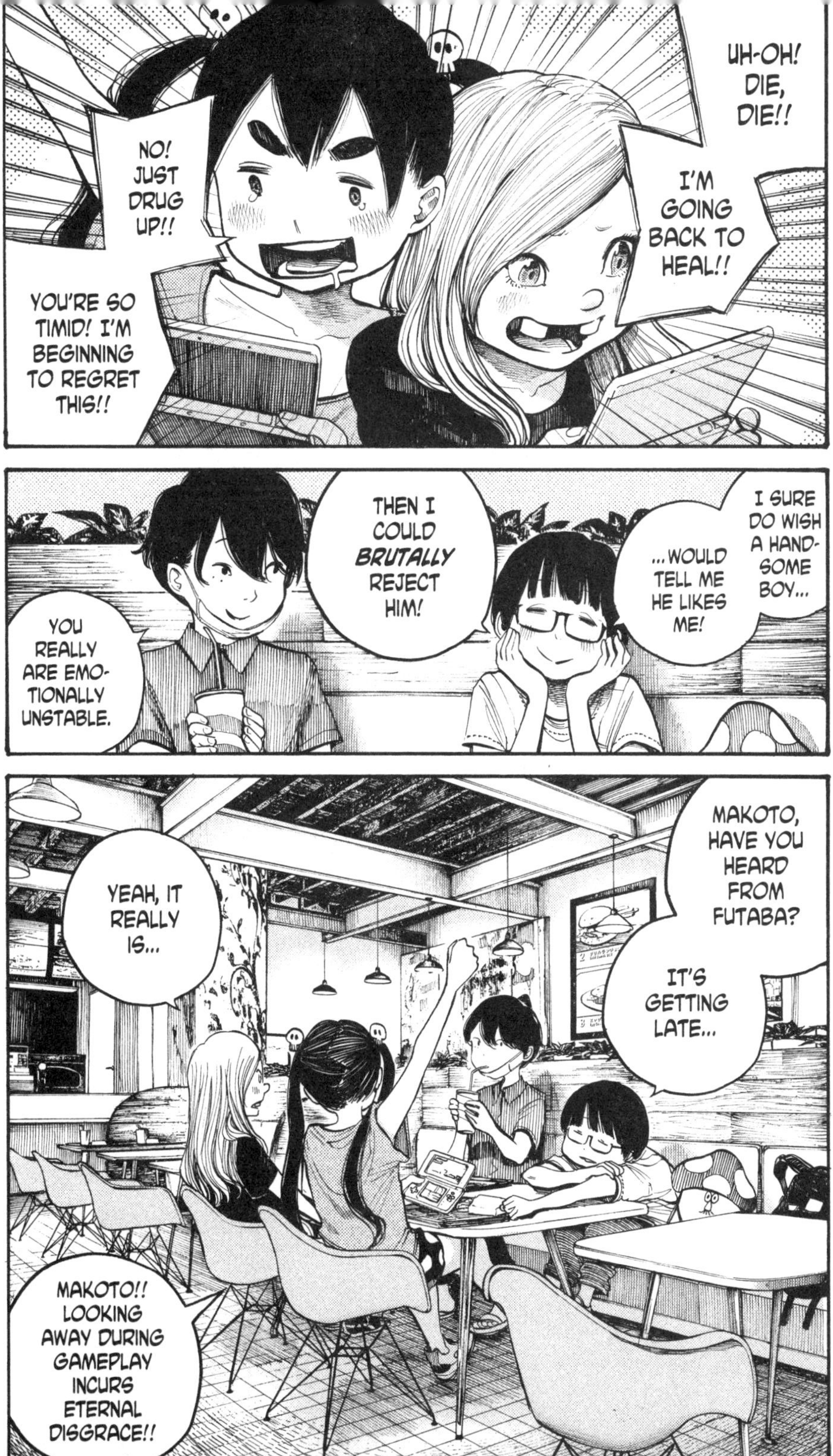
UH-OH! DIE, DIE!!
I'M GOING BACK TO HEAL!!
NO! JUST DRUG UP!!
YOU'RE SO TIMID! I'M BEGINNING TO REGRET THIS!!
I SURE DO WISH A HANDSOME BOY...
...WOULD TELL ME HE LIKES ME!
THEN I COULD *BRUTALLY* REJECT HIM!
YOU REALLY ARE EMOTIONALLY UNSTABLE.
MAKOTO, HAVE YOU HEARD FROM FUTABA?
IT'S GETTING LATE...
YEAH, IT REALLY IS...
MAKOTO!! LOOKING AWAY DURING GAMEPLAY INCURS ETERNAL DISGRACE!!

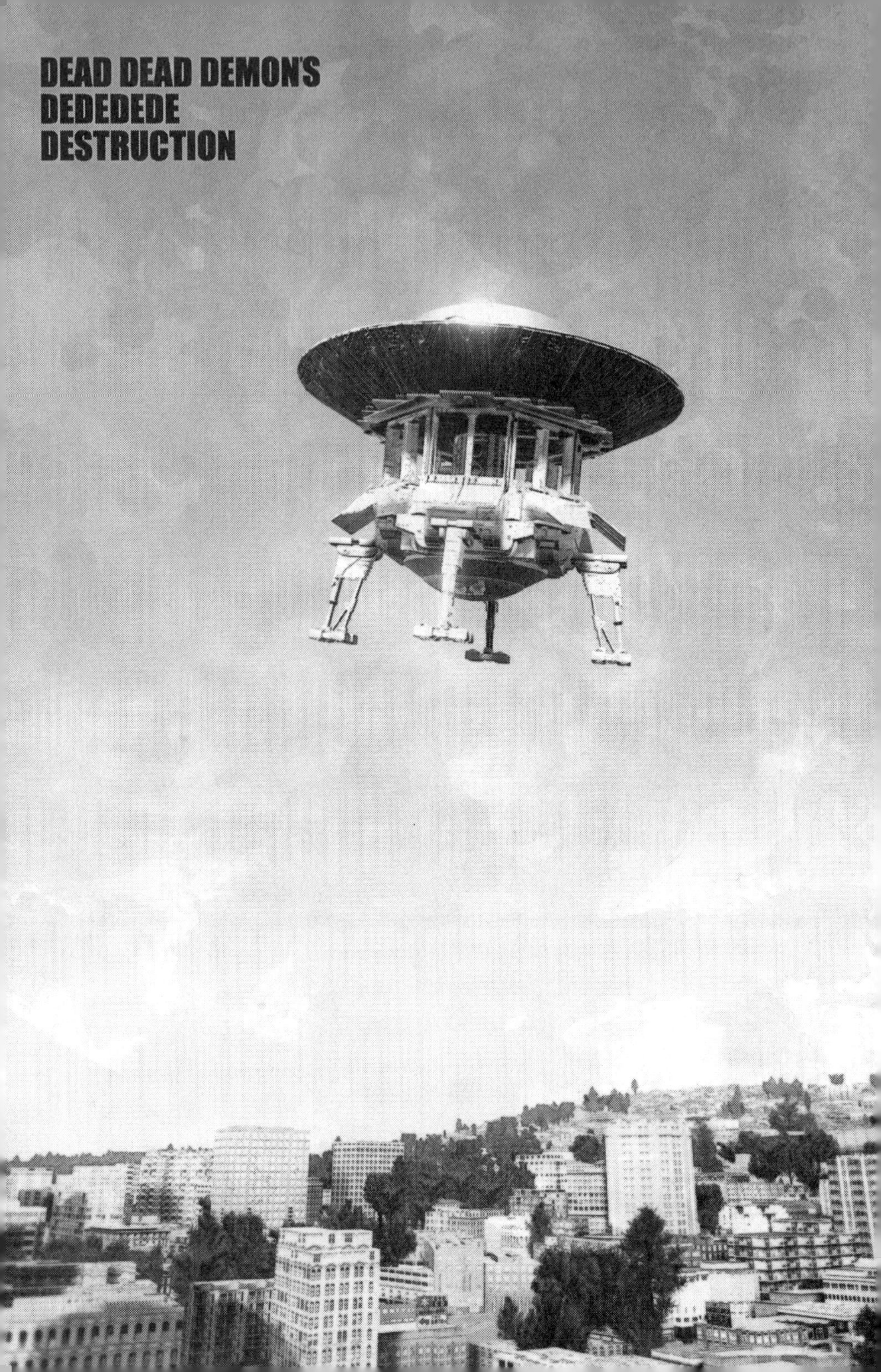
DEAD DEAD DEMON'S
DEDEDEDE
DESTRUCTION

DEAD DEAD DEMON'S DEDEDEDE DESTRUCTION

INIO ASANO

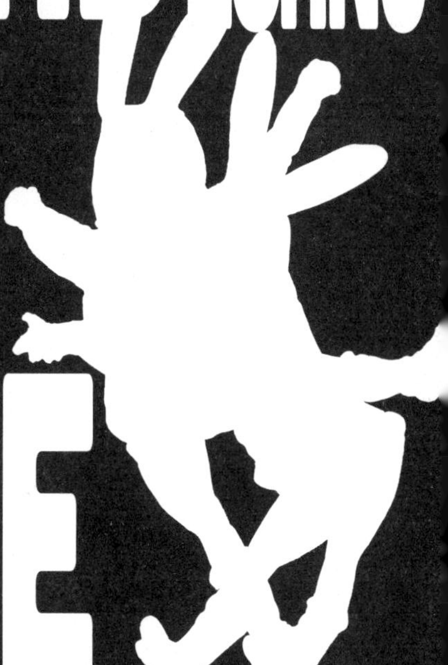

CHAPTER 47

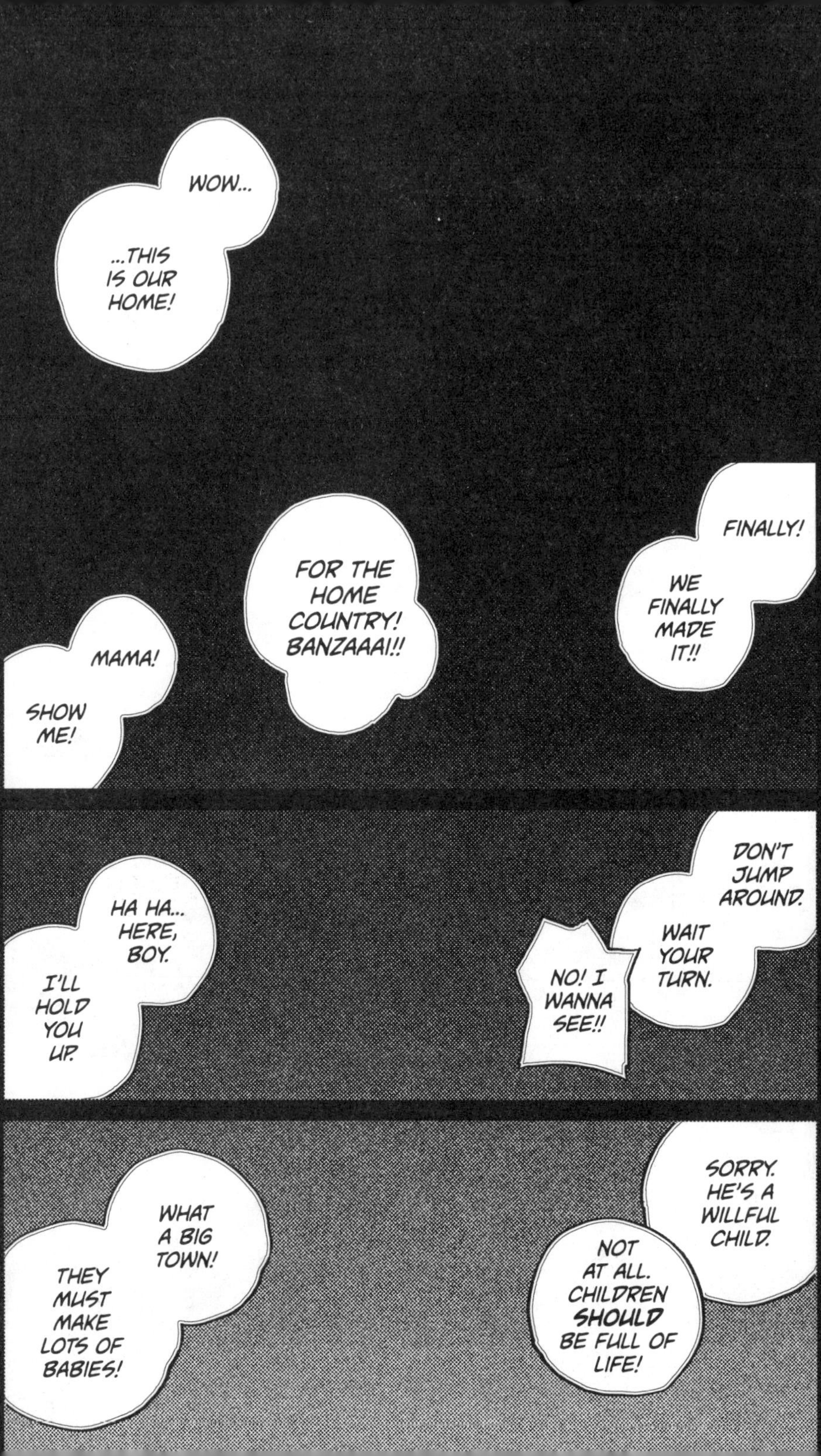
WOW...
...THIS IS OUR HOME!
FINALLY!
WE FINALLY MADE IT!!
FOR THE HOME COUNTRY! BANZAAAI!!
MAMA!
SHOW ME!
DON'T JUMP AROUND.
WAIT YOUR TURN.
NO! I WANNA SEE!!
HA HA... HERE, BOY.
I'LL HOLD YOU UP.
SORRY. HE'S A WILLFUL CHILD.
NOT AT ALL. CHILDREN **SHOULD** BE FULL OF LIFE!
WHAT A BIG TOWN!
THEY MUST MAKE LOTS OF BABIES!

WOW!!
横浜
Yokohama

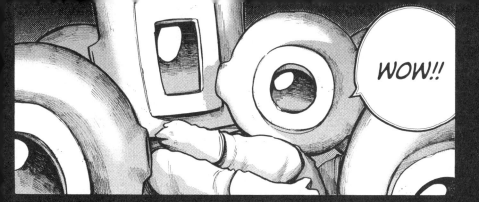

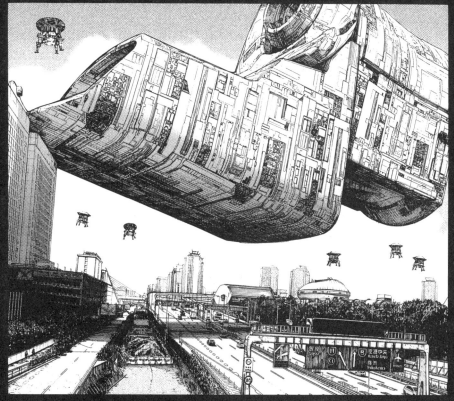

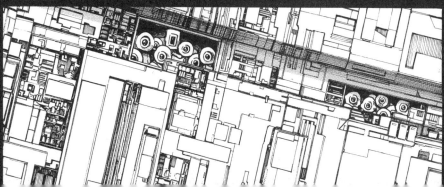

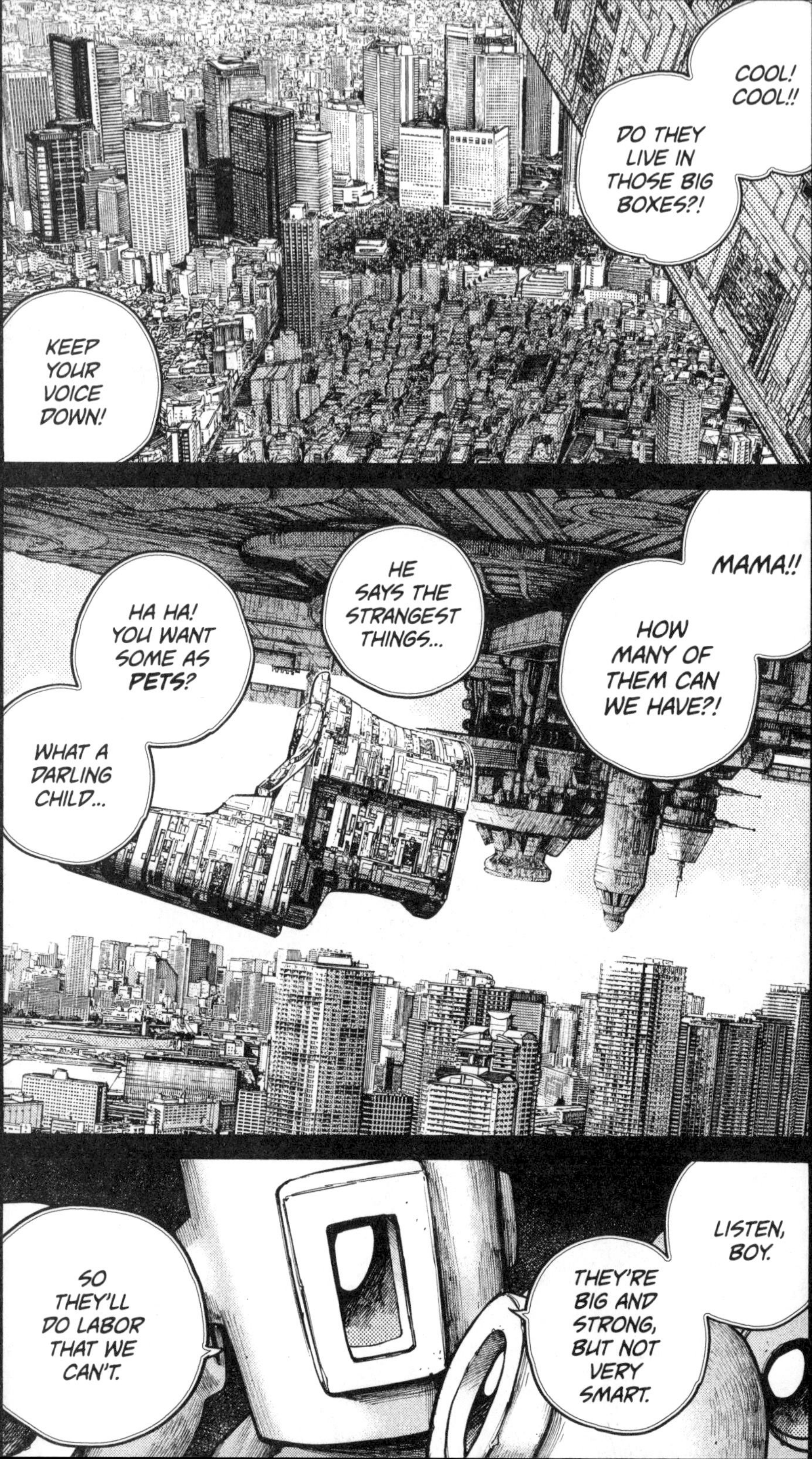

COOL! COOL!!
DO THEY LIVE IN THOSE BIG BOXES?!
KEEP YOUR VOICE DOWN!
MAMA!!
HOW MANY OF THEM CAN WE HAVE?!
HE SAYS THE STRANGEST THINGS...
HA HA! YOU WANT SOME AS PETS?
WHAT A DARLING CHILD...
LISTEN, BOY.
THEY'RE BIG AND STRONG, BUT NOT VERY SMART.
SO THEY'LL DO LABOR THAT WE CAN'T.

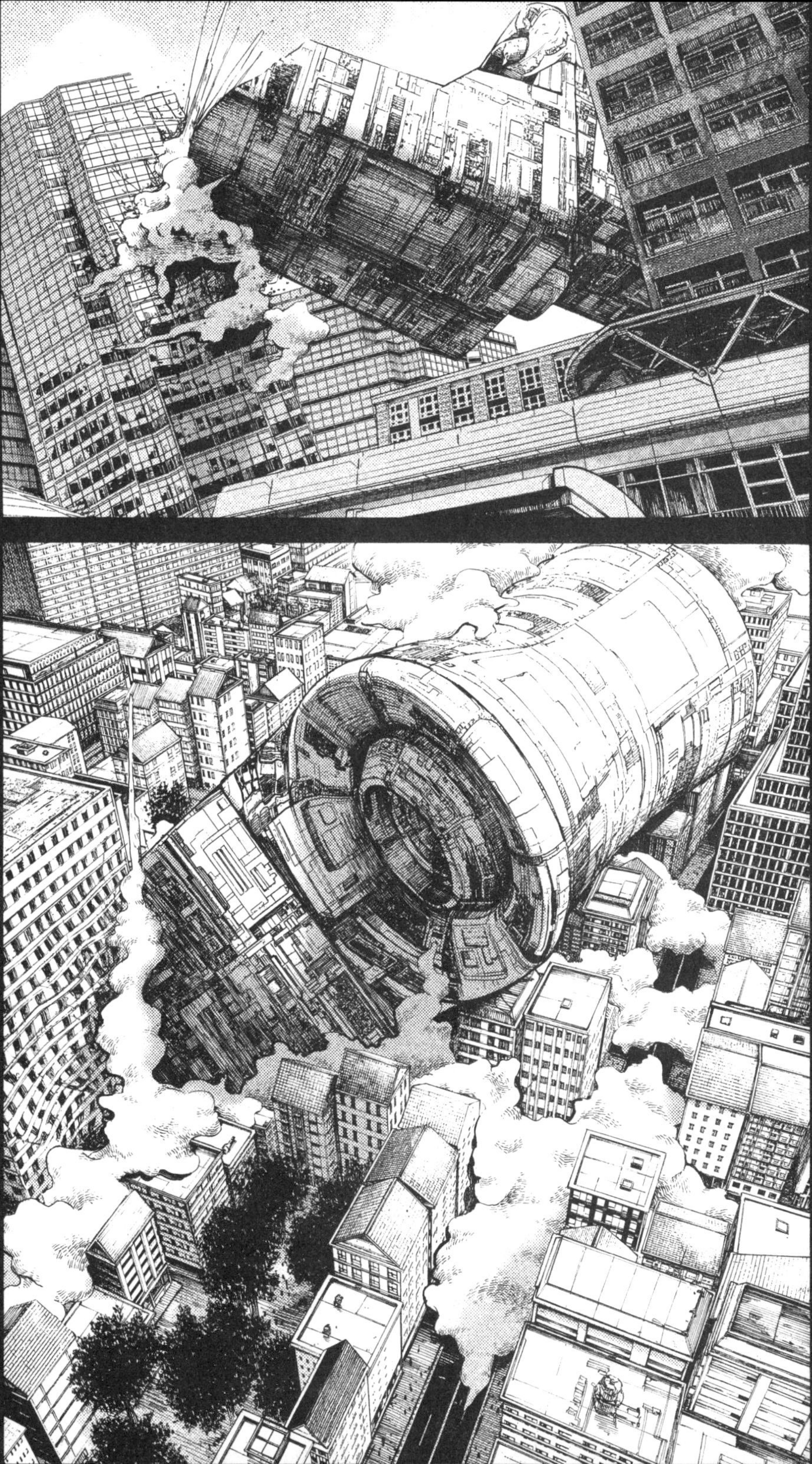

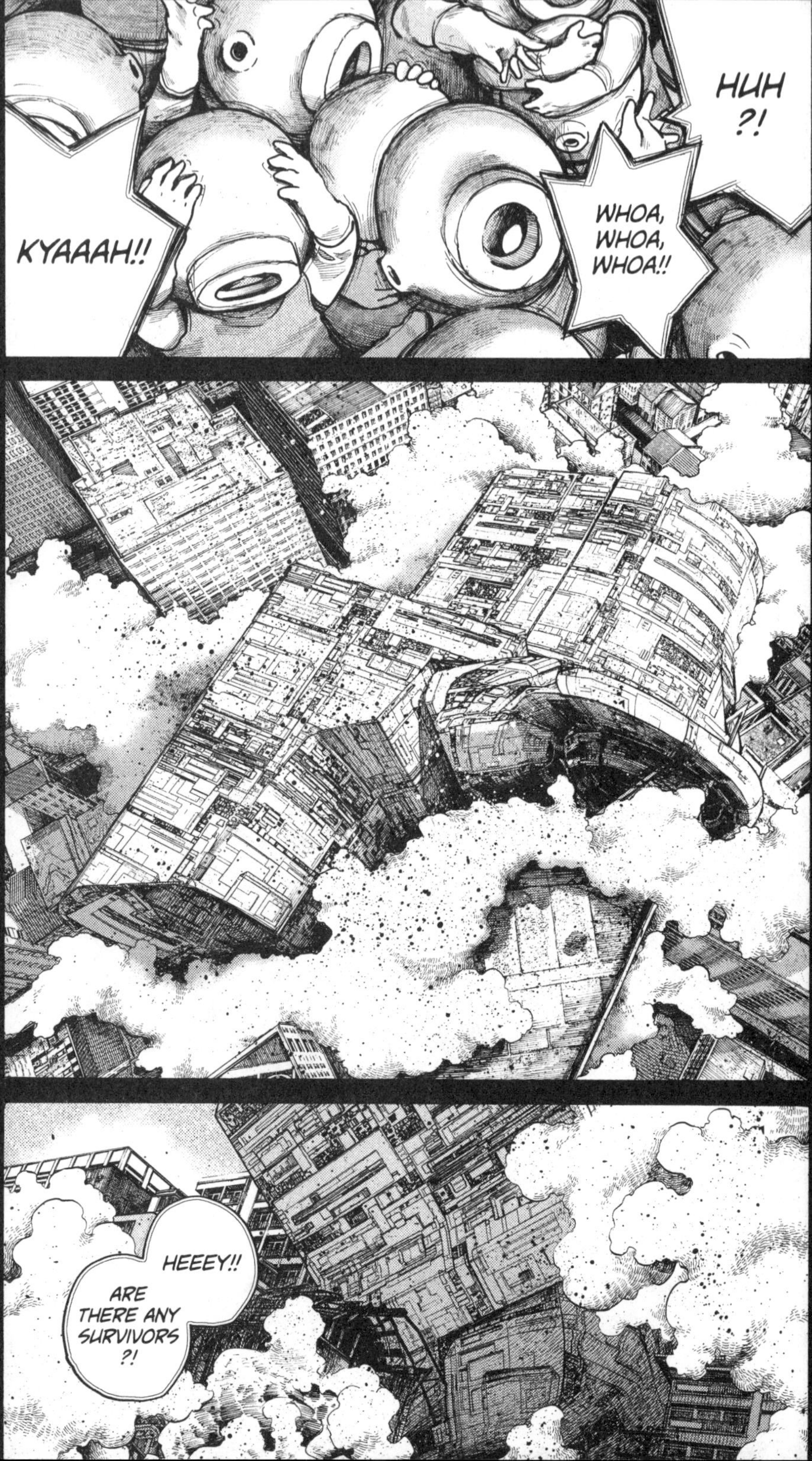
HUH ?!
WHOA, WHOA, WHOA!!
KYAAAH!!
HEEEY!!
ARE THERE ANY SURVIVORS ?!

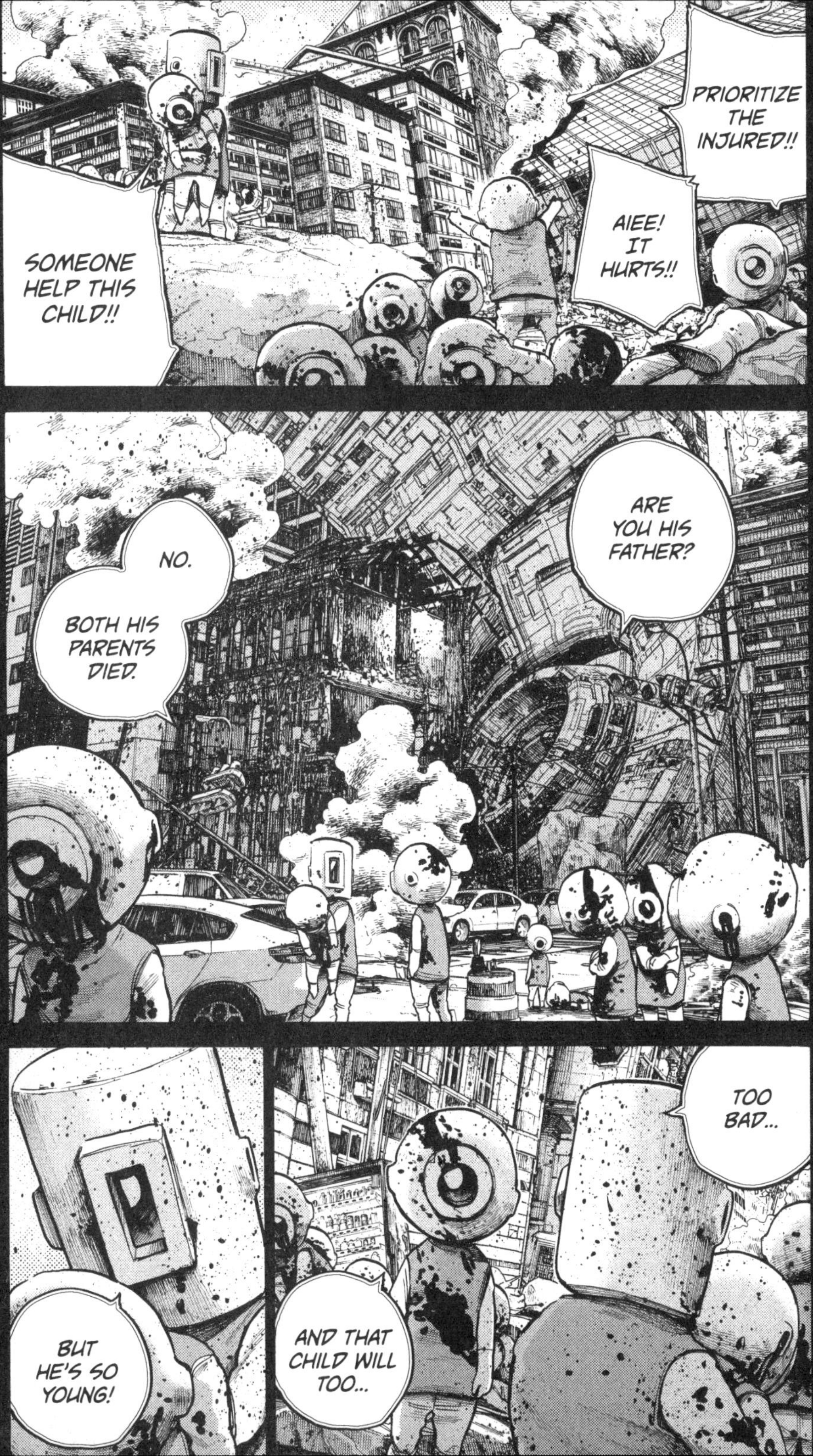
PRIORITIZE THE INJURED!!
AIEE! IT HURTS!!
SOMEONE HELP THIS CHILD!!
ARE YOU HIS FATHER?
NO.
BOTH HIS PARENTS DIED.
TOO BAD...
AND THAT CHILD WILL TOO...
BUT HE'S SO YOUNG!

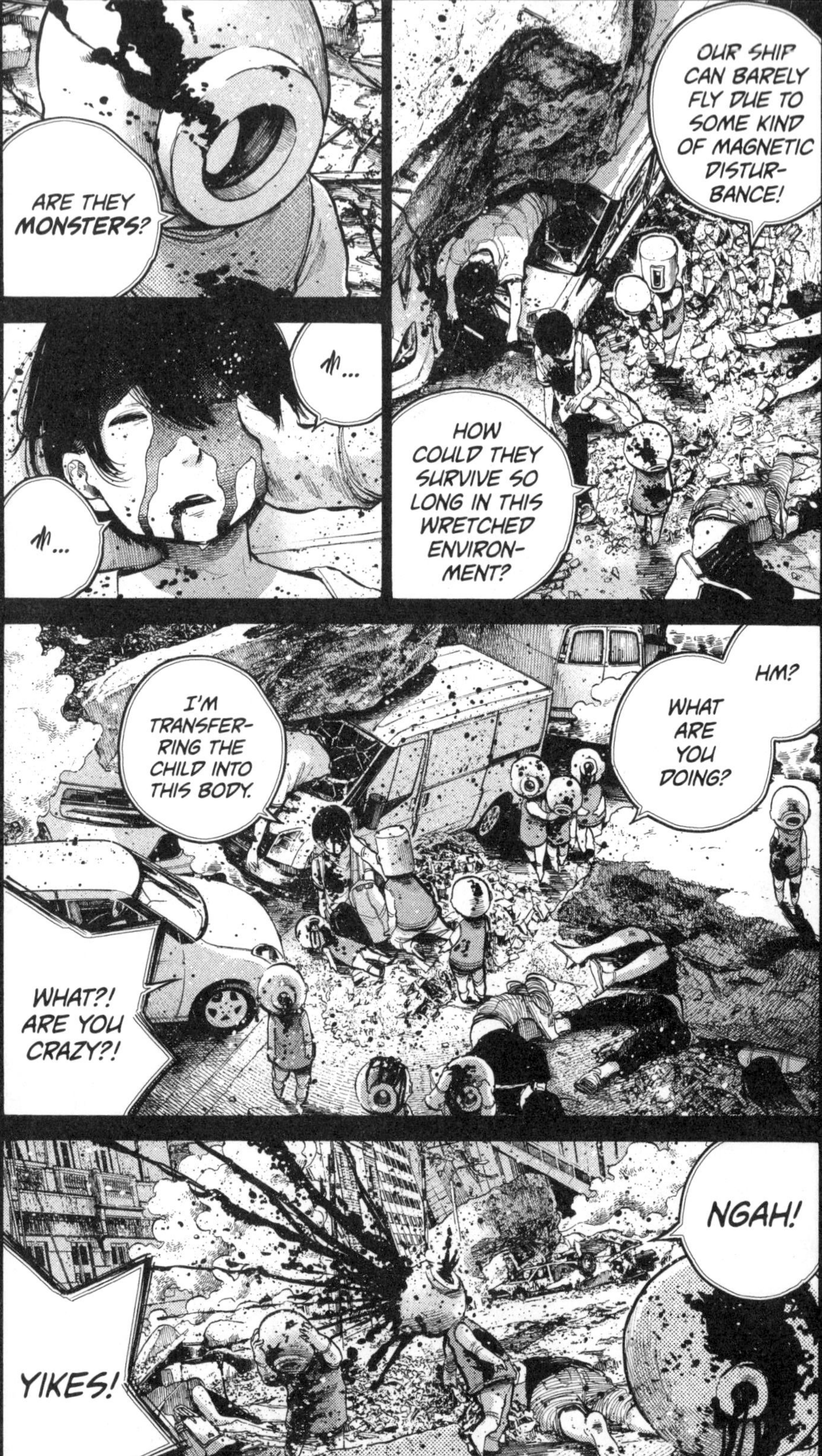
OUR SHIP CAN BARELY FLY DUE TO SOME KIND OF MAGNETIC DISTURBANCE!
HOW COULD THEY SURVIVE SO LONG IN THIS WRETCHED ENVIRONMENT?
ARE THEY MONSTERS?
Mn...
Mn...
HM?
WHAT ARE YOU DOING?
I'M TRANSFERRING THE CHILD INTO THIS BODY.
WHAT?! ARE YOU CRAZY?!
NGAH!
YIKES!

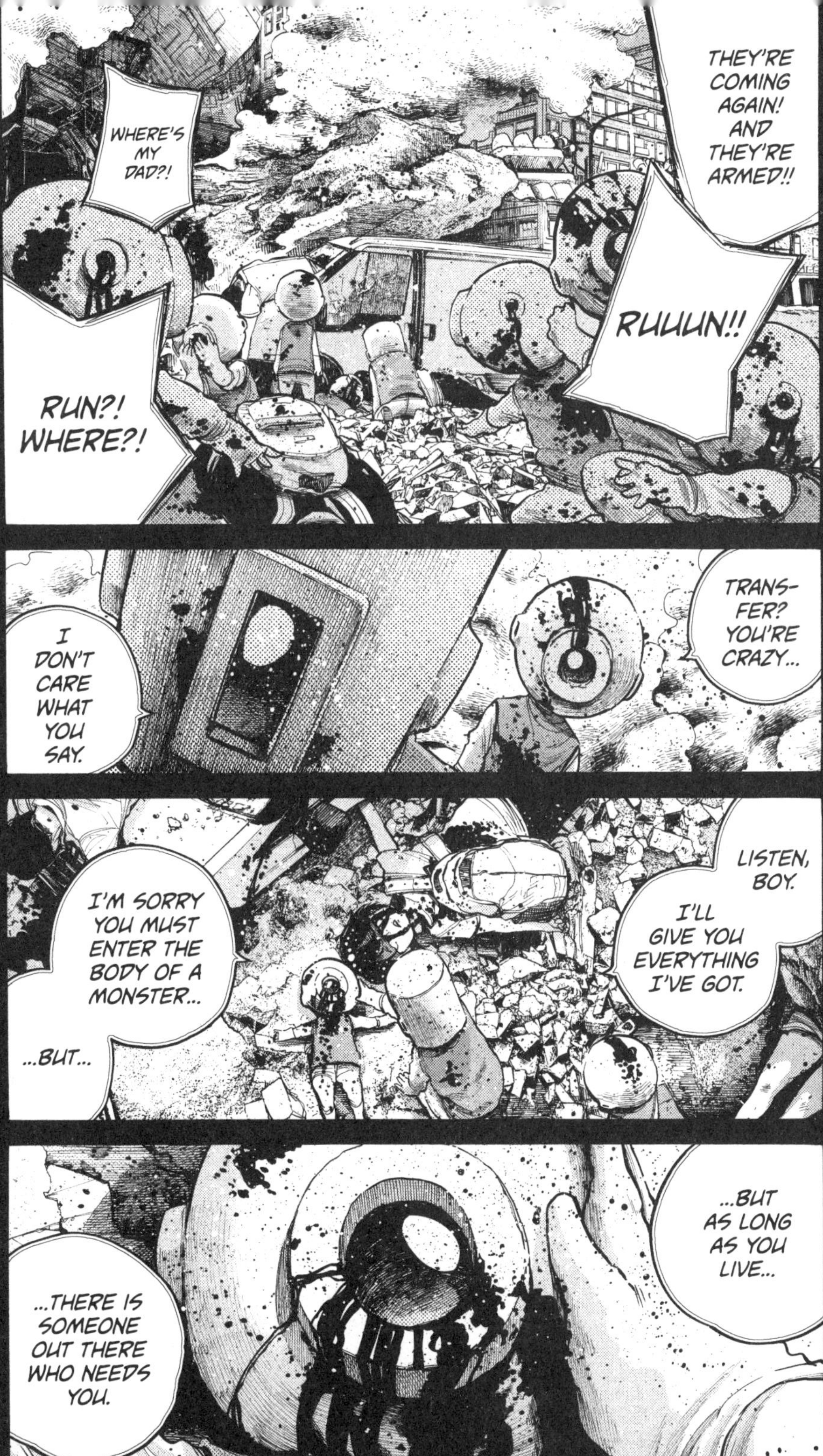
THEY'RE COMING AGAIN! AND THEY'RE ARMED!!
RUUUN!!
WHERE'S MY DAD?!
RUN?! WHERE?!
TRANSFER? YOU'RE CRAZY...
I DON'T CARE WHAT YOU SAY.
LISTEN, BOY.
I'LL GIVE YOU EVERYTHING I'VE GOT.
I'M SORRY YOU MUST ENTER THE BODY OF A MONSTER...
...BUT...
...BUT AS LONG AS YOU LIVE...
...THERE IS SOMEONE OUT THERE WHO NEEDS YOU.

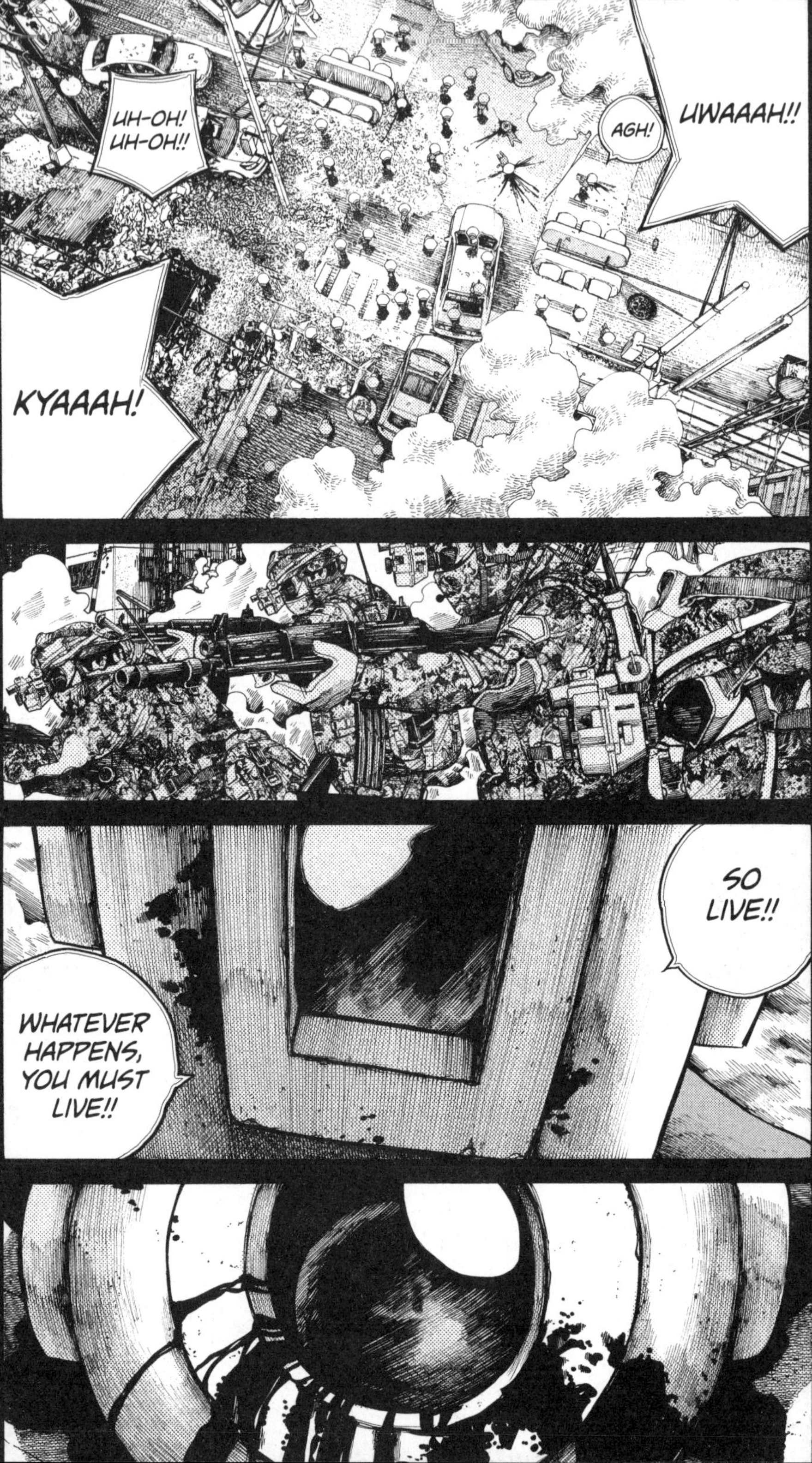
UWAAAH!!
AGH!
UH-OH! UH-OH!!
KYAAAH!
SO LIVE!!
WHATEVER HAPPENS, YOU MUST LIVE!!

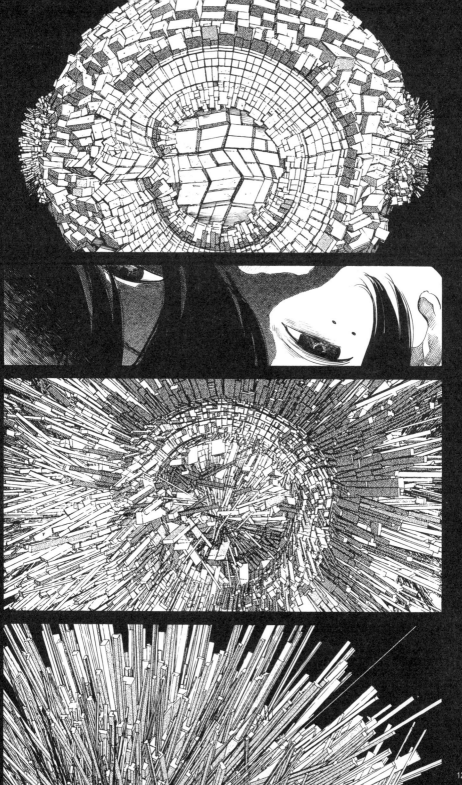

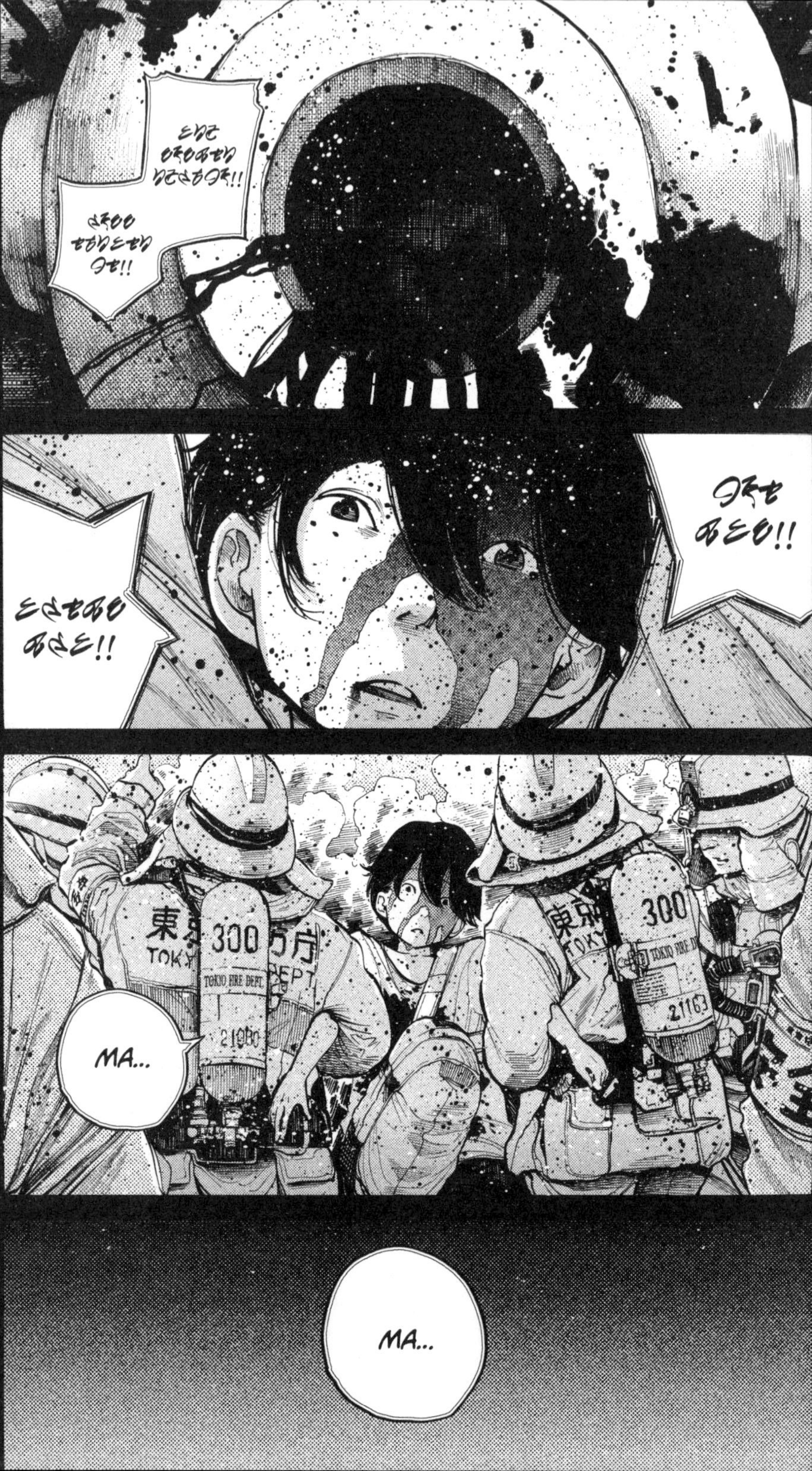
MA...
MA...

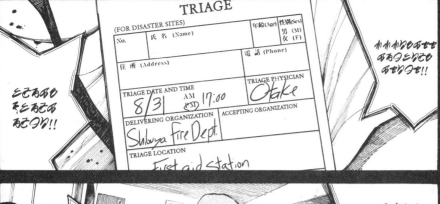

TRIAGE

(FOR DISASTER SITES)

No.	氏名 (Name)		年齢(Age)	性別(Sex)
				男 (M) 女 (F)

住 所 (Address)	電 話 (Phone)

TRIAGE DATE AND TIME	TRIAGE PHYSICIAN
8/31 AM 17:00	Otake

DELIVERING ORGANIZATION	ACCEPTING ORGANIZATION
Shibuya Fire Dept.	

TRIAGE LOCATION

First aid station

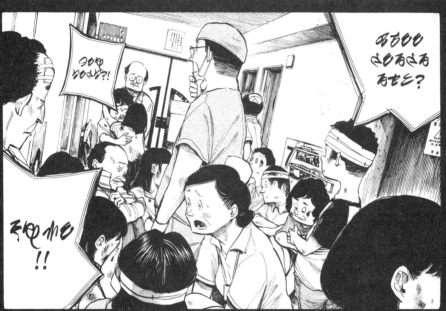

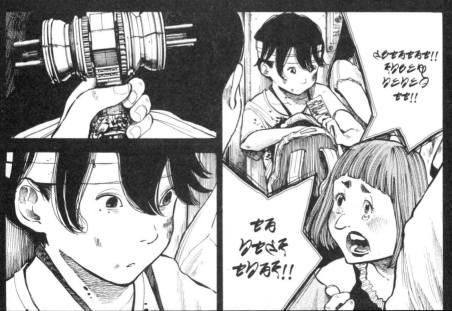

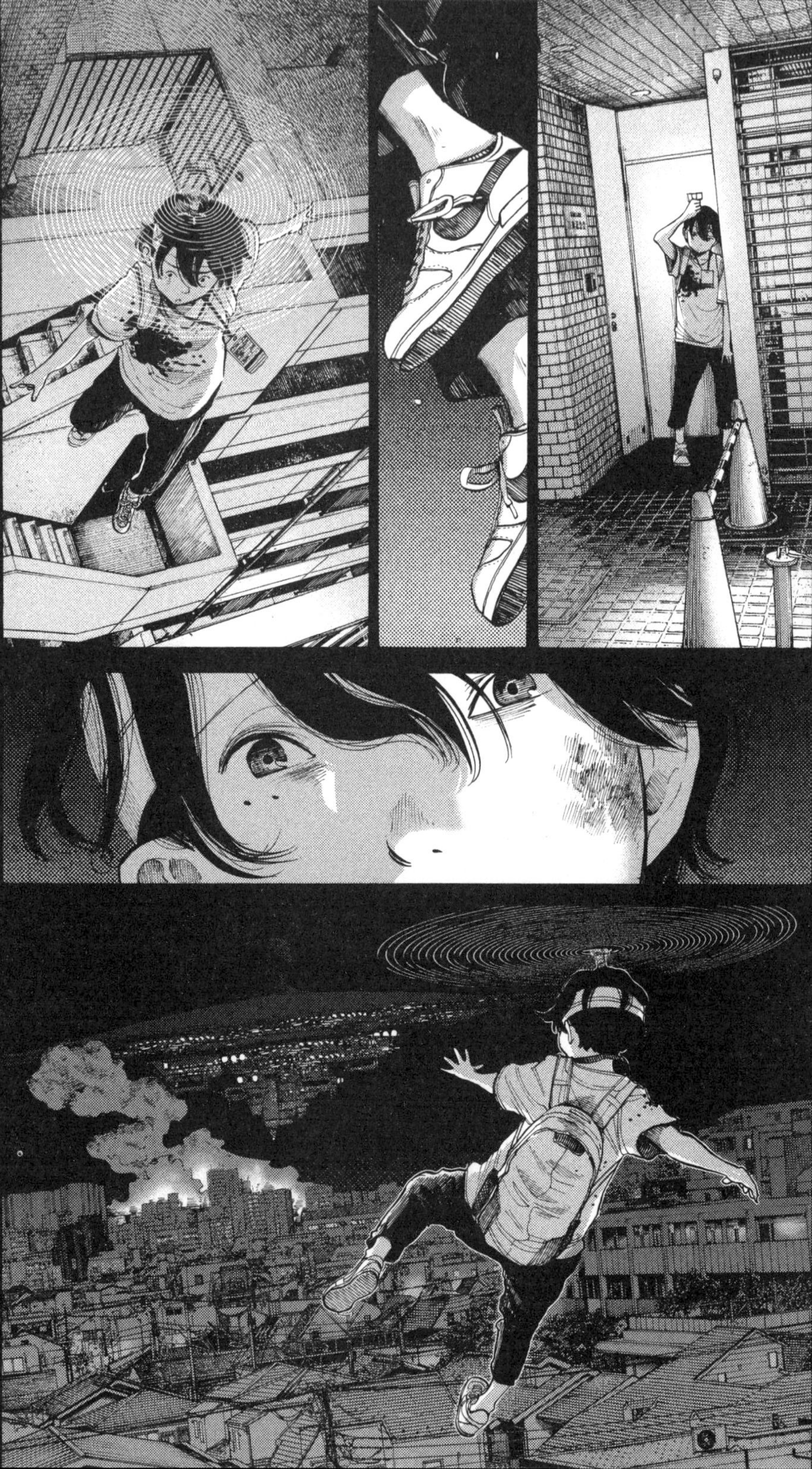

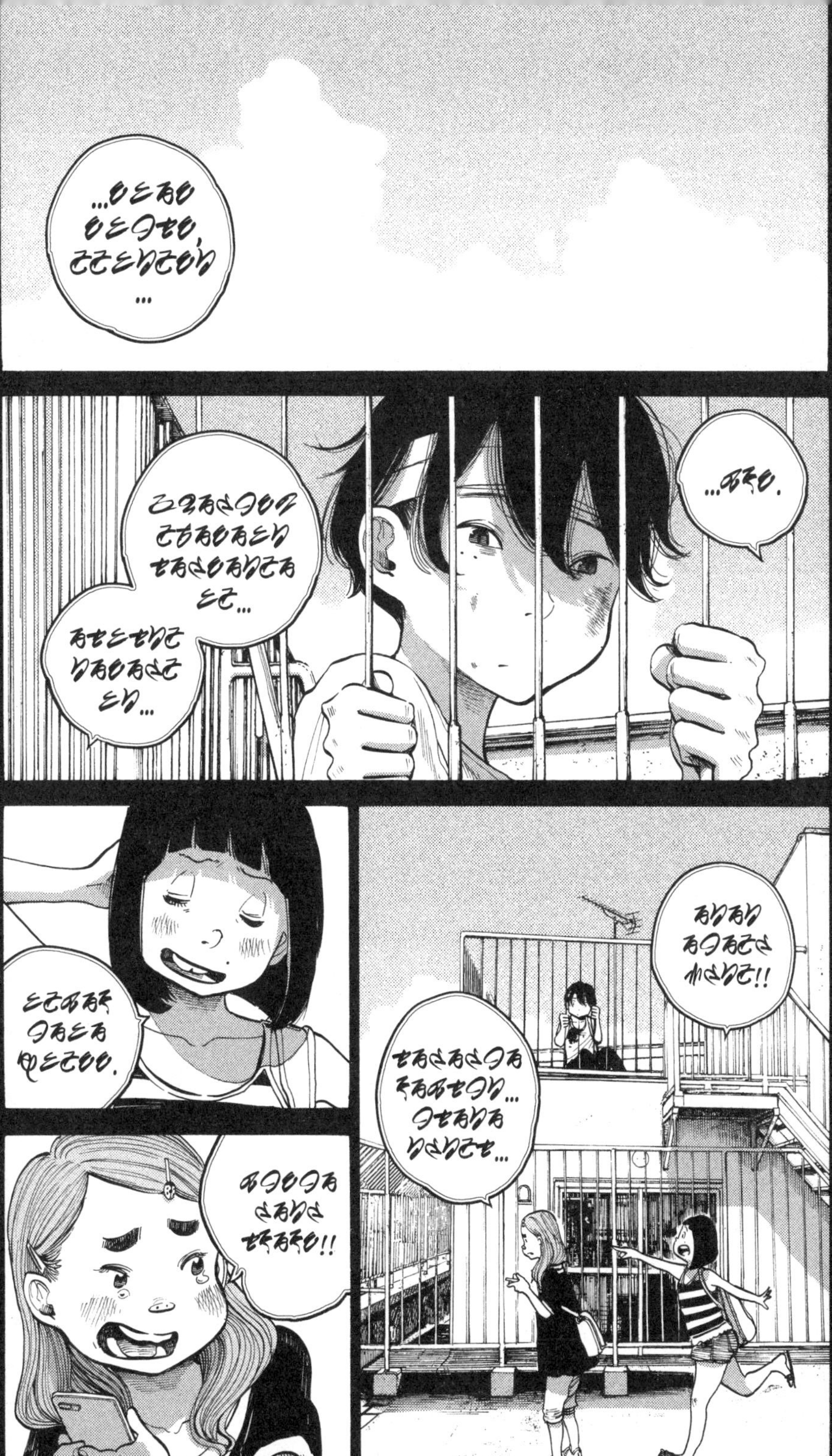

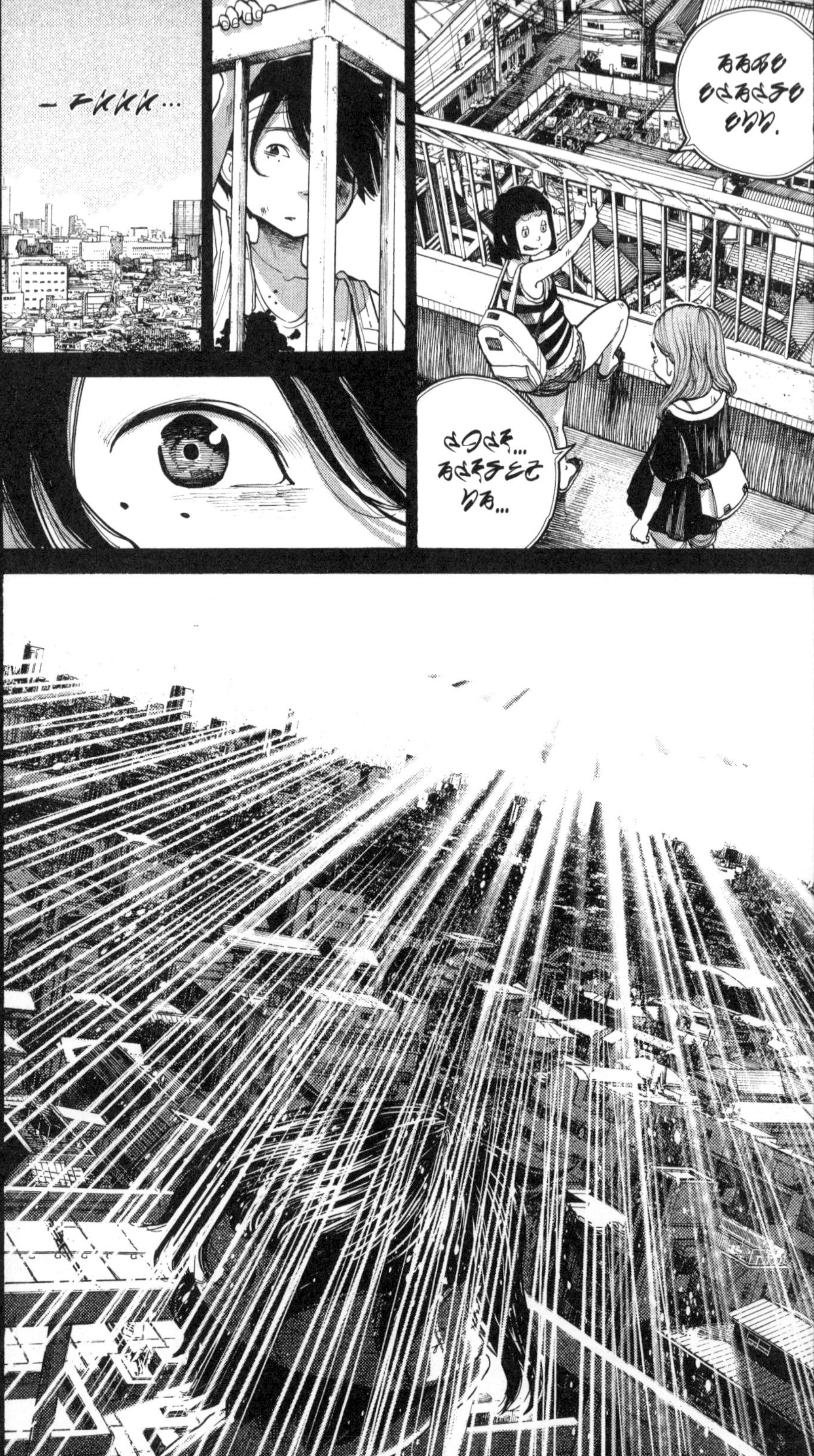

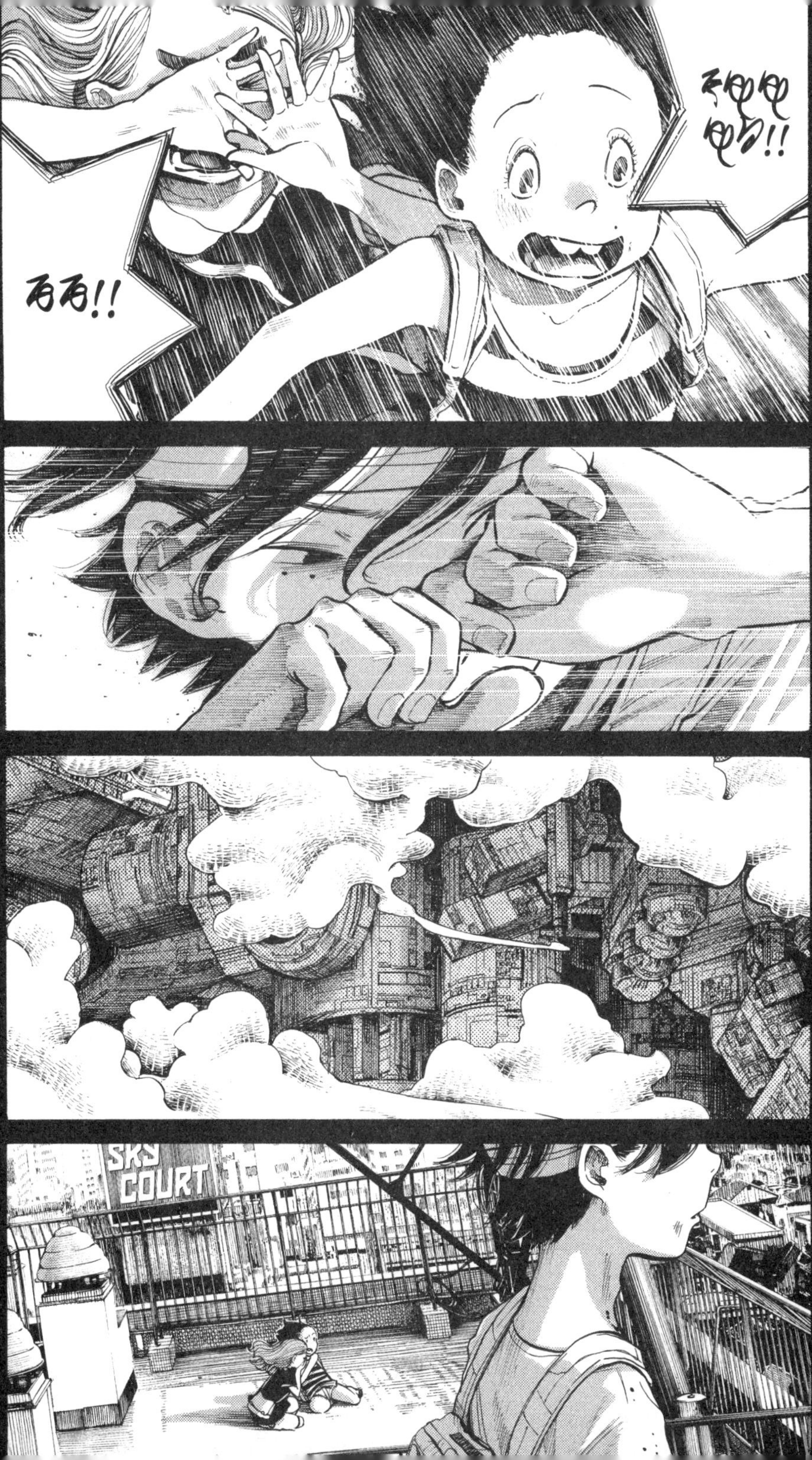

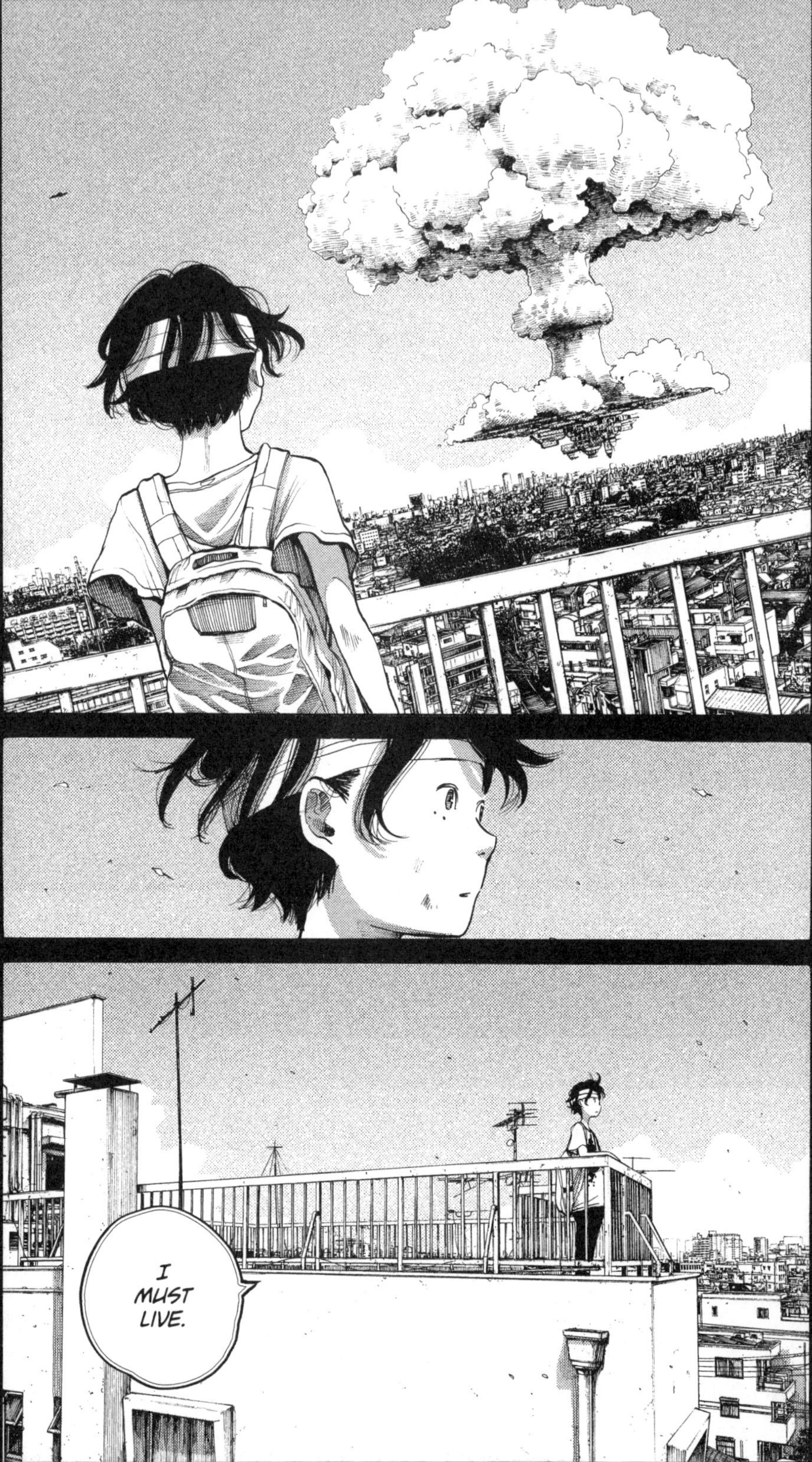
I MUST LIVE.

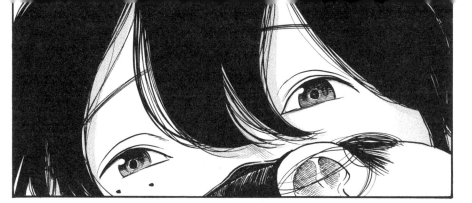

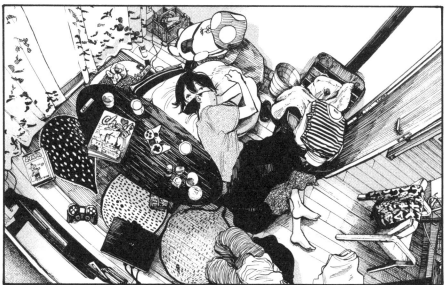

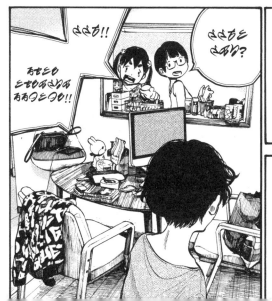

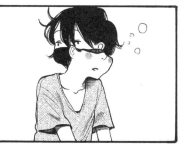

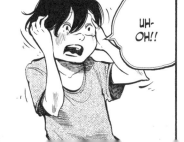

UH-OH!!

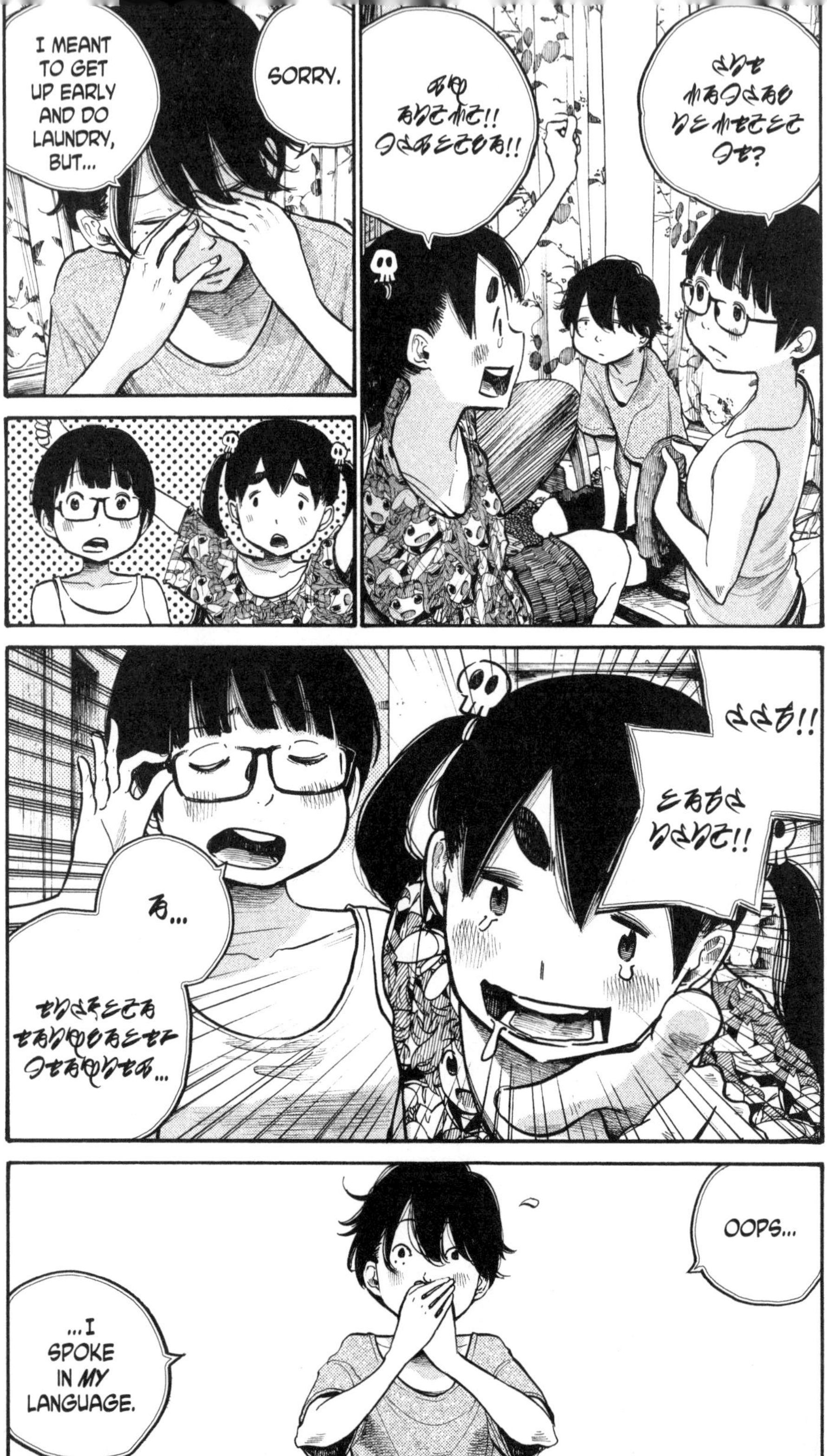
SORRY.
I MEANT TO GET UP EARLY AND DO LAUNDRY, BUT...
OOPS...
...I SPOKE IN *MY* LANGUAGE.

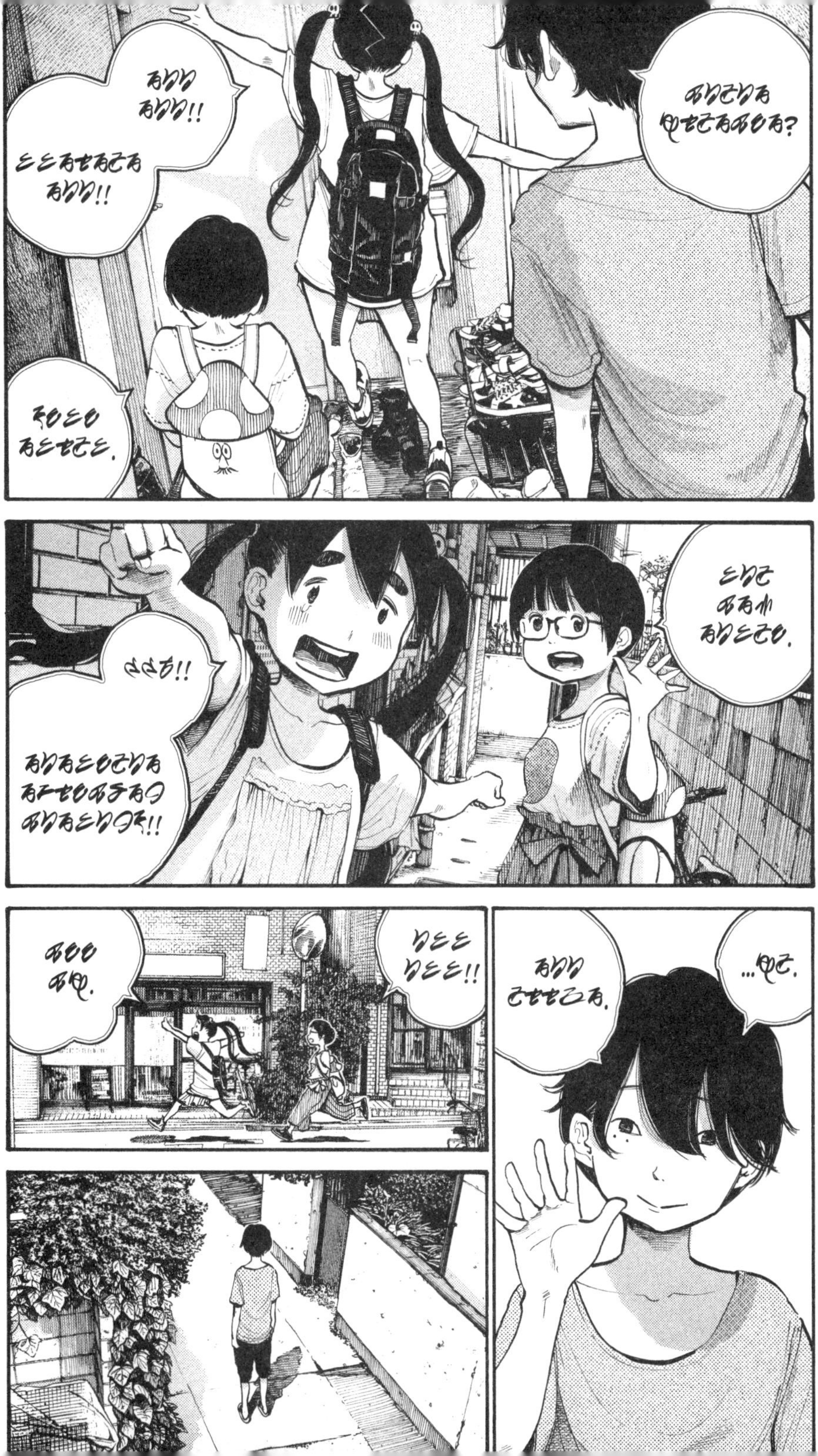

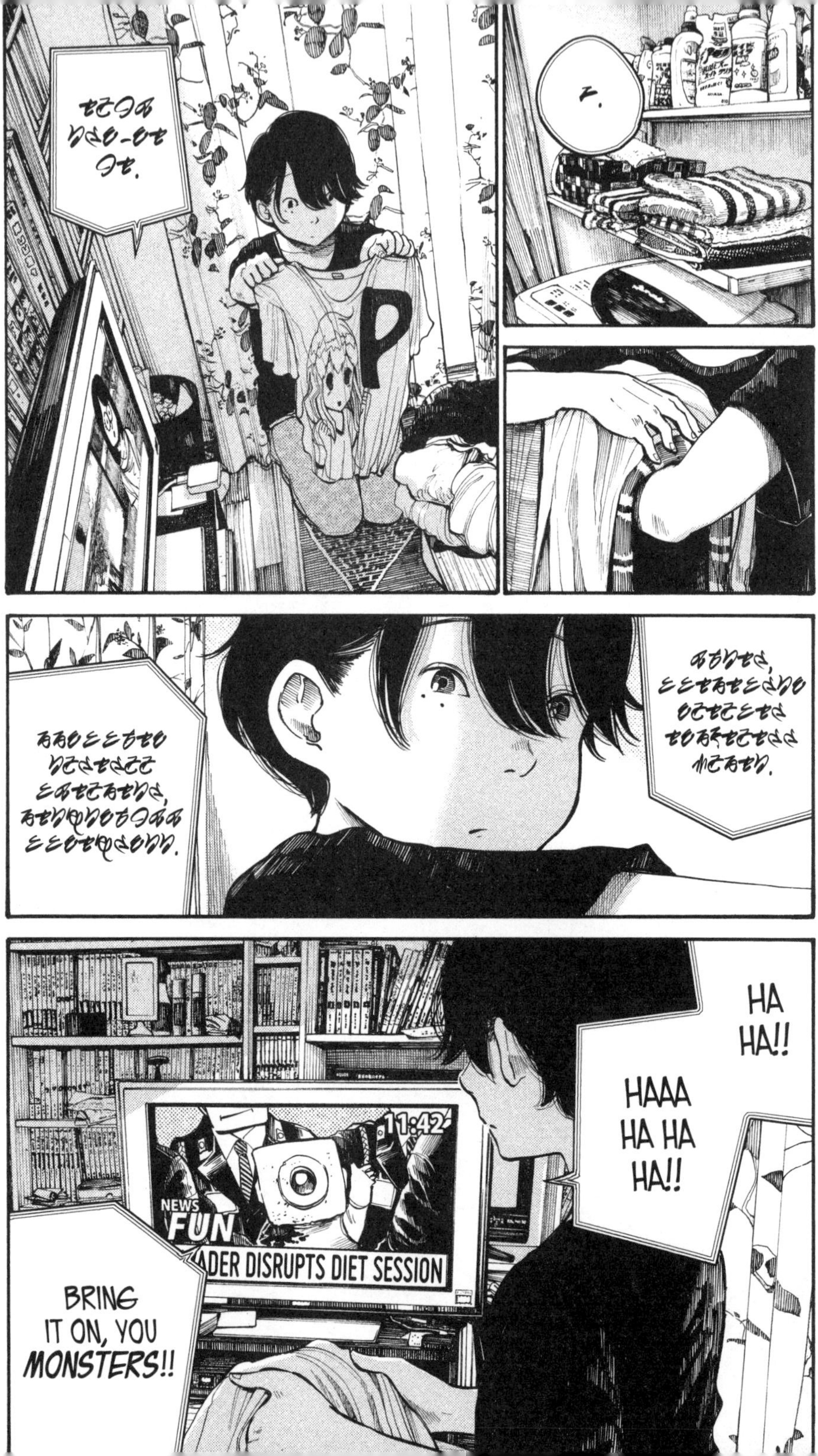
HA HA!!
HAAA HA HA HA!!
11:42
NEWS FUN
ADER DISRUPTS DIET SESSION
BRING IT ON, YOU MONSTERS!!

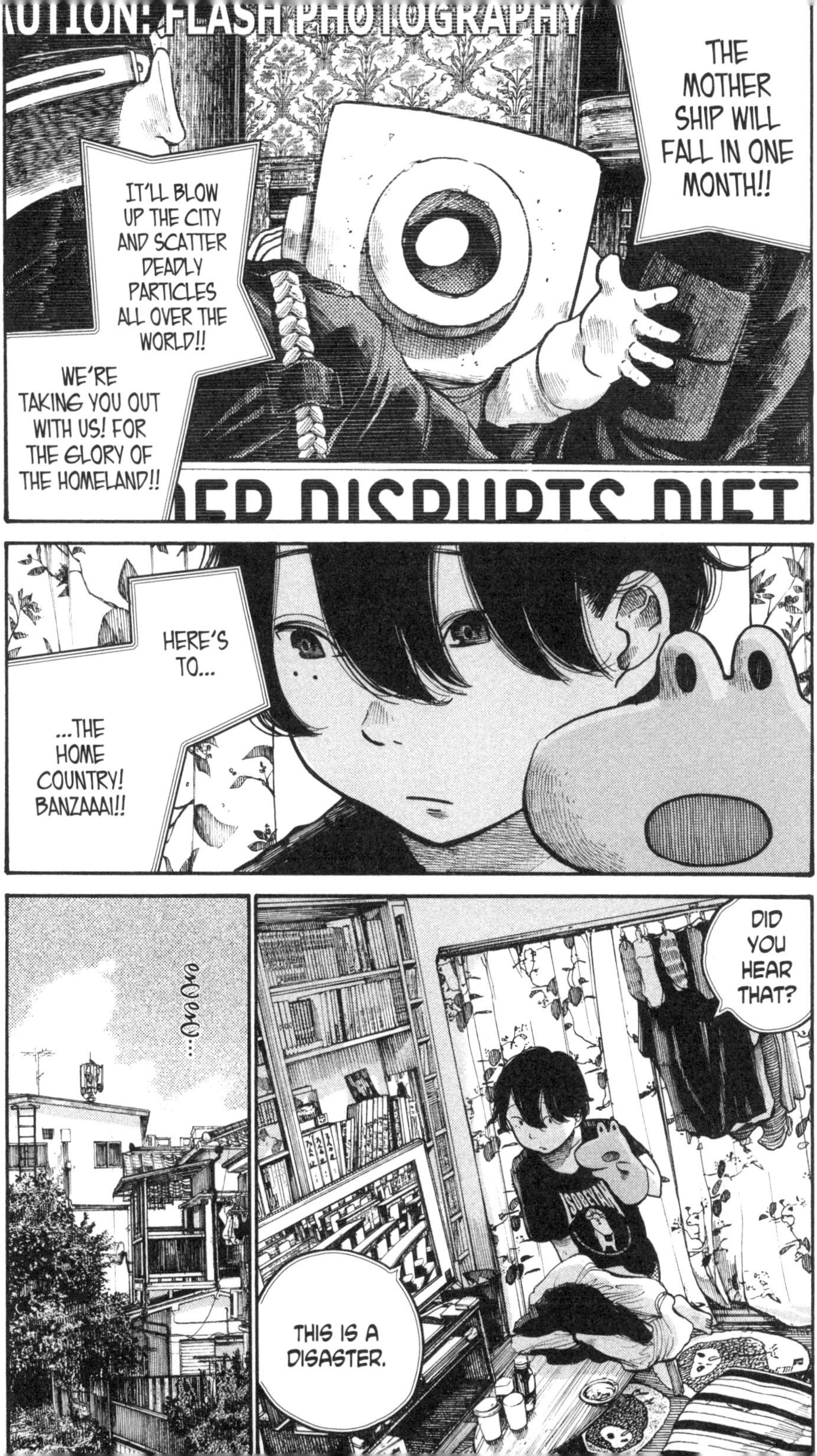
FLASH PHOTOGRAPHY
THE MOTHER SHIP WILL FALL IN ONE MONTH!!
IT'LL BLOW UP THE CITY AND SCATTER DEADLY PARTICLES ALL OVER THE WORLD!!
WE'RE TAKING YOU OUT WITH US! FOR THE GLORY OF THE HOMELAND!!
DISRUPTS DIET
HERE'S TO...
...THE HOME COUNTRY! BANZAAAI!!
DID YOU HEAR THAT?
THIS IS A DISASTER.

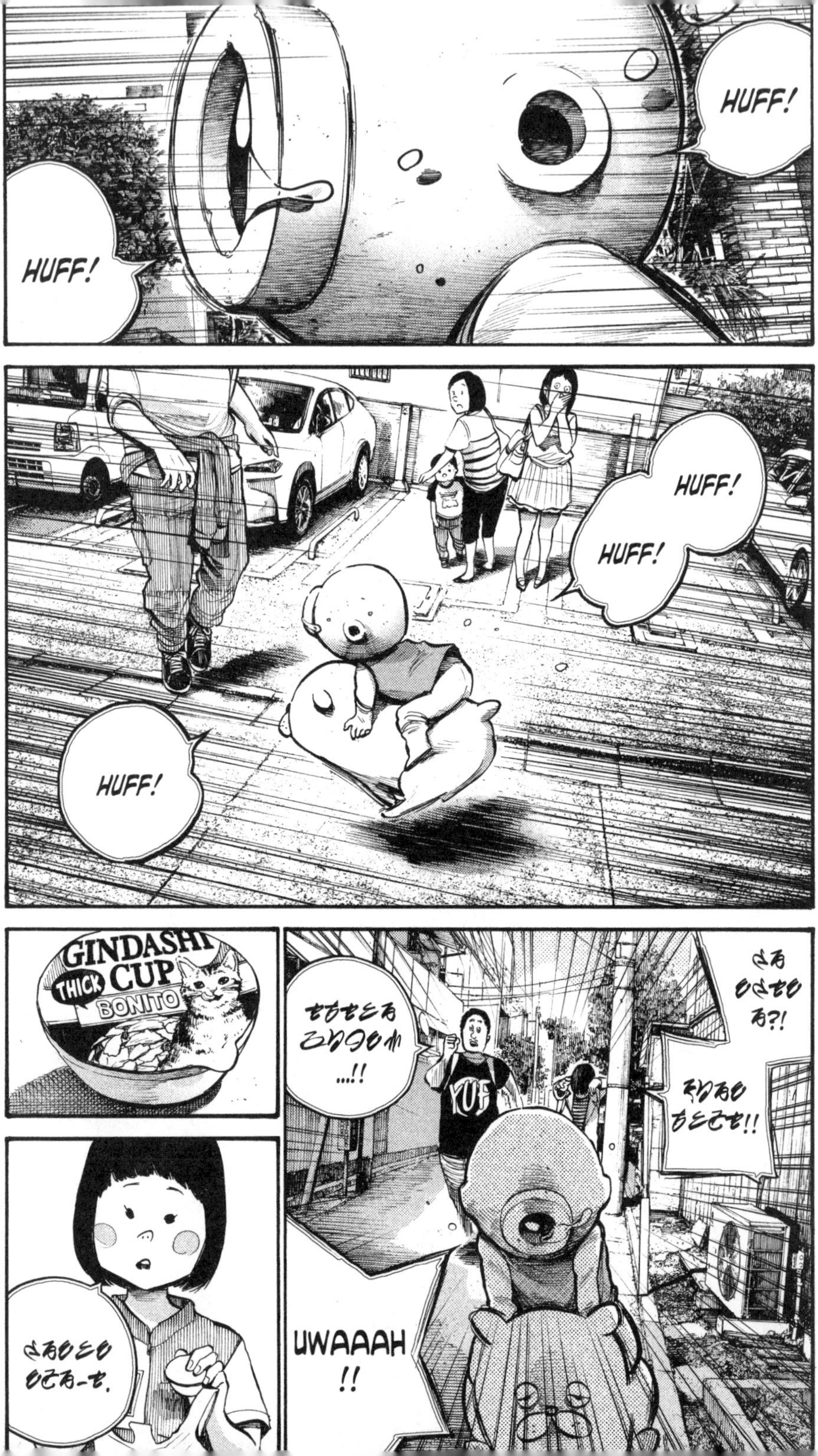
HUFF!
HUFF!
HUFF!
HUFF!
HUFF!
...!!
UWAAAH !!
GINDASHI CUP
THICK
BONITO

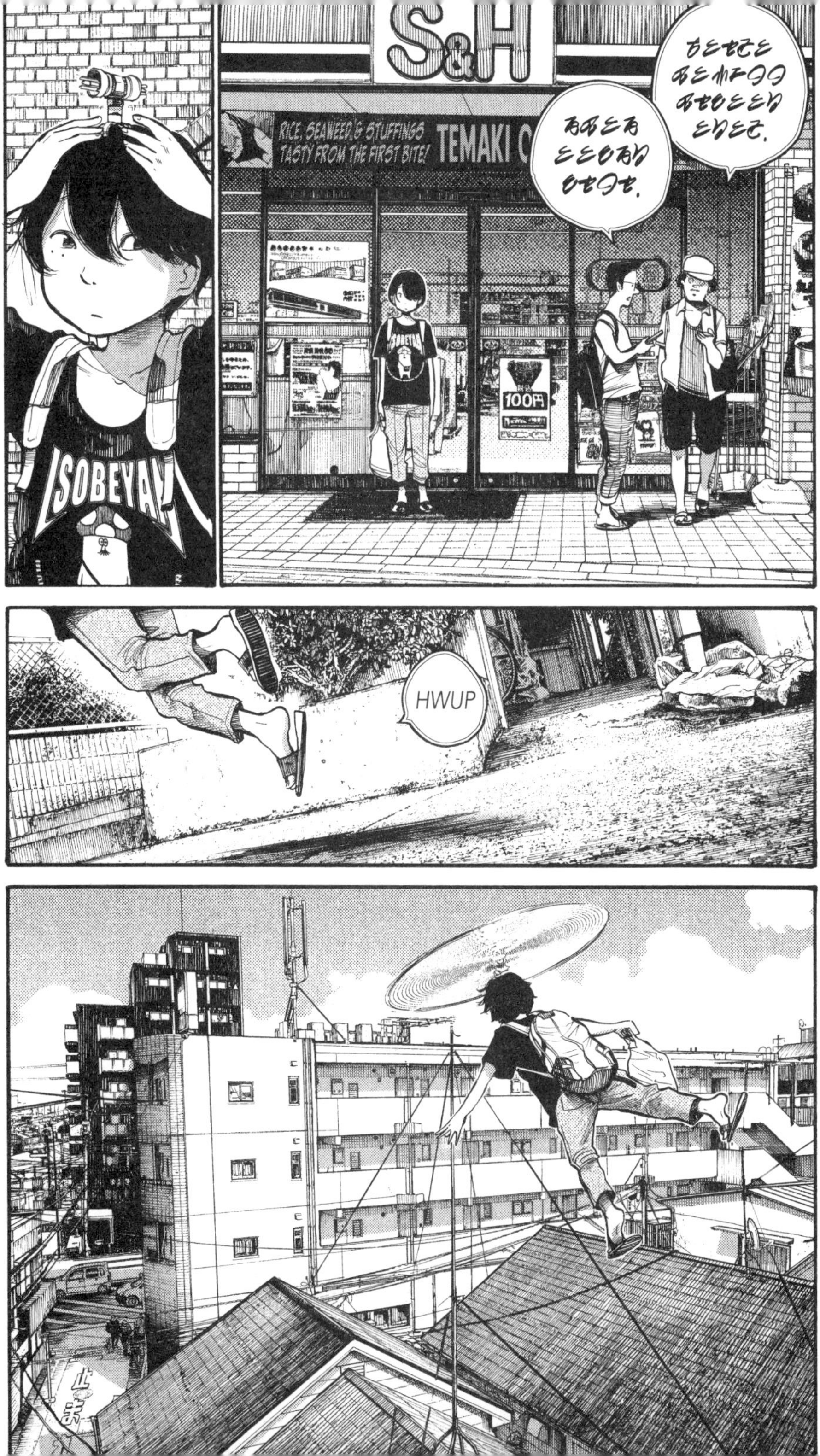
S&H
RICE, SEAWEED & STUFFINGS
TASTY FROM THE FIRST BITE!
TEMAKI C
100円
ISOBEYA
HWUP

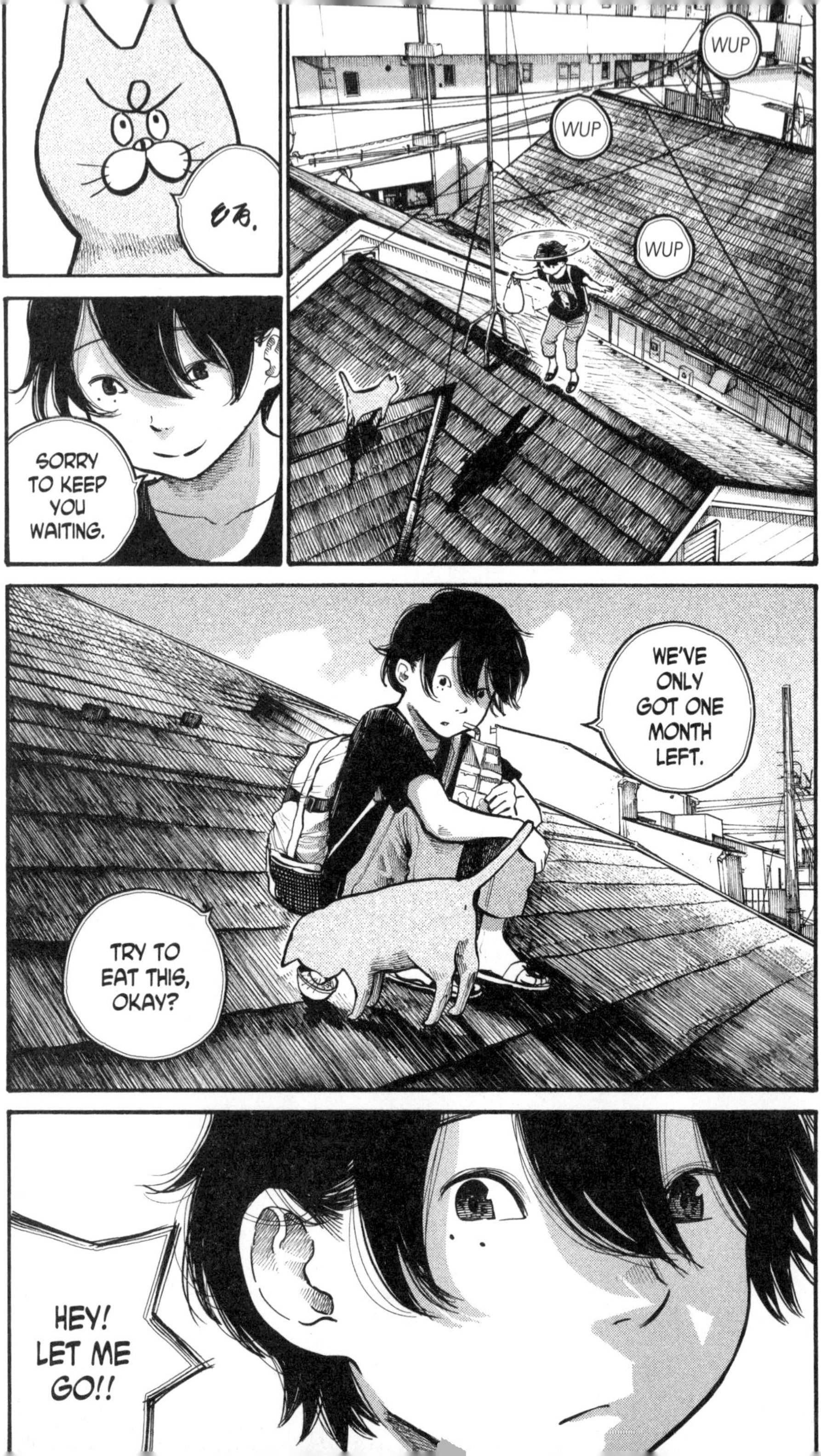
WUP
WUP
WUP
SORRY TO KEEP YOU WAITING.
WE'VE ONLY GOT ONE MONTH LEFT.
TRY TO EAT THIS, OKAY?
HEY! LET ME GO!!

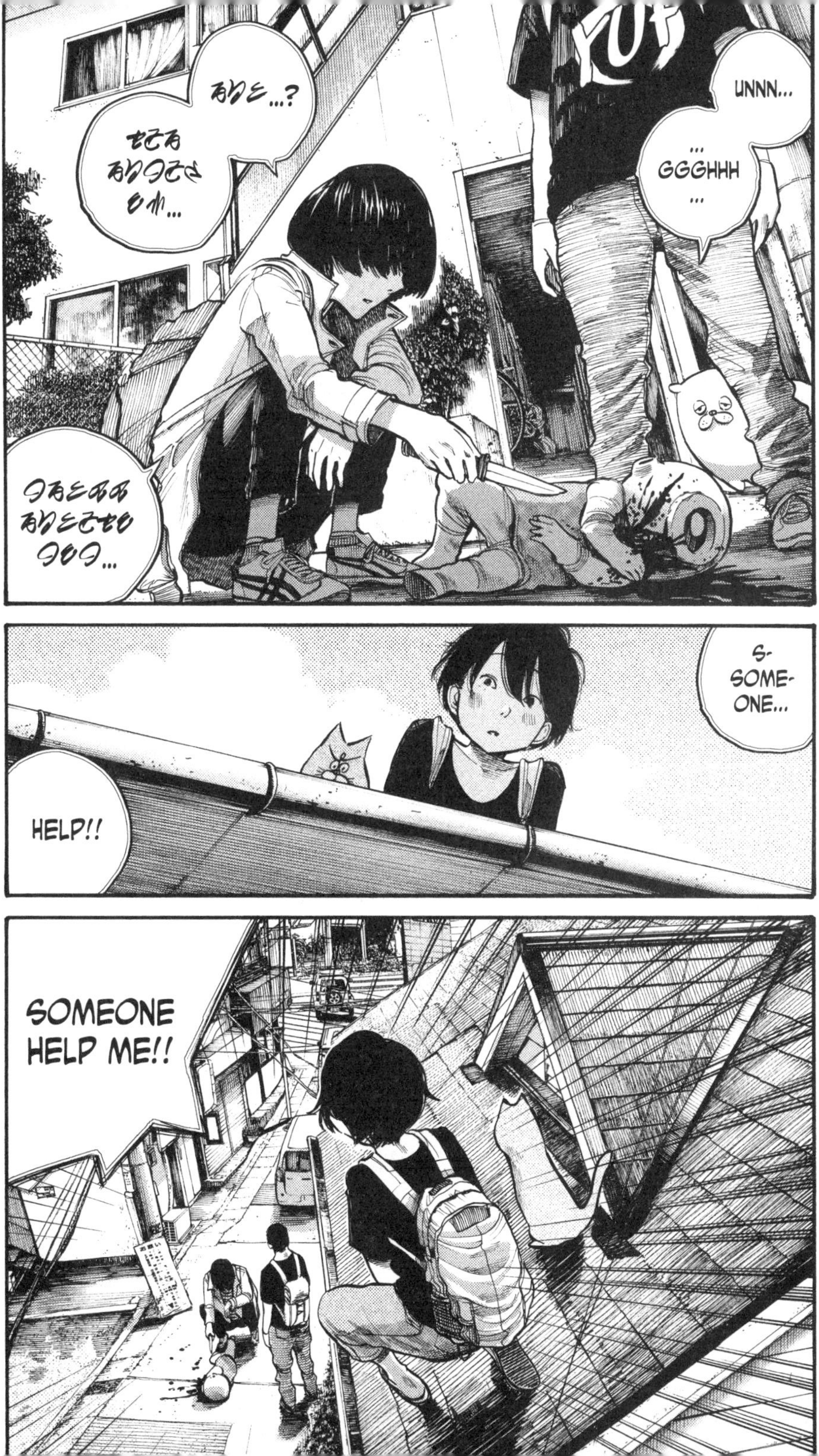
UNNN...
... GGGHHH ...
S-SOME-ONE...
HELP!!
SOMEONE HELP ME!!

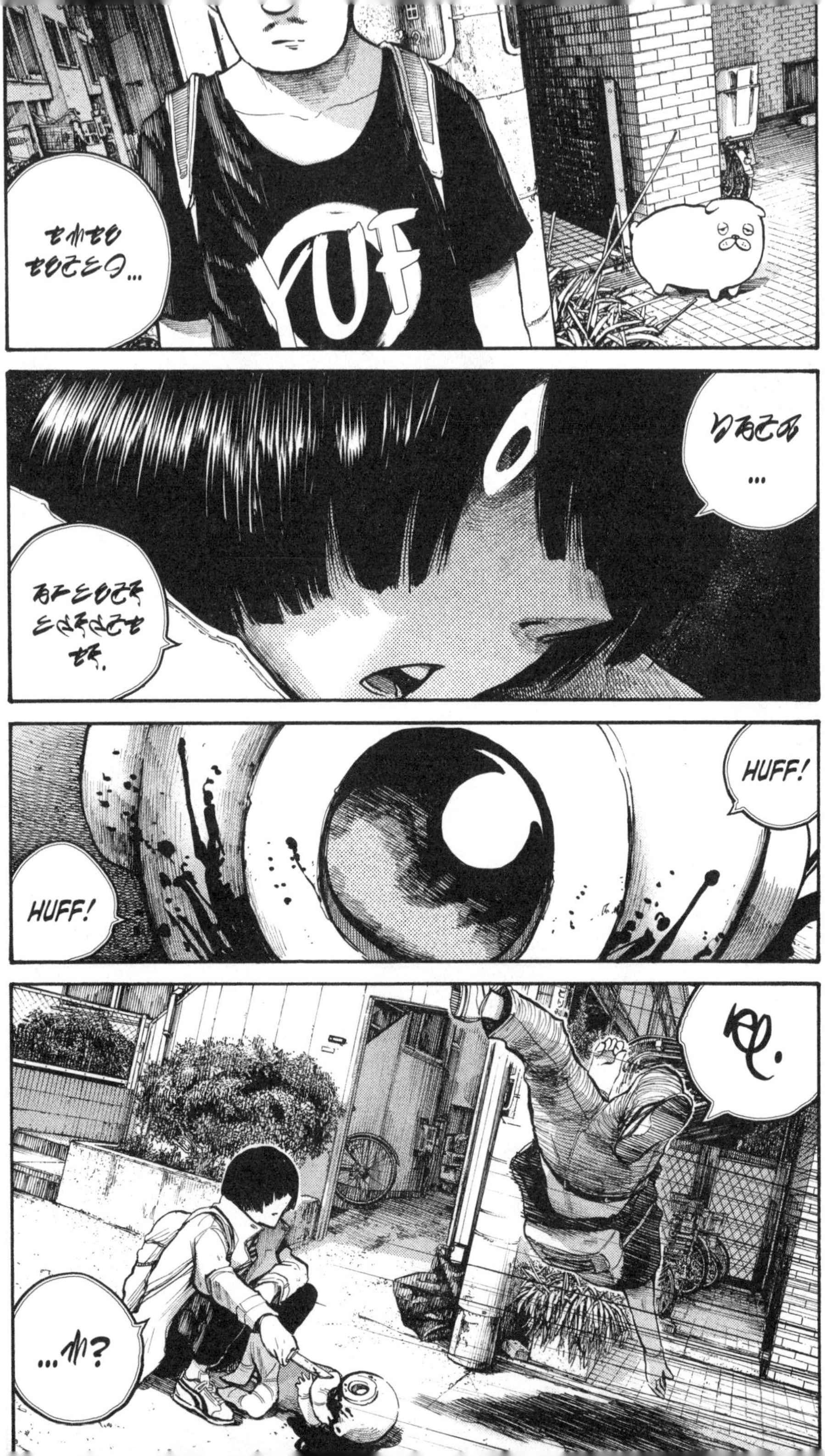
HUFF!
HUFF!

CHAPTER 48

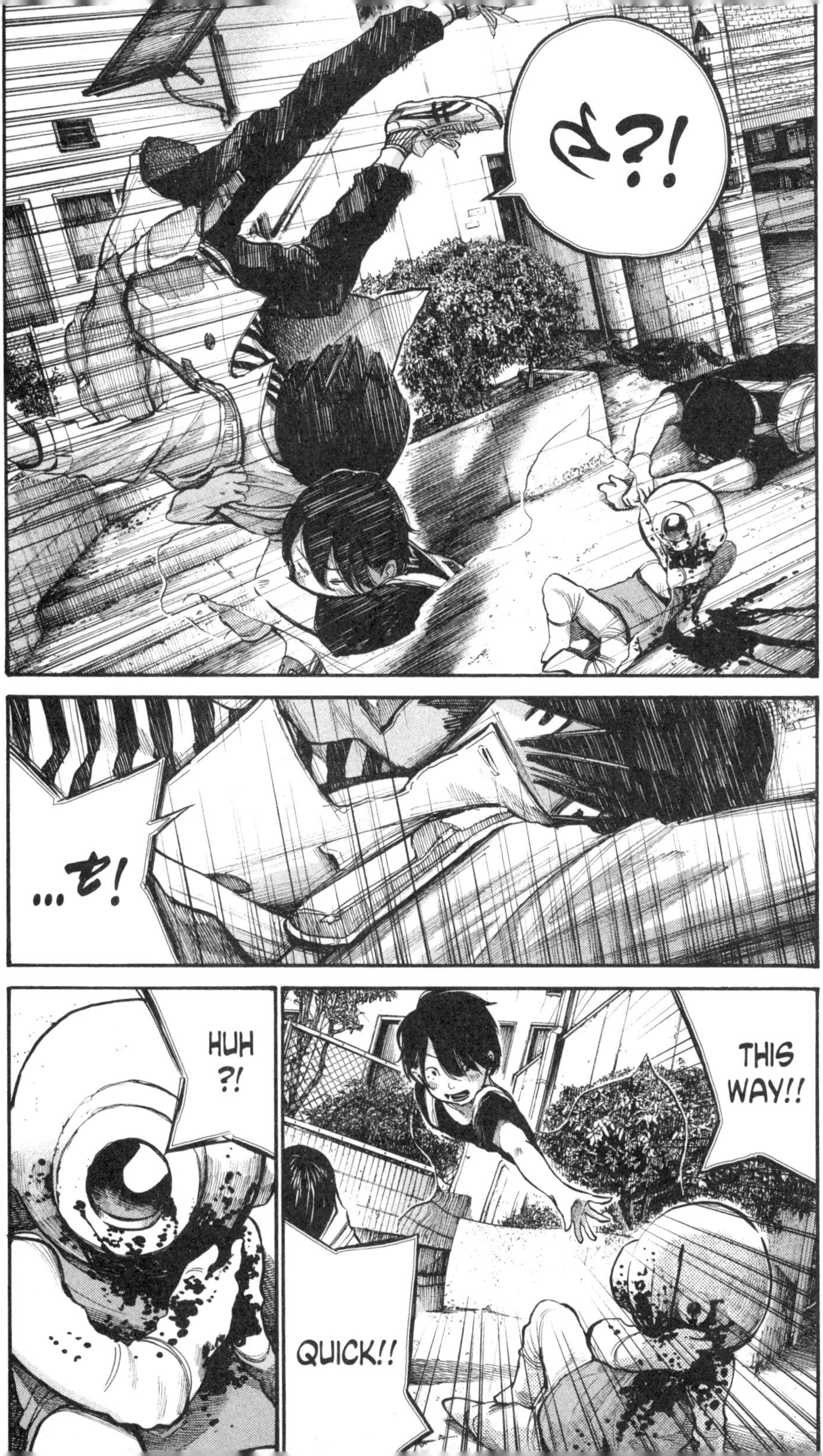
THIS WAY!!
QUICK!!
HUH ?!

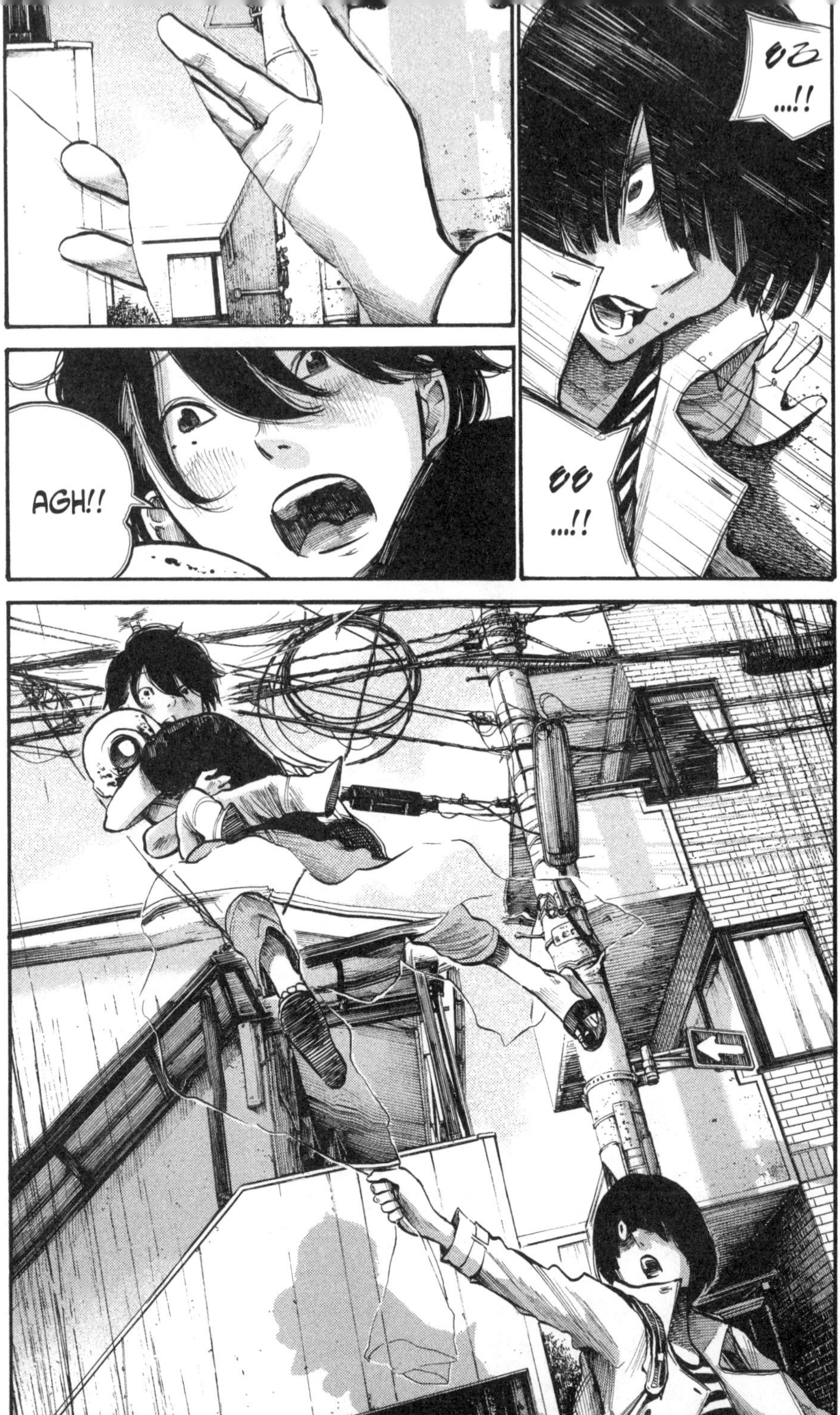
OO ...!!
OO ...!!
AGH!!

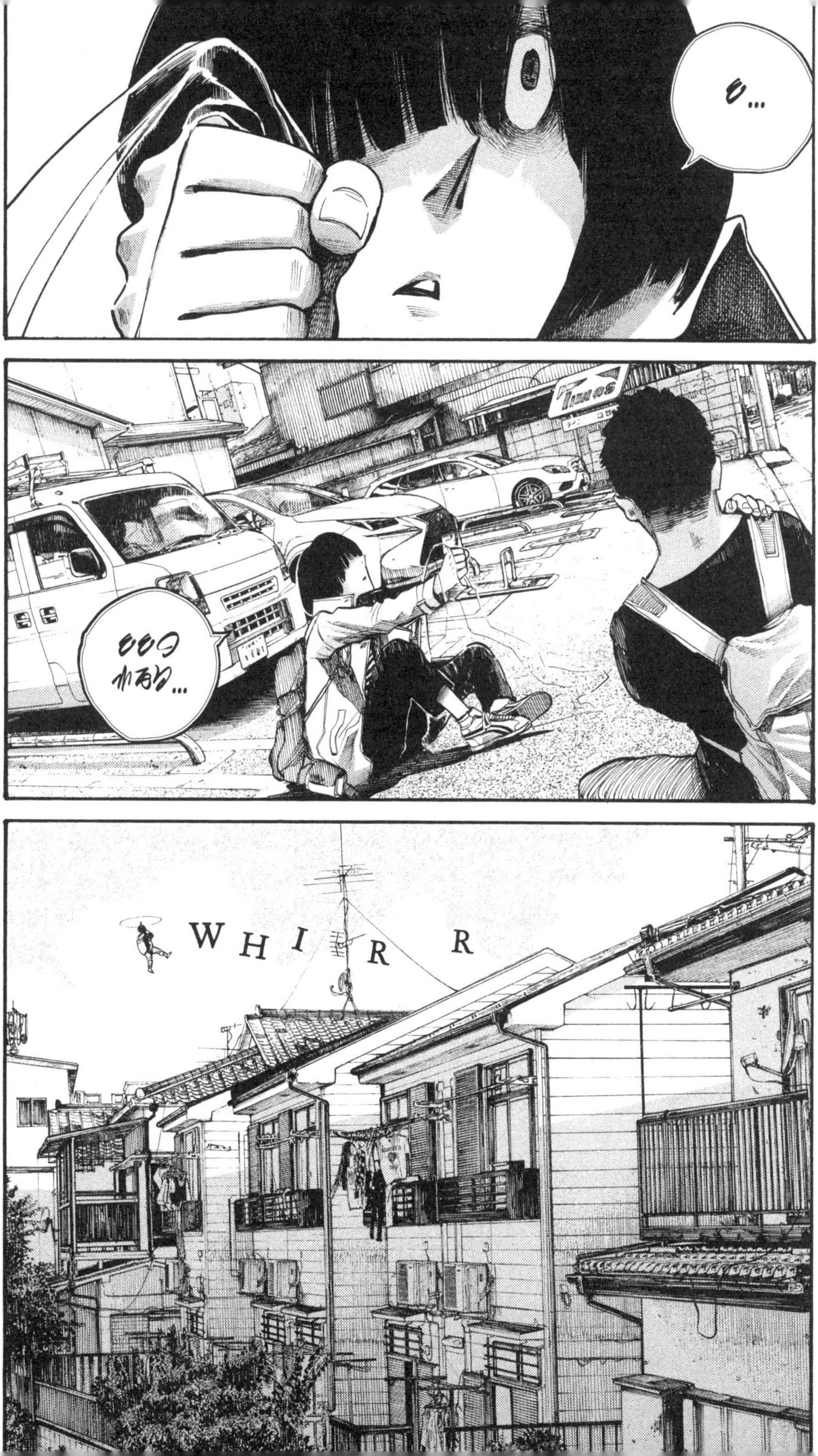
WHIRR

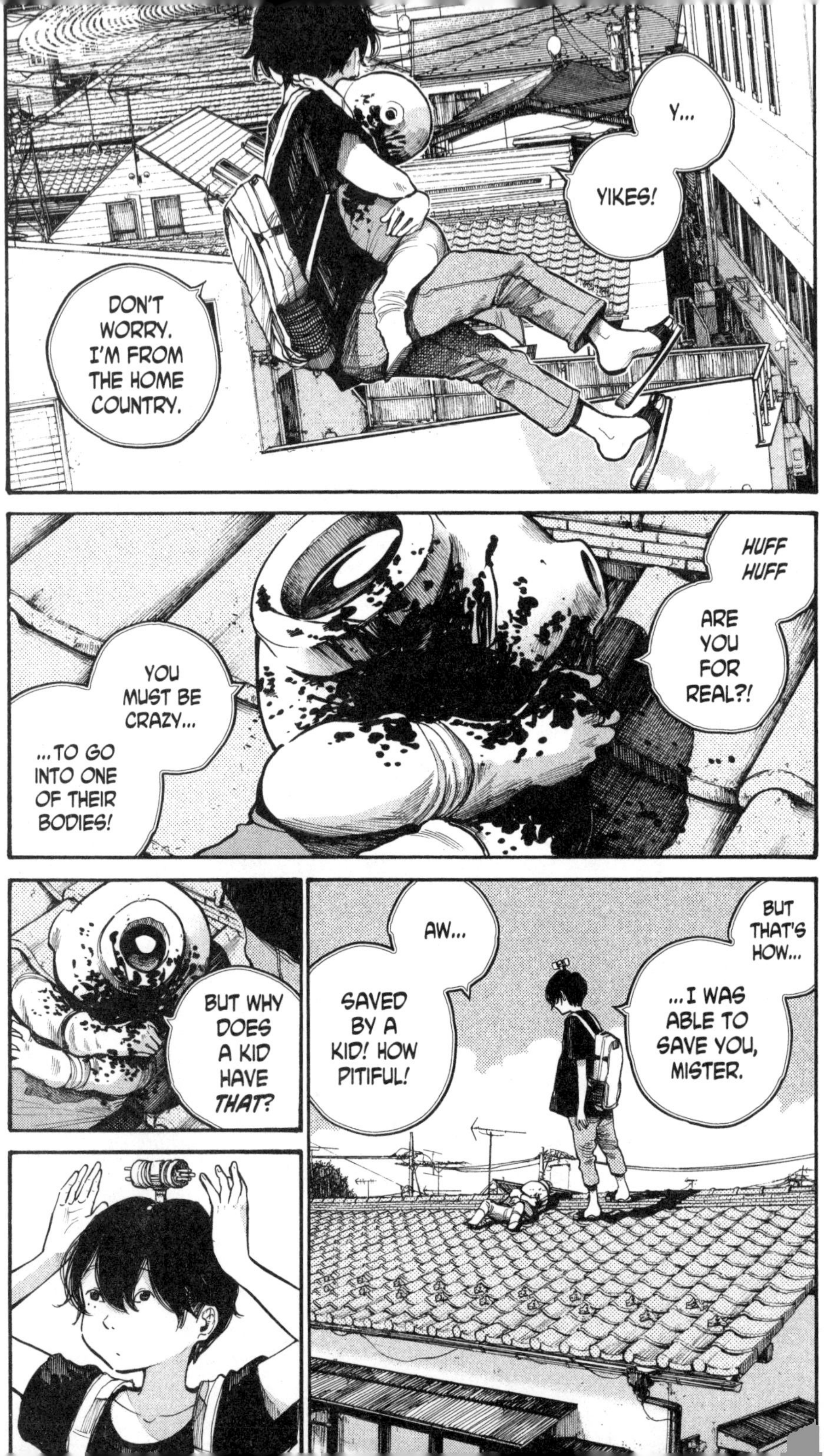
Y...
YIKES!
DON'T WORRY. I'M FROM THE HOME COUNTRY.
HUFF HUFF
ARE YOU FOR REAL?!
YOU MUST BE CRAZY...
...TO GO INTO ONE OF THEIR BODIES!
BUT THAT'S HOW...
...I WAS ABLE TO SAVE YOU, MISTER.
AW...
SAVED BY A KID! HOW PITIFUL!
BUT WHY DOES A KID HAVE *THAT*?

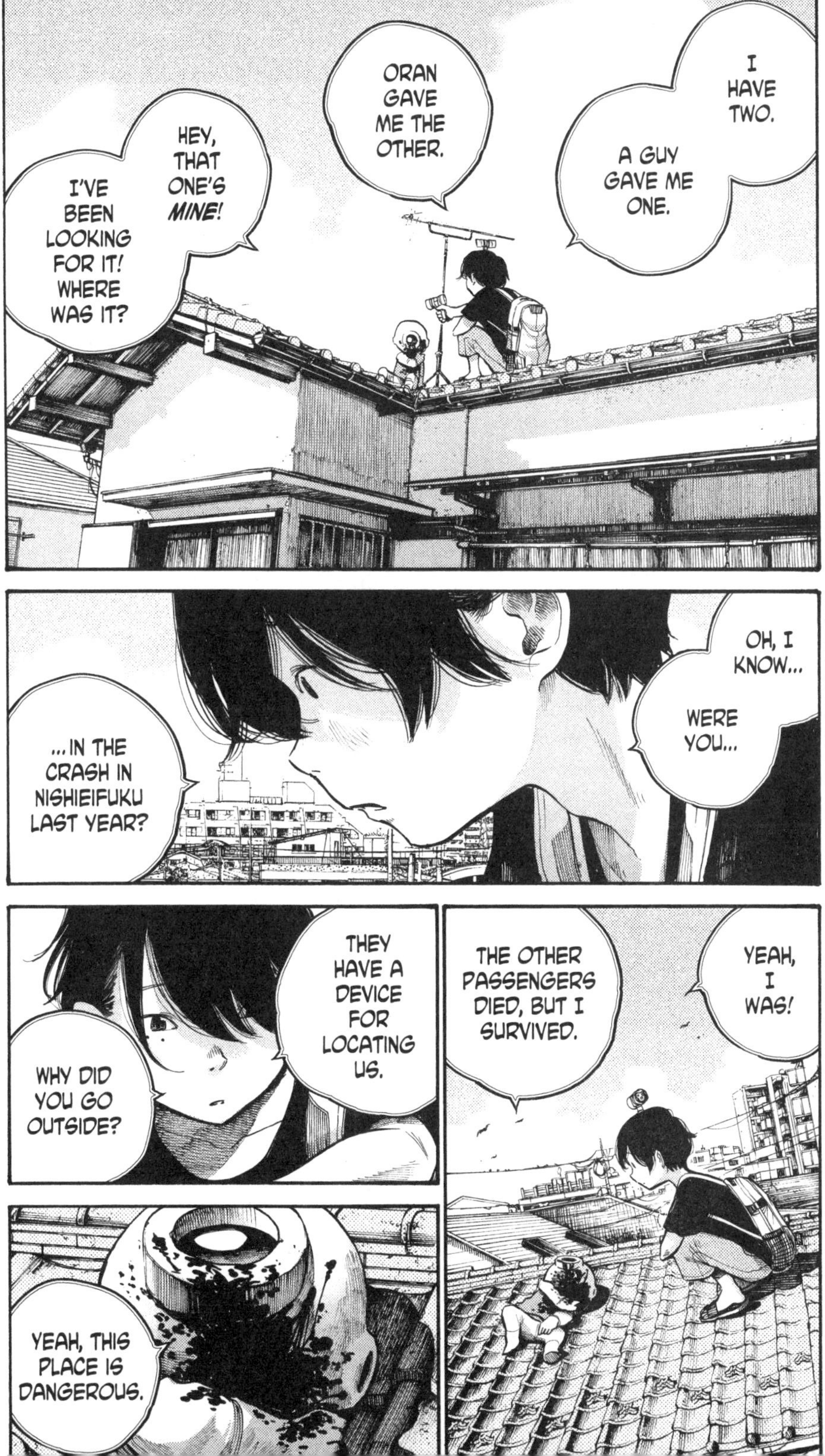
I HAVE TWO.
A GUY GAVE ME ONE.
ORAN GAVE ME THE OTHER.
HEY, THAT ONE'S *MINE*!
I'VE BEEN LOOKING FOR IT! WHERE WAS IT?
OH, I KNOW...
WERE YOU...
...IN THE CRASH IN NISHIEIFUKU LAST YEAR?
YEAH, I WAS!
THE OTHER PASSENGERS DIED, BUT I SURVIVED.
THEY HAVE A DEVICE FOR LOCATING US.
WHY DID YOU GO OUTSIDE?
YEAH, THIS PLACE IS DANGEROUS.

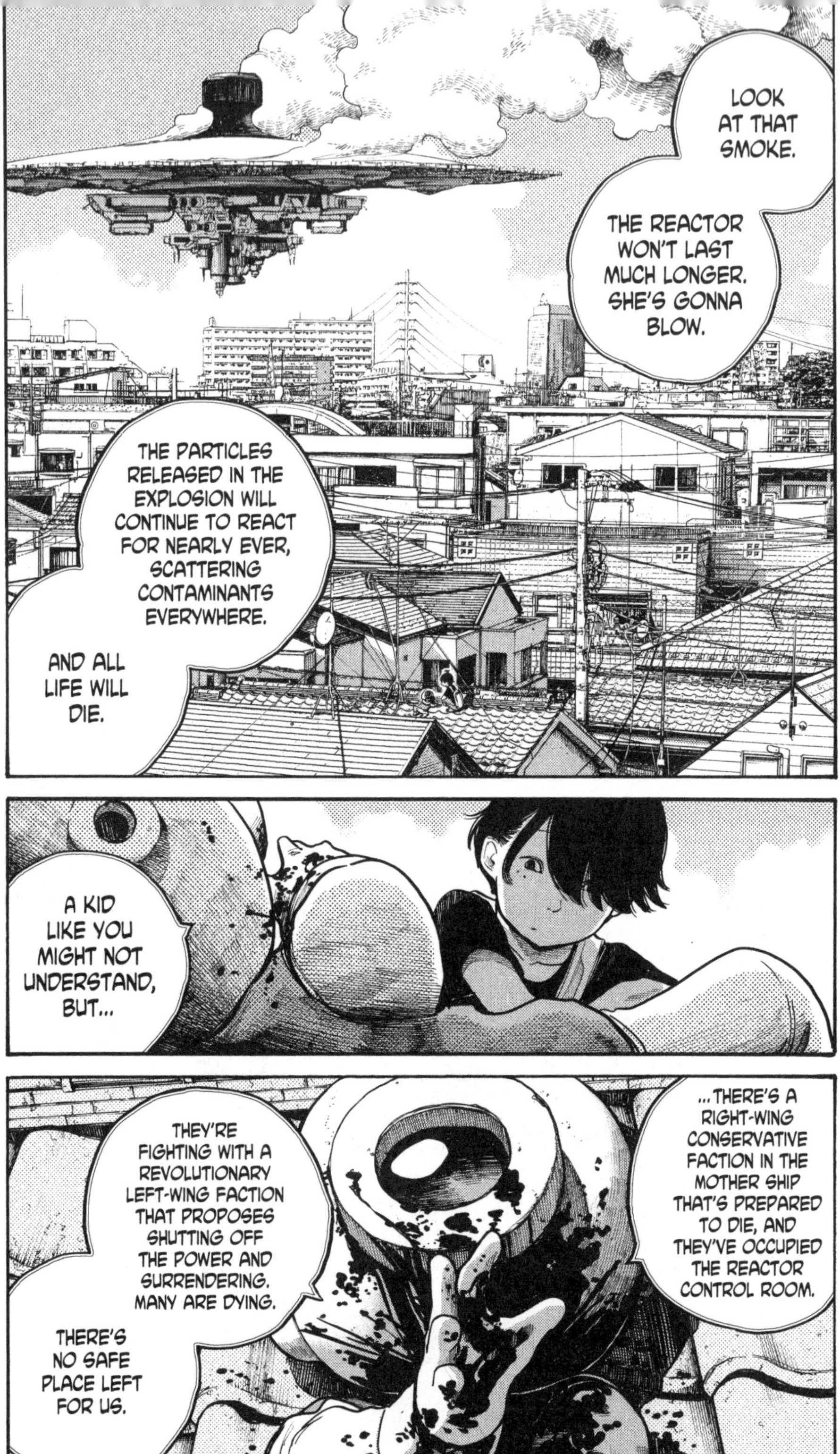
LOOK AT THAT SMOKE.
THE REACTOR WON'T LAST MUCH LONGER. SHE'S GONNA BLOW.
THE PARTICLES RELEASED IN THE EXPLOSION WILL CONTINUE TO REACT FOR NEARLY EVER, SCATTERING CONTAMINANTS EVERYWHERE.
AND ALL LIFE WILL DIE.
A KID LIKE YOU MIGHT NOT UNDERSTAND, BUT...
...THERE'S A RIGHT-WING CONSERVATIVE FACTION IN THE MOTHER SHIP THAT'S PREPARED TO DIE, AND THEY'VE OCCUPIED THE REACTOR CONTROL ROOM.
THEY'RE FIGHTING WITH A REVOLUTIONARY LEFT-WING FACTION THAT PROPOSES SHUTTING OFF THE POWER AND SURRENDERING. MANY ARE DYING.
THERE'S NO SAFE PLACE LEFT FOR US.

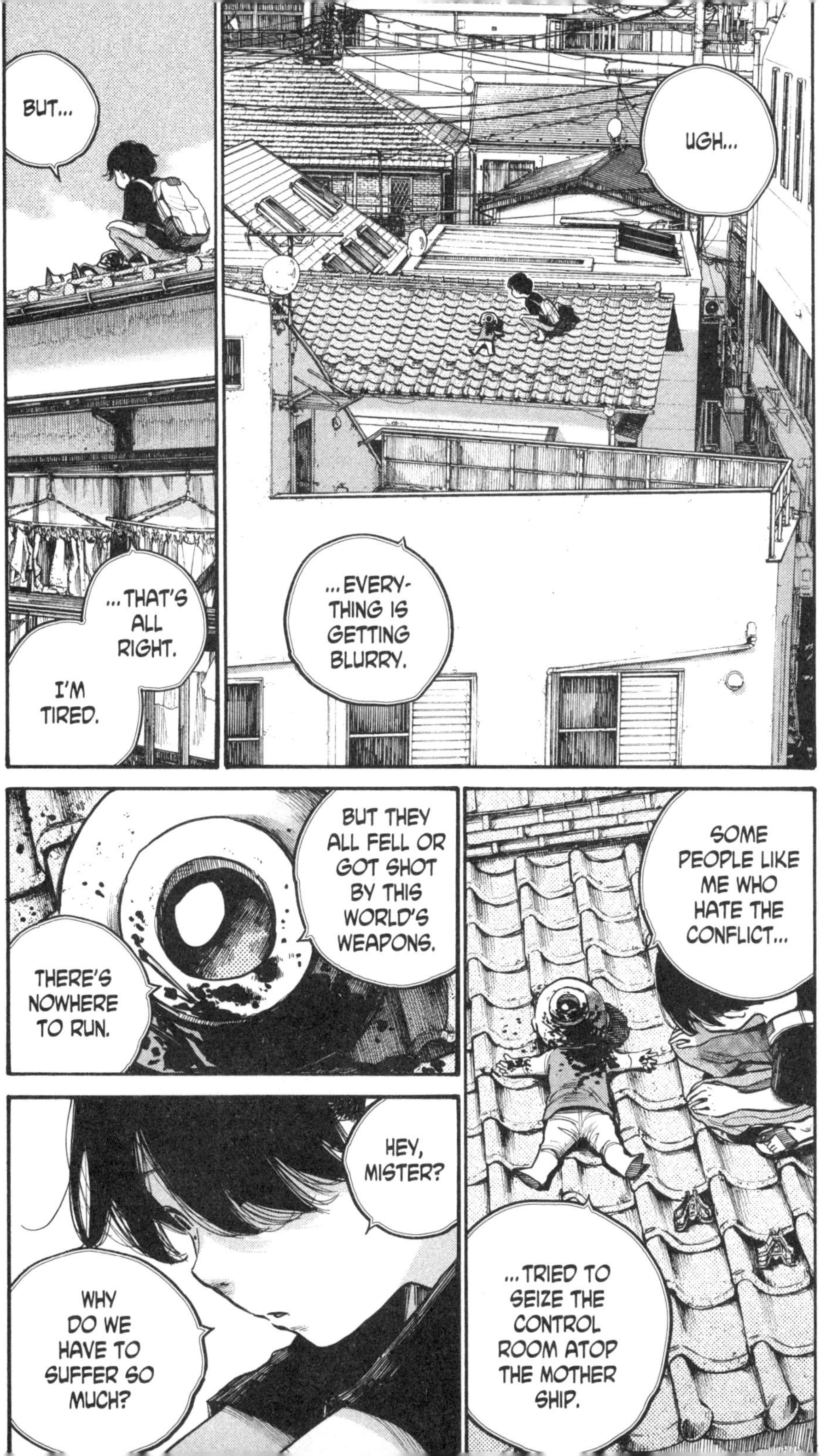
UGH...
...EVERYTHING IS GETTING BLURRY.
BUT...
...THAT'S ALL RIGHT.
I'M TIRED.
SOME PEOPLE LIKE ME WHO HATE THE CONFLICT...
...TRIED TO SEIZE THE CONTROL ROOM ATOP THE MOTHER SHIP.
BUT THEY ALL FELL OR GOT SHOT BY THIS WORLD'S WEAPONS.
THERE'S NOWHERE TO RUN.
HEY, MISTER?
WHY DO WE HAVE TO SUFFER SO MUCH?

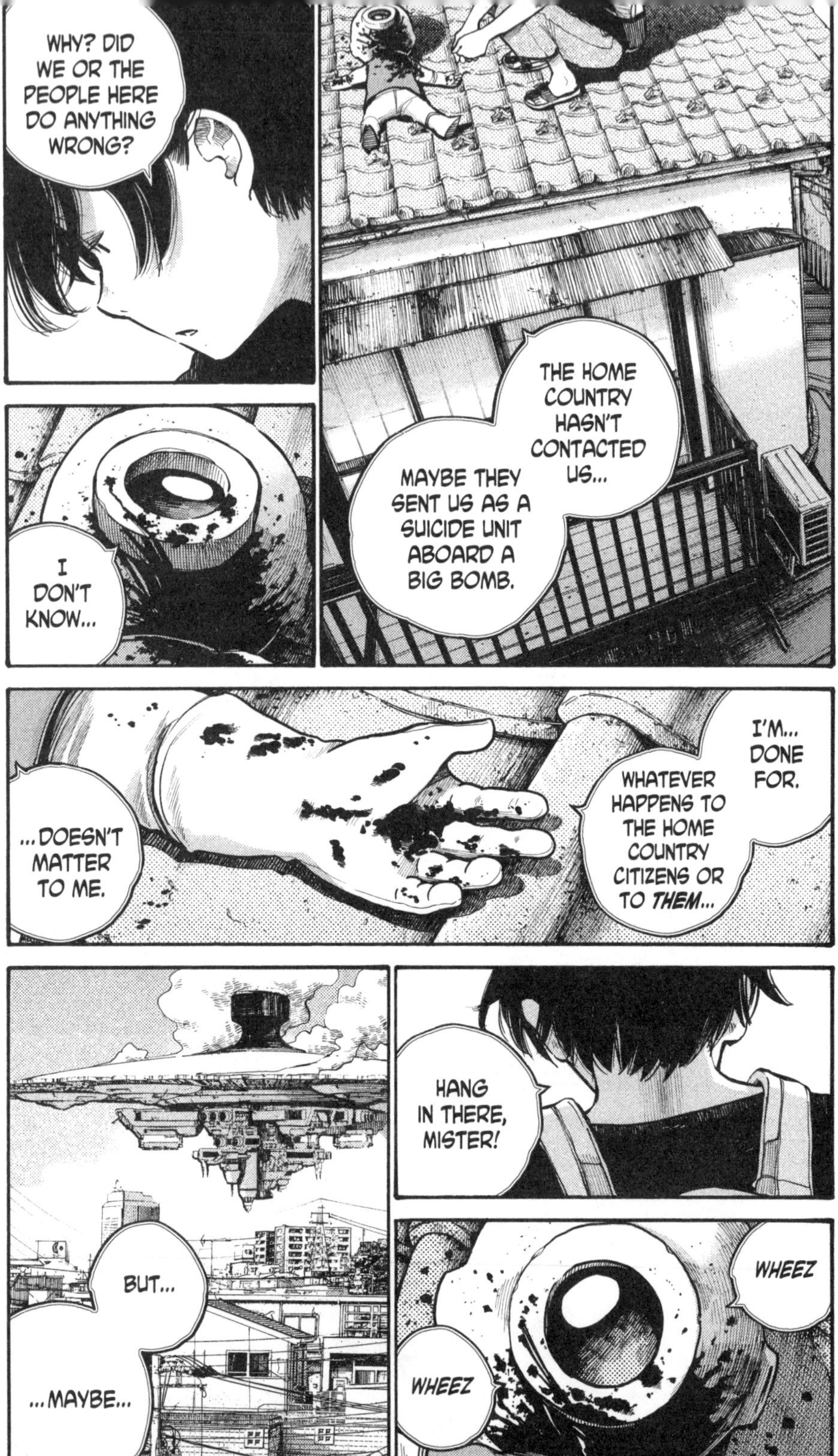
THE HOME COUNTRY HASN'T CONTACTED US...
MAYBE THEY SENT US AS A SUICIDE UNIT ABOARD A BIG BOMB.
WHY? DID WE OR THE PEOPLE HERE DO ANYTHING WRONG?
I DON'T KNOW...
I'M... DONE FOR.
WHATEVER HAPPENS TO THE HOME COUNTRY CITIZENS OR TO *THEM*...
...DOESN'T MATTER TO ME.
HANG IN THERE, MISTER!
WHEEZ
WHEEZ
BUT...
...MAYBE...

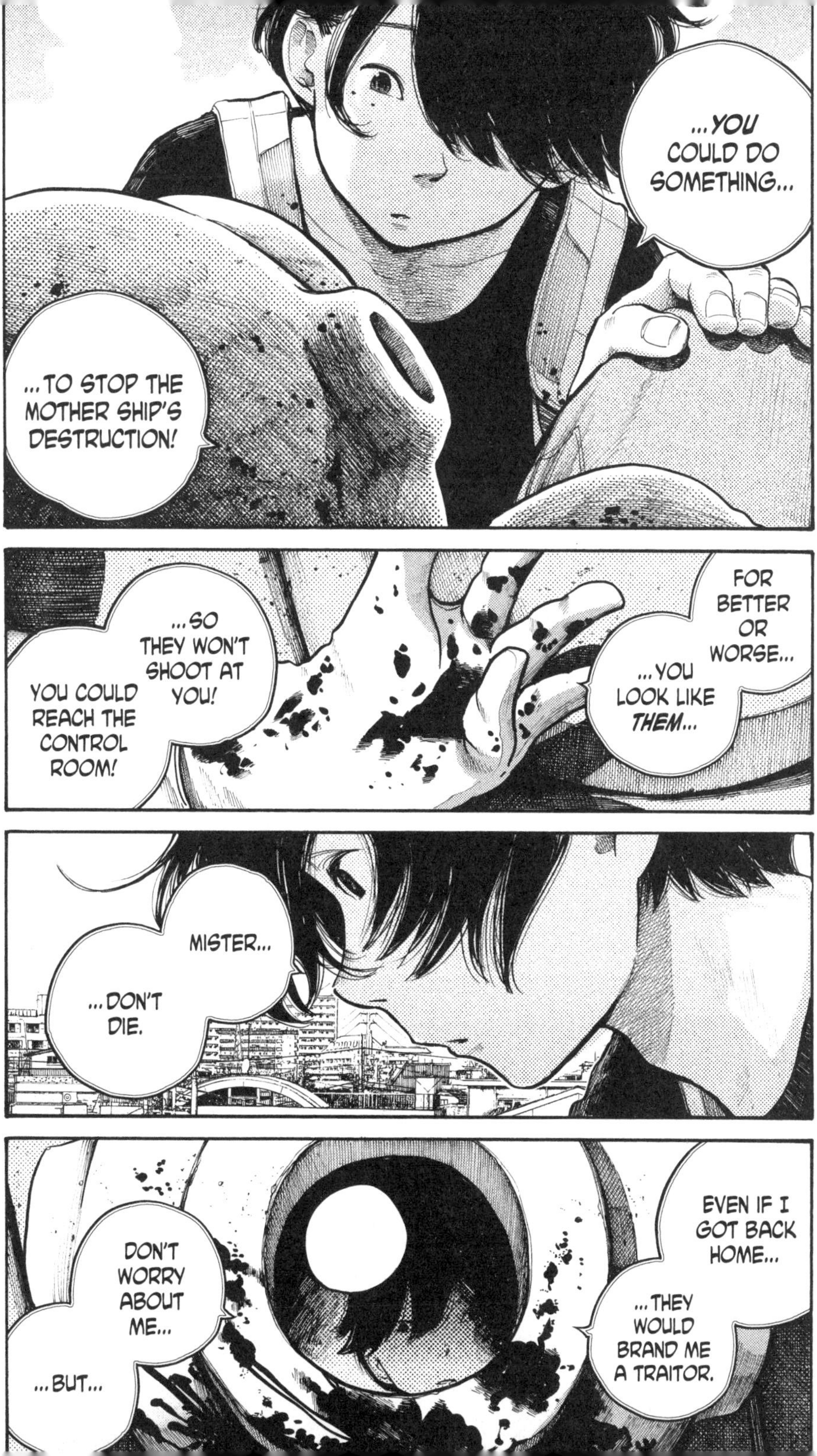
...*YOU* COULD DO SOMETHING...
...TO STOP THE MOTHER SHIP'S DESTRUCTION!
FOR BETTER OR WORSE...
...YOU LOOK LIKE *THEM*...
...SO THEY WON'T SHOOT AT YOU!
YOU COULD REACH THE CONTROL ROOM!
MISTER...
...DON'T DIE.
EVEN IF I GOT BACK HOME...
...THEY WOULD BRAND ME A TRAITOR.
DON'T WORRY ABOUT ME...
...BUT...

HERE AT THE END...
...MY ONLY CONCERN...
...IS FOR MY FRIEND AND COMPANION...
...IN THIS HELL.
PLEASE ...
... PROTECT ...
...MY FRIEND.

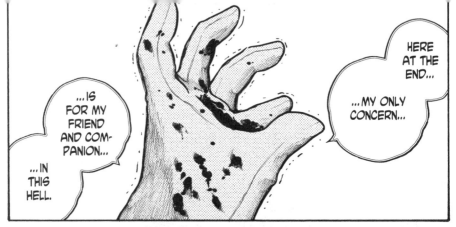

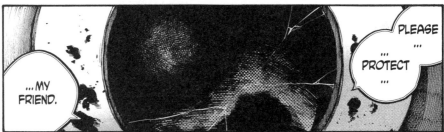

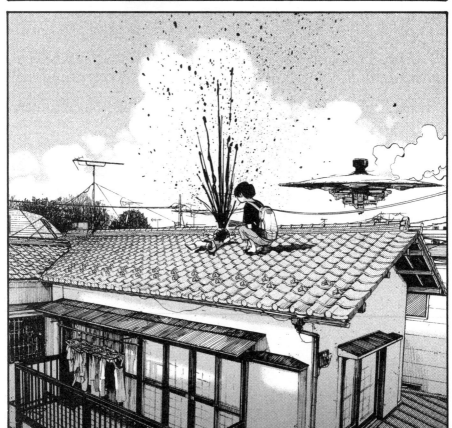

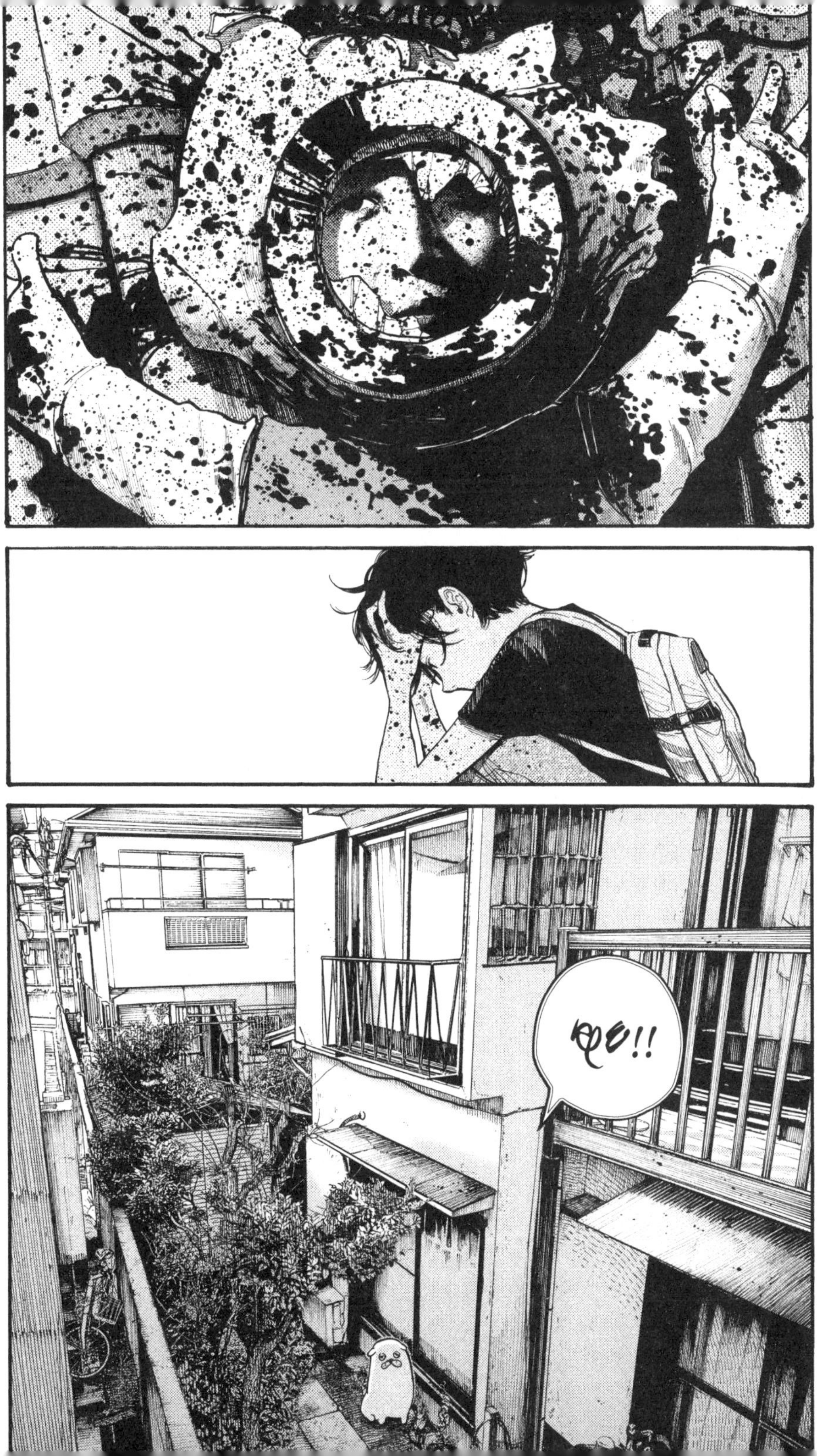

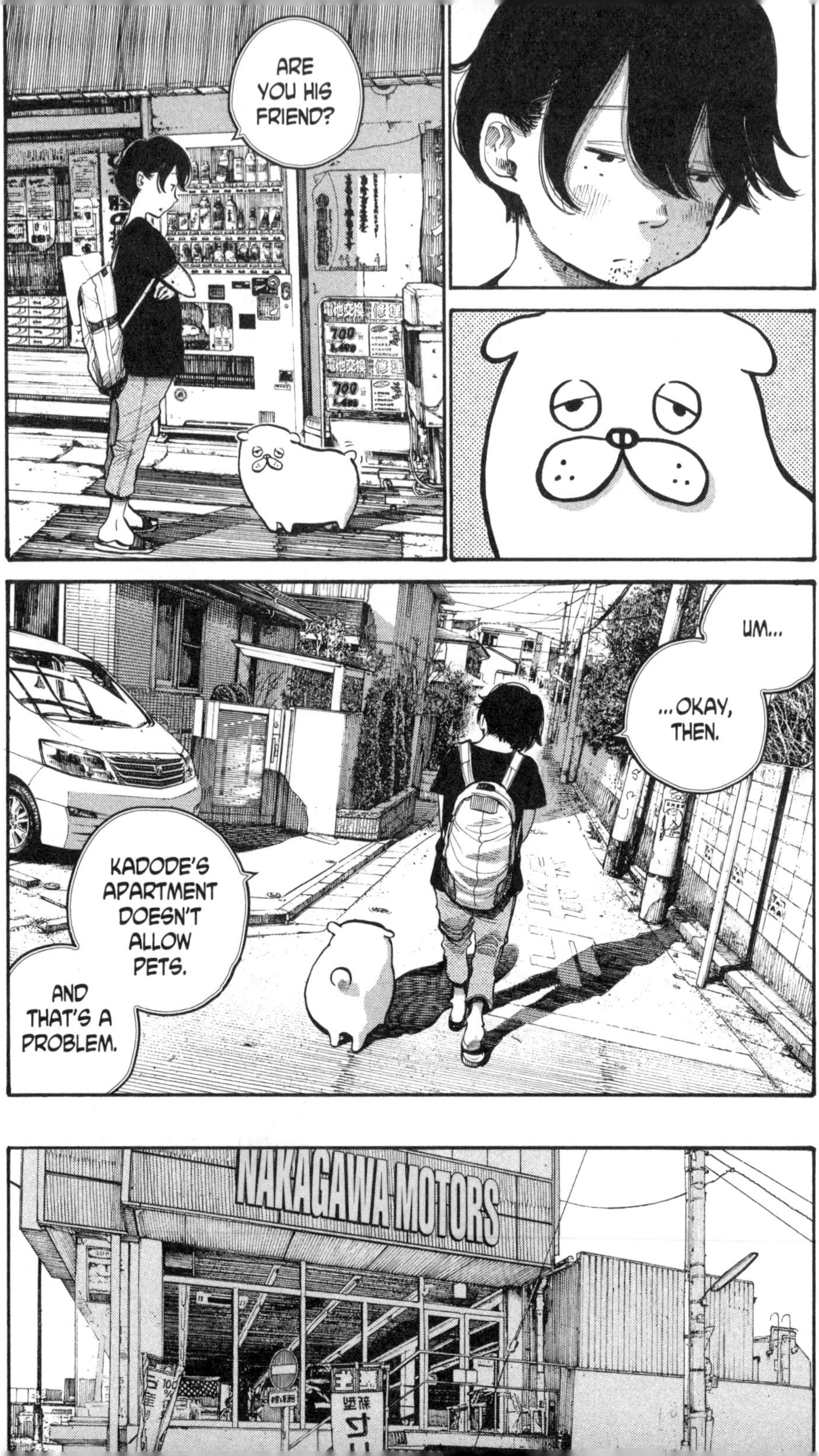
ARE YOU HIS FRIEND?
UM...
...OKAY, THEN.
KADODE'S APARTMENT DOESN'T ALLOW PETS.
AND THAT'S A PROBLEM.
NAKAGAWA MOTORS

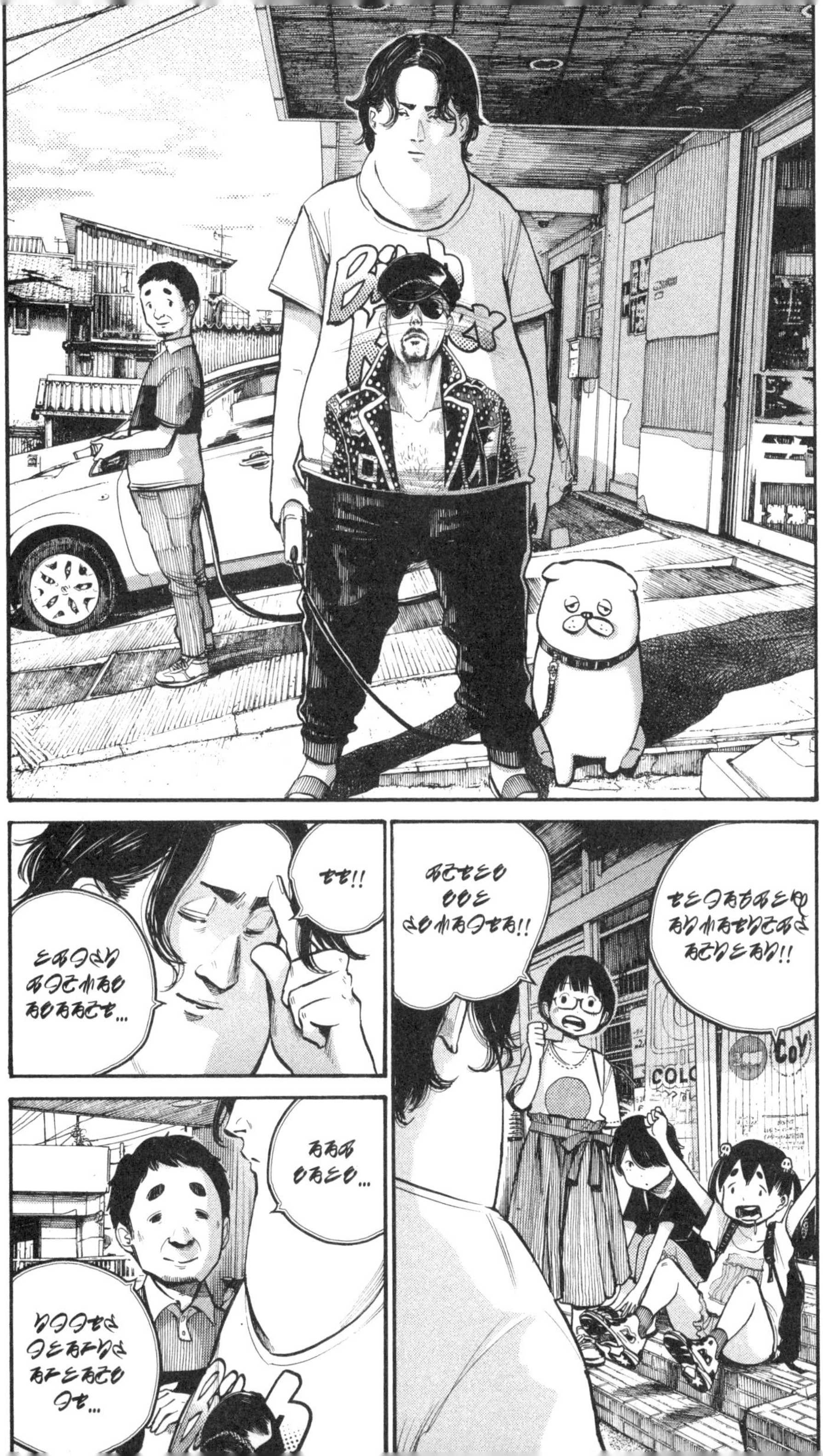

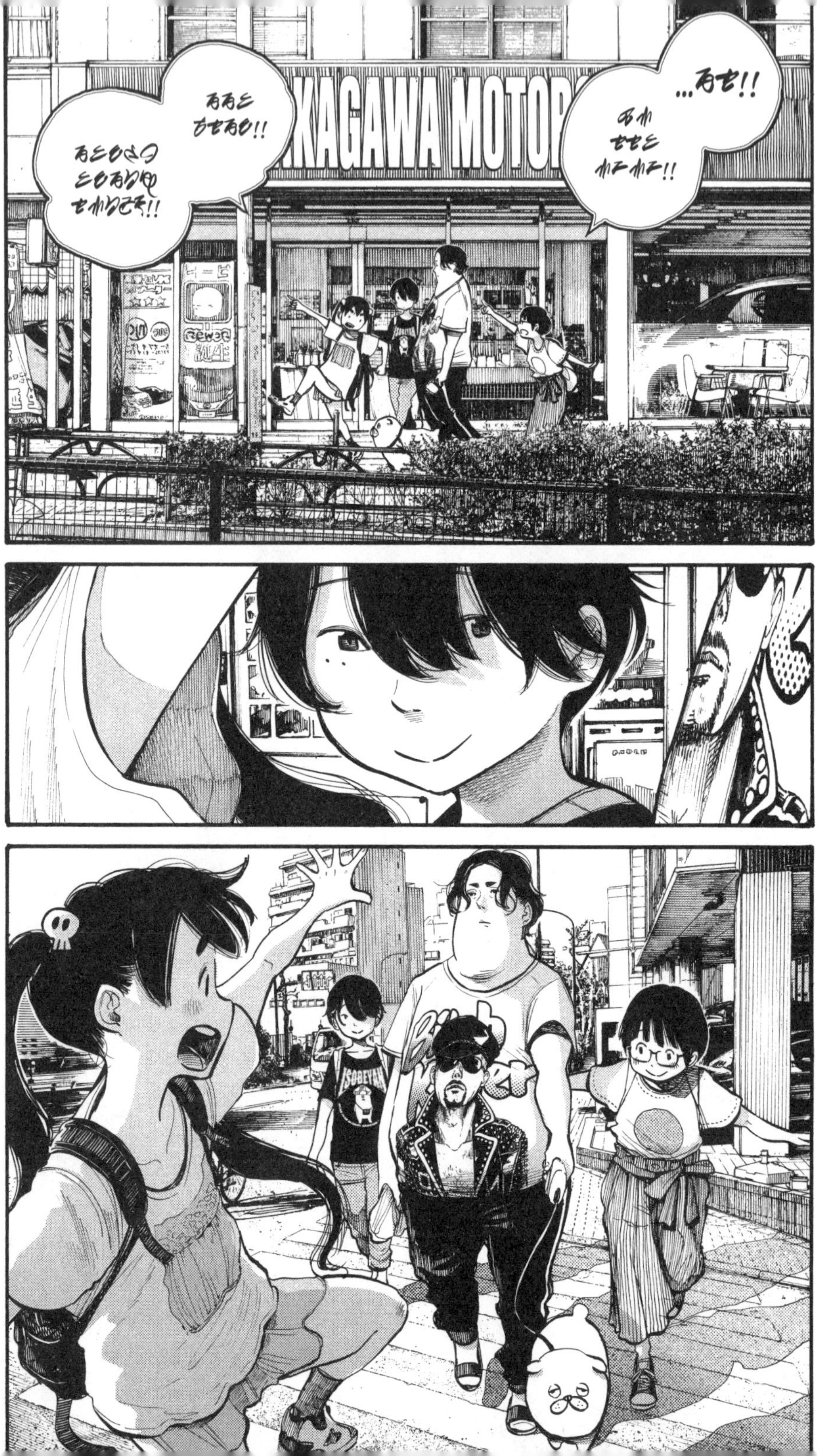
KAGAWA MOTOR
ISOBEYAN

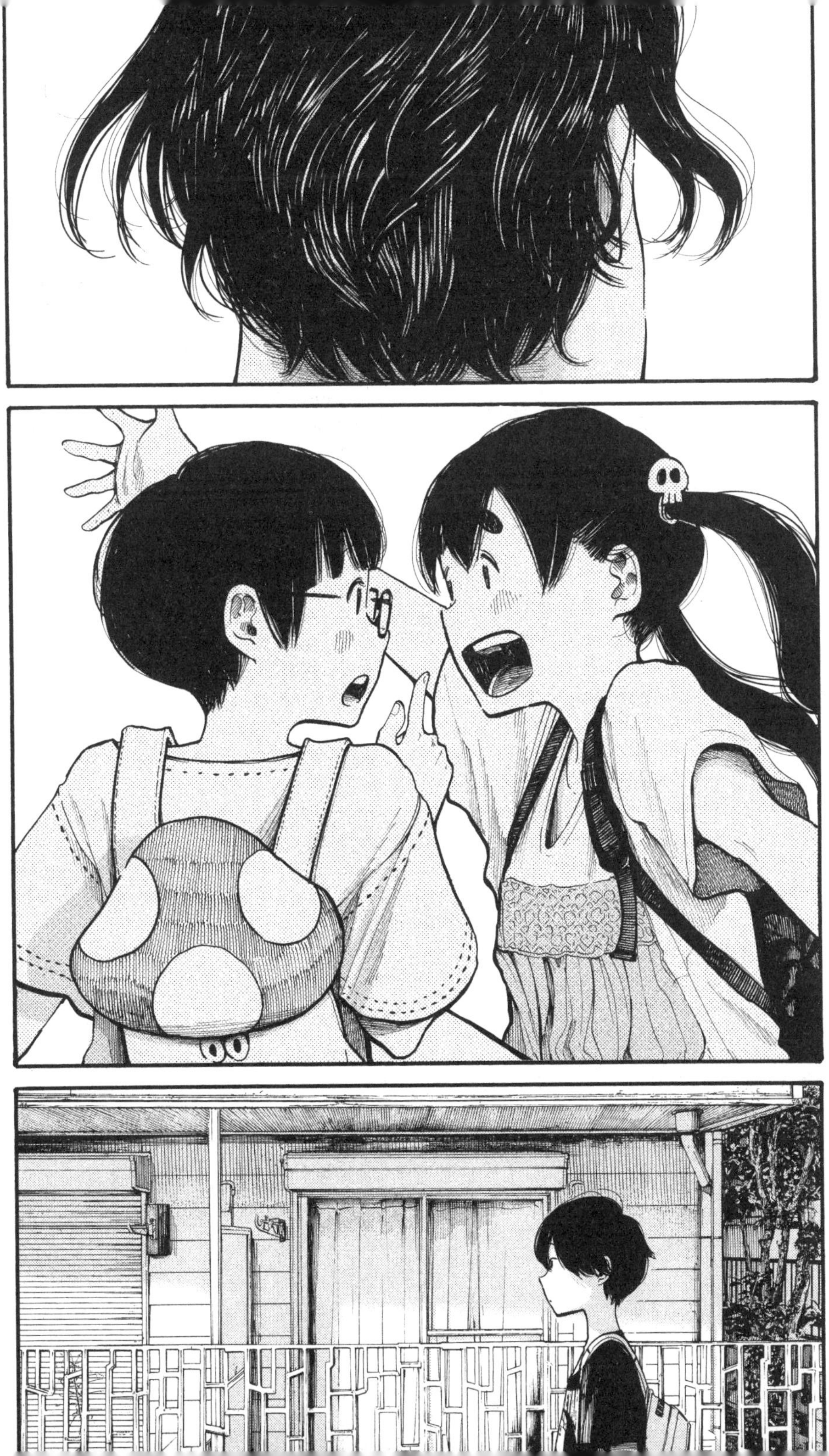

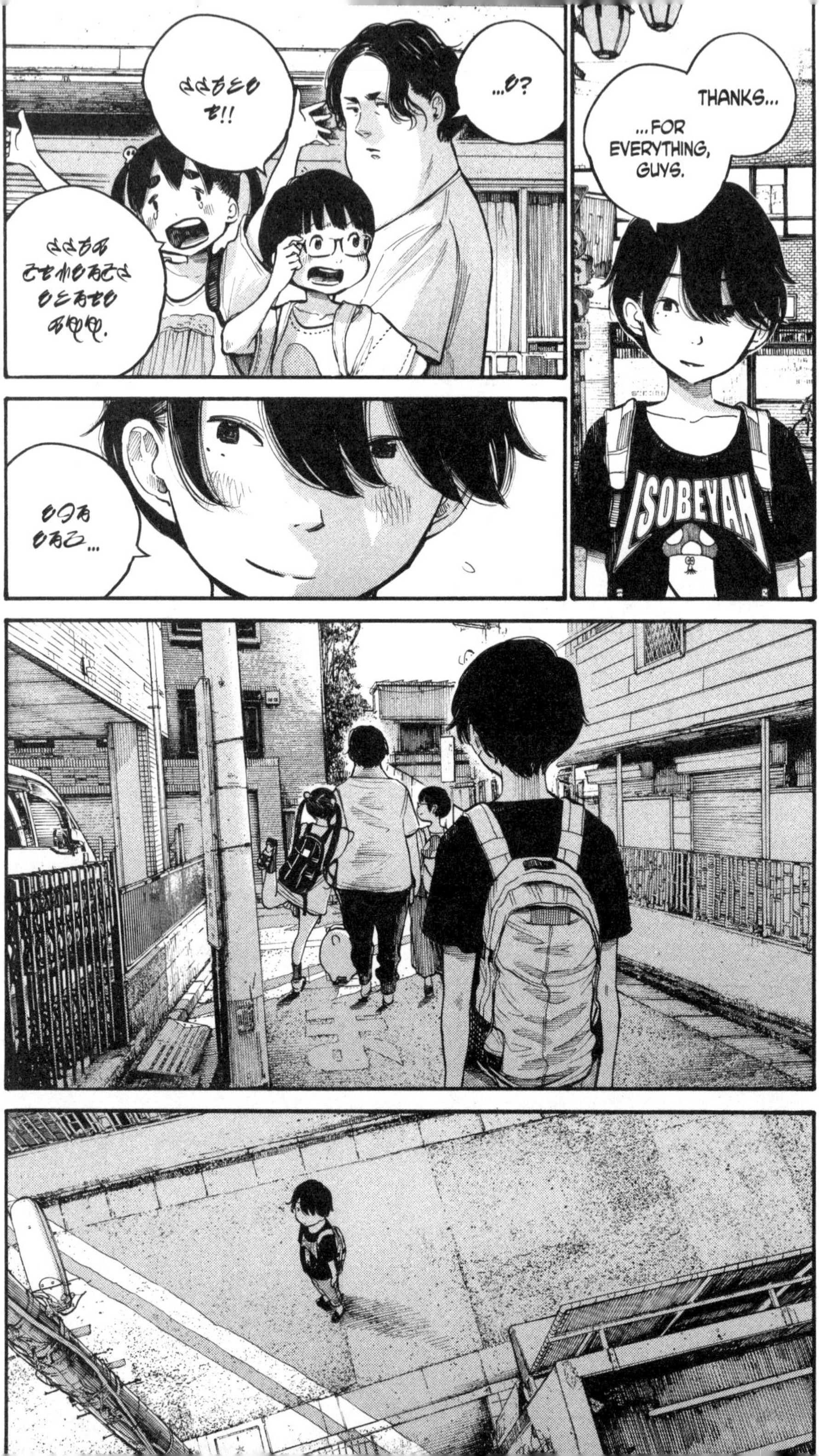
THANKS...
...FOR EVERYTHING, GUYS.
ISOBEYAH
...?

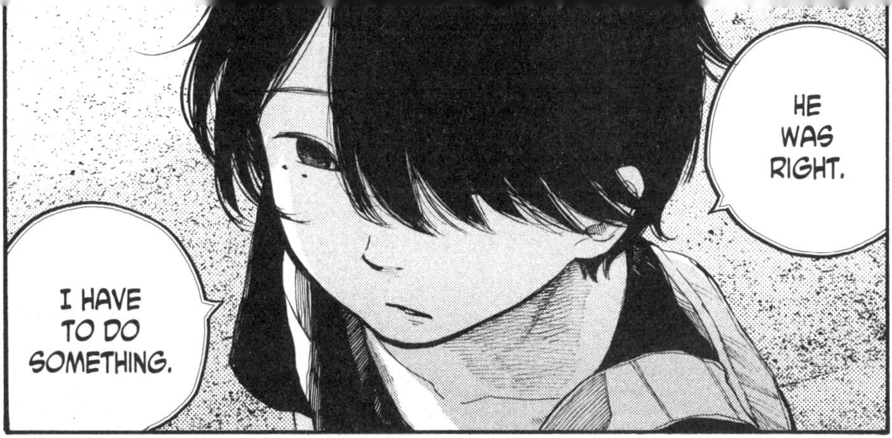
HE WAS RIGHT.
I HAVE TO DO SOMETHING.

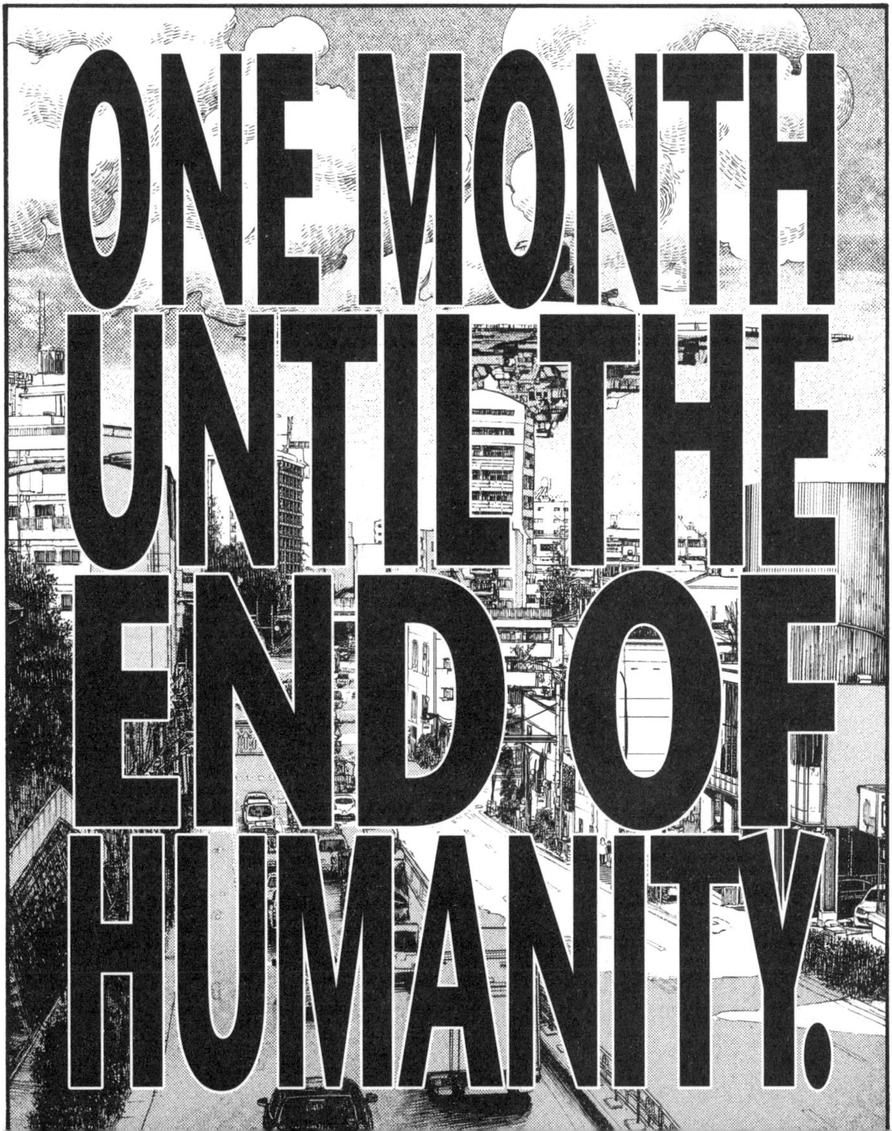
ONE MONTH UNTIL THE END OF HUMANITY.

Dead Dead Demon's
Dededede Destruction Volume 6
Inio Asano

Background Assistants: Satsuki Sato
Ran Atsumori
Buuko

CG: Naoto Tomita

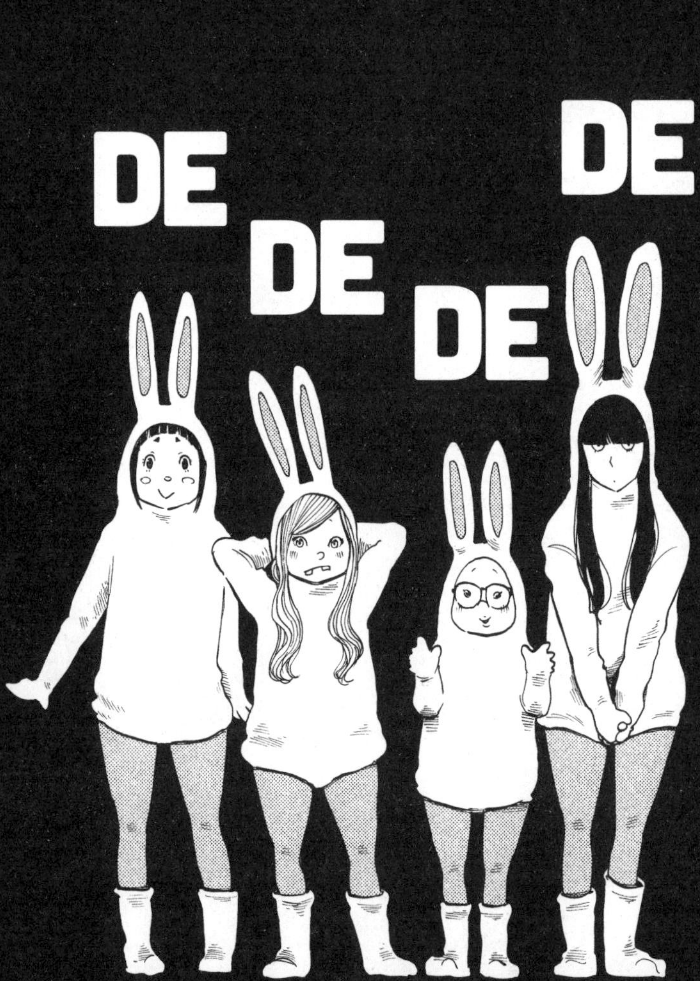
DE
DE
DE
DE

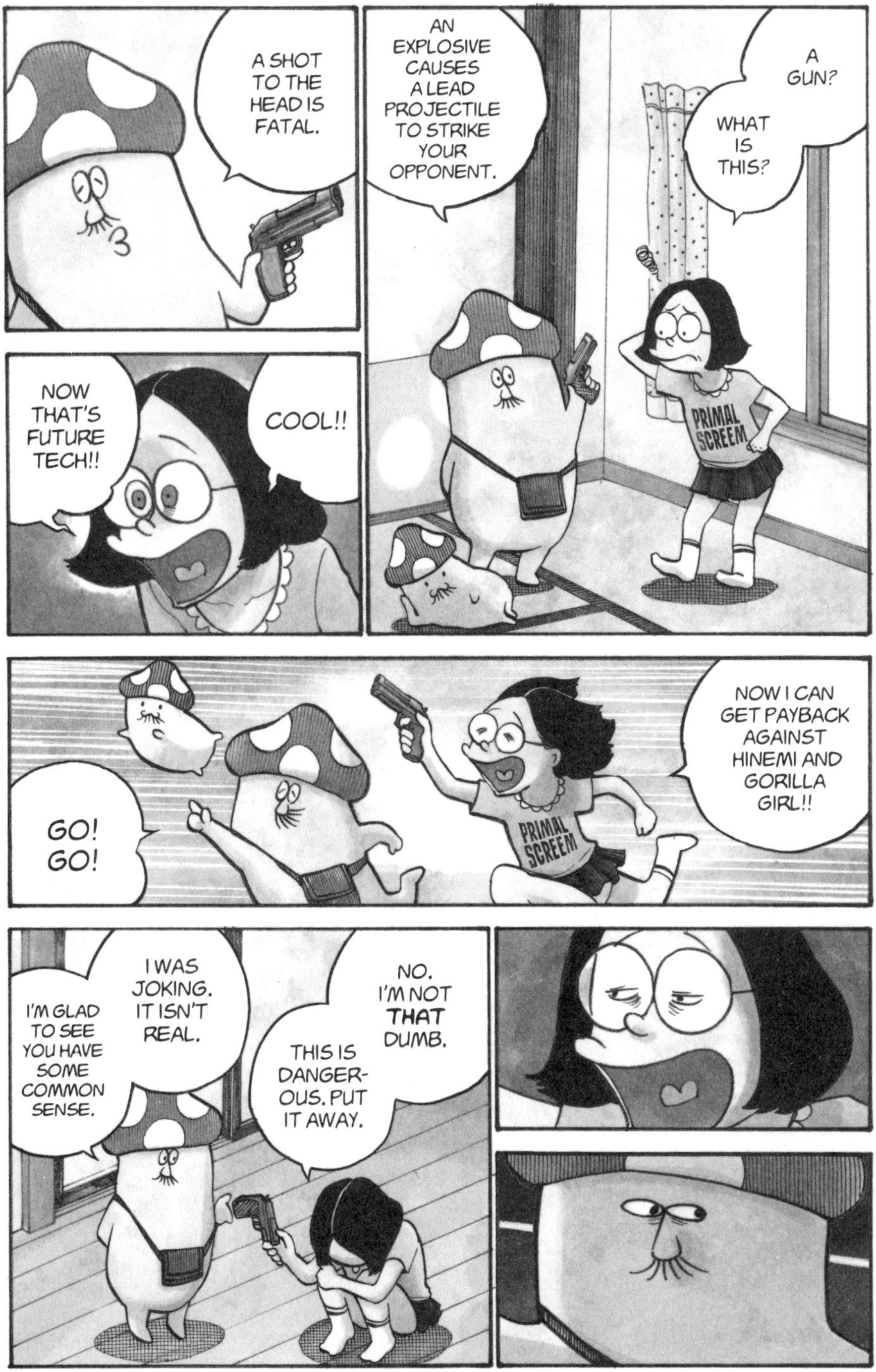
A GUN?
WHAT IS THIS?
AN EXPLOSIVE CAUSES A LEAD PROJECTILE TO STRIKE YOUR OPPONENT.
PRIMAL SCREEM
A SHOT TO THE HEAD IS FATAL.
COOL!!
NOW THAT'S FUTURE TECH!!
NOW I CAN GET PAYBACK AGAINST HINEMI AND GORILLA GIRL!!
PRIMAL SCREEM
GO! GO!
NO. I'M NOT **THAT** DUMB.
THIS IS DANGER-OUS. PUT IT AWAY.
I WAS JOKING. IT ISN'T REAL.
I'M GLAD TO SEE YOU HAVE SOME COMMON SENSE.

☆Volume 7 releases October 2019, so start getting excited now!

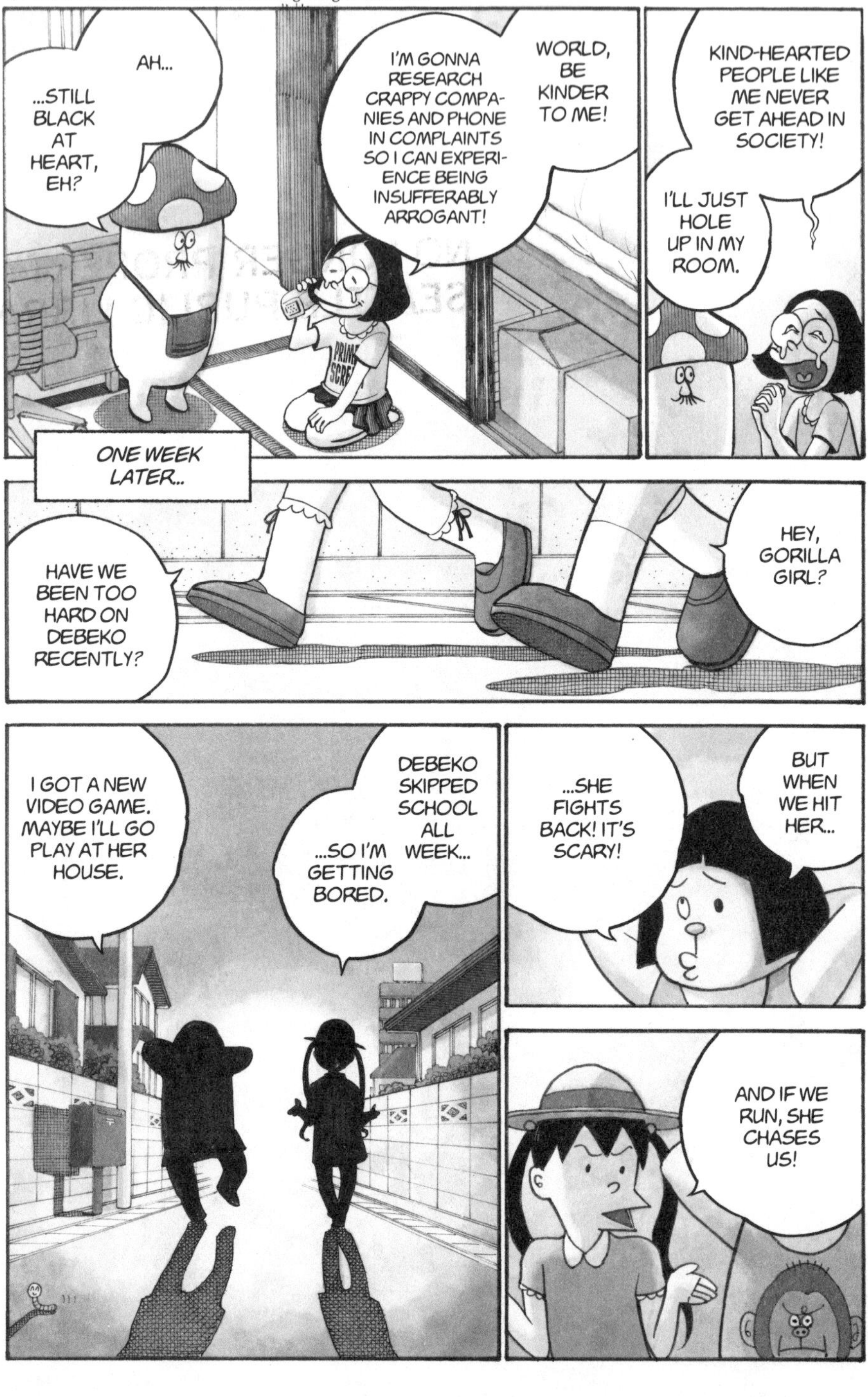
KIND-HEARTED PEOPLE LIKE ME NEVER GET AHEAD IN SOCIETY!
I'LL JUST HOLE UP IN MY ROOM.
WORLD, BE KINDER TO ME!
I'M GONNA RESEARCH CRAPPY COMPANIES AND PHONE IN COMPLAINTS SO I CAN EXPERIENCE BEING INSUFFERABLY ARROGANT!
AH...
...STILL BLACK AT HEART, EH?
ONE WEEK LATER...
HEY, GORILLA GIRL?
HAVE WE BEEN TOO HARD ON DEBEKO RECENTLY?
BUT WHEN WE HIT HER...
...SHE FIGHTS BACK! IT'S SCARY!
AND IF WE RUN, SHE CHASES US!
DEBEKO SKIPPED SCHOOL ALL WEEK...
...SO I'M GETTING BORED.
I GOT A NEW VIDEO GAME. MAYBE I'LL GO PLAY AT HER HOUSE.

DEAD DEAD DEMON'S DEDEDEDE DESTRUCTION

Volume 6
VIZ Signature Edition

Story and Art by **Inio Asano**

Translation **John Werry**
Touch-Up Art & Lettering **Annaliese Christman**
Design **Shawn Carrico**
Editor **Pancha Diaz**

DEAD DEAD DEMON'S DEDEDEDE DESTRUCTION Vol. 6
by Inio ASANO
© 2014 Inio ASANO
All rights reserved.
Original Japanese edition published by SHOGAKUKAN.
English translation rights in the United States of America,
Canada, the United Kingdom, Ireland, Australia and
New Zealand arranged with SHOGAKUKAN. .

Original Cover Design:
Kaoru KUROKI·Chie SATO+Bay Bridge Studio

The stories, characters and incidents mentioned
in this publication are entirely fictional.

Printed in Canada

Published by VIZ Media, LLC
P.O. Box 77010
San Francisco, CA 94107

10 9 8 7 6 5 4 3 2 1
First printing, July 2019

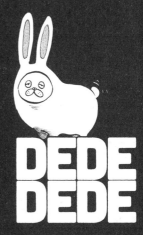

**DEDE
DEDE**

VIZ MEDIA
viz.com

VIZ SIGNATURE
vizsignature.com

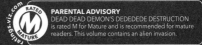